THOMAS BROWNE
AND THE WRITING OF
EARLY MODERN SCIENCE

Claire Preston argues that Thomas Browne's work can be fully understood only within the range of disciplines and practices associated with natural philosophy and early-modern empiricism. Early-modern methods of cataloguing, collecting, experimentation, and observation organised his writing on many subjects from medicine and botany to archaeology and antiquarianism. Browne framed philosophical concerns in the terms of civil behaviour, with collaborative networks of intellectual exchange, investigative selflessness, courtesy, modesty, and ultimately the generosity of the natural world itself all characterising the return to 'innocent' knowledge, which, for Browne, is the proper end of human enquiry. In this major new evaluation of Browne's *oeuvre*, Preston examines how the developing essay-form, the discourse of scientific experiment, and above all Bacon's model of intellectual progress and cooperation determined the unique character of Browne's contributions to early-modern literature, science, and philosophy.

CLAIRE PRESTON is Fellow and Lecturer in English at Sidney Sussex College, and Newton Trust Lecturer in the Faculty of English, University of Cambridge. She is the editor of *Sir Thomas Browne: Selected Writings* (1996) and author of *Edith Wharton's Social Register* (2000) and *Bee* (2005), and has published widely on early-modern and American literature.

THOMAS BROWNE
AND THE WRITING OF
EARLY MODERN SCIENCE

CLAIRE PRESTON

CAMBRIDGE
UNIVERSITY PRESS

PUBLISHED BY THE PRESS SYNDICATE OF THE UNIVERSITY OF CAMBRIDGE
The Pitt Building, Trumpington Street, Cambridge, United Kingdom

CAMBRIDGE UNIVERSITY PRESS
The Edinburgh Building, Cambridge, CB2 2RU, UK
40 West 20th Street, New York NY 10011–4211, USA
477 Williamstown Road, Port Melbourne, VIC 3207, Australia
Ruiz de Alarcón 13, 28014 Madrid, Spain
Dock House, The Waterfront, Cape Town 8001, South Africa

http://www.cambridge.org

First published 2005

Printed in the United Kingdom at the University Press, Cambridge

Typeface Adobe Garamond 11/12.5 pt.   *System* LaTeX 2ε   [TB]

A catalogue record for this book is available from the British Library

ISBN 0 521 83794 4 hardback

for
Kevin Jackson
and in memory of
Dick Preston

'Shall I not have intelligence with the earth? Am I not partly leaves and vegetable mould myself?'

Henry David Thoreau, *Walden* (1854)

Contents

Illustrations

Acknowledgements

Thomas Browne's horizons were, as Samuel Johnson said, larger than the hemisphere of the world, and although he has had countless imitators, no one writing about his learned imagination can hope to keep up with him except with heroic assistance. Although this book gestated for a long time and was often interrupted by other projects which threatened its completion, a great many generous and alert friends and colleagues remembered it and offered their own reserves of knowledge. I have been very much aided by contributions from David Abulafia, Bill Ashworth, James Basker, Max Beber, the late Bob Boutilier, Douglas Brooks, James Carley, Helen Castor, Anne Dunan, R. J. W. Evans, Elizabeth Flowerday, Daniel Grimley, Sir Gabriel Horn FRS, Richard Humphreys, John Kerrigan, Raphael Lyne, Judith Maltby, Alex Marr, the late Jeremy Maule, Christopher Parrish FRCS, Margaret Pelling, Neil Rhodes, Clare Robertson, Nicholas Rogers, Andrew Rosenheim, James Rosenheim, Keith Straughan, Colin Tite, John Wands, Jonathan Woolfson, and Andrew Zurcher.

I thank the three anonymous readers who commented so carefully on parts of the draft, and especially William West, who later declared his identity and generously allowed me to consult him further in the final stages of revision. Anne Barton, Adrian Poole, Howard Erskine-Hill, Clive Wilmer, Kevin Jackson, and Kate Bennett read and criticised all or part of the book at various stages, and provided much-needed encouragement. I have profited very much from their comments; any surviving errors and infelicities are entirely my own. I should like to record apologies also to Thomas Browne himself for what are certain to be errors in construing his sometimes difficult prose and recondite learning. Heather Lane, Gabrielle Rose, Patrick Gates, and Dario Iacopucci gave invaluable and often time-consuming technical advice on computers and the internet; and Heather Lane has additionally tracked down many necessary books. James Eason, creator of the University of Chicago's Thomas Browne website, advised on the arcana of search-engines. The Master and Fellows of Sidney Sussex

College granted me a year's leave in which to finish the book, and I thank in particular Professor Dame Sandra Dawson, Master of Sidney, for giving me an invaluable hint on the timing of sabbaticals. Rob and Blythe Edwards and Ron and Michèle Royal in America, and Vincenzo and Marion Iacopucci in Italy hospitably provided beautiful and quiet places of retirement, scholarly refuge, and electronic expertise in which to work. I cannot omit tribute to the magisterial work of Sir Geoffrey Keynes, C. A. Patrides, and Robin Robbins, the great editorial triumvirate without whom no modern reader of Browne can hope to flourish; and to recognise, in my own thinking, the influential work of Steven Shapin, Michael Hunter, and Peter Miller on civility and early-modern science.

Victoria Cooper of Cambridge University Press, the model of a civil editor, encouraged and guided the book from its embryonic stage with enthusiasm and patience; Maartje Scheltens steered it through the production and editorial process with grace and efficiency. To them, both scholars in their own right, and to Caroline Howlett, who combines rigorous copy-editing with a fine sense of humour, my affectionate and grateful thanks.

I was fortunate to be invited to present much of this material, in somewhat different form, to the following gatherings, where my thinking was deepened and corrected by my audience on many points: the Renaissance Computer Conference, University of St Andrews (convened by Neil Rhodes and Jonathan Sawday); the Literature and History Seminar, Oxford University (convened by Susan Brigden and Andrew McCullough); the Cabinet of Natural History, Cambridge University (convened by Katie Whitaker); the Curiosity Seminar, Oxford University (convened by Alexander Marr); the Renaissance Seminar, Cambridge University (convened by Gavin Alexander and David Hilton); and the Claribelle Woods Memorial Lecture, Oklahoma State University (convened by Martin Wallen).

The staff of the following libraries have been unfailingly helpful and resourceful: Cambridge University Library, especially the Rare Books Department and Photographic Services; the English Faculty Library, Cambridge; the British Library (Books and Manuscripts); Sidney Sussex College (Cambridge) Library and Muniment Room; the Hawthorne-Longfellow Library of Bowdoin College; Pembroke College (Cambridge) Library; the Firestone Library (Robert Taylor Collection) of Princeton University; the Beinecke Library, Yale University; and the Osler Library, University of Montreal. I am grateful to the British Library; the University Library, Cambridge; the Whipple Library, Cambridge; and the Biblioteca Universitaria, Bologna for permission to reproduce engravings and illustrations from their collections.

Versions and portions of some chapters first appeared elsewhere. Parts of Chapter Two and Chapter Six derive from ' "Unriddling the World": Thomas Browne and the Doctrine of Signatures', *Critical Survey* 5 (1993); parts of Chapter Three and Chapter Five from 'In the Wilderness of Forms: Ideas and Things in Thomas Browne's Cabinets of Curiosity' in *The Renaissance Computer: Knowledge Technology in the First Age of Print*, ed. Neil Rhodes and Jonathan Sawday (Routledge, 2000); Chapter Five as 'The Jocund Cabinet and the Melancholy Museum in Seventeenth-Century English Literature' in *Curiosity and Wonder from the Renaissance to the Enlightenment*, ed. Alexander Marr and R. J. W. Evans (Ashgate, 2005).

The republic of letters, miraculously a still-viable state of mind, is tended and maintained by a circle of friends whose constant generosity reminds me of the privilege of association they grant me: for this I specially thank Susan Brigden, Anne Barton, Kate Bennett, Anne Dunan, Kevin Jackson, Christopher Page, Martin Wallen, and Clive Wilmer. Another of its citizens, Richard Preston, physicist and man of letters, did not live to see the completion of this book, but it is to his lifelong example that I owe my admiration for literary-scientific polymaths like Thomas Browne. To his memory, and to Kevin Jackson, companion and guide in that interesting nation, I dedicate it with much love.

South Bristol, Maine
Christmas Day, 2004

Notes on the text

All quotations from primary works are given in their original spelling and punctuation. In references in the notes, the place of publication is London unless otherwise stated. Subsequent references do not give a title abbreviation unless there is more than one work by that author in the bibliography.

Abbreviations

CM	*Christian Morals* in Keynes I, 243–95 (references are given in the notes as part and section numbers)
GC	*The Garden of Cyrus* in Keynes I, 175–227 (references are given in the notes as chapter and page numbers)
GC. Bacon	'To my worthy and honoured friend Nicholas Bacon of Gillingham, Esquire' in *Garden of Cyrus*
Keynes	*The Works of Sir Thomas Browne*, ed. Geoffrey Keynes, 2nd revised edn, 4 vols. (Chicago: University of Chicago Press, 1964). (Keynes I indicates vol. I.)
Keynes Selected	*Sir Thomas Browne: Selected Writings*, ed. Geoffrey Keynes (London: Faber and Faber, 1968)
LF	*Letter to a Friend* in Keynes I, 101–21
MC	*Musæum Clausum* in *Miscellany Tracts* in Keynes III, 109–19
MT	*Miscellany Tracts* in Keynes III, 3–120
NCB	*Miscellaneous Notes from Commonplace Books* in Keynes III, 272–330
NE	*Notes and Experiments in Natural History* in Keynes III, 347–60
NHN	*Notes on the Natural History of Norfolk* in Keynes III, 401–31
OA	*Observations in Anatomy* in Keynes III, 333–44
ON	*Observations and Notes* in Keynes III, 239–71
Patrides Approaches	*Approaches to Sir Thomas Browne: The Ann Arbor Tercentenary Lectures and Essays*, ed. C. A. Patrides (Columbia, MO: University of Missouri Press, 1982)
Patrides STB	*Sir Thomas Browne: The Major Works*, ed. C. A. Patrides (Harmondsworth: Penguin, 1977)
PE	*Pseudodoxia Epidemica*, ed. Robin Robbins, 2 vols. (Oxford: Clarendon Press, 1981) (references are given in the notes as book, section, and page numbers)
PE. Reader	'To the Reader' in *Pseudodoxia Epidemica*

RM   *Religio Medici* in Keynes I, 3–93 (references are given in the
              notes as part and section numbers)
RM.Reader   'To the Reader' in *Religio Medici*
Robbins *PE* Robbins's Introduction and editorial apparatus, in *Pseudo-
              doxia Epidemica*, ed. Robbins
Robbins *STB* *Sir Thomas Browne: 'Religio Medici', 'Hydriotaphia', and 'The
              Garden of Cyrus'*, ed. Robin Robbins (Oxford: Clarendon
              Press, 1972)
U-B   *Hydriotaphia, or Urne-Buriall* in Keynes I, 131–72 (references
              are given in the notes as chapter and page numbers)
U-B.LeGros 'To my worthy and honoured friend Thomas Le Gros of
              Crostwick, Esquire' in *Urne-Buriall*

Introduction

The City of Norwich's handsome bronze monument to its most famous man of letters was erected in 1905, the tercentenary of Browne's birth. The large effigy is seated in a chair contemplating the fragment of a funeral urn in its outstretched right hand, its head resting thoughtfully in its left. On a summer's day early in the twenty-first century, this memorial was in the middle of a large flock of little boys furiously skateboarding in the Haymarket; a few yards beyond them the outdoor market stalls were doing a brisk trade; and Sir Thomas himself was wearing an orange plastic traffic cone on his head. In the midst of business and pleasure, no one was paying the slightest attention to this grave figure, even with its unusual headgear. The scene is so quintessentially Brownean that it defies comedy and even irony: time makes pyramids pillars of snow, and monuments, he concludes in *Urne-Buriall*, are 'but the irregularities of vainglory, and wilde enormities of ancient magnanimity'. To be apparently derelict and unknown in the bustle of future ages is no more than the fate of Methusaleh, whose long life has become his only chronicle; by the same token, a day-glow plastic traffic cone is no more than the cold consolation of eternity.

This monument is not Browne's tomb. His bones lie nearby, under the floor in the chancel of St Peter Mancroft, the large, incomparably beautiful parish church which dominates the Haymarket. By a curious coincidence, his remains suffered the kind of fate he so often refers to in *Urne-Buriall*. Disturbed in 1840 during repair work in the church, the coffin was robbed of Browne's skull in mysterious circumstances, but not before a plaster cast had been made of it. Later in the decade a skull reputedly Browne's and matching the cast was presented to the Norfolk and Norwich Hospital. There it remained, while the plaster cast was put on display at the local museum. The skull was not reinterred in St Peter Mancroft until 1922. Before this was done, biometric studies were made comparing the skull with the known and purported portraits of Browne, the results of which confirmed that the skull was indeed his. 'Who knows the fate of his bones, or how often he is to be buried?' he asks, and the rumination is prophetic, with the serial in- and exhumation, multiple relics (varyingly authentic), grave-robbery, and antiquarian examination of his bodily fragments sounding like a vignette of his own invention.

Browne was primarily interested in fragments, remains, tokens – material, textual, and conceptual clues to a ruined or lost order. An organising structure of all his major works, this book proposes, is the restitution – attempted, achieved, or failed – of that order. The following chapters examine his work in the light of a range of related disciplines and practices loosely grouped under the heading of natural philosophy or the new empiricism of the late-sixteenth and seventeenth centuries, disciplines which include reparative cataloguing, collecting, experimentation, observation, and antiquarianism (in artefactual and documentary forms). These categories are linked to Browne's writing through the areas of study especially interesting to him, including certain forms of medical diagnosis, the study of physic and botany, archaeology, numismatics, etymology, scientific nomenclature, and anatomy. The spectrum of his interests and accomplishments is informed, I argue, by the developing and conventionless essay-form (a form which in his hands is sometimes a primitive dramatic monologue), by the necessity for an authenticating discourse of scientific experiment, report, and analysis, and above all by the overwhelmingly influential Baconian model of intellectual progress and cooperation, all features of what was then termed, by scientist and layman alike, 'civility'.

In my first chapter I argue that Browne's writing and themes must primarily be understood in terms of civil behaviour, a concept essential both to polite social interaction and more importantly to the developing culture of scientific and antiquarian investigation, for which civility is the foremost tool in the advancement of learning. I use the initiating event of his literary career, the pirating of *Religio Medici* in 1642, as the referent for his understanding of cooperation and tolerance, ideas which inform all his subsequent work.

Religio Medici is a first and very immature work, one in which the young Browne is trying out effects, is not always in control of his material, and is attempting, not always convincingly and even occasionally comically, to make an intellectual *summa* despite his youth. The second chapter discusses the competing 'voices' of *Religio*, that of the original compositional moment (*circa* 1635), and that of ten years on in the 1643 preface and in the additions to the authorised version; this bivocalism, I argue, can be read as a nascent dramatic monologue. Despite its earliness, the contingent nature of Browne's thought is fully on display in *Religio Medici*, and my discussion notes the important connexions this early style has with the essays of Montaigne and Bacon, and how it represents what would become in the later works a link between the early form of essay-writing and the post-Restoration scientific report as practised by Hooke, Boyle, and other members of the Royal Society. It extends the concept of learned sociability by examining Browne's use of natural civility in certain insects, who become for him a signature of the cooperative endeavour he is about to join.

Browne participated in networks of civil intellectual exchange between virtuosi, naturalists, and doctors, and Chapter Three considers *Pseudodoxia Epidemica* in terms of the polarities of vulgarity and civility which govern such networks and their activities, and of the rhetoric of technological and scientific advancement and social improvement. A textual cabinet of curiosities, a Baconian compilation which civilly displays Browne's vast learning for the benefit of other civil investigators and readers, *Pseudodoxia* is conceptually linked with early-modern collections and with the history of museums. The optimistic tone of *Religio Medici*, however, which ought to be foremost in *Pseudodoxia*, begins to fail by the end of the book, and we detect the emergence of the darker and more sceptical Browne of *Urne-Buriall*.

The themes of Urne-Buriall discussed in Chapter Four introduce specifically antiquarian cooperation between Browne and his colleagues in learning, and situate Browne's own style of open-minded antiquarianism in relation to the great English tradition that begins with Camden and flourishes well beyond the end of the seventeenth century. But this essay on cremation and burial finally disparages the antiquarian project: using his archaeological learning Browne explodes the myth of preservation and shows that the true theology of the past is that which reminds us of the end of days. This resurrection theme is one which has been indicated from the beginning of my book and which will cumulatively be shown to colonise much of his thought.

Chapter Five offers a brief excursus on *Musæum Clausum* and other spoofs of antiquarian learning and natural philosophy. Although out of chronological order, it serves as a foil to *Urne-Buriall*, one which alerts us to Browne's uneasy sense of the Baconian project to restore 'a knowledge broken', and which in a quite different mode from *Urne-Buriall* examines the futility of collecting and compiling.

Chapter Six discusses *The Garden of Cyrus*, Browne's last major investigative work. Here he most fully integrates his investigative antiquarianism with his natural theology and his empirical botany and embryology. The *decussis* or the quincunx is for Browne a mystical signature of renewal and resurrection, but it is one which he must piece out as a practising, empirically rigorous scientist, one who is most at home with the observation of seeds and insects, two categories of life which were of special interest to biologists working on generation, and to craftsmen attempting to perfect the technologies of observation. The discussion considers theories of generation, the development of microscopes, and the ways in which these ideas and tools allowed Browne to construct a theory of life from the smallest observable parts of nature. This chapter links *Cyrus* with ideas of retirement and of paradise, and proposes that with its outstanding central scientific digression on generation it be read as a *structural*, and not simply a thematic, counterpart to *Urne-Buriall*.

Chapter Seven considers Browne's fugitive writings – the remains of his experimental and observational life included in his notebooks and tracts – and concludes the book as a whole.

If I have omitted two substantial minor compositions (*Letter to a Friend* and *Christian Morals*) from extended treatment it is because they repeat the more powerful themes of the four major works and the *Tracts* without usefully extending them in the terms of my own discussion. It may be objected, too, that I have chosen to refer to Browne without the title of his knighthood. Although virtually every book and electronic database which includes him lists him as 'Sir' Thomas Browne, the honour was granted in the final decade of his life, possibly as a mere formality to please the visiting King, and seems to me essentially unconnected with the spirit of his civil behaviour and of his voice in the compositions of 1635–72.

If Browne had doubts about the afterlife of human relics, his own literary remains have survived with extraordinary vigour in the imaginative universe of English letters. My own enthusiasm began very prosaically during an otherwise dull morning sitting an SAT (American college entrance) examination in a bland high-school classroom. The setters of the multiple-choice exercise had (quite improbably as it now seems) chosen the rhapsodic passage from *Urne-Buriall* V where oblivion blindly scattereth her poppy and diuturnity is a dream and folly of expectation. With this transfixing prose reverberating in my mind, it was not easy to complete the test; and because it was unattributed I did not discover its source for some years. One quotable fragment – 'and Methusaleh's long life his only chronicle' – casually dropped into an unrelated undergraduate essay caught the attention of my tutor, who informed me, at last, whom I was plagiarising with such delight.

Browne has also lived in many great imaginations. His powerful tropes so exercised the splenetic Presbyterian controversialist Alexander Ross that he issued lengthy rebuttals of *Religio Medici* and *Pseudodoxia Epidemica* shortly after their publication, rebuttals whose fury only magnifies the cool brilliance of his target. Other seventeenth-century voices did Browne the honour of mimicking his title and manner, such as MacKenzie's *Religio Stoici* (1663), Meriton's *Religio Militis* (1672), T. A.'s *Religio Clerici* (1681), Dryden's *Religio Laici* (1682), and Bridgwater's *Religio Bibliopolae* (1691), and further 'Religios' – *Philosophi, Chemici, Grammatici, Obstetrici, Bibliographici, Journalistici, Libertini, Mathematici, Poetae, Religiosi*, and *Veterum* – have been appearing unabated since the eighteenth century.

Johnson committed his only essay on a writer solely of prose in *Lives of the Poets* to Browne, of whom he said 'the horizon of his understanding was much larger than the hemisphere of the world',[1] but whose foibles and eccentricities he characterised with elegant, affectionate irony; indeed, Walter Pater detected in Johnson's own 'slow latinity' an imitation of Browne.[2] Noah Webster was not so temperate in his criticism of Johnson's injudicious selections of Browne for the *Dictionary*: 'the style of Sir Thomas is not English; and it is astonishing that a man attempting to give the world a standard of the English language should have ever mentioned his name but with a reprobation'.[3] Coleridge, on the other hand, carefully annotated a copy of *Religio Medici* for Sara Hutchinson, with special symbols to apprise her of 'sublimity', 'majesty', 'ingenuity', and 'quaintness'.[4]

Charles Lamb named Thomas Browne and Fulke Greville as the two literary personages he would most wish to have met in their nightgowns and slippers. James Russell Lowell compared him to Shakespeare. The American Romantics and Transcendentalists of the mid-nineteenth century were avid readers of Browne: Poe commended Browne as 'a model of manners, with a richly marginalic air', by which he meant that Browne expresses himself 'freshly – boldly – originally – with abandonment – without conceit';[5] Emerson took pleasure in recommending him to Margaret Fuller; Melville, who called Browne 'a crack'd Archangel', had much inspiration for *Mardi* and *Moby-Dick* from *Pseudodoxia Epidemica* and *Religio Medici*; Emily Dickinson told Thomas Higginson in 1862 that Ruskin, Revelation, and Browne were the indispensable prose works she kept by her.[6] Thoreau

---

[1] Samuel Johnson, *The Life of Sir Thomas Browne* in Patrides *STB*, 502.   [2] Patrides *STB*, 481.

[3] To David Ramsay, 1807 (*The Letters of Noah Webster*, ed. Harry H. Warfel (New York: Library Publishers, 1953), 286).

[4] Samuel Taylor Coleridge, *Marginalia* in *The Collected Works of Samuel Taylor Coleridge* (London: Routledge and Kegan Paul, and Princeton: Princeton University Press, 1985), XII, 765.

[5] Edgar Allen Poe, 'Marginalia', *Democratic Review* (November 1844), 484–94; reprinted in Poe, *Marginalia* (Charlottesville: University of Virginia Press, 1981), 1.

[6] Emily Dickinson to Thomas Higginson, 26 April 1862 in *The Letters of Emily Dickinson*, ed. Thomas H. Johns, 3 vols. (Cambridge, MA: Harvard University Press, 1958), II, 404.

mimicked *Urne-Buriall* in his remarks in *Walden* on the *vanity* of opu-
lence;[7] and no one reading Thoreau on old clothes can avoid detecting this
inflection:

if my jacket and trousers, my hat and shoes, are fit to worship God in, they will
do; will they not? Who ever saw his old clothes, – his old coat, actually worn out,
resolved into its primitive elements, so that it was not a deed of charity to bestow
it on some poor boy, by him perchance to be bestowed on some poorer still, or
shall we say richer – who could do with less? I say, beware of all enterprises that
require new clothes, and not rather a new wearer of clothes.[8]

Bram Stoker read *Religio Medici* in preparation for writing *Dracula*,
perhaps gathering ideas and material for the character of van Helsing; and
in the annals of scholarship there can be few more surprising developments
than the serendipitous discovery of Stoker's reading list in which this fact
is revealed, an anecdote of a discovered fugitive manuscript which would
make part of a modern *Musæum Clausum*: two scholars, expecting to be
shown an early German woodcut of Vlad the Impaler which they had
come to Philadelphia to examine, were casually asked by the curator of
the Rosenbach Foundation Library if they would be interested in seeing
Stoker's working notes for *Dracula*. 'At first we could not believe our ears.
No scholar had ever found Stoker's notes.'[9] The relics of many lie, as Browne
says, in all parts of the earth; these may seem to have wandered far.

E. M. Forster made Browne, along with Dante and Shelley, one of the
drivers of the celestial omnibus which travels to a place where literary
characters and motifs are real, and Browne is imagined as a more than
usually philosophical English cab-driver who refuses the hero's watch in
lieu of a ticket:

Tickets on the line, whether single or return, can be purchased by coinage from no
terrene mint. And a chronometer, though it had solaced the vigils of Charlemagne,
or measured the slumbers of Laura, can acquire by no mutation the doublecake
that charms that fangless Cerberus of Heaven!¹⁰

One Benjamin Dockray claimed to have discovered the dialogue suggested by Browne in *Urne-Buriall* 'between two Infants in the womb concerning the state of this world [which] might handsomely illustrate our

⁷ See Robin Grey, The *Complicity of Imagination: The American Renaissance, Contests of Authority, and
  17th-Century English Culture* (Cambridge: Cambridge University Press, 1997).
⁸ Henry Thoreau, *Walden*, ed. J. Lyndon Shanley (Princeton: Princeton University Press, 1971), 23.
⁹ Raymond McNally and Radu Florescu, quoted by Elizabeth Miller, '[Stoker's Research]' in *Three
  Vampire Tales*, ed. Anne Williams (Boston: Houghton Mifflin, 2003), 47.
¹⁰ 'The Celestial Omnibus' in *Collected Short Stories of E.M. Forster* (London: Sidgwick and Jackson,
  1948), 45.

ignorance of the next'. Published in 1855, it sounds nothing like Browne, a fact explained by Dockray as the effect of translation back into English from an early German translation of the lost original.[11] It has been suggested that the thirteenth variation in Elgar's *Enigma Variations* (1899) is based on *Religio Medici*; and indeed, Browne seems to generate a certain kind of mystery. J. B. Priestly, hearing that the plaque at number 12 Orford Place commemorating Browne's residence there was once mistaken for a doctor's surgery by Kelley's *Directory of Norwich 1929*, told the following ghost story to his friend:

> 'Don't you see it? The year is 1929, after the publication of that directory. Late at night, with everything closed solid, a woman is suddenly taken ill and her husband, frantic, grabs for the directory to look for a physician. There is no telephone, but the nearest doctor is a man named Browne, a few squares away. The husband snatches his hat, rushes out into the darkened streets, and in a few minutes is standing before the tablet in Orford Place. Yes, there he is! – "*Thomas Browne, M.D.*" He plunges his thumb into the bell and –'
> 'And what?'
> 'Gets him'.[12]

Who, indeed, knows the fate of his bones? Even gravestones tell the truth scarce forty years, and to be read by bare inscriptions, by enigmatical epithets or first letters of our names, to be studied by antiquaries who we were, are cold consolations unto the students of eternity.

Other admirers of Browne have included Thomas de Quincey, Lytton Strachey, Virginia Woolf, Cyril Connolly, and Jorge Luis Borges. A massive project, the construction of a universal encyclopaedia of an apparently lost civilisation, is accidentally discovered by the narrator in Borges' 'Tlön, Uqbar, Orbis Tertius' (1941). The *First Encyclopaedia of Tlön*, itself now vanished but for a single volume, signals the melancholy dispersion of a culture and of its only record – beautifully Brownean themes. The narrator eventually discovers that Tlön had in fact been the creation of an early-seventeenth-century hermetic group somewhere in Europe, a fictional world which has since been insinuated into the realm of learning like an intellectual virus. Borges's narrator retreats in despair to the only consolation he can think of, the translating into Spanish of *Urne-Buriall*. The very real Kingdom of Redonda – a Tlön-like state consisting of a tiny guano island

---

[11] Benjamin Dockray, 'Reminiscences of the Unborn Life of Twins, 1683' in *Conjectural Restoration of the Lost Dialogue between Two Twins* (1855).

[12] Originally told by Vincent Starrett, *Books Alive* (New York: Random House, 1940); quoted by Jeremiah Finch, *Sir Thomas Browne: A Doctor's Life of Science and Faith* (New York: Henry Schuman, 1950), 26–7.

in the Caribbean ruled by Javier I – has its own publishing house (Reino de Redonda), much of whose output consists of Spanish translations of Browne's works by his royal admirer, Javier Marias.

W. E. Sebald (dedicatee of the Redondan translations) produced in *The Rings of Saturn* a perambulation of the Norfolk-Suffolk borders in the style of, and suffused with references to, the Norfolk doctor.[13] Susan Sontag, Allen Kurzweil, and Philipp Blom have used curious and natural histori-cal collecting as themes in recent works, Blom with reference to Browne himself.[14] J. A. Cuddon's magisterial memoir of Istanbul in the 1950s finds words expressive of that great city in *Religio Medici*.[15] Tony Kushner's ec-centric play *Hydriotaphia* is remotely connected to Browne's writings, and even more remotely to Browne himself, who features as the main character: Kushner characterises him rather improbably as a 'nasty bloated logorrheic old bugger', a series of epithets even his arch-enemy Alexander Ross would have resisted.[16]

Certain modern artists, even if they do not read Browne, neverthe-less respond to the same impulses of collecting and encyclopaedic as-semblage. Brian Catling cites Browne as a favourite as he discusses the 'half-remembered pattern of observance' in his own work.[17] In the same spirit, Joseph Cornell's cabinets of memory, Mark Dion's bio-installations, and the curious artefacts made by Man Ray, André Breton, Luigi On-tani, Ian Hamilton-Finlay, Yves Klein, Claudio Parmiggiani, Pino Pascali, Kurt Schwitters, Jean Arp, and Marcel Broodthaers respond to the same collecting and ordering impulses to which Browne reacted in early muse-ums and cabinets of curiosity, arrays and displays strongly reflected in their work.[18] Perhaps the most extended and brilliantly Brownean project of all is the Museum of Jurassic Technology in Culver City, California, a scholarly

---

[13] W. E. Sebald, *The Rings of Saturn* (1995), trans. from the German by Michael Hulse (London: Harvill, 1998). Sebald's encounter with *Musæum Clausum* generates unacknowledged additions of his own to the catalogue, an effect Browne seems to have on some of his fans. See my next note on Philipp Blom.

[14] Susan Sontag, *The Volcano Lover* (1992); Allen Kurzweil, *A Case of Curiosities* (1992); and Philipp Blom, *To Have and to Hold: An Intimate History of Collectors and Collecting* (London: Allen Lane, 2002). Blom is one of the few writers to interest himself in *Musæum Clausum* (although has con-fused some of Browne's imaginary books with those of Rabelais and of Johann Fischart (187) – an occupational hazard, apparently, for those who read this work (see my previous note on Sebald).

[15] J. A. Cuddon, *The Owl's Watch-Song: A Study of Istanbul* (London: Barrie and Rockliff, 1960), 84, 183, 197–8.

[16] Tony Kushner, *Death and Taxes: Hydriotaphia and Other Plays* (New York: Theatre Communications Group, 2000), 31.

[17] Brian Catling, *Tending the Vortex: The Works of Brian Catling*, ed. Simon Perril (Cambridge: CCCP Books, 2001), 45.

[18] Mark Dion, *Natural History and Other Fictions* (Birmingham: Ikon Gallery, Hamburg: Kunstverein, and Amsterdam: De Appel, 1997); Adalgisa Lugli, *Wunderkammer* (Torino: Umberto Allemandi, 1997).

collection of meticulously catalogued and ironised items – a map of the siege and battle of Pavia, a scale model of Noah's ark, a wall of antlers, microscopic carving of unfeasible complexity, a selection of mouse-cures, and a vitrine of inhaled objects – which seem like refugees from *Musæum Clausum*.[19]

Like the commemorands of the Walsingham urns, little might Browne have expected the curiosity of future ages to honour his memory in quite these ways, although it is tempting to believe that the author of *Musæum Clausum* would have appreciated the wit and invention of such 'after-considerations'. It is one of the undertakings of this book to show why.

---

[19] See Lawrence Wechsler, *Mr Wilson's Cabinet of Wonder* (New York: Vintage Books, 1995).

CHAPTER I

Browne's civility

Happy are they whom privacy makes innocent.

(*U-B* v, 170)

THE PRESS AND THE APOCALYPSE

In the fourth act of Seneca's *Thyestes*, fearful Chorus imagines a universal cataclysm which issues from the murder of Thyestes' young sons by their uncle Atreus, who means to secure the kingdom for himself and his heirs. Thyestes is about to learn that he has cannibalised his own sons at Atreus' banquet, and for this, says Chorus, the heavens will revolt, the seasons will be confused, and chaos will come again. This vision ends in a desperate apostrophe:

> And are we chosen out of all earth's children
> Of a disjointed universe? Are we
> To see the world's end come?
> A cruel fate brought us to birth, if we
> Have lived to lose the Sun, or if our sins
> Have driven him away.
> But we must not complain, nor fear;
> *Too fond of life is he who would not die*
> *When all the world dies with him.*[1] [italics mine]

It is with a paraphrase of the final lines of this apocalyptic passage that Thomas Browne chooses to open his preface 'To the Reader' in the 1643 *Religio Medici* authorising the previously anonymous essay as his own.

It is always useful to unpack such prefaces, especially one linked to the later printing of a much earlier work; and *Religio Medici*, written at

---

[1] Seneca, *Thyestes*, ll. 875–84 (in Seneca, *Four Tragedies and Octavia*, trans. E. F. Watling (Harmondsworth: Penguin, 1966), 83. Seneca offers a related sentiment in *Troades*, lines 162–4: 'Happy Priam, happy is any man who dying in war has taken with him all things spent' (*Seneca's 'Troades': A Literary Introduction with Text, Translation, and Commentary*, trans. Elaine Fantham (Princeton: Princeton University Press, 1982), 136–7).

some point between 1633, when Browne completed his medical training in Leiden, and 1636, roughly the date which he assigns to it when he claims it was composed 'about seven yeares past', may be as much as ten years older than the 1643 preface (*RM*.Reader, 9). Returning at the age of twenty-eight from Holland with his foreign doctorate of medicine, he spent a period of about four years in medical apprenticeship, probably in Oxfordshire, in order to qualify to practise in England; it is possible that the essay was begun as early as this.[2] By 1642 there were a number of manuscripts of *Religio Medici* in circulation, one of which reached a printer who brought out two editions of it in that year.

The very form of the essay may also have worried its author: then as now generically unclassifiable, *Religio Medici* is a series of claims, remarks, and enquiries based on Browne's faith and its application to worldly conduct. It is a 'cento', to use one of his preferred terms, of assembled fragments, an assemblage of thoughts apparently, but not entirely convincingly, aimed at systematic coherence. In its seventy-one more or less discrete, more or less related sections (seventy-five in the 1643 edition), each concerned with an opinion or a belief enunciated in varying registers of authority and insistence, *Religio Medici* is a disconcertingly personal self-portrait which is neither autobiography nor confession, and Browne probably feared the consequences of its tonal and rhetorical diversity, that it would be misunderstood as more absolute than it was ever intended to be.

In 1643, distressed by the sudden notoriety of these privately circulated meditations, and perhaps alarmed by the potential danger of exposing his views to an increasingly intolerant establishment and opposition, he corrected the offending 1642 edition(s), prefaced it with the apologetic 'To the Reader', and allowed it to be printed for the third time in authorised form by Andrew Crooke, the opportunistic pirating publisher of the earlier versions.

---

[2] Raymond Waddington places the date of composition between December 1633 and October 1635 ('The Two Tables in *Religio Medici*' in Patrides *Approaches*, 86). For other discussions of the date of composition of *Religio Medici*, see *Sir Thomas Browne's Works*, ed. Simon Wilkin, 4 vols. (London: William Pickering, 1835–6), 11, iv–vii; Keynes 1, 3–7; Frank Livingstone Huntley, *Sir Thomas Browne: A Biographical and Critical Study*, 2nd edn (Ann Arbor: University of Michigan Press, 1968), 90–103; Patrides *STB*, 23; *Thomas Browne, Religio Medici*, ed. Vittoria Sanna (Cagliari: Universitá di Cagliari, 1958), viii–xi, xxxiv–xli; *Sir Thomas Browne: Religio Medici*, ed. Jean-Jacques Denonain (Cambridge: Cambridge University Press, 1953), ix–xxi; and Michael Wilding, '*Religio Medici* in the English Revolution' in Patrides *Approaches*, 100–14. The debate about the place of composition of *Religio Medici* is covered by Huntley, *Sir Thomas Browne*, 90–7. He finished his apprenticeship and was incorporated M.D. at Oxford on 10 July 1637 (Anthony à Wood, *Athenae Oxoniensis, to which are added the Fasti*, ed. Philip Bliss, 5 vols. (1815), 1, 498). Direct internal evidence for the date of composition occurs in 1.41: 'nor hath my pulse beate 30 yeares'; and in 11. 11: 'now for my life, it is a miracle of 30 yeares'. This would place these sections, at least, in 1635 or earlier.

Browne claims in his prefatory letter that this corrected version is 'a full and intended copy of that Peece which was most imperfectly and surreptitiously published before' (*RM*.Reader, 1). It is likely that Crooke *was* surreptitious, but it is exceedingly difficult to credit Browne's charge of extreme imperfection: Crooke's was not a heroic sloppiness, and most of the many corrections are quite minor.[3] The four sections in Part I which Browne added to the 1643 edition emphasise his own subsequently developed views and do not represent corrected misprintings or erroneous omissions in the earlier versions.[4] Indeed, his alterations of this kind (notably sections 1.8 and 1.56) seem designed to situate him in opposition to various radical sects, which were increasingly active in the early 1640s. The most important revisions of the 1642 version are the complement of the author's name, and the insertion of the prefatory letter itself. Indeed, the 'authorisation' which Browne seems to give *Religio Medici* is literal – he legitimises it by acknowledging it as his own in order to say a thing or two about illicit publication.

The serving up of children at a feast of reconciliation is a violation of hospitality which portends the radically uncivil fate of the Achæan royal house, a bloody cycle of guest- and host-crimes which in the *Oresteia* of Aeschylus has consequences for the Trojan War, a cycle broken only by the divine intervention which issues in the founding of the Athenian Areopagus.[5] Thus, Browne's invocation of Seneca directs us to perhaps the most ferocious example of barbarity in the western canon, and notifies us that

[3] L. C. Martin thinks that Browne could not or would not give proper attention to the revision of *Religio*, and speculates that he had no involvement in the correction of proofs or collation of errata (*Religio Medici and Other Works*, ed. L.C. Martin (Oxford: Clarendon Press, 1964), xiv); Geoffrey Keynes deems Browne to have forgiven Crooke for the original piracy because he allowed him to reprint the book in its authorised version on a number of occasions between 1643 and Crooke's death in 1674 (Keynes 1, 4); Browne's nineteenth-century editor, Simon Wilkin, believed that *Religio Medici* was widely circulated in manuscript before 1641, and that Browne wished to acknowledge it once it was published because it had sold well and been given a good reception (Wilkin, 11, v–vi); see also Elizabeth Cook, who judges that there is nothing to suggest that Crooke's editions were based on a garbled manuscript ('The First Edition of *Religio Medici*', *Harvard Library Bulletin* 2 (1948), 22).

[4] Browne's holograph proof corrections in the partial 1642 edition held in the Robert H. Taylor Collection at Princeton University show either relatively trifling semantic alterations (e.g., 'throughly' for 'truly') or substantive afterthoughts and reworkings which could not have been omissions or errors by Crooke. Denonain flags more than 650 corrections of the 1642 edition which appear in 1643 (Denonain, xxvii).

[5] Browne's interest in, and perhaps horror of, the Thyestes story is signalled again in *Musæum Clausum*, where one of the curious paintings catalogued in 'Draughts of three passionate Looks' includes 'Thyestes when he was told at the Table that he had eaten a piece of his own Son'; the other two 'looks' are those of Bajazeth going into his cage and Oedipus discovering his crimes against his parents (*MC*, Keynes 111, 114). See also the fish that looked like Theodoric's son in 'Of fishes eaten by our saviour' in *MT* (Keynes 111, 55). James Wise discounts Browne's use of *Thyestes* as merely 'hyperbolical' (James N. Wise, *Sir Thomas Browne's 'Religio Medici' and Two Seventeenth-Century Critics* (Columbia, MO: University of Missouri Press, 1973), 12).

the threat to order, or what the early-modern period termed 'civility', is of unexampled importance to him. In the following discussion I will propose the nature and extent of Browne's understanding of this threatened civility, and suggest the important bearing the *mentalité* comprehended by the word 'civility' has on the wide range of intellectual and social practices connected with his professional life as a doctor, writer, and investigator.

'Certainly that man were greedy of life', Browne begins the letter, 'who should desire to live when all the world were at an end, and he must needs be very impatient who would repine at death in the societie of all things that suffer under it' (*RM*.Reader, 9). It is in keeping with Browne's millenarian thought that his Senecan paraphrase describes the expectation of the last times.[6] That crisis, however, is not usually for him the universal convulsion and 'generall combustion of this world' associated with Christian eschatology, nor does he picture it as a violent Thyestean dismemberment.[7] Instead of catastrophic and ruinous natural and supernatural events, he tends to imagine a sort of cosmic housekeeping or spiritual tidiness: he prefers the re-memberment of Ezekiel's vision of the valley of bones, that curious slice of Old Testament prophecy in which a charnel heap of human remains knit themselves together and rise up to heaven at the voice of God, a vision reiterated in *Religio Medici*, *Pseudodoxia Epidemica*, and *Urne-Buriall*. William Camden had noted that St Paul calls 'the place of burial ... *seminatio*, in respect of the assured hope of Resurrection'.[8] It is with this sense of the end of the world that Browne imagines 'the graves shall shoot up their concealed seeds, and in that great Autumne, men shall spring up, and awake from their Chaos againe' (*PE* VI.i.442). Elsewhere in *Religio Medici* he imagines a satisfying sorting-out operation on Judgement Day:

I beleeve that our estranged and divided ashes shall unite againe; that our separated dust, after so many pilgrimages and transformations into the parts of mineralls, Plants, Animals, Elements, shall at the voyce of God returne into their primitive shapes, and joyne againe to make up their primary and predestinated formes ...

[6] Browne was, however, no precise millenarian: claims that the end would come in 1653 or 1656 by various authorities he regarded as mere 'statute madnesse' (*RM* 1.46); but he certainly believed that the world was entering the final days of the years of Grace. (See C. A. Patrides, 'Renaissance and Modern Thought on the Last Things: A Study in Changing Conceptions', *Harvard Theological Review* 51 (1958), 171; Frank Livingstone Huntley, '*The Garden of Cyrus* as Prophecy' in Patrides *Approaches*, 136; and Derek Hirst, *England in Conflict, 1603–1660* (London: Arnold, 1999), 256–8, 259–60, 276–7, 298.

[7] Godfrey Goodman, *The Fall of Man, or the Corruption of Nature* (1616), 397. For literal readings of the apocalypse, see the discussion by Florence Sandler, '*The Faerie Queene*: An Elizabethan Apocalypse' in *The Apocalypse in English Renaissance Thought and Literature: Patterns, Antecedants, and Repercussions*, ed. C. A. Patrides and Joseph Wittreich (Manchester: Manchester University Press, 1984), 149.

[8] William Camden, *Remains Concerning Britain* (1605), ed. R. D. Dunn (Toronto: University of Toronto Press, 1984), 389.

at the last day, when these corrupted reliques shall be scattered in the wildernesse of formes, and seeme to have forgot their proper habits, God by a powerfull voyce shall command them backe into their proper shapes, and call them out by their single individuals. (*RM* 1.48)

This encouraging account of last things – of decay followed by restoration – is one which will reappear in his later writing. In *Religio Medici*'s prefatory letter Browne's apocalypse is, however, imagined much more desperately and (significantly) socially – as the triumph of death over 'the *society* of all things that suffer under it'. His translation of Seneca in the first sentence tellingly connects *greed* and unsociability to indicate the totality of selfishness, incivility, or inhospitability in the ancient Atrean crime which Browne distinctively and paradoxically opposes to his normally more hopeful vision of the Last Day.

'Happy are they whom privacy makes innocent', he remarks in *Urne-Buriall*. It is – perhaps bathetically and hyperbolically – Browne's privacy which has been insulted by the illicit publication of *Religio Medici*. This small but piercing injury prompts the extreme reconfiguration of the apocalypse as, for the only time in his career, social chaos, as the kind of fundamental incivility which, in earlier instalments of human history, founders states and families, in which uncivil assaults on individuals are obviated only by the divine imposition of a legally based civil society. As he explains in the preface, his notion of social order and hierarchy, represented in King and Parliament, is being catastrophically eroded by civil affronts from the press, so that even his own injury – a rude, helpless exposure to the general view – is owing to the same foundered proprieties. With this uncharacteristically dismal vision of the apocalypse, Browne seems to suggest that his personal misadventure with the press is a microcosmic signature of the end of days, as if his sense of insult and distress were profound enough to have warped his usual vision of the orderliness of the Last Judgement – of that ultimatum as the re-establishment of satisfyingly trim proprieties. Even syntactically, the Thyestean allusion seems to invade – indeed, commandeer – our reading of the rest of the opening passage about incivility.

With scant biographical information about Browne before 1660, we are likely to remain virtually ignorant of his political reaction to the events of the 1640s and 1650s, the period in which his four major works were published, and, with the exception of *Religio Medici*, the period in which they were wholly produced. There has never been any real doubt, however, that his sympathies were broadly Royalist, if by that title we can roughly group the many prosperous, innately conservative members of the middle and upper classes who preferred peace and quiet rather than chaos and turmoil, and who were suspicious especially of the potential for chaos among the lower orders, without necessarily being much enamoured of the Stuart monarchy and episcopacy, or much opposed to some sort of gentle reform of their excesses. There is some evidence that Browne was one of many citizens who refused to give money toward the Parliamentary retaking of Newcastle in 1643, and his name appeared in the *Vox Norwici* of 1646, a pamphlet defending the Anglican clergy; in 1660 he may have signed a petition from the gentry of Norfolk urging General Monck to make government reparations to the localities against the depredations of the wars. For Browne, the potential for chaos, as I have already pointed out, is almost entirely imagined as intellectual rather than political disorder; except for a remark in his natural history notes about the fearsomeness of republics and his regret at the execution of the King, he left no political opinions of any kind.[9]

The unauthorised publication of *Religio Medici* during extreme civil unrest in early 1642 had been immediately preceded by the horror of the Irish Revolt and subsequent massacre of (it was claimed) 30,000 Protestants in October 1641.[10] That year had also produced the abolition of the episcopacy and Parliament's Grand Remonstrance with Charles. December 1641 was a month of riots and demonstrations; and in early January 1642 the King fled London. If Browne imagines the incivility of the pirating printer as a serving up of his literary offspring unbeknownst to the father, then this alarming series of political, social, and ecclesiastical breakdowns – each in some sense an upsetting of the established rules of order, hierarchy, deference, and restraint – must have reinforced that vision of chaos, of 'a tragical age', as Cowley observed, 'best to *write of*, but worst to *write in*'.[11] The inseparability of intellectual and political civility, phrased very often in expressions of courtesy and civil social conduct, originates for the mid-seventeenth century in the Latin roots *civilitas* and *civilis* – the art

---

[9] Browne's identity is not, however, clearly established in relation to these documents. Jeremiah Finch, somewhat recklessly, regards them as clear indications of a 'staunch Royalist . . . openly supporting the King's cause and using his influence to further it as opportunity arose' (*Sir Thomas Browne: A Doctor's Life of Science and Faith* (New York: Henry Schuman, 1950), 125–6, and 128; see also Jonathan F. S. Post, *Sir Thomas Browne* (Boston: Twayne Publishers, 1987), 50; and Kitty Scoular Datta, 'Sir Thomas Browne and *Vox Norwici*', *Notes and Queries* 231 (1986), 461).

Browne's disparaging comment about storks as harbingers of a commonwealth may indicate a certain Royalist bias (*NHN*, 416); the association of the stork with non-monarchical systems was apparently proverbial: 'commonwealth from ill birds doth begin' is a saw quoted by Stephen Bann, *Under the Sign: John Bargrave as Collector, Traveler, and Witness* (Ann Arbor: University of Michigan Press, 1994), 19.

[10] Exaggeration did its work in England: the toll, though grievous, was likelier 4,000 (Hirst, 183).

[11] Abraham Cowley, *Poems* (1656), a2ᵛ.

of government and the qualities of citizenship.[12] It is a yoking evident in *Religio Medici* from the opening sentence of its preface.

In the complex Stoic metaphor of Browne's prefatory letter, death and the press are likened: like repining at the tyranny of death, to which we are all subject, there is almost no point deploring the tyrannies of the press, since we are just 'as hopelesse of their reparations'(*RM*.Reader, 9).[13] With no modern legal concept of intellectual property, the primitive version of copyright operated by the Stationers' Company heavily favoured the printer over the writer, and printers were able to possess literary property if they could get hold of it and enter it in the Stationers' Register.[14] Thus, even though among writers a modern conception of intellectual ownership had long since emerged, the law lagged far behind, and piracy by a printer against a writer had little legal meaning – only, perhaps, in the emotional complaints of writers.[15] The messiness of this arrangement would have been current in Browne's mind: printers and their output had proliferated remarkably during the period after the abolition of the Star Chamber and the cessation in 1641 of the authority of its publishing decrees; Parliament's legislation of 1642 and 1643, which might have rectified his somewhat anomalous situation, instead failed him.[16]

Since Browne could not claim explicit illegal affronts to him by the press in general or by Crooke in particular, and because some blame must accrue to the facilitator of the piracy who surrendered the manuscript,

---

[12] On the genealogy of civility, see Anna Bryson, *From Courtesy to Civility: Changing Codes of Conduct in Early Modern England* (Oxford: Clarendon Press, 1998), 49–58.

[13] George Wither more explicitly names booksellers (closely associated with and often identical to printers) as enemies of the commonwealth who usurp the labours of writers and upset the proper systems of commodity exchange which underwrite social well-being and prosperity (*The Schollers Purgatory Discovered in the Stationers Commonwealth* [London, 1624], :1ᵛ–10).

[14] See Mark Rose, 'The Author as Proprietor: *Donaldson v. Becket* and the Genealogy of Modern Authorship', *Representations* 23 (1988), 54–5; the situation is also discussed by Arthur F. Marotti, 'Shakespeare's Sonnets as Literary Property' in *Soliciting Interpretation: Literary Theory and Seventeeth-Century English Poetry*, ed. Elizabeth D. Harvey and Katherine Eisaman Maus (Chicago: University of Chicago Press, 1990), 143–4.

[15] Printers, Wither laments, 'publish bookes contrived, altered, and mangled at their owne pleasure, without consent of writers' (Wither, 10).

[16] The press, essentially unregulated at this point, was subsequently, in the Signature Order of 1642, enjoined to print nothing without the consent of the author; but since *Religio Medici* was still anonymous, Crooke was probably not bound by it. The Licensing Order of 1643 expressly forbade piracy, but came too late for Browne. See Ernest Sirluck, 'Milton's Pamphlets' in *The Complete Prose Works of John Milton*, ed. Sirluck, 8 vols. (New Haven: Yale University Press, 1959), 11, 158–61; Abbe Blum,'The Author's Authority: *Areopagitica* and the Labour of Licensing' in *Re-Membering Milton: Essays on the Texts and Traditions*, ed. Mary Nyquist and Margaret W. Ferguson (New York and London: Methuen, 1987), 74–96; and Samuel R. Gardiner, *History of the Great Civil War 1642–1649*, 4 vols. (London: Longmans, Green, 1904), 1, 149. Robin Robbins notes that Browne's allusion to a work 'Counterfeitly imprinted' refers to the forged commission from Court at Edinburgh in December 1643 inciting Irish Catholics to rebel in support of Charles (Robbins *STB*, 191, note 1).

Browne's complaint in 'To the Reader' is therefore only partly personal. Although to suffer silently would otherwise be the appropriate response of 'private persons', it is, he insists, the public injury not to himself but to *truth* that elicits the preface, and the broadcasting of untruths augmented by 'things of truth most falsly set forth'. '[I]n this latter', he says, 'I could not but thinke my selfe engaged . . . the reparation being within our selves'. This competition between private agency and externally or publicly imposed necessity is familiar from Milton's *Areopagitica*: both writers are characteristic of the early-modern shift in what Norbert Elias has called an increasingly 'internalized' individual autonomy.[17] Thus Browne is now perforce willing to offer 'a full and intended copy' of what had been 'most imperfectly and surreptitiously published before' (*RM*.Reader, 9). In other words, while admitting that he cannot repair the fragmentation of the English polity which will apparently accept from a wild and unregulated press any number of affronts to King, Parliament, and private individuals, he will none the less control the publicity of the insult to himself by rebuking publicly the incivility of that general social disorder which seems to have coalesced for him in this episode of sloppy, inaccurate, impermissible publication.

Although Browne has been described as 'less than distressed' by the illicit publication of his essay in 1642, this judgement, based on the apparent insouciance of his dealings with the printer, is hard to reconcile with the tone and themes of the preface.[18] For one thing, *Religio Medici* was an old work, practically a *juvenilium*, written during the transitional period between years of studenthood and entry into the professional world of medicine. His shock was clearly genuine, as it would likely not have been for the Royalist poet Abraham Cowley, who claimed that his adolescent poems had been shown to the world like premature infants. Cowley had made a public cult of his youthful precocity (those first poems were published in 1633, when he was at school), and he never allowed that fact to be forgotten.[19] For Browne, on the other hand, *Religio Medici* was the work he almost never mentioned in later years, as if he hardly reckoned it among his serious works. It had always been intended as private, meant only for friends to read in manuscript and not for vulgar consumption.

[17] Norbert Elias, *The Civilizing Process* (1969), quoted in Blum, 78.   [18] Patrides *STB*, 23.

[19] Cowley, 'Preface of the Author', *Poems*, a3^v–a4^r. That juvenile volume was *Poeticall Blossoms* (1633). For a discussion of Cowley's attitude toward publication, see Arthur F. Marotti, *Manuscript, Print, and the English Renaissance Lyric* (Ithaca, NY: Cornell University Press, 1995), 264; and Richard Helgerson, *Self-Crowned Laureates: Spenser, Jonson, Milton and the Literary System* (Berkeley: University of California Press, 1983), 215–17.

Religio Medici is mainly a précis, Browne insists in the preface, of his beliefs at the time of writing; his 'advancing judgement' cannot be held to account for them. This earliness of the essay is, indeed, one of its essential features: it is clearly marked as a young man's book, its innocence of tone and outlook only barely masked by its magisterial phrasing, written from the perspective of his relatively tranquil mid-1630s. By contrast to the well-known juvenilities of *Religio Medici*, the tone of the 'To the Reader' is *not* naive: if he had once upon a time recorded his bizarre regret that coition is 'the foolishest act a wise man commits in all his life', and eccentrically wished that we could procreate like trees,[20] the older and more experienced Browne of the preface looks back on the naiveté of his essay, the juxtaposition of the two personae indicating the hopelessness of maintaining such innocence with the uncivil forces of the press and of rebellion arrayed against him. His own journey from the innocence of eight-and-twenty to sceptical late-thirty-something is one of Browne's many temporal conceits: *Religio Medici* is the tract, to use a phrase from *Urne-Buriall*, of an embryon philosopher still *in utero*, still discoursing in Plato's den *(U-B* IV, 162); and by 1643 it was either stillborn or ripped untimely from the womb. It is that innocence, in Browne's account, which seems to have been rudely awakened into worldliness and embarrassment by the unauthorised publication of his manuscript, which he floridly reckons to have been virtually deflowered by publicity, 'common unto many', 'corrupted', and 'depraved' (*RM*.Reader, 9).

It is interesting to compare Browne's charges of textual corruption with those of his near-contemporary, Godfrey Goodman. To his 1616 *The Fall of Man* (which Browne knew well) Goodman appended a brief *envoi* noting and apologising for certain errata which residence outside London prevented him from correcting:

> but presently I called to mind, that the subject of my booke, was onely to prove a generall corruption; which corruption I should in effect seeme to disprove and denie, unlesse it might everywhere appeare, and therefore a necessitie did seeme so to ordaine it, that it should first begin in the author, then in the pen, then in the presse, and now I feare nothing so much as the evill and corrupt exposition of the Reader, for thus there is a generall corruption. How happie was I to make choice of such a subject, which seemes to excuse all the errors of my pamphlet.[21]

---

[20] Daniela Havenstein briefly wonders if this odd wish is the 'unnatural Phancy of a frigid young man, or . . . a joke', but concludes that it is part of Browne's conception of privacy (*Democratizing Sir Thomas Browne: 'Religio Medici' and its Imitations* (Oxford: Clarendon Press, 1999), 63). It might, clearly, be linked to Marvell's desire for prelapsarian solitude.
[21] Goodman, [446].

Like the errors in *The Fall of Man*, the 1643 *Religio Medici* figures itself as a lesson in human fallibility, and can be read as an antiphonal between the two voices of Browne's experience – the mature one of 'To the Reader' and that of his late youthful innocence in the essay itself. If the 'generall corruption' of the world is to Goodman's mind echoed in the corruption of his work, Browne's 'full and intended' copy of *Religio Medici* in its authorised edition presents the history of Browne's own journey from innocence to recognition. This account of textual and personal fallenness introduces the intellectual and natural consequences of the original Fall which largely organise each of his major works.

PRIVACY PROTESTED

In defence of prefaces like Browne's, Harold Love writes that 'more credence than is customary should be given to the claims made by authors . . . that they had been forced to the press by the fear or fact of an unauthorized printing from a corrupt manuscript . . . Far from being coy attempts to disarm criticism, such pleas identify a real and pressing dilemma for scribally publishing authors'.[22] Scribal publication, the authorially initiated circulation of a manuscript copy or copies among friends or colleagues, was a private practice over which the writer could not necessarily maintain control. Scribal transmissions flourished between equals, within recognised client-patron relationships, or among like-minded specialists, text-exchange extending mutual sociability and preserving exclusive social and intellectual coteries.[23] We will probably never know whom Browne had to thank for handing *Religio Medici* to Crooke; nor have we any record of his response to what he might reasonably have construed as a betrayal of trust. It may have been an act of carelessness or downright unkindness which Browne might well have labelled 'uncivil'.[24]

Our judgement of the preface depends partly on the status of privacy itself, which was deeply contested in this period. The nature of Browne's claims to it – although possibly passé by 1643 – will assist our understanding of his political and social positions insofar as they can be determined. Kevin Dunn notes some important developments in the relation of the writer to his public: in the seventeenth century, he argues, the rhetoric of

---

[22] Harold Love, *The Culture and Commerce of Texts: Scribal Publication in Seventeenth-Century England*, 2nd edn (Amherst, MA: University of Massachusetts Press, 1998), 72.

[23] Love, 44; 179.

[24] The proliferation of non-holograph manuscripts of *Religio Medici* is strong evidence that the initial publication was entrepreneurial, not authorial (Love, 77).

self-authorisation was almost completely developed, together with the understanding of authorship as ownership; and this had consequences for the
reigning classical rhetorical elements of the exordium. The classical modesty
topos, by claiming powerlessness, subsumes the speaker as 'an unmotivated
function of the case'; disclaimers of unwonted publicity are therefore not
expressions of a private voice or idiom, but a species of *insinuatio* aimed
at forestalling hostility.²⁵ By contrast, a seventeenth-century complaint like
Browne's *is* the voice of violated personal and intellectual privacy, and the
scribal and vocal evidence in *Religio Medici* seems to support the gravity
and sincerity of the preface: for Browne, the failure of respect for ownership
and inwardness of text figures the failure of major proprieties in the public
sphere, in the very commonwealth.

When *Religio Medici* was first issued anonymously in 1642, the Earl of
Dorset read it with approval and recommended it to his imprisoned protégé,
Sir Kenelm Digby, Royalist, experimentalist, and cookery expert. Digby
read through the night of 21 December 1642 (by his own account) in order
to write what were to become his *Observations on 'Religio Medici'* (1643) as
a letter to his patron. This document, Digby claims, was like Browne's also
then given to a printer without his knowledge.²⁶ When Browne heard of
the imminent appearance of what were reported to be Digby's 'animadver-
sions', he immediately wrote begging him to await the authorised edition
before bringing out such remarks. As he explained, *Religio Medici* was produced 'with no intention for the Presse, or the least desire to obliege the
Faith of any man to its assertions'.²⁷ Forced only by its gathering fame to
present a correct version of the essay, Browne plaintively reiterated to Digby
that claim of privacy in 'To the Reader': 'the intention was not publick:
and being a private exercise directed to my selfe, what is delivered therein
was rather a memoriall unto me than an example or rule unto any other'

²⁵ Kevin Dunn, *Pretexts of Authority: The Rhetoric of Authorship in the Renaissance Preface* (Stanford:
Stanford University Press, 1994), 2–9; see also Cecile Jagodzinski, *Privacy and Print: Reading and
Writing in Seventeeth Century England* (Charlottesville: University of Virginia Press, 1999), 11–12.
²⁶ For the relentlessly self-publicising Digby, this seems an unlikely claim. It is somewhat more probable
that the stigma of print required it of him – an interesting contrast to Browne's disclaimer. Jackson
I. Cope discusses Digby's 'manipulation of the public rhetoric of forms' in 'Sir Kenelm Digby's
rewritings of his life' in *Writing and Political Engagement in Seventeenth-Century England*, ed. Derek
Hirst and Richard Strier, (Cambridge: Cambridge University Press, 1999), 52–68. See also Wise,
57–63; Allardyce Nicholl, 'Kenelm Digby, Poet, Philosopher, and Pirate of the Restoration', *Johns
Hopkins Alumni Magazine* 21 (1933), 330–50; and R. J. Petersson, *Sir Kenelm Digby* (Cambridge,
MA: Harvard University Press, 1956). On Digby's reputation, see also Huntley, *Sir Thomas Browne*,
143. Henry Stubbe described Digby as 'the Pliny of our Age for lying' (*The Plus Ultra Reduced to a
New Plus* (1670), 161).
²⁷ Thomas Browne to Kenelm Digby, [3 March 1642/3] (Keynes IV, 235).

(*RM*.Reader, 9–10). The Montaigneian savour of this remark is very strong, as it is at many points in *Religio Medici*: Montaigne insists in *On the Education of Children*, 'these are but my humors and opinions, and I deliver them but to show what my conceit is, and not what ought to be beleeved'.[28] And yet Montaigne's self-scrutiny partly aims at public self-portrait, at self-revelation. Unlike Browne's, Montaigne's essays – although purposed, initially at least, for his friends and family – were works he revised and published again and again during his lifetime. Browne, by contrast, invokes the word 'private' four times in the brief prefatory letter to *Religio Medici*, a word which had been relatively uncommon in English before the sixteenth century, and which during the early-modern period was coming to signal a category of experience rather than merely a behavioural type.[29] All his protestations – that the views expressed are out of date, that the quotations are at times incorrect, that ideas are to be understood tropically and flexibly, not rigidly – are overridden by his even clearer sense of having been publicly embarrassed by exposure; the revisions of 1643 are not Montaigne's leisurely and multiple reconsiderations, but hurried redactions to suit unfortunate and unsought conditions.

Once Browne had revealed his identity to Kenelm Digby, he was quickly reassured by that famous savant that no insult had been intended. Although the vainglorious Digby is almost certainly not to be believed in his account of how his *Observations* were produced and published, he too claimed injury to his privacy, the liberty of his remarks about *Religio Medici* addressed to the Earl of Dorset supposedly 'to be attributed to the security of a private letter'.[30] Digby, Browne's first serious critic, was also his least astute and least honest, the *Observations* little more than a catalogue of self-serving quibbles;[31] nevertheless, it is difficult to concur with the view that scouts mocking irony in Digby's letter to Browne, even if its tone is inconsistent with his

---

[28] Michel de Montaigne, *The Essayes of Michel Lord of Montaigne*, trans. John Florio, ed. A. R. Waller, 3 vols. (London: J. M. Dent and Sons/Everyman, 1910), III, 152. Browne insisted in later life that he had never read more than a few lines of Montaigne, despite the constant comparisons of their work.

[29] See Ronald Huebert, 'Privacy: The Early Social History of a Word', *Sewanee Review* 105 (1997), 28–9.

[30] Kenelm Digby to Thomas Browne, [20 March 1642/3] (Keynes IV, 237).

[31] Digby's *Observations* are a Heepish mix of obsequiousness (to Dorset), faint praise (of Browne), and extended sneering cavils (with Browne and *Religio Medici*). Digby condescendingly allows that Browne is fascinating on the occurrences of everyday life, but advises that a person of such low rank, conception, and *otium ignobile* should stay clear of abstraction, speculation, and metaphysics (Digby, *Observations on 'Religio Medici'* (1643), 119, 75–6). Digby's work, warned a notice appended to the Browne–Digby correspondence reproduced in the 1643 edition, consists of 'discourses collateral and digressions of his own, not at all emergent from this discourse' (Robbins *STB*, 89).

book.[32] Digby addressed him, in the traditional manner of one courteous
gentleman to another, in terms of the utmost civility, heaped praise upon
Browne's 'great parts' and 'learned and ingenious discourse', denigrating his
own 'superficiall besprinkling [of knowledge]'. 'I dare assure you', he said,
'that nothing shall ever issue from me but savouring of all honor, estime and
reverence both to yr selfe and that worthy production of yrs.'[33] And, indeed,
Digby's inept and envious critique of *Religio Medici* served to publicise it
by appending a famous name to the essay of the obscure Dr Browne.

'The reciprocal civility of authors', Samuel Johnson remarked impatiently of this exchange, 'is one of the most risible scenes in the farce of
life'.[34] These important rituals of gentility, however, Johnson misjudges:
Browne's nervous anticipation of slight, and the ceremonial obeisance of
Digby – who must have recognised the undeniable and rankling superiority
of Browne's writing and thought – invoke the sincere diction of civility: by
'civility' I mean (for the moment) simply the orderliness of social exchange,
a form of mannerliness, or politeness, which 'teaches to dispose our words
and actions in their proper and just places',[35] which each seems to take as
vital to mutual discourse. When Browne claims in the letter that it is only
'the importunitie of friends and the allegeance I must ever acknowledge
unto truth' which compel him to issue a correct version of *Religio Medici*,
he is confessing the social and intellectual obligations which combine to explain his reluctant decision to acknowledge the initial injury. And although
he himself has been coerced both by untoward circumstance and by the
obligations of civility to authorise the work, he is restrained, even eirenic:
his remarks, he claims, can neither advantage his advocates nor disable his
detractors, and he will not even vouch for the accuracy of his quotations.
The newly authorised *Religio Medici* is offered by Browne politely, mod-
estly, with the licence owed by a civil writer to civil and courteous readers,
who are invited to read it as flexibly and tropically as he has written it. By
appending the prefatory letter, Browne seeks to re-establish the terms of
civility which the appearance of the pirated essay has violated.

Browne's diction and assumptions of civility raise a number of questions.
Some of the conventions of what Stephano Guazzo and others had styled
'civil conversation' are certainly in play: Guazzo named reservation, dex-
terity, patience, humility, civility, affability, and dissimulation as the key
virtues of such conversation, and Browne seems to take most of these as

[32] Wise, 60; and Huntley, *Sir Thomas Browne*, 143.
[33] Kenelm Digby to Thomas Browne, [20 March 1642/3] (Keynes IV, 236–7).
[34] Samuel Johnson, *Life of Sir Thomas Browne* in Patrides *STB*, 486.
[35] Antoine de Courtin, *The Rules of Civility* (1678), 4.

données.[36] Hobbes develops a more universal precept of consideration of others (what he calls *commodus*), which he regards as a precept of nature – without it war and violence break out – and which is the opposite of inhumanity.[37] But because Browne writes as a scientist as well as a gentleman, does this model of social, transactional civility – a model of polite exchange based on deference, modesty, and necessity – enhance our understanding of Browne's authorial and professional practice in his later, more obviously investigative works? To what extent do the Stoic, Baconian, and Hobbesian models of civil society and social benefit inflect his tasks as writer and as practising medic and virtuoso; and in what way does his knowledge of natural history condition his thoughts on civil behaviour? And finally, is it reasonable to connect Browne with the specifically scientific model of civil interaction invoked by Bacon and by virtually every Baconian practitioner between 1605 and 1700? There exists some fascinating work which delineates this scientific civility, but it is not work which interests itself much in its associated literary tropes.[38] We must look to literary figures like Browne, Cowley, Evelyn, Butler, and others – scientific in bent but not major contributors to the scientific enterprise – to expand upon the imaginative, literary space of scientific, 'learned sociability'.[39]

When Lodovick Bryskett explains that his *Discourse of Civil Life* (1606) was written only for 'private exercise' and 'has long layne by me, as not meaning... to communicate the same to others' but for the importunity of his friends, he is employing what may, by Browne's time, have been a completely evacuated privacy-modesty trope.[40] George Hakewill can similarly excuse his *Apologie of the Power and Providence of God* (1627) as 'long since in my younger yeares begunne by me for mine owne private

---

[36] Stephano Guazzo, in *The Art of Complaisance, or the Means to Oblige in Conversation* (1677), 8 (originally published in English as *Civile Conversation* (1575)).

[37] Thomas Hobbes, *On the Citizen* (*De Cive*), ed. and trans. Richard Tuck and Michael Silverstone (Cambridge: Cambridge University Press, 1998), 48.

[38] See Steven Shapin's '"The Mind is its Own Place": Science and Solitude in Seventeenth Century England', *Science in Context* 4 (1990), 191–218; his '"A Scholar and a Gentleman": The Problematic Identity of the Scientific Practitioner in Early Modern England', *History of Science* 29 (1991), 279–327; and his *A Social History of Truth: Civility and Science in Seventeenth-Century England* (Chicago: University of Chicago Presss, 1994); and also Robert G. Frank, Jr, *Harvey and the Oxford Physiologists: A Study of Scientific Ideas* (Berkeley: University of California Press, 1980).

[39] I borrow this useful phrase from Peter Miller, *Peiresc's Europe: Learning and Virtue in the Seventeenth Century* (New Haven: Yale University Press, 2000), 49.

[40] Lodovick Bryskett, *A Discourse of Civil Life* (1606), A2v. His friend Sidney had much earlier perfected this trope with his arrogantly modest exordium in the *Defence of Poetry*, in which he describes himself as having unintentionally 'slipped into the title of a poet... my unelected vocation' (*A Defence of Poetry* in *The Miscellaneous Prose of Sir Philip Sidney*, ed. Katherine Duncan-Jones and Jan van Dorsten (Oxford: Clarendon Press, 1973), 73). The development of this trope in the seventeenth century is discussed in Dunn, 2–137.

exercises and satisfaction', and claim to have given it over for publication '*permissu superiorum* and none otherwise'.[41] Godfrey Goodman insists in 1616 with perhaps more than conventional acerbity 'that no man did ever more abhorre the Presse than my selfe: solemnly protesting that I would sooner bee rakt or prest to death for silence rather the[n] any words of mine should once hinder the Presse'.[42] The suave John Evelyn much later describes his *Publick Employment* (1667) as 'but the Effects of a very few hours, a cursory pen, and almost but of a sitting'.[43] These assertions, all within a well-established set of conventions, may be sincere or simply formal – it is difficult to tell, and perhaps difficult therefore to judge Browne's tone securely.

A more specialised trope – one also congenial to Browne – exists alongside the generalised modesty-privacy convention. The poet's gentility is pitched against the apparently vulgar evidence of publication, as in John Eliot's querulously entitled 'To the Printer, if these papers should unhappily come to the Press', and in 'To his Stationer, if need be'.[44] Metaphors for the abuses of the press – economic, ethical, and sexual – collaborate in portraying the entire process of publication as a violation of civil behaviour and exchange. George Wither compares it to the enslavement of authors (whose work is unremunerated by piratical booksellers), and to the bondage of the whole hierarchy of book-related trades (compositing, binding, claspmaking); civil and commercial transaction is reduced to robbery.[45] Goodman even suggests 'some generall vacation, that new bookes might for a time cease' lest we continue to 'content . . . ourselves with patcht peeces, and broken sentences'.[46]

That posture of defence against exposure to the common marketplace elsewhere mutates into a specifically genealogical anxiety about inheritance and promiscuity: Philip Sidney, for example, prefatorily describes his new *Arcadia* as 'this child which I am loth to father' but for the insistence of his sister, the Countess of Pembroke.[47] Abraham Cowley, himself the son of a London stationer, prefaced the 1656 edition of his poems with a strikingly

---

[41] George Hakewill, *Apologie of the Power and Providence of God* (Oxford, 1627), c1ʳ.

[42] Goodman, A6v.

[43] John Evelyn, *Publick Employment and an Active Life Prefer'd* (1667), A7ʳ.

[44] John Eliot, *Poems* (1658). Eliot, MP and prisoner in the Tower from 1629, was a neo-Stoic. See Eliot's 'To His Book' and 'Paul's Churchyard'. See also Marotti, *Manuscript, Print*, 263.

[45] Wither, 10.

[46] Goodman, A6ʳ. Browne makes a related suggestion in *Religio Medici* when he proposes that most books ought to be burned to make the most of those few worthy of our attention (*RM* 1.24). See my discussion of this passage in Chapter Two.

[47] Philip Sidney, *The Countesse of Pembroke's Arcadia*, ed. Albert Feuillerat (Cambridge: Cambridge University Press, 1912), 4–5.

similar complaint. An inferior play had been falsely attributed to him, and other works of his own had more recently been published 'without my consent or knowledge, and . . . so mangled and imperfect, that I could neither with honour acknowledge, nor with honesty quite disavow them'.[48] In each case the confusion of rank and identity in unwilling exposure through publication is evoked as the disarray of social hierarchy: the bad play (Heywood's *The Iron Age*) is like an impostor falsely claiming Cowley's paternity against the legitimate claims of his own offspring. Cowley's masqueraded name, he implies, violates literary sumptuary law in dressing an inferior work above its station; and the pirated later works, damaged in the press, are like false or debased coinage. Hence his determination to publish this book of poems himself, despite his modesty and discretion, lest similar violations be visited on it. Like Browne, Cowley is forced to produce true copy in response to, or to forestall, the depredations of the press. The proper civil order (and even biblio-genetic propriety) is upset as avaricious stationers and booksellers 'diminish the value of the *Author*, so they may encrease the price of the *Book*', and literary reputation is 'thus Executed'.[49]

For Browne, writing made promiscuous ('indiscriminately mixed') through publication is akin to sexual disorder: he describes the illicit text of *Religio Medici* as a printer's Cressida, 'being communicated unto one, it became common unto many, and was by transcription successively corrupted untill it arrived in a most depraved copy at the presse' (*RM.*Reader, 9).[50] What may have been his own strange but approving elegy on the posthumous publication of Donne's poems employs the same hyperbole: Donne's 'loose raptures' are a 'Wanton Story' in danger of being misread by the dull. In this poem's subtitle – 'Upon the Promiscuous printing of his Poems, the Looser sort, with the Religious' – the word 'promiscuous' (or 'mixed') alerts us to this same worry about the failure of hierarchy and category which the elegy itself attempts to discount.[51] The promiscuity of printers is a social epidemic which carries the taint of genetic and generic miscegenation, of

---

[48] Cowley, *Poems*, (a)IV.   [49] *Ibid.*

[50] 'Promiscuous' as sexual mixing and indiscrimination did not enter the language until the nineteenth century, but the sense is latent in seventeenth-century use, including Browne's.

[51] Thomas Browne, 'To the deceased Author' in *Donne: Poetical Works*, ed. Herbert J. C. Grierson, 2nd edn (Oxford: Oxford University Press, 1971), 340–1. This bizarre poem has been attributed to Sir Thomas Browne by some editors (Edmund Gosse and Herbert Grierson, for example); Sidney Gottlieb merely describes it as the 'most extravagant' of the elegies, but offers no opinion of its provenance ('*Elegies upon the Author*: Defining, Defending, and Surviving Donne', *John Donne Journal* 2 (1983), 30). W. Milgate, however, considers it 'tasteless' and thus unlikely to be Browne's (*John Donne: The Epithalamiums, Anniversaries, and Epicedes* (Oxford: Clarendon Press, 1978), 221. Geoffrey Keynes, cited by Milgate, proposed a Revd Thomas Browne of Christ Church as a much

destabilising familial disorder. Browne seems to quote Sidney when he compares *Religio Medici* to progeny he cannot acknowledge, and to a miscarried foetus, an intertextual gestational journey from the glorious Elizabethan high noon of the 1580s and Sidney's confident masterpiece to the troubled evening of the early Stuarts and Browne's nervous disavowals.

It is these traditional habits of disclaimer which have prompted some critics to question Browne's sincerity in the preface.[52] But Browne does not confront us with that merely ceremonial disavowal and personal modesty which we see in some other letters and prefaces; rather, in making a specific complaint of damage and even of theft – the theft is less of the text itself than of his privacy and peace of mind – he claims damage by extension to readerly and writerly 'ingenuity', that civil, contractual generosity by which the republic of letters governs itself, the Senecan contract of mutual respect.[53] Thus his original Thyestean metaphor compels us to consider the whole range of incivilities figured by the relation of parents and their children or of writers and their works: infanticide (with dismemberment) is the most extreme of a spectrum of cognate crimes – illegitimacy, miscegenation, abduction – which printing commits on writing.[54] And the trespasses

more plausible candidate. But the argument against Dr Browne is no stronger than that for the Revd Browne: both were very young men still engaged in their studies (the future Dr Browne on the Continent, the Revd Browne at Oxford) when Donne died in 1631. Dr Browne, however, might have a stronger claim, having made an early mark for himself as the single student orator at the refoundation of Broadgates Hall as Pembroke College in 1624, a ceremony attended by Sir Sidney Godolphin (who would also contribute an elegy to the Donne volume); and the collection of commendatory verse published after the Pembroke dedication included a contribution from Donne himself. The young Browne might well have occurred to various minds as an appropriate representative of recent Oxford talent. There is, however, no getting around the peculiar and almost disagreeable character of the Browne elegy, and I remain open-minded about its attribution.

52 Dr Johnson dryly observes: '[Browne] was not very diligent to obstruct his own praise by recalling his own papers [i.e., the mss of *Religio Medici* in circulation among friends], but suffered them to wander hand to hand, till at last, without his consent, they were in 1642 given to a printer.' Johnson thinks it unlikely that a long treatise of this kind could have reached the press nefariously, and that Browne must have sanctioned it (485). Frank Huntley notes that 'The *Religio* is not completely innocent of rhetoric', which seems to mean that he does not accept Browne's sincerity (Huntley, *Sir Thomas Browne*, 95). See also Leonard Nathanson, *The Strategy of Truth: A Study of Sir Thomas Browne* (Chicago: University of Chicago Press, 1967), 73. Wise, however, admits that Browne's charges of piracy have been 'largely validated' by recent editors (Wise, 13).

53 The Senecan enthusiasm for cooperation prompts that contract: 'if wisdom were given me under the express condition that it must be kept hidden and not uttered, I should refuse it. No good thing is pleasant to possess, without friends to share it' (Seneca, 'On Sharing Knowledge' in *Ad Lucilium Epistulae Morales*, trans. Richard M. Gunmere, 3 vols. (Cambridge, MA: Harvard University Press, 1917), 1, 27. Ideas of intellectual cooperation and generosity and of friendship were closely bound together among seventeenth-century advancers. For a discussion of Senecan civility in early-modern Europe, see P. Miller, 49–53.

54 I am most grateful to Douglas Brooks for allowing me to read in draft the forthcoming collection *Printing and Parenting in Early Modern England* (Aldershot: Ashgate Press, 2004), which has been particularly helpful to me in thinking about the bastardisation of writing by the press.

on *Religio Medici* deform Browne himself, who is forced to violate the usual boundaries of polite civil interchange by literalising a normally tropic and conventional disclaimer. All of these amount to a form of generative deca-dence which fragments and disorders understanding. It is a decay which is directly addressed by the restorative purposes of civil cooperation.

CIVILITY AND COOPERATION

Several related but distinct categories of civility are invoked by Browne, each signalling an important range of ideas and behaviours. The standard courtesy literature constructs a pleasant and convenient model of social or-ganisation from signals of respect for comfort, honour, and privacy, a system of gestures and verbal codes which assert and invite that respect. Civility, according to Antoine de Courtin, is 'the exactness and punctilio . . . so indis-pensably necessary in the Conversation of the World'.[55] Hobbesian political civility more pragmatically promotes a concept of civility which regulates otherwise potentially chaotic human impulses – greed, self-interest, and the violent maintenance of natural rights and ownership – by posing the coun-terbalancing human inclination for safety and the security of natural rights as controlling mechanisms. This kind of civility, as Hobbes argues it, is not a system of mutual respect but a contractual system of mutually cancelling self-interest: 'all society', he says, 'is a product of love of self, not love of friends'.[56] Whereas courtesy literature advances a cooperative enhancement of individuals by one another, with the result that society emerges teleolog-ically as the end of good behaviour, political theory describes something less generous, society as merely the means and consequence of checks and balances between competing individuals. As a *tertium quid* there exists a Baconian conception of scientific civility where self-interest and disinter-est are indistinguishable, with a 'brotherhood' of investigators producing knowledge aimed at the enhancement of all members of the group and of the wider world.[57]

---

[55] de Courtin, A3^r.
[56] Hobbes, *De Cive*, 24; see also *Leviathan*, ed. Richard Tuck (Cambridge: Cambridge University Press, 1991), Part 1, Ch. xv.17 ('Of Other Laws of Nature').
[57] Bacon's hierarchy of Salomon's House includes the 'Dowry-Men or Benefactors' who 'cast about how to draw out of [experiments] things of use and practice for man's life' (*New Atlantis*, ed. Arthur Johnston (Oxford: Clarendon Press, 1974), 246). Rose-Mary Sargent describes *New Atlantis* as 'a fable designed to provide . . . readers with a vivid image of what it would be like to live in a land where his vision of the scientific enterprise provided the overriding structure for society' ('Bacon as an Advocate for Cooperative Scientific Research' in *The Cambridge Companion to Bacon*, ed. Markku Peltonen (Cambridge: Cambridge University Press, 1996), 152).

This model of learned sociability, which might be described as 'investigative civility', is the one most apparent in Browne's literary productions. It is a combination of the polite social postures and lexis exemplified by Guazzo and the civic, specifically intellectual, cooperation advocated by Bacon. In Browne's writing we notice that the texture of the prose is partly governed by what would have been virtually reflexive expressions of social courtesy and partly nuanced by necessary and sincere cues of intellectual cooperation and generosity. We detect his commitment to an outward-looking, active civility even in his family dealings. Advising his son Thomas – travelling for enrichment in France before university – he enjoins him to 'be courteous and Civill to all, put on a decent boldness and avoid *pudor rusticus*, not much known in France';[58] in another letter he reminds young Thomas that without a 'Commendable boldness' he will be unable to put forward 'the good parts wch God hath given you'.[59] Putting oneself forward with decency is a form of civility, and the manner of Browne's own address to savants like Evelyn is a model of this commendable boldness couched in civil disclaimers: in offering notes and corrections to Evelyn's *Elysium Britannicum*, he says, 'I have presumed to present these enclosed lines unto you, which I beseech you to accept as hints & proposalls, not any directions unto your judicious thought.'[60] Evelyn replied praising Browne's 'communicable nature, . . . the most obliging of all my correspondents'.[61] Browne, an admirer of Lipsius and of Seneca (Lipsius' antique model), would have derived templates for neo-Stoic community from the emerging link between sociability and learning, and the construction of civility among the intellectual elite in England as the republic of letters.[62]

As John Evelyn somewhat impatiently declares: 'The *Common-wealth* is an assembly . . . which would fall to universal confusion and solitude indeed, without continual care and publick intendency.'[63] Worldly conversation is the lifeblood of the properly disposed state, of the commonwealth which favours virtuous and socially productive action and interaction either to foster our naturally virtuous impulses or to contain our naturally brutish incivility. Such a commonwealth must thrive, as the courtesy rulebooks of this period insist, on the central attribute of civility, modesty. 'Indeed',

[58] Thomas Browne to young Thomas Browne, 22 December [1660] (Keynes IV, 3).
[59] Thomas Browne to young Thomas Browne, 31 January [1660/1] (Keynes IV, 5).
[60] Thomas Browne to John Evelyn, 21 January 1659/60 (Keynes IV, 273).
[61] John Evelyn to Thomas Browne, 28 January 1659/60 (Keynes IV, 273–4).
[62] For instance, from Seneca, *De Beneficiis*, and Lipsius, *De Constantia* (1584). It is also possible that Browne was influenced by Gassendi's life of Peiresc (*Viri illustris Nicolai Claudii Fabricii de Peiresc senatoris aquisextiensis vita* (Paris, 1641)). See P. Miller, 37–48.
[63] Evelyn, *Publick Employment*, 14.

says Courtin, '[modesty] is the only civility.' A personal quality, modesty fosters public virtue: it encourages 'not only a meek and moderate opinion of ourselves, but ... a gentile [genteel] preference of the satisfaction and accommodation of other people before our own; and an abhorrence and detestation of any thing that may disoblige them'.[64] Disobliging behaviour prevents cooperative action and promotes dissension. Civil modesty can only be practised socially, and thus solitude is the other bugbear of the courtesy-writers: 'Man is a conversible creature', says Guazzo; therefore 'account Solitude as a *Poyson*, and company as an *Antidote* ... cast off Solitude as a Concubine, and esteem Company as your lawful [*sic*] Spouse'.[65] The emphasis on social exchange, on the lasciviousness and turpitude of isolation, gives cooperative, corporate, public behaviour a moral pitch far above the apparent self-indulgence and selfishness of retirement. Civility, for Guazzo and for Browne's Baconian investigative model, is sociality.

This model of cooperative civility is especially important to the project of mid- and late-seventeenth century English experimental and natural philosophy. Robert Frank, Steven Shapin, and others have discussed at length the civil interaction and cooperative enterprises of the members of the so-called Invisible College in London during the 1640s and the Experimental Philosophy Club in Oxford in the following decade, groups in which Harvey, Charleton, Hooke, Boyle, Cowley, and Wilkins and their circles subsumed individual glorification within, or at least joined it to, the greater projects to which all contributed – the measurement of air pressure, for example, or the technology of blood tranfusion, and the purpose and mechanism of the lungs.[66] This disinterested mutuality, in part a reaction against the perceived futility of Scholastic natural philosophy, was specifically codified under the auspices of the Royal Society. The Schoolmen, Thomas Sprat explains,

retire[d] from humane things, and shut themselves up in a narrow compass, keeping company with a very few, and that too in a solemne way; [they] addict[ed] themselves ... to some melancholy contemplations, or to devotion, and the thoughts of another world ... But what sorry kinds of Philosophy must they needs produce, when it was a part of that *Religion*, to separate themselves ... from the converse of mankind?

There are works, Sprat says, 'which require as much aid, and as many hands, as can be found'; and such works will not wait upon private seclusion.[67]

---

[64] de Courtin, 7 and 9.   [65] Stephano Guazzo, *The Art of Conversation* (1738), 8.
[66] See Frank, *Harvey*, 63–89, for dates and associations among these scientists.
[67] Thomas Sprat, *The History of the Royal Society* (1667), ed. Jackson Cope and Harold Whitmore Jones (St Louis, MO: Washington University Studies, 1958), 52–72 and 19–20.

'Certainly', says Cowley, 'the solitary and inactive Contemplation of Nature, by the most ingenious Persons living, in their own private Studies, can never effect [the advancement of learning]'.[68] Francis Bacon himself was the counter-example to the School philosophers, an amateur experimentalist, and patron and theoretician of scientific culture who was at the heart of the state, first as a lawyer and later as an MP and Lord Chancellor.[69]

The tension between retirement and public employment, between privacy and publicity, complicates the formerly highly differentiated roles of scholar and gentleman. These were, as Steven Shapin has argued, being reconfigured in the seventeenth century, especially by the gentleman-scientists, whose learning aligned them with the traditional scholarly isolate denigrated by Sprat, but whose ability to improve and to transact knowledge increasingly depended upon social conditions which favoured the traditionally 'gentle', a class by definition supposed to play a civic and social role.[70] Experimentally inclined gentleman-scholars had leisure, means, and space to conduct acts of research which required equipment, laboratories, materials, travel, and assistance in order to maintain the ideal of group enterprise which could take account of various experimental and observational data from diverse hands (from among their own social and national groups, of course, but also from foreign and corresponding scientists). This was an enterprise specifically cited as equivalent to or even an integral part of the more generally prevailing ideology of civic participation. Like the celebrated Robert Boyle, such gentlemen 'lived in the due methods of civility';[71] John Evelyn claimed 'there lives not a *Person* in the *World*, whose *moments* are more *employ'd* than Mr *Boyles* . . . there is nothing more *publick*, than the *good* he's always *doing*'.[72]

[68] Cowley, Preface, *A Proposition for the Advancement of Experimental Philosophy* (1661) in Abraham Cowley, *Complete Works in Verse and Prose*, ed. Alexander Grosart, 2 vols. (London: Chertsey Worthies' Library, 1881), 11, [285]. Cowley's description of the new college of experimental philosophy notes a rule that the 'professors' and scholars of the college are to dine together every evening and discuss their work (289).

[69] Courtesy as well as policy seems to restrain Sprat's recollection of Bacon's imprisonment for accepting bribes; also suppressed is the fatal outcome of Bacon's last experiment with frozen chicken – he caught a chill and died.

[70] Shapin, '"A Scholar and a Gentleman"', 286–9; see also George C. Brauer, *The Education of a Gentleman: Theories of Gentlemanly Education in England 1660–1775* (New York: Bookman Associates, 1959), 34–51; and Jay Tribby, 'Cooking (with) Clio and Cleo: Eloquence and Experiment in 17th-century Florence', *Journal of the History of Ideas* 52 (1991), 417–39. Henry Peacham says: 'nobility is . . . knowledge, culture of the mind, or . . . some glorious action performed . . . [which is] useful and beneficial to the commonwealths' (*Compleat Gentleman* [1612], ed. Virgil B. Heltzel (Ithaca, NY: Cornell University Press for the Folger Shakespeare Library, 1962), 12).

[71] Gilbert Burnet, 'Character of a Christian Philosopher' in *Lives, Characters, and an Address to Posterity*, ed. John Jebb (1883), 366–7.

[72] Evelyn, *Publick Employment*, 118–19.

But that civic model was not monolithic. In his *Discourse on Method* (1637) René Descartes gives the well-known account of his Montaignean decision to withdraw to a city where he had no acquaintances and 'where I have been able to live a life as solitary and retired as though I were in the most remote desert'.[73] Alone in his well-heated room he worked out his thoughts on method and wrote the discourse which he intended for public consumption. This interesting case of private, indeed, intentionally uncommunal work designed for publicity is particularly modern, rather than Scholastic, Descartes preferring his own autonomous project before a corporate one, self-benefiting retirement and seclusion instead of inefficient civic and social exchange. In his essay 'Of Solitude' Cowley, like Bacon, argues that solitude is an important privilege from which only the very few who are truly wise can profit: it is their opportunity to perfect '[t]he Habit of Thinking . . . Cogitation is the thing which distinguishes the Solitude of a God from a wild Beast'; and he emphasises the godliness of human solitude when he notes that it was the original blessed condition of Adam.[74] We require these notions of scientific civility and gentlemanly tradition, and of retirement, privacy, and solitude, in order to think more clearly about Thomas Browne's place in (or his absence from) such networks. Browne, I suggest, participates in both the Cartesian and the Boylean models of intellectual behaviour. Like Cowley, Browne equates privacy with virtue but is necessarily secluded in his professional work in any case (and he has, along with Burton and Montaigne, been described as a 'philosophical solitary'[75]); like his admirer John Evelyn, he acknowledges and embraces 'publick employment' in his investigative activity and in his writing.

Browne himself was undoubtedly 'gentle'. The son of a prosperous London mercer but, crucially, the stepson of a knight, Browne was sent to Winchester and Oxford, and could finance (possibly out of his moderate patrimony) extensive Continental medical training.[76] He was, somewhat

---

[73] Descartes, *Discourse on Method* in *René Descartes: Philosophical Writings*, trans. and ed. Elizabeth Anscombe and Peter D. Geach (Edinburgh: Nelson, 1963), 30. This episode in Descartes's career is discussed by Shapin, '"The Mind is its Own Place"', 201.

[74] Abraham Cowley, *Essays, Plays and Sundry Verses*, ed. A. R. Waller (Cambridge: Cambridge University Press, 1906), 39, 396. The claim of godliness was still being rehearsed in 1665 by George MacKenzie, one of Browne's imitators, in *A Moral Essay Preferring Solitude* (1665), 3.

[75] Morris Croll, '"Attic Prose" in the Seventeenth Century' in *Style, Rhetoric, and Rhythm*, ed. J. Max Patrick *et al.* (Princeton: Princeton University Press, 1966), 95.

[76] Browne's father's will of 1613 eventually left approximately £600 to each of his five children, but this was established only after the stepfather, Sir Thomas Dutton, threatened to injure that patrimony through fraud; Browne's uncle stepped in as executor to take control of disbursement of the estate on their behalf (see Huntley, *Sir Thomas Browne*, 6; and Trevor Hughes, 'The Childhood of Sir Thomas Browne: His Relationship to His Mother and Stepfather', *London Journal* 23 (1998), 21–9).

unusually, an eldest (and only) son professing physic when this occupation was not typical among the gentry. Probably because the practice of medicine was more characteristically middle class, it was associated with the Parliamentary/Republican cause, an allegiance which Browne did not share.[77] He is a case-study in the difficulty, emphasised by Margaret Pelling, of designating medicine in this period as a trade or a profession when medical occupations – from apothecary to doctor of medicine – comprised such a heterogeneous social range. Although he practised a profession for which he was specifically qualified, and indeed must have worked for his living since he was probably without further substantial inherited funds, as a university-trained physician Browne would have been something of a hybrid in the social hierarchy.[78] Some, like Harvey, had treated Charles I, and Browne's eldest son Edward achieved or maintained social cachet as a fashionable doctor (Edward attended Charles II); Robert Fludd was the notoriously haughty son of a knight. Others in this social range were academic medics, which meant either that they lectured from Galen and did not practise, or that they used their scientific training to join in gentlemanly congeries of experimenters in the two universities, or in London, or attached to some great aristocratic household such as Arundel's, the Cavendishes', or Shaftesbury's. But even within this ambit Browne is slightly unusual. As a local and general practitioner in the modern sense in Norwich, where, it has been estimated, the ratio of medical practitioners to population was 1:200 and the consumption of medical services was high,[79] Browne treated both rich and poor, and it is quite clear from his letters that he was called out or interrupted, like any local doctor, at inconvenient, 'uncivil' times of day and night to attend his sometimes troublesome patients.[80]

---

[77] William Birken, 'The Social Problem of the English Physician in the Early 17th Century', *Medical History* 31 (1987), 203, 214.

[78] Margaret Pelling, *The Common Lot: Sickness, Medical Occupations, and the Urban Poor in Early Modern England* (London: Longman, 1998), 230–58.

[79] Pelling, 226. That very respectable figure is consonant with the economic health of Parliament-inclining Norwich, then the second city of England and a major port. Although we do not know exactly why the young Browne chose to settle there (Jeremiah Finch argues that Thomas Lushington, his former Oxford tutor, and Nicholas Bacon, Charles Le Gros, and Justinian Lewyn, all also friends from Pembroke College, Oxford and already established there, encouraged this move), the reason may be as obvious as the prospect of good business. See Jeremiah Finch, 'The Norfolk Persuaders of Sir Thomas Browne: A Variant Copy of the 1712 Posthumous Works', *Princeton University Library Chronicle* 11 (1950), 45; and Huntley, *Sir Thomas Browne*, 98.

[80] He mentions treating Alderman Wisse, a chronic hypochondriac, who called on him on a Sunday evening in 1679. In the autumn of the same year an ague was rife among the population of Norwich, and Browne notes that 'extraordinarie sickly seasons woorie physitians, & robbeth them of their health as well as their quiet'. Despite his conviction that at an advanced age ''tis either a folly or a shame to use meanes to live longer', he notes: 'this day a poore woeman being a hundred & 3 yeares and a weeke old sent to me to give her some ease of the colick' (Keynes IV, 108, 139, 144).

At the same time, however, and especially after the publication of *Pseudodoxia Epidemica* in 1646, he was a celebrated savant with a pan-European reputation who corresponded with many of the leading scientists of his day. He was, as would be expected, a member of the Royal College of Physicians, though he was never a Fellow of the Royal Society, as his fame and accomplishment might lead us to suppose. There is in fact nothing very remarkable about this: not only was the new-minted Royal Society less prestigious than the Royal College, but Browne would not have been able to attend the weekly London meetings regularly, and may have elected to save his subscription money when he could receive few benefits of membership.[81] Browne was thus in later life disabled by location if by little else to consort with Boyle, Hooke, Charleton, and their colleagues. These facts indicate how very much outside certain norms of scientific and social gentility Browne was in some respects, while being in others very much within them. In some ways he reminds us of Descartes, his contemporary, or even Montaigne, barricaded in places of mildly anti-social but hardly hermetic or even scholarly retirement.[82]

But physical proximity to scientific fashion is only one measure of civil involvement. If we consider Browne's vast correspondence, and the evidence of his reading (both of the latest books, and of papers and transactions of the Royal Society and the Royal College), we have a very different picture.[83] This was the celebrated polymath Dr Browne whose *Religio Medici* was on the Holy Roman Emperor's reading list and banned by the Papal Index in 1645, and whose *Pseudodoxia Epidemica* was noted and admired by scholars in all the scientifically active European countries.[84] John Aubrey, who noted that his 1642 reading of *Religio Medici* 'first opened my understanding', sought his biography for *Brief Lives*.[85] He was a neighbour and acquaintance of the great Townshend family of Raynham Hall, Norfolk. John Evelyn and other distinguished visitors called

---

[81] This speculation is made by Finch, *Sir Thomas Browne*, 263.

[82] By 1672, William Ramsey's *The Gentleman's Companion*, a courtesy-book, was recommending Bacon, Boyle, Digby, Descartes, and Browne as appropriately 'gentle' reading (it also suggested that the gentleman establish a laboratory in which to pass his time (128, 132)).

[83] In 1668, for example, he was awaiting new works by Merrett, Mayow, and Boyle (*New Experiments concerning the Spring and Weight of the Air*); 'I keep the sheets of the transactions [of the Royal Society] as they come out monethly' (Thomas Browne to Edward Browne, 23 December 1668 (Keynes IV, 39)).

[84] The *Index Librorum Prohibitorum* banned *Religio Medici* on 18 March 1645 (Finch, *Sir Thomas Browne*, 5). It was still on the index in 1949.

[85] John Aubrey, *Brief Lives*, ed. Oliver Lawson-Dick, 2nd edn (London: Mandarin, 1992), xxviii. Browne's tersely modest recital of his accomplishments must have made the gossipy Aubrey despondent; he did not write a life of Browne. See Browne's letter of 14 March 1672/3 to Aubrey in Keynes IV, 376.

on him.[86] He had friendships with Robert Paston and Henry Power, and his surviving correspondence includes letters to and from Kenelm Digby, John Evelyn, Elias Ashmole, William Dugdale, Christopher Merrett, John Ray, and Henry Oldenburg, some of whom were early, powerful members of the Royal Society. Browne and his work were admired by Boyle, who was willing to test Browne's assertions about the coagulation of *aqua fortis* in oil three times until he could corroborate the findings of 'so faithful and candid a naturalist';[87] and by Hooke and Grew, who stole the same phrase from *The Garden of Cyrus*.[88] And although it will not do to over-emphasise the disinterestedness and altruism of the medical occupations, some of Browne's most characteristic letters depict team diagnosis in several fields: with Edward his son, with Henry Power, and with medics with whom he had little or no direct acquaintance, he discusses cases; with Christopher Merrett, the ornithologist, he confers about the proper nomenclature of birds; William Dugdale consults him about fossils, and Browne offers a number of helpful ideas.[89] Browne is very much a cooperating Baconian scientific correspondent, if not always a direct participant.

It is not necessarily an easy triangulation, therefore, to assemble a picture of Browne in relation to the civil theory and civil practices of his

[86] He knew and admired Raynham Hall, the Townshend seat, to which he refers approvingly, along with its owner, Sir Horatio (shortly to be Lord) Townshend, in *Urne-Buriall*'s dedicatory epistle (see James M. Rosenheim, *The Townshends of Raynham* (Middletown, CT: Wesleyan University Press, 1989), 170). The Raynham household account-books of 1671–86 show that Browne's horse was stabled there 3–10 May 1673, and that the family paid for journeys made by a surgeon and doctors from Norwich to Raynham, 10–17 May 1673, undoubtedly to attend Lady Townshend in her final illness (private communication with James Rosenheim). John Evelyn accepted an offer to visit Norwich with Lord Howard, 'having a desire to see that famous Scholar and Physition Dr T. *Browne*... with whom I had sometime corresponded by Letters but never saw before' (*The Diary of John Evelyn*, ed. E. S. de Beer (London: Oxford University Press, 1959), 561–2 (17–18 October 1671)). Other visitors were John Ray, Christopher Merrett, Henry Oldenburg, Samuel Tuke, and possibly Robert Paston (the Earl of Yarmouth) and John Aubrey (see David Tylden-Wright, *John Aubrey: A Life* (London: HarperCollins, 1991), 182).

[87] 'Two Essays concerning the Unsuccessfulness of Experimentes' in *The Works of the Honourable Robert Boyle* (1744), 1, 349–50. Joseph Glanvill was also pleased to confirm what Browne had said about magnetised needles in *Pseudodoxia Epidemica* (Glanvill, *The Vanity of Dogmatizing* (1661), quoted in Finch, *Sir Thomas Browne*, 258).

[88] 'Nature geometrizes' (Robert Hooke, *Micrographia* (1665), 54; and Nehemiah Grew, *Anatomy of Plants* (1682), 160).

[89] On medical altruism, see Pelling, 236–7. On joint consultations, see Browne's letters to his son Edward of 17 May 1679, 5 January 1679/80, 27 February 1679/80, and 24 January 1680/81 in Keynes IV, 107, 146, 180; the Browne-Power correspondence; and his correspondence with Drs Bave and Maplet (Keynes IV, 239–51). See Browne's correspondence with Merrett in Keynes IV, 343–62. On Browne's correspondence with Dugdale, see Keynes IV, 301–27; and also Claire Preston, 'In the Wilderness of Forms: Ideas and Things in Thomas Browne's Cabinets of Curiosity' in *The Renaissance Computer: Knowledge Technology in the First Age of Print*, ed. Neil Rhodes and Jonathan Sawday (London: Routledge, 2000), 170–83; and Chapter Four, below.

day. In the preface to *Religio Medici* we detect a Browne perhaps somewhat out of character, a bruised sensibility who would normally make merely a phatic allusion to prevailing gentlemanly, elite cooperation, generosity, and modesty. However, embattled by the rising mid-century civil confusion, and in Parliament-leaning Norwich perhaps lacking the supporting presence enjoyed by like-minded gentlemen of science in the Royalist sanctuary that was Oxford in the 1640s, Browne's construction of civility and intellectual exchange is sorely tried.[90] He himself suggests as much in *Pseudodoxia Epidemica*'s prefatory letter: in attempting the project of making this encyclopaedia of misapprehension, he remarks,

more advantageous had it been unto Truth, to have fallen into the endeavours of some cooperating advancers [experimenters], that might have performed it to the life, and added authority thereunto: which the privacie of our condition and unequall abilities cannot expect. Whereby notwithstanding wee have not been diverted, nor have our solitary attempts beene so discouraged, as to despaire the favourable looke of learning upon our single and unsupported endeavours. (*PE*.Reader, 1)

And although he never claims the isolation of the closet, the cloister, or the garden, as a scientifically trained and practising experimentalist he would have understood the principle of timely demonstration or publication of results. In this sense, *Religio Medici* is a private thought-experiment among friends, prematurely or inappropriately divulged to the public in uncooperative 1643. That much cooperative experimentation and investigation – in Oxford and London especially – was performed by coteries insisted, if only tacitly, on a propriety governing confidentiality and divulgation, a form of gentility still in force, in spite of contrary claims, in the work of the Royal Society.[91] *Religio Medici* therefore occupies an uncertain ground where the competing ethics of publicity and privacy, each vulnerable to abuses within scientific, intellectual culture, are uneasily in play.

---

[90] One of Browne's patients, Dr Joseph Hall, Bishop of Norwich, saw his palace and cathedral sacked by Parliamentary troops in 1642 (Joseph Hall, *The Works of the Right Reverend Joseph Hall* (1863), 1, lxiv–lxviii). Browne at this time lived in Tomblands, a street fronting the cathedral close, and probably had already witnessed an attempted sacking in the previous year by local Presbyterians and other diasaffected elements (see Anon, *True News from Norwich* (1641)).

[91] The civil practices of the Oxford experimenters from the 1640s to the 1660s are described by Frank, *Harvey*, 216–20. There was, however, disagreement within the early Society about the propriety and practice of divulgation of scientific information to the public; this was sometimes evidence of class-snobbery and sometimes merely pragmatic and economic (see Sargent, 167–8).

UNCIVIL LEARNING AND THE FALL OF MAN

That *Religio Medici*'s added sections (written when the massive and designedly 'public' *Pseudodoxia* was almost certainly already underway) couch
their discussion of sectarian controversy in plentiful allusions to incivility
('improperations and termes of scurrility betwixt us' (*RM* 1.3)) indicates
the way in which Browne's sense of scientific cooperation and his sense of
civil order can be understood as virtually identical.[92] For example, Browne
believes Protestant England is unconscionably rude to the Pope (with 'popular scurrilities and opprobrious scoffes' offered to him), the Pope after
all a temporal prince to whom we in fact 'owe the duty of good language' (*RM* 1.5).[93] When we 'erre . . . in points, not onely of our own, but
one anothers salvation' (*RM* 1.56), we practise a species of 'uncharity'. His
own temperament, he explains, prompts him to a radical civility which he
defines as a form of charity: 'averse from nothing' – including, it turns
out, the peculiar foodstuffs of foreigners – he is happy to share his learning
with the 'community in learning'; indeed, he regards intellectual generosity
as 'the cheapest way of beneficence' (*RM* 11.3).[94]

In his later work civility becomes even more embedded in Browne's
vision, where his theology of incivility lies not specifically with controversialist censures or piratical printers, but with the Devil himself, the original
uncivil being, the villainy of whose 'first Schisme' was to promote civil
unrest in heaven and earth. In consequence, Browne argues, those who are

complexionally propense to innovation, are naturally indisposed for a community,
nor will ever be confined unto the order or oeconomy of one body, . . . [and] do
subdivide and mince themselves almost into Atomes.[95] (*RM* 1.8)

I have been suggesting that the subtext of Browne's letter in *Religio Medici*
is the sense of fallenness, social and individual, that the violation of privacy
and of civility is a declension equivalent to the sea-change of Adam and
Eve, a declension which roughly hurls the persona of the young Browne of

---

[92] This identity is specifically Baconian. See Andrew Barnaby and Lisa J. Schnell, *Literate Experience: The Work of Knowing in Sevententh-Century English Writing* (New York and Basingstoke: Palgrave Macmillan, 2002), 43.

[93] In this remark we must suspect Browne of baiting the sectarians.

[94] Browne introduces his modes of charity with a charming approbation of the idiosyncratic French taste for 'frogges, snailes, and toadstooles' (*RM* 11.1).

[95] This section was added to the 1643 edition. Reid Barbour points out that Browne is here using the terms of Epicurean atomism associated during the Civil War with democratical and anarchic tendencies (*English Epicures and Stoics: Ancient Legacies in Early Stuart Culture* (Amherst: University of Massachusetts Press, 1998), 59.

the mid-1630s into the wearier, discordant world of 1643. But paradoxically, that highly principled sense of injury, and the concept of world-enhancing civility itself, is supererogatory *except* in a fallen world, where only artificial systems of order – behavioural and intellectual – can reinstate good behaviour in spite of, or precisely because of, the fallenness of things. Innocence, fallenness, and the needful intermediation of civility which arises from that fall are the impulses of nearly all Browne's work. Civility, with its cognate systems of intellectual order, is the consquence of the *felix culpa.* The practice of civility is a form of regeneration.

The fall of man produced an ongoing disobedience in the world, not simply active human infractions of divine ordinance, but a more pervasive misbehaviour or failure of right order, a primarily chaotic condition against which all subsequent human labour, intellectual or manual, must strive. Discussion of the exact causes and consequences of the fall were commonplace, and works describing these are a feature of sixteenth- and seventeenth-century theology. Browne was well-versed in the details of that discussion.[96] Godfrey Goodman, high-churchman and Bishop of Gloucester, produced one of the most exhaustive and literal accounts of the innate corruption of the world, with man as the Jonah in the ship of nature, the cause of its incivility and disorder.[97] Many of Goodman's metaphors for this damage in *The Fall of Man* (1616) are civic, social, and governmental: just as a well-governed state, he observes, cannot flourish with internal factions, so nature itself totters on its civil foundations because 'creatures . . . trespasse upon creatures, and offend each other', and man in particular, 'breaking his owne bounds, being *nexus & naturae vinculum*, it must necessarily follow, that all the rest of the creatures . . . should likewise be inordinate, & overflow their owne banks';[98] the very animals are 'disjoyned in their affections . . . play tyrants amongst themselves; and like Common Pyrates and robbers, seaze upon booties and preyes'.[99] Man exhibits his comprehensive fallenness in everything from his physiology to his ceremonies of courtesy: sudden death

---

[96] Some examples include Jean Bodin, *Methodus ad facilem historiarum cognitionem* (1566) and *Republique* (1576); Francis Shakelton, *A Blazyng Starre* (1580); Philip Stubbes, *Anatomy of Abuses* (1583); Philippe de Mornay, *Traité de la vérité de la religion chrétienne* (1581); Thomas Burnet, *The Sacred Theory of the Earth* (1689); and John Ray, *Miscellaneous Discourses concerning the Dissolution and Changes of the World* (1692). Spenser, Donne, Herbert, Raleigh, and Heywood (whose *The Iron Age* annoyed Cowley and was part of a series of works on nature's decay) all incorporate the theme, as do Burton and Bacon, Archbishop Ussher, John Wilkins, and Henry Power. Browne's library contained a number of these works. For a general discussion of the debate, see Victor Irwin Harris, *All Coherence Gone: A Study of the Seventeenth Century Controversy over Disorder and Decay in the Universe,* 2nd edn (London: Frank Cass, 1966).
[97] Goodman, 27.   [98] Goodman, 17.   [99] Goodman, 20.

is attributed to 'privie conspiracies';[100] and the heart itself, prey to inflammations, can 'purloine and presse upon the poore commons'.[101] Signs of respect and reverence such as removing one's hat and bowing are 'mans voluntarie punishment of his owne disobedience'; oaths and vows are needful hedges against our assumed falsehood.[102] Study is, for Goodman, the only supply of such defects, and 'God in revenge of sinne . . . punisheth man with the heavie yoake of ignorance . . . [and] the immoderate desire of knowledge'.[103]

There can be little doubt that Browne knew *The Fall of Man*: he seems to have replicated some of Goodman's rhetorical flourishes almost wholesale.[104] But George Hakewill's riposte to Goodman, *An Apologie of the Power and Providence of God* (1627), was a more congenial theory of the post-lapsarian condition, and also offered Browne subjects and styles.[105] Hakewill argues, against Goodman, that the 'malice and faintnesse of our *owne wills*' are to answer for our defects. Where Goodman takes human and natural imperfection to be of one house, Hakewill believes that we must not call into question the perfection of God's creation, and decries the doctrine of decay of nature as a type of vulgar error.[106] Browne seconds this when he agrees that human intellectual disorder is merely a distorting lens through which we seem to detect natural chaos: man has 'fallen away from his Creator', but the world itself is 'neither old nor decayed' (*RM* 1.45). This is an essentially Baconian response to the fragmented order of

---

[100] Goodman, 40.

[101] Goodman, 101. The physiology of the heart was incorporated into various monarchic and democratic allegories, notably by Harvey himself.

[102] Goodman, 60.

[103] Goodman, 391, 393–4.

[104] For example, Goodman's disparagement of insects in comparison with more prodigious animals (lions, unicorns, tigers, elephants) is converted by Browne into the opposite figure, in which prodigies amaze only 'ruder heads'(*RM* 1.15). Goodman's witty observation that even chickens can expect a more acceptable interment than man, since they are delivered on silver salvers and damask cloth, whereas man is wrapped in a sheet and thrust into the ground for worms' meat (107) flavours some of the conceits of *Urne-Buriall*. An expostulation on human mortality yields another almost Brownean phrase: 'as if [man's] body were ordained to be the compost of the earth, and did only serve to make the Churchyard fat with the oyle of his flesh, and to pave the high wayes with the sculs and bones of dead men' (Goodman, 332).

[105] Indeed, Browne's debt to Hakewill is even more pronounced in *PE* (see Robbins, *PE*, xxi–xxiv). Hakewill favours 'For mine owne part', one of Browne's characteristic locutions (40); he quotes Romans II.33, the source of Browne's celebrated 'oh altitudo!' (Hakewill, c[2r]). He quotes *Thyestes* (and much other Seneca): 'where there is no modesty, in such a kingdom there can be no stability' (Hakewill, c3ᵛ). Many of the errors corrected in *Pseudodoxia Epidemica* also appear in *An Apologie*, as does an extended examination of excessive admiration of antiquity (Hakewill, 22).

[106] Hakewill, 272–3, and b4ʳ. This view is elaborated again at mid-century by John Jonston, *An History of the Constancy of Nature* (1657).

knowledge: it is the nature of virtue and of approaches to prelapsarian civility to attempt the restoration of understanding in spite of human and natural degradation.

In *Religio Medici* Browne imagines even within the individual conscience an untoward, Goodmanesque competition between the forces of order and disorder: 'There is another man within mee, that's angry with mee, rebukes, commands, and dastards mee', he announces (*RM* 11.7), evoking a disturbed mental society whose factions do not hold civil conversation. The essentially uncivil tendencies of this personal psychomachia must be kept in fetters, especially 'those powers whose rebellions, once Masters, might bee the ruine of all' (*RM* 11.7). The defiance of ignorance through civil learning and investigation has, in other words, a public and communal, as well as a private and personal, register. What Browne fears as 'the unruly regiment' within himself is equivalent to, or even identical with, 'that unruly rebell' (*RM* 11.10), the Devil, who always attends our thoughts, ready to stir up disorder, and Browne regards the Devil as *uncivil* as much as *evil*, allying that devilish incivility to human incivility in manners and thought. His imagined psychomachia is almost always represented in terms of political or social truculence – the individual conscience is a commonwealth subject to uprisings and rebellions, inhabited by that grand schismatic the Devil, or it is troubled by quarrels among acquaintances who rebuke and dastard each other.

That the consequences of the original temptation by our Grand Foe introduced behavioural incivility to the world we already knew, of course – Cain murdered Abel, the lion and the lamb would no longer lie down together, and fell 'but like the whole world' (*RM* 1.43) – and this species of fallenness colours *Religio Medici*. Just as momentously, the fall exacted a further price: no longer would there be, he reminds us in a melancholy phrase from *Pseudodoxia Epidemica*, 'a Paradise or unthorny place of knowledge' (*PE* 1.v.30). The intellectual confusion which arose from what he terms 'the severall wounds of constitution' (*PE* 1.ii.5) incurred in the fall promoted the dominion of the senses, of the appetite, of what he derogates as 'the irrationall and brutall part of the soule, which lording it over the soveraigne faculty, interrupts the actions of that noble part' (*PE* 1.iii.17). The dominion of sense over intellect is figured in this passage as a commonwealth in rebellion, in which the king or 'soveraigne part' is falsely 'lorded' over by what had been the subaltern faculties. Satan, or his legacy within us, is 'an invisible Agent, and secret promoter without us ... the first contriver of Error, and professed opposer of Truth' (*PE* 1.x.58). Not only is the Devil imagined as an infiltrator or quisling practising disruptive dirty tricks in us; he stands accused of introducing an idolatry which takes the form of credulous adherence to ancient and unsubstantiated authority rather than to evidentiary proof (*PE* 1.vi.32), a form of intellectual incivility which is the theme of *Pseudodoxia Epidemica*. Thus, Browne's vision of chaos directs itself in *Religio Medici* to incivility and ignorance (related concepts) as the primary consequences and motivating intellectual conditions of the fall, a vast social, civil catastrophe which, in the Baconian programme, summons 'cooperating advancers' to the front lines of learned investigation to restore order in the form of correct knowledge, knowledge which we have forgotten and which can only be reconvened by 'reminiscentiall evocation' (*PE*.Reader, 1).[107]

To recuperate our original unpolluted understanding we must deliberately become 'innocent' again: 'to purchase a clear and warrantable body of Truth', Browne observes, 'we must forget and part with much wee know' (*PE*.Reader, 1). Out of the age-long, ruinous state of ourselves and of the world, therefore, and out of the impending catastrophe waiting in the wings of the English political drama, Browne from the outset of his public career in 1642 salvages three primary fields of civil action and reparation. Through ideas, first, of human social intercourse, second, of intellectual rigour and conception, and, third, aspects of the natural world itself, the prospect of and capacity for orderly behaviour and maintenance of order become Browne's civil subject.

We have been alerted to the importance of the rules of civil social transaction and order by *Religio Medici*'s 'To the Reader'. Features of natural order prevailing against disorder elsewhere in his work, and the reparation of learned untruths and false authority, are proposed as a kind of civility and security in a world of ideas which had itself sustained injury in the general fall. Certain kinds of encyclopaedias, natural history collections, and cabinets of curiosity – physical embodiments of intellectual patterns which have a clear influence on the structures of *Pseudodoxia, Urne-Buriall,* and *The Garden of Cyrus* – are assemblages designed partly to reinstate that lost order and clarity of natural knowledge.[108] The animal, mineral, and vegetable kingdoms are, in such arrays, managed by (sometimes apparently eccentric) rules of cognate relation or correspondence; these arrays

---

[107] This is one of Goodman's themes, too: '*cognitio nostra est reminiscentia*, our learning or knowledge is only a kind of remembrance; supposing that men had formerly some naturall knowledge ... though it was lost by some ill accident, and therefore must be renewed againe, as it were called to minde, or better remembered by learning' (Goodman, 389).

[108] See Preston, 'In the Wilderness of Forms', 170–2. These assemblages will be considered in detail in Chapter Three.

are very often as materially and visually arresting in their orders as they are intellectually and abstractly satisfying. And such artificial restitutions are not the only resort of Browne and other seventeenth-century naturalists. They detect surviving signatures of innocence, order, and civility in the natural world, 'goe[ing] to Schoole to the wisedome of Bees, Aunts, and Spiders' because 'the civilitie of these little Citizens . . . neatly sets forth the wisedome of their Maker' (*RM* 1.1), indications apparently from on high that civil structures are the inherent structures of creation. The far-reaching implications of the concept of civility are to be found throughout Browne's work and the nature and progress of his enquiry, its social context, and the literary patterns he imposes on its results will form the basis of the rest of this book.

CHAPTER 2

Religio Medici: *the junior endeavour*

> Physick and preaching ill agree,
> There is but one *Religio Medici*.
> Alexander Brome, 'The Answer' in *Songs and*
> *Other Poems* (1664), 199.

His patterns of composition and structures of thought indicate Browne's debt to prevailing paradigms of contemporary natural philosophy, natural history, and the ancillary disciplines of antiquarianism. Browne was generally a careful and deliberate rather than a spontaneous writer, and I will argue that his work is consistently formed by ideas of compilation, collection, and the organisation of objects and information, ideas associated with the Baconian project to advance learning; by the theological notion of innocence, a notion which determines early-modern understanding of the attainment of knowledge; and by the cooperative, collaborative themes of intellectual civility and social organisation which developed with the rise of empiricism and the intellectual curriculum of the New Philosophy. *Religio Medici* introduces most of these themes in one way or another: in it we are notified of Browne's signaturism, his experimental urgency, and his resurrectionism (which reappear in *The Garden of Cyrus*); his antiquarian deliberation, and his neo-Stoic humility (also in *Urne-Buriall*); his enquiry-mode, his polymathic engagement with authorities, and his ideas of intellectual civility (characteristic of *Pseudodoxia Epidemica*, the *Miscellany Tracts*, and his abundant correspondence). Indeed, *Religio Medici* even has comic elements, a delicate humour and irony which we encounter again in *Musæum Clausum*.

These features of *Religio Medici* allow it to perform, for the purposes of this discussion, an introductory role for the whole *oeuvre*, as well as to illuminate its own peculiar *earliness*. By this last I mean that too often the Browne of *Religio Medici* has been admired for his apparently tranquil and finished prose, as if he had sprung fully formed as a writer and thinker (a view of him largely originating with Coleridge), and this has tended to deform our understanding of the work and the man.[1] Instead, I will argue that Browne's work follows a discernible developmental path, with *Religio Medici* an establishing essay in which the inexperienced and youthful writer is unselfconsciously trying out ideas, playing with authorial personae, writing for himself and possibly for friends but in no way as a public or especially deliberative writer, at least not in the manner of his later output. Without this sense of the immature Browne, the writer not fully master of his themes or of his effects, we can have no real appreciation of how that mastery develops, and how remarkable it is when fully evolved.

Religio Medici must therefore be examined for the local landscape and weather of its interesting immaturity; thereafter it can be analysed as a catalogue and thematic introduction to several key elements of the more measured and deliberate productions of Browne's literary prime, namely their essayistic qualities, their engagement with experimental culture, their structural components, the Senecan or neo-Stoic ideas underpinning them, and the various forms of natural theology which govern certain aspects of Browne's thought. This survey of *Religio Medici* risks dethroning it from the apex of his achievement, where it has been stationed since his own lifetime. Although there is no question that it is Browne's most personal work – the most accessible, the least *recherché*, the most transcendental, and also the most immediate to his own and to subsequent ages – it is nevertheless almost certainly his least typical production.

EARLINESS: JUNE AND DECEMBER

The often-mentioned but rarely explored earliness of *Religio Medici* is a significant gauge of an immature brilliance. For all his expressions of distress in its prefatory letter of 1643, Browne's pronouncements and attitudes in *Religio Medici* are quite clearly those of a far more idealistic, even naive, man whose outlook is quite remote from that of the Learned Doctor Browne of the subsequent major works closely grouped in the mid-1640s to the mid-1650s. They are, rather, that of Young Man Browne, perhaps about twenty-eight years old when he took up his task, and if not, strictly speaking, young in the world, only recently entering his profession after a lifetime

---

[1] Coleridge's celebrated, enthusiastic marginalia in *Religio Medici* construct a rather anachronistically Romantic Browne of almost mage-like powers (Coleridge, 741–99). For a brief discussion of Coleridge on Browne, see my ' "Unriddling the World": Sir Thomas Browne and the Doctrine of Signatures,' *Critical Survey* 5 (1993), 263–70.

of study. One way of thinking about the essay is to imagine the Browne of 1633–5 (the probable period of composition) producing a set of establishing tenets, occasionally enunciated with the reckless temerity of youth – in this case, highly educated and to some extent cosmopolitan youth. What has been criticised as unforgivable self-confidence in *Religio Medici* in fact sounds more like a sophomoric, not always very pragmatic, template for life, a quasi-manifesto descended from Sidney and Augustine, exhibiting a certain almost adolescent bravado. As far as can be from the self-conscious young Milton of the seventh sonnet, Browne's voice is strangely reminiscent of much more recent fictional young men at the beginning of their careers such as Pip Pirrip and Jay Gatsby, vowing undertakings and absolutes which can only be contemplated by those who have not yet had to sustain them in the real world.[2]

The 1643 edition of *Religio Medici* with its sober, appended preface and grave additional sections is thus a bipartite portrait of Browne: the foibles of his much younger persona are refracted through, and even excused and forgiven by, the mature considerations of his later self. But if the acknowledgement of Browne's youth (a confession he himself makes and insists on) is a way of understanding some peremptory aspects of the essay's pronouncements, its voice apparently argues against this. The stately sententiousness, the beautiful aphorisms which so enchanted his Romantic admirers, are curious modes for so young a man: the aphorism and the solemn sentence are perhaps more appropriate (though not exclusive) to age and experience, delivered to, not by, those unseasoned in life. 'I have . . . enlarged that common *Memento mori* [remember you must die], into a more Christian memorandum: *Memento quatuor novissima* [remember the Four Last Things]' shows him in the very act of producing such aged effects, of mimicking a Senecan maturity of demeanour and expression (*RM* 1.45). If twenty-eight is not strictly immature, fragments of the eggshell are visible: as hard as it is to resist the grace of a remark such as 'It is a brave act of valour to contemne death, but where life is more terrible than death, it is then the truest valour to dare to live', it is a maxim generated not from experience but from books, specifically the examples of Cato, Job, and Stoic philosophy (*RM* 1.44). Yet with only rarefied academic training to his name, and not yet ascended even to the height of qualified physician, he nevertheless writes as if he were a somewhat detached, even world-weary observer of the human comedy noting the hobby-horses of his time through the lens of a

---

[2] *Religio Medici*'s most powerful post-Enlightenment equivalent is Thoreau's *Walden*, whose first-person authority is similarly inventive, impractical, and full of youthful bravura. Thoreau, along with a number of the great American Romantics, was greatly influenced by Browne.

life of incident and care. *Religio Medici* has, bizarrely, the air of a *summa*, of a carefully thought-out, time-tested rule and epitome. It is in fact one delivered from the depths of inexperience.

He achieves this effect partly by playing with our sense of his age. Although he proclaims his youth late in *Religio Medici* when he tells us that he has not yet lived thirty years (*RM* 1.41), in the first paragraph he claims grandly to 'having, in my riper yeares, and confirmed judgement, seene and examined all' (*RM* 1.1). He is especially fond of playing the *senex* or at least the prematurely aged:

I have outlived my selfe, and begin to bee weary of the Sunne; I have shaked hands with delight in my warme blood and Canicular dayes; I perceive I doe Anticipate the vices of age, the world to mee is but a dreame, or mockshow, and wee all therein but Pantalones and Anticks to my severer contemplations. (*RM* 1.41)

As he considers the piling up of sins with years, he continues to ventriloquise age:

I would not live over my houres past, or beginne again the thred of my dayes: not upon *Cicero*'s ground, because I have lived them well, but for feare I should live them worse; . . . I finde in my confirmed age the same sinnes I discovered in my youth; I committed many then because I was a child, and because I commit them still I am yet an Infant. Therefore I perceive a man may bee twice a child before the dayes of dotage, and stand in need of *Aesons* bath before threescore. (*RM* 1.42)

In the phrases suggesting advanced age, besides referring to himself as being 'in my riper yeares, and confirmed judgement'(*RM* 1.1), he looks back to the 'greener studies' of his youth (*RM* 1.6) and congratulates himself on the maturer wisdom of his 'setled yeares'(*RM* 11.7). He repeatedly surveys the history of his life, and the long tale of his struggle with religious doubts, as if it were of decades' duration, packed with incident, and now remote (*RM* 1.53, 1.17, 1.19). The sins of the sixteen-year-old, he concludes, are swelled and intensified at age forty, speaking as if he himself were well beyond this. But at the age of twenty-eight or so he is precisely in the middle of that range, twelve years away both from sixteen and forty.

Coleridge was bemused by Browne's poses: 'He says, he is a Batchelor, but he talks as if he had been a married man.'[3] That Browne should propose himself as in his dotage at something less than onescore and ten may be a kind of sly humour. He notes that he is saturnine and melancholic, that his manner is reserved and austere, 'full of rigour, sometimes not without morosity' (*RM* 1.3), 'in no way facetious, nor disposed for the mirth

---

[3] Coleridge, 754.

and galliardize of company' (*RM* II.II). Yet this same sensibility is one
which is humorously self-indicting: 'I thanke God . . . I have escaped . . .
Pride', he exclaims, but immediately proceeds to list his considerable linguistic attainments ('besides the *Jargon* and *Patois* of severall Provinces, I
understand no less than six Languages'); his wide experience in foreign
countries and his knowledge of their laws and customs; his understanding of astronomy, botany, theology, and ancient philosophy. He concludes,
perhaps waggishly, 'it is better to sit downe in a modest ignorance, & rest
contented with the naturall blessing of our owne reasons' (*RM* II.8). The
oscillating tone of grave and ripe wisdom coupled with extreme youth, of a
certain arrogance with a bathetic self-accusation, of grave self-scrutiny with
comic irony, could be designedly humorous, or entirely unconscious.[4]

Allusions to his real age, therefore, seem to invite admiration for preco-
cious virtuosity, even as he confesses in one of the poems of *Religio Medici*
that 'in the midst of June I feele December' (*RM* 1.32). He plays not only
on his own, but also on more general concepts of age. The declaration that
'there is no man more paradoxicall than my self' (*RM* 1.6) produces a series
of temporal conundrums: we are all of us older by nine months than we
realise (*RM* 1.39); yet he reckons his own age not from his conception or
birth but from his enrollment as a Christian (*RM* 1.45); because our sins
do not alter as we age, we are still infants in our prime and in our dotage in
youth (*RM* 1.42); as children we are our parents' graves (*RM* II.14); Adam
was thirty at his creation (*RM* 1.39); he gives his own age as thirty and as
not yet thirty (*RM* II.II; *RM* 1.41); but in any case, those who die at thirty
are *not* immature (*RM* 1.43). Finally, taking to its logical extreme the belief
in God's eternal present, he declares:

I was not onely before my selfe, but *Adam*, that is, in the Idea of God, and the
decree of that Synod held from all Eternity. And in this sense, I say, the world was
before the Creation, and at an end before it had a beginning; and thus was I dead
before I was alive; though my grave be *England*, my dying place was Paradise, and
Eve miscarried of mee before she conceiv'd of *Cain*. (*RM* 1.59)

This tone slightly resembles the ludic oscillation between *propria persona*
and Democritus Junior in *The Anatomy of Melancholy*, but it is neither
as consistent nor as contrived as Burton's. It is genuinely variable and
uncertain, sometimes actually unstable, sometimes comically extreme and
paradoxical, and sometimes unironically sententious: in short, Browne is

---

[4] Frank Warnke detects various examples of playfulness in *Religio Medici* ('A Hook for Amphibium:
Some Reflections on Fish' in Patrides *Approaches*, 55–6). I note some Brownean humour in *PE* in
Chapter Three.

not in full control of his medium. However specific passages are judged, to read *Religio Medici*, I suggest, is hardly to encounter the magisterial and authoritative finale which it pretends at times to be, and for which critics have ransacked its pages; rather, it is to read an unsure, presumptuous, self-abasing, possibly sportive *juvenilium* written in a voice in the process of finding itself out, by a sensibility half in love with the still-distant end of life, or at least with the notion of sober wit and climacteric wisdom. There is more than a little of the self-dramatising in it: like Donne's various poses in undone lover's laces or winding-sheet, or Burton's vocal antics and histrionic attitudes, Browne's narratorial chicanery (or indecision) is greatly at odds with the gravity of his subjects and the composure he seems to be aiming at. Although he claims that *Religio Medici* has emerged as a 'senior' work out of 'first studies', its effect is that of an initial trying-on of poses, attitudes, and tones.

Coleridge, recognising this quality in Browne, recommended that *Religio Medici* be 'considered as in a *dramatic* & not a metaphysical View'.[5] If, either deliberately or accidentally, Browne is ventriloquising the vocal style of a much older person, we might consider *Religio Medici* as a primitive form of dramatic monologue, and one moreover whose unstable tone is deliberately, or at least characteristically, playful, a playfulness that is significantly absent from the 1643 preface and the four inserted sections. The designation as a dramatic monologue is not necessarily anachronistic. Although the prevailing critical history of English letters configured by Eliot's tendentious 'dissociation of sensibility' would have it that only an early-Enlightenment fracturing of feeling and thought could inaugurate the kind of Romantic subjectivity found in the classic dramatic monologues of Tennyson and Browning,[6] and although it is true that certain features of *response* to the nineteenth-century dramatic monologue could not have been present in readers of mid-seventeenth-century writing, in other ways *Religio Medici* strongly resembles, and could almost be a precursor of, the post-Romantic form.[7] Donne and his metaphysical contemporaries, after all, used dramatic exclamation and sudden emotional shifts to suggest a dramatic role in poems like 'The Apparition' and Herbert's 'The Collar'.

[5] Coleridge, 758. Patrides also thinks *Religio Medici* should be read dramatically (Patrides *STB*, 22).
[6] Robert Langbaum, *The Poetry of Experience: The Dramatic Monologue in Modern Literary Tradition* (London: Chatto and Windus, 1972), 38–47.
[7] Clive Wilmer traces the dramatic monologue from Theocritus through Ovid and Propertius, with important examples in English by Chaucer, the Earl of Surrey, Marvell, and Rochester; existing both as *prosopopoeia*, a school exercise related to oratory, and as complaint, the dramatic monologue has a vigorous history before and during the seventeenth century ([Clive Wilmer], 'Dramatic Monologue' in *A Dictionary of Literary Terms and Literary Theory*, ed. J. A. Cuddon, 4th edn (Oxford: Blackwell, 1998), 237–40). See also Alan Sinfield, *Dramatic Monologue* (London: Methuen, 1977), 42, 9–11, 14.

One of the Renaissance precursors of the dramatic monologue was the epistle; and some of Browne's later *Miscellany Tracts*, essentially forms of the essay, are addressed as letters to enquirers such as Dugdale, Evelyn, Ray, Nicholas Bacon, and others, and presuppose, by their epistolary form, an asking and listening persona whose voice is not present, but is sometimes strongly indicated or paraphrased, and whose influence is felt in the tract (one of the features of the dramatic monologue).[8] The early-modern essay has been described as an 'implied dialogue', a dialectical performance of authorship *and* readership,[9] and this is a feature, too, of Seneca's letters to Lucilius, the precursors of the early-modern essay, with Seneca likening his correspondence with the younger man to a conversation. *Religio Medici* is not a letter (except to the extent that the preface is an epistolary address 'To the Reader') but implies a listener (one of those friends or colleagues to whom he passed the original manuscript);[10] nor is it an essay in the manner of Bacon or of his own *Tracts*. Instead, it exists somewhere between these two forms. With its two speaking voices, one heavily represented by the bulk of the text, the other framing and modifying certain of its statements, it presents an alienated *ur*-speaker who, by the process of aging, is no longer 'the writer'.[11] These two authorial voices – of 'now' and 'then' – supply two sensibilities, both explicit speaking voices, with the Senecan implication of exchange, of civil conversation. The 1630s voice has the crucial dramatic quality of being in the moment, with inconclusive, specific, and momentary arguments pitched as conclusive; equally, the contemporaneity of the 1643 voice, expressing sternly fundamental and developed ideas, gives it another kind of fervour, but one that is quite distinct from the earlier incarnation.[12]

Robert Langbaum has observed how, in a Victorian monologue like Tennyson's *Ulysses*, the implication of a younger, more robust protagonist is indicated in the 'enervated cadence' of the much older man, so that the poem in effect delivers two selves, past and present; and further, how Tennyson and Eliot dwell, in their *earliest* monologues, on the debilities of age. That 'early' Tennysonian world-weariness is a feature already noted

---

[8] Sinfield, 7.

[9] Michael L. Hall, 'The Emergence of the Essay and the Idea of Discovery' in *Essays on the Essay: Redefining the Genre*, ed. Alexander Butrym (Athens, GA: University of Georgia Press, 1989), 82.

[10] The necessity of an implied reader is by no means absolute: neither Tennyson's *Maud* nor *Locksley Hall* nor Browning's *Caliban upon Setebos*, three of the greatest dramatic monologues, has such a presence.

[11] The classic formulations of the dramatic monologue all refer to poems. There are, of course, prose works in the genre, such as Beckett's *Not I* and *Krapp's Last Tape*, which like *Religio Medici* engages with the sense of the younger self as a different and distinct persona.

[12] Langbaum, 90. I am very grateful to Clive Wilmer for helping me to understand aspects of the Victorian dramatic monologue.

in *Religio Medici*. If the dramatic monologue depicts the alienation of the author from himself via his willingness to play and inhabit a role, *Religio Medici* – as a pair of separated voices – performs the unwillingly alienated selves of 1635 and 1643, the latter explicitly renouncing the positions and emotions of the former as 'a memoriall unto me . . . plausible unto my passed apprehension . . . not agreeable unto my present selfe' (*RM*.Reader, 10), while insisting on the quality of the times as the agent of alienation. And even within the 1630s *Religio* he alludes to yet another, distinctive former self of yet earlier years whose 'greener studies [were] polluted with two or three' heresies (*RM* 1.6). Indeed, he seems to speak of an evolving persona when he says 'every man is not onely himselfe' (*RM* 1.6). All but one of the four new sections of 1643 concern themselves with sectarian wrangling, schism, the damaged social economy, and the nearing end of the world,[13] subjects which seem suited to the increased chaos and darkness of the moment; none of these solemn issues allows for the deliberately extreme, even semi-comic reasoning of 1635 that, for example, lets him claim to be as happy with the picture of a horse as with one of a beautiful woman (*RM* 11.9). Part of the 'drama' of *Religio Medici* is maintained by precisely those sections of 1643 that are not ludic, that are tonally and thematically different from the 1635 body of the work. The measured binarisms with which he alludes in the 1630s to sectarian controversy in 1.4 ('angry'/'calm', 'extreme'/'mediocre') – whose debate will be reconciled, like the union of the two poles, in heaven – are quite unlike his grimmer discussion of the same ideas in 1.56 (a 1643 insertion), where the sectaries are characterised as damning, reprobating, and vulgar, and where their arguments work against each other's salvation.

Other features usually noted in discussions of the dramatic monologue are a specific occasion, interaction between speaker and listener, and various temporal markers.[14] Browne is perfectly precise about his age, and about the compositional moment, that first transitional period between studenthood and professional life (the 1630s *Religio*), and the later occasion of the illicit publication (the 1643 *Religio*). There are, in consequence of this specificity, many temporal markers which remind us not only of his age but also of his experience up to the time of initial composition – travel, education, domestic situation – and even more precise ones which guide our reading of

---

[13] Sections 8, 43, and 56. Section 28 complains about belief in relics.

[14] See, for example, Ina Beth Sessions, *A Study of the Dramatic Monologue in American and Continental Literature* (San Antonio: Alamo Printing Co., 1933). Later theorists of the dramatic monologue have, however, questioned the taxonomical rigour of this early formulation, since it excludes many of the most important examples of the form (Langbaum, 76; and Glennis Byron, *Dramatic Monologue* (London: Routledge, 2003), 31.

the 1643 insertions: deteriorating political and social structures, the parlous condition of the monarchy and the intransigent position of the church, and the unregulated condition of the press.

Religio Medici is thus primarily a naive monologue which, by a retrospective conversion at the hands of the older Browne, is made into a *dramatic* monologue with the bifurcation of the voices alienating the earlier from the later, a temporal act which highlights, moreover, the ultimately momentary, transient authority of the younger voice, demoting it from any claim to summary and abstract finality. This younger Browne is by implication manipulated by the older self, so that, as in a full-fledged dramatic monologue of a much later era, we are sympathetic to, but not disarmed or compelled by, this young first-person voice. As in a canonical dramatic monologue, Browne does not require or expect his auditor's acceptance of his arguments; he seeks only attention and permission to be heard. And this is the outstanding point: by inviting his audience without expecting or requiring its agreement, Browne reiterates formally the burden of his major eirenic claim: it is safe and civil to have distinct, and even antithetical, visions and ideology as long as the contract of civility holds and can entertain the variety of belief. The bivocal 1643 *Religio Medici* enacts its own message of toleration.

Written more than a decade before the publication of his next work, *Pseudodoxia Epidemica* (1646), *Religio Medici* thus requires a special kind of reading: although its sonorities and its measured opinions have suggested a comprehensive mentality to its many admirers and imitators, it should be taken much more tentatively, more as a kind of manifesto whose real viability – philosophical and even stylistic – would be revised and adjusted in the succeeding works of greater learning and of different times. The position and function of *Religio Medici* as an establishing work, a prelude of sorts to a life of investigation, is immensely useful in framing a baseline of what were as yet unmodulated personal categories of thought.

SUNDRY PARTICULARITIES: DESIGN AND REGISTER

I have already proposed that the protestations of the 1643 preface should be read as genuine, that Browne was not feigning the pose of the surprised author. He did, it is clear, take advantage of that trope; but beyond its conventional employment, I will argue, Browne invented his own medium in *Religio Medici*, a work of complete formal originality. His subsequent works, though new *literary* forms, at least allude to some recognisable paradigm of intellectual organisation – the curiosity cabinet, for example, the encyclopaedia, or the antiquarian survey. *Religio Medici* does not neatly suggest itself as anything so familiar: it is neither essay in the Montaignean style, nor treatise in the format of the collection or the scientific anatomy. It glances at the confessional mode and offers a few apparently personal anecdotes (some of them mildly eccentric), yet it is by no means an auto-biography or in any exact sense an example of the life-writing typical of Donne, Walton, Hutchinson, or Aubrey. It is casually digressive, enough so to confound any purely linear narrative pattern, and yet there is no hint of Burton's self-conscious disruption. It makes a case for a general style of belief, but with so little overt rhetorical aggression that as a manifesto it hardly exists in the same tonal universe as Sidney's *Defence* or Milton's *Areopagitica*. But it is notoriously difficult to prove a negative, and so it has been the task of Browne scholars to discover a form or a structure for *Religio Medici* rather than to admit that none exists. It is, however, its formlessness, its innocence of design which is outstanding, and which, by comparison, highlights the formal precision of his subsequent works.

The many descriptive analyses of *Religio Medici*'s form, tone, and purpose have the air of theological speculation, and the variety of approaches make an unruly heap which inadvertently indicates the essay's own unruliness. He meant to present his revulsion for the mob and sectarianism, goes one argument.[15] He preferred sectarian controversy to repressive control by an established church, goes another, and set out to demonstrate the tolerant position that could accept many varieties of belief.[16] His way of thinking about the nature of belief and devotion was complacently Anglican, remote from the issues of the day, and he transmitted this by a 'play of art'.[17] He was pleading for the freedom of individual conscience.[18] He merely wished to show off his prose style and draw attention to himself,[19] and he was especially in love with rhetorical flourishes.[20] He wanted to defend doctors against the charge of atheism by offering his sincere personal credo.[21] With so many competing readings, the questions of genre and tone and

---

[15] Wilding, 102; and Huntley, *Sir Thomas Browne*, 106–7.

[16] Post, 54.

[17] Joan Webber, *The Eloquent 'I': Style and Self in Seventeenth-Century Prose* (Madison: University of Wisconsin Press, 1968), 4, 8.

[18] Finch, *Sir Thomas Browne*, 4.

[19] Stanley Fish, 'The Bad Physician: The Case of Sir Thomas Browne' in *Self-Consuming Artifacts: The Experience of Seventeenth-Century Literature* (Berkeley: University of California Press, 1972), 353–73; and Walter Pater (quoted in J. R. Mulryne, 'The Play of Mind: Self and Audience in *Religio Medici*' in Patrides *Approaches*, 61).

[20] Alexander Ross, *Medicus Medicatus* (1645), A2r and 20.

[21] Andrew Cunningham, 'Sir Thomas Browne and his *Religio Medici*: Reason, Nature and Religion' in *Religio Medici: Medicine and Religion in Seventeenth-Century England*, ed. Ole Peter Grell and Andrew Cunningham (Aldershot: Scolar Press, 1996), 12.

style are consequently also vexed: rescued from the criticisms of Fish and Pater, among others, *Religio Medici* has been understood as a Pascalian *peinture de la pensée*; as a demonstration consistent with other seventeenth-century prose essays which relentlessly remind the reader that the subject is the authorial self; as Senecan; as neoclassical-baroque, mannerist or anti-Ciceronian, paradoxical, guileful, Latinate.[22]

The same wish for order has prompted the discovery of overarching design in *Religio Medici*. Thus, an implicit tripartite form based on faith, hope, and charity has for some years been established and widely accepted. Founded exclusively (and fortuitously) on the opening remark in Part II which seems to move to 'that other virtue of charity', this argument retroactively proposes that the first and longer section of the essay must therefore be about faith and hope, a circular argument at best, and one which does not explain why charity, the greatest of the three Christian virtues, receives a relatively paltry treatment (fifteen sections compared to sixty for the other two combined).[23] Another analysis discovers an allusion to the two branches of 'charity' as they were understood by seventeenth-century catechism – love of God and love of neighbour; it is, in this argument, the latter that is being considered in Part II as 'that other virtue of charity' after Part I's illumination of the first.[24] But the disclaimer at the end of Part I in which he defers the 'many things singular and to the humour of my irregular selfe' to the better understanding of 'maturer judgements' (*RM* I.60) feels like an ending; the much briefer Part II might almost be an afterthought rather than a structured conclusion, so that such explanations require large exceptions.[25] Discussions of his style often resort to the kinds of extravagant descriptive flourishes employed by Coleridge and Pater (and Coleridge advises Browne's reader not to expect consistent philosophy but to lie back and enjoy his mannerisms[26]); or they attempt unsustainable verbal-visual

---

[22] Croll, '"Attic Prose"', 87; Webber, 4–8; Robert Adolph, *The Rise of Modern Prose Style* (Cambridge, MA: Harvard University Press, 1968), 212; Murray Roston, 'The "Doubting" Thomas' in Patrides *Approaches*, 76–80; several of Morris Croll's essays reiterate the assignment of the Ciceronian style; Margaret Wiley, *The Subtle Knot: Creative Scepticism in Seventeenth-Century England* (London: George Allen and Unwin, 1952), 137–60; Mulryne, 63; George Williamson, *The Senecan Amble: A Study in Prose Form from Bacon to Collier* (Chicago: University of Chicago Press, 1951), 213–14. The valiant attempts of Croll, Williamson, Adolph, and others to define and categorise seventeenth-century prose styles have not, for the most part, been especially helpful in the case of Browne.

[23] Huntley, *Sir Thomas Browne*, 107. The themes of the first part do not, in any case, especially bear out the case for faith and hope.

[24] Waddington, 81–99. Robbins also gives the two tables argument (Robbins *STB*, xi).

[25] The play on *fathering* and *authorizing* and the throwaway alliteration ('further father') in this last section is borrowed from the concluding sentence of the 1643 preface, as if the remark's final position in Part I appealed to him as a guiding and concluding one for his statement of intent.

[26] Coleridge, 765.

analogies, likening a Browne paragraph to Poussin or El Greco;[27] or they attempt to liken *Religio Medici* to a Donne sermon or a Montaigne essay, even though the work is too various and resistant to settle easily in such analogies; or they imply *a priori* expectations of the essay or devotional tract, and condemn *Religio Medici* for having no obvious designs on us.[28]

Let us therefore entertain the possibility that *Religio Medici* is actually messy, that if it seems disorganised, fundamentally unstructured, conversational, tonally inconsistent, that is precisely what it is. We must seek patterns of thought, rather than patterns of composition, since insisting on some subtle formal regularity only imposes an artificial and arbitrary shape upon the essay while failing to honour and actively notice what *Religio Medici* actually is.[29] Let us instead contemplate the spectacle of an artist in undress rather than, in Coleridge's phrase, in 'his best clothes', genuinely hapless, careless, and inexperienced, and forget the cunning, adroit Browne producing calculated and premeditated effects. Despite the attempt of Johnson and many another critic to wish it away, if the 1643 preface is sincere Browne really did pen the essay informally and as a private exercise as he claims, and its messiness is therefore likely to be that of casual composition, of informality, almost of notebook scribbling (a practice of his for which there is much evidence), his untrammelled enthusiasms often quite winsome in their certitude. There is no reason to doubt, and many reasons to accept, his claim of having written it only 'at leisurable hours' (during what would have been a busy apprenticeship) and without 'the assistance of any good book whereby to promote my invention' (at a point when he would have been far from libraries and too poor to own an extensive one of his own) (*RM*.Reader, 10).[30] If this most personal and least settled composition has any governing shape or pattern, it is that of the catalogue or extended enumeration, rendered as parataxis, the least artful of rhetorical figures.

The casual macro-structure of *Religio Medici* is readily apparent. The sixty sections of Part 1 (including the additions of 1643) fall into several roughly and sometimes only coincidentally linked thematic groups. In the declarative early sections, for instance, he identifies his own stripe of

[27] Roston, 75–9.

[28] Fish, *Self-Consuming Artifacts*, 365; see also Warnke's riposte, 49–59.

[29] The essential lack of structure has, of course, been acknowledged in the past, but this has been salved by the suggestion that, for instance, it is a 'sequence of linked thought' (Cunningham, 'Sir Thomas Browne', 23), or by avoiding the issue altogether and instead concentrating on the nature of Browne's beliefs (which are themselves hard to pin down because they are often apparently contradictory).

[30] The nature of such practical training – even when it was carried out – varied widely among doctors. Without further knowledge of Browne's whereabouts and connexions in these years, it is impossible to be sure that this excuse was not merely a trope. I am indebted to Margaret Pelling for advising me on this aspect of Browne's experience.

Christianity in relation to others (1–8). In another group (45–52) he moves from his own (mildly) millenarian beliefs to a series of discussions of the last judgement, resurrection, and the afterlife. These groups have a progressive and logical structure interrupted by sudden diversions: an important set of ideas about divine purpose and cause in the creation ('there are no *Grotesques* in nature' (13–16)) and a subsequent section on the varieties of faith and on the credit of the Bible (20–3) are interrupted first by a digression on fortune (which might more easily have sat next to his later consideration of miracles), and then by one on the competition of reason and faith in the human soul. In other words, large, perhaps orchestrated, sections of the essay are punctuated by apparently unrelated material, and some sections seem to be taking up earlier points as if they had previously been forgotten or short-changed. Together with the cumulative effect of his enumerative parataxis, these punctuations give the work the immediacy of an inconsistent statement of ideas and principles by someone still finding his way. There is nothing, for example, of the measured pace and structure of *Urne-Buriall*; *Religio Medici* does not build toward a transcendental (or any other kind of) conclusion beyond a brief prayer. Indeed, this loose intellectual semi-organisation is a felicitous disarray more reminiscent of Browne's notebooks and commonplace books than of his later formal works.

Such a style is of course not necessarily consonant with youth and inexperience; however, a younger man, as he admits in the preface, has not accumulated all the ideas and interests of his older self, and the 1635 Browne betrays this when he seems to ignore or dismiss areas which would later become central to his intellectual disposition. He has, for example, only scorn for the *piae fraudes* represented by sacred relics, and has but 'slender and doubtfull respect . . . unto Antiquities' (*RM* 1.28), sentiments which would be reversed or transformed in *Musæum Clausum* and *Urne-Buriall*.

Except that its paratactic joining of subjects is an early rendition of a rhetorical habit central both to his later work and to the Baconian project as a whole, I would argue that *Religio Medici* is only locally, and not comprehensively, coherent. This lack of structure may itself be its most important structural feature, and analyses of it which insist on a recognisable form because Browne is the sort of writer who generally feels, and is, measured and formally exact discount the likelihood that he had not yet become that coherent writer. Thus, the essay may possibly be gathered into the fold of life-writing – as a strange and reserved specimen, admittedly – not because it conforms to any standard narrative pattern but because, willy nilly, it enacts a sensibility, a sensibility which it is not entirely within Browne's power to govern or fashion. It might be described as a kind of thinking aloud, where the act and the pattern of thought is at least as revealing as the conclusions reached. But another possibility is that *Religio Medici* mimics the structure of material assemblage and encyclopaedic convening: the influences of the physical and thematic arrays of items and information so characteristic of early-modern investigation would have been primary in Browne's intellectual formation in the 1620s and 1630s, and we might consider the work as a cabinet of at least locally ordered thoughts, the elements of personal creed on display. Such arrays are discussed more fully in the next chapter; here it is convenient to note that the analogy between such compilations and the recuperative restoration of decayed knowledge might fittingly be applied also to *Religio Medici*: the convened pieces of Browne's philosophy represent the kind of regeneration of coherence symptomatic of the whole Baconian programme. *Religio Medici* proposes its tentative conclusions in the civil mode.

EXPERIMENTATION AND ESSAY-STRUCTURE IN *RELIGIO MEDICI*

One of the enquiries of this chapter is to establish – if possible – *Religio Medici*'s relation to the developing essay-form, a genre to which we might at least casually assign all his works. What are the traits of essays of this period? How is Browne's writing related to scientific enquiry; and how are we to understand his striking vocal features? As an essayist, Browne has been usefully compared with Montaigne and Bacon, the founders of the early-modern essay tradition.[31] Quite apart from his insistence on having 'never read 3 leaves of that Author [i.e., Montaigne] & scarce any more ever since', and that similarities between them are often 'butt coincidence' (*NCB*, 290), the exercise is far from straightforward. The essay – established and enlarged by Montaigne and Bacon but perhaps reasonably extending, in the minds of English practitioners, as far back as Seneca – had few conventions or rhetorical rules and offered a liberating absence of formal expectations and constraints. This formal freedom of enquiry and consideration coincided, as has often been observed, with the rise of empirical investigation and the need for writing which either itself enacted the mental journey of discovery, or re-enacted the already-performed process (often experimental) by which truth was arrived at.[32] The elaboration, however, of the scientific essay is

---

[31] Ted-Larry Pebworth, 'Wandering in the America of Truth: *Pseudodoxia Epidemica* and the Essay Tradition' in Patrides, *Approaches*, 166–77; and Michael L. Hall, 76–89.

[32] Peter Dear, 'Narratives, Anecdotes, and Experiments: Turning Experience into Science in the Seventeenth Century' in *The Literary Structure of Scientific Argument*, ed. Peter Dear (Philadelphia:

usually located at a somewhat later moment – in the 1650s and 1660s – so that *Religio Medici* would be an unusually early instalment of that form. But Montaigne's felicitous 1580 coinage '*essai*' ('trial, assay') insists on this sense of process and experiment, and that quality of trial, as well as of patchedness, is a feature of Browne's writing, too. Browne is, however, rarely so deliberately disruptive, even in *Religio Medici*, as Montaigne claims to be when he describes his work as 'antike', 'monstrous', 'patched and hudled up together of divers members, . . . having neither order, dependencie, or proportion, but casuall and framed by chance',[33] his short tracts, as well as his major works after *Religio Medici*, generally observe, on the contrary, a rigorous framework of enquiry which would influence Robert Boyle among others.[34]

It is the aphoristic style of Bacon, whose *Essays* in their final form were published while Browne was an undergraduate, which offers a clearer model, as do Seneca's letters and tracts such as *De Beneficiis*, staples of the humanist curriculum.[35] The Baconian essay in some ways sounds and moves like a Browne essay, the sometimes abrupt transitions and sudden interjections building to a total picture which reminds the reader simultaneously of its incompleteness, of the essayist's inability to supply a comprehensive, rhetorically polished answer to such questions as 'what is truth?' Browne is no natural aphorist, and where the Baconian aphorism is designedly terse and even cryptic, Browne prefers a more generous and extended period. His aphorising, where it exists, is part of his mimicry of grave sententiousness as an effect of age.

Bacon's concision is rhetorical rather than substantive, and Browne's essayistic forays are also highly contained, even if less sparely expressed. In some of the *Miscellany Tracts* and in one or two other uncollected late works which most nearly approximate the Baconian and the later scientific essay, he writes on such concise subjects as the location of Troas, on artificial hills, and on the genealogy of languages, and his expositions are somewhat difficult to compare to the earlier and more diffusely philosophic (as opposed to the scientific or antiquarian) Bacon. The unexpectedly Senecan

University of Pennsylvania Press, 1991), 162–3; and Frederick L. Holmes, 'Argument and Narrative in Scientific Writing' in *Literary Structure*, ed. Peter Dear, 165–6. See also Steven Shapin, 'Pump and Cicumstance: Robert Boyle's Literary Technology', *Social Studies of Science* 14 (1984), 484–91.

33 Montaigne, 'Of Friendship' in *The Essayes of Michel Lord of Montaigne*, trans. John Florio, ed. A. R. Waller, 3 vols. (London: Dent, 1910) I, 90.

34 Pebworth, 176.

35 Bacon calls Seneca the originator of the essay-form. We have Browne's direct assurance that he was ill-acquainted with Montaigne's work; and there is no conclusive evidence that he knew Bacon's *Essays* when he wrote *Religio Medici*, although *Pseudodoxia* shows the influence of *The Advancement of Learning*, and the Bacon essay is most influential in *U-B*.

tone of parts of *Religio Medici* – the tone of deliberation and of occasional emphasis and insistence delivered in rhetorically finished assertions which have an aphoristic ring – is marked wherever he is attempting to lay down his personal credo ('I can hold there is no such thing as injury; that if there be, there is no such injury as revenge, and no such revenge as the contempt of an injury' (*RM* 11.7)). Even with features of Bacon and Seneca, and of the Montaignean tradition, blended and altered in *Religio Medici*, Browne is an original. His prose works, if they are essays, are *sui generis*: they have some coincidental and deliberate likeness to their predecessors, but we must allow them their own format and mannerisms.

To evaluate *Religio Medici* as an original form and as an early essay it is therefore helpful to observe Browne at work in a more established essay-form at the other end of his career, in the *Miscellany Tracts* (*op.post.* 1683), and in other miscellaneous writings of the post-*Religio Medici* period. 'Of the Fishes Eaten by our Saviour' is a brief and characteristic epistolary tract, and like most of the other twelve *Miscellany Tracts* it responds to a question proposed by some unnamed, learned correspondent. The question restated at the outset by Browne – what kinds of fish did Christ eat with the Disciples after his resurrection? – invites 'farther inquiry' because Scripture itself is indeterminate. The opening section establishes one range of evidence with a brief enumeration of problematic fish stories in the Bible – those of Tobit, Jonah, and the Israelites. The discussion then moves into a development section which addresses the correspondent's question and frames another range of evidence as the territory of solutions: as a naturalist Browne asks what species of fish live in the Sea of Galilee, how large they become, and whether or not their size is consonant with the expression 'great'. As a naturalist familiar with Middle-Eastern geography, Browne gives the straightforward answer that the kinds of fish taken in this lake must be freshwater species, since the Sea of Galilee is landlocked. So the fish eaten by Christ could only have been trout, pike, chevin (chub), or tench, all of which, Browne assures us, are species identified in that region by the 'learned Traveller, Belonius' and 'answerable' to the Scriptural designation 'great,' if we understand the expression to mean 'large *in their own kinds*,' rather than 'large species' [my emphasis] (*MT*, 53).

This purely informative survey of Biblical fish, incorporating textual and natural-historical evidence, then shifts away from the post-resurrectionary meal to the earlier story of the tribute money, when Christ instructed Peter to open the mouth of the first fish he caught, there to find two coins. *Faber marinus*, the Peterfish, Pennyfish, or John Dory, Browne explains, so-called because the two marks on either side are said to be Peter's fingerprints and a 'signature of money', is wholly fabulous, not because he doesn't believe in such signatures, but because it is a pelagian, not a freshwater, species – another mingling of textual and natural facts. The essay ends with a counter-query for the corrrespondent: what fish was it that appeared to the Gothic King Theodoric in the guise of his recently executed son as it lay in the dish at table, a meal which caused his death?[36] Having moved from Christ's meals to the related category of fish in the Christian narrative, the essay thus drifts associatively outside the confines of the Bible into the realm of amazing stories involving fish, and from fish eaten after death to fish eaten just before it. In doing so, however, the essay follows a simple developmental order: 1.) statement of topic; 2.) discussion of the kinds of evidence from which it arises; 3.) natural-historical focus on the fauna of the Holy Land; 4.) a related misapprehension about Peterfish; 5.) a counter-query in a related but distinct category about Theodoric's fish supper. This is in the main a straightforward assessment of the stated topic, although its tendency to wander slightly beyond the bounds of the enquiry is a more pronounced feature of his other writing.

Some of the *Miscellany Tracts* are neither as firmly managed nor as open to digression. One is no more than a list of plants and one a list of coronary plants, another a series of comparative passages in Anglo-Saxon and seventeenth-century English, and another a blow-by-blow interpretation of a prophecy of the New World. These have little structure beyond that of simple paratactic accumulation.[37] Other works (not all of them included in the *Tracts*) feel more like fully developed essays, and some display, as 'Of the Fishes' does not, Browne's distinctive stylistic cadences. 'On Dreams', an unpublished work probably from late in his career, opens with the kind of balanced proposition so familiar from *Urne-Buriall* and *The Garden of Cyrus*, expressed in useful, unextravagant metaphors.[38] Indeed, it is an announcement, an investigative and philosophical premiss, from which the rest of the essay will develop:

Half our dayes wee passe in the shadowe of the earth [i.e., night], and the brother of death [i.e., sleep] exacteth a third part of our lives. A good part of our sleepes is peeced out with visions, and phantasticall objects wherin wee are confessedly

---

[36] Browne had read of this in Procopius, *De bello Gothici*, but he misremembered the story, and it is a telling misprision: it was not, in fact, Theodoric's own son, but the son of Boethius whom he had had executed and whose face appeared in the fish. Procopius, *History of the Wars*, ed. H. B. Dewing, 3 vols. (Cambridge, MA: Harvard University Press, and London: Heinemann, 1961), III, v. i. 32–9.

[37] 'Of Plants in Scripture', 'Of Garlands', 'Of Languages', 'A Prophecy Concerning the Future State of Several Nations' (*MT*, 3–108).

[38] Browne had already considered dreams in *RM* II.II, and more briefly in *PE* I.x. His conclusions in these three separate sallies on dreams are rather distinct.

deceaved. The day supplyeth us with truths, the night with fictions and falshoods which unconfortably divide the natural account of our beings. And therefore having passed the day in sober labours and rationall enquiries of truth, wee are fayne to betake ourselves unto such a state of being, wherin the soberest heads have acted all the monstrosities of melancholy, and which unto open eyes are no better then folly and madnesse (*MT*, 230).

These first remarks are presented in a tone reminiscent of the prefatory dedication of *Urne-Buriall*, with sententious and formally balanced opening concepts (night-sleep, day-night, truth-falsehood, sobriety-madness) indicating a confidently established framework from which he then concocts an initial (and very simple) theory of dreams: as we live, so shall we dream, with virtuous daytime thoughts yielding composed sleep. The most pious and best of men will dream almost divinely; and the rest of us will tend to dream of whatever has most occupied us in waking hours. That uncontentious assertion is quickly modified, however: no sooner is it formulated than he warns of the vulnerability to upset of such straightforward arithmetic by the 'phantasticall spirit', which may in sleep set out on 'unrulie wandrings', wherein the 'soberest heads have acted all the monstrosities of melancholy'. The apparently easy equation of waking and sleeping thoughts turns out suddenly to be unreliable (*MT*, 230).

The subsequent body of the essay departs from these initial, partly unstable, propositions about the spiritual logic of dreams to consider their interpretation. Here Browne introduces paratactic accumulation in an impressive oneirocritical survey of the ancient world. Such 'phantasticall' dreams, he says, may be read as signatures (or 'mysterie[s] of Similitude'), rebuses, visual puns, encouragements, warnings, or even mere digestive disruptions, but they mainly follow the waking-sleeping equation of the first remarks, with, at their coarsest, a diet of beans being held to account for Daniel's visions.[39] It is a survey not so much interpretive as informational, much as *Urne-Buriall* is until its final chapter a survey of local and international obsequial customs. But, like the conclusion of *Urne-Buriall*, the final paragraphs of 'On Dreams' are its most provocative ones, seeming to suggest a purpose for the preceding enumeration higher than mere cataloguing. If the dreams of Alexander, Pharaoh, and Cato are in fact merely 'innocent delusions' (*MT*, 233), there is also, he warns, 'a sinfull state of dreames; . . . & there may be a night booke of our iniquities' – in other words, 'mortal sinnes in dreames aris[e] from evill precogitations'. The arithmetic of dreams is retrospectively and horribly vindicated – if we dream of crimes it is because

---

[39] In *Pseudodoxia* he quickly dismisses the dreams of the ancients as delusions practised by the Devil (*PE* 1.x.62).

we have already considered them awake. He tells of Dionysus who executed a man for dreaming of having killed him, and of Lamia who tried to sue a man who dreamt lasciviously of her.

This set of remarks opens up a potentially vast and troubling debate: does thinking of an action carry the same moral weight as performing it, and is dreaming therefore a kind of thought which in waking would make us guilty? He has thrown up the possibility that we are sometimes subject to 'evill precogitations', but at the same time he casts into doubt the reliability of such analogies when he notes that even the best of men will dream in antithesis of their waking selves. He observes that in law the dreamer and the sleepwalker are not regarded as responsible actors, but adds that 'if there be such debts [i.e., responsibility for deeds done in sleep], wee owe deeply unto sympathies [i.e., the spiritual/mystic connexion between the dreamer and the dreamt]', and inconclusively decides that 'the common spirit of the world must bee judg in such arrearages' (*MT*, 233).[40] This momentary and teasing meditation, beautifully characterised under the suggestive, quasi-legal term 'arrearages' (outstanding debts), has a Baconian deftness, a laconic delicacy which refuses to milk its theme.[41] All he will avouch at the end is that everyone dreams, and he waggishly suggests that any exempting theory – that infants and others do not – is itself a phantasm.

'On Dreams', in sum, shows Browne in a far more speculative and suggestible mode than the essay on Biblical fish. Although 'On Dreams' also offers sturdy catalogues of exemplary dreams and their meanings, its thought-patterns are contingently, but not necessarily, progressive: the middle section on the interpretation of dreams serves only as workmanly grounding in 'fact' for the much more adventurous and meaningful speculations on the nature and cause of thought in sleep and on the moral heft of dreams. The essay represents a passage among, rather than a structure of, related ideas which are opportunistically seized upon as they arise, neither designedly 'antic' nor deliberately arrived at. Browne is never uninterested in factual assemblage, but this gathering of elements is more than the worthy, essentially random compiling which was the hallmark of some amateur Baconians.[42]

---

[40] See my discussion below of *RM* ii. ii, which also remains inconclusive about the responsibility of dreamers.

[41] *OED* meanings 1, 2, and 3 define 'arrearage' as indebtedness or being behind in payment; backwardness; or an outstanding sum on an unpaid balance.

[42] See Harold Cook, 'The Cutting Edge of a Revolution? Medicine and Natural History Near the Shores of the North Sea' in *Renaissance and Revolution: Humanists, Scholars, Craftsmen and Natural Philosophers in Early Modern Europe*, ed. J.V. Field and Frank A. J. L. James (Cambridge: Cambridge University Press, 1993), 48–9; and Marie Boas Hall, 'Thomas Browne, Naturalist' in Patrides *Approaches*, 179.

The unconventionalised format of the essay allows Browne's own thought-processes to meander, suspending the polemical and procedural requirements of proof and conclusion, permitting him to move from the concrete to the speculative by an associative, rather than by an accumulative, process. The thoughts on arrearages are in no way couched in or built upon the examples of antique dreams, nor authorised by those examples; and yet those ancient dreams establish a topical environment of dream-lore which conduces to the discussion of dream-metaphysics. Baconian compiling, an essentially *material* task in the gathering of objects and facts, and Baconian parataxis, the anti-rhetorical, adventitious assembly of ideas and remarks (especially in aphoristic style), together offer a useful way of introducing speculations far removed from predictable oneirocriticism. This strategy – of co-opting Baconian compilation and aphoristic contingency to produce what we can conveniently characterise as a Montaignean fluidity – is one already developed in *Religio Medici*.[43]

Virtually all of Boyle's writing excuses its own incompletion and disorganisation.[44] Boyle's approach to the scientific essay – certainly influenced in part by Browne – is proposed in the *Proemial Essay . . . Touching Experimental Essays* (1661): the essay is to be 'the Narrative of what I had try'd and observ'd'.[45] It is not to be 'systematical', and by dispensing with formal rhetorical structure and comprehensive surveys it can emphasise not only the experimentalist's 'peculiar notions' (i.e., what is new in his work), but by being 'competently stock'd with experiments' it can also demonstrate the experimental process by which new information is gained'.[46] This process is what Shapin calls the 'literary technology' of scientific writers, and what Dear calls scientific 'narratives'.[47] It is a useful way of thinking about *Religio Medici*. An anticipator of Boyle, Browne's not precisely scientific, sometimes complacent *Religio Medici* has the character of a narrated self-interrogatory investigation. Casual and naive self-scrutiny in *Religio Medici* inadvertently takes the form and colouration of the later scientific essay.

---

[43] Compare *Religio Medici*'s passage on dreams with one in *Letter to a Friend* (*c.* 1656) (Keynes I, 108–9). Here, straightforward oneirocritical '*arithmetic*' which assigns specific divinatory meaning to specific dream-images is disparaged by Browne as 'easie and feminine' – i.e., irrational and merely 'curious' – in the case of the dead Loveday, whose female relations hoped his dreams presaged a return to health. Here, Browne's medical assessment of Loveday's phthisical symptoms categorically rules out any such possibility: consumption is invariably fatal.

[44] On this feature of Boyle's work, see Sergei Zakin, 'Inside the Book of the World: Issues of Textual Interpretation in Mid-Seventeenth-Century Discourse on Knowledge', unpublished Ph.D. thesis, University of Cambridge (1998), 76.

[45] Robert Boyle, *A Proemial Essay . . . Touching Experimental Essays* (1661), 15.

[46] Boyle, *Proemial Essay*, 9. Barnaby and Schnell discuss this aspect of Boyle's thought (40).

[47] Shapin, 'Pump and Circumstance', 484; Dear, 'Narratives', 135–6.

Compare, for example, 'On Dreams' to the discussion of dreams in *Religio Medici* (11.11). In the latter, the nature of dreams is Stoically described as 'real' or more real than, and as satisfactory as, waking life, and moreover as supplying us with a reality we may long for but miss awake; this is linked with the metaphysical suggestion that dreams are an intimation of death's liberation of the soul (and I quote the passage at length):

> In briefe, I am content, and what should providence adde more? Surely this is it wee call Happinesse, and this doe I enjoy, with this I am happy in a dreame, and as content to enjoy a happinesse in a fancie as others in a more apparent truth and reality. There is surely a neerer apprehension of any thing that delights us in our dreames, than in our waked senses . . . I thanke God for my happy dreames . . . , for there is a satisfaction in them unto reasonable desires, and such as can be content with a fit of happinesse; and surely it is not a melancholy conceite to thinke we are all asleepe in this world, and that the conceits of this life are as meare dreames to those of the next, as the Phantasmes of the night, to the conceits of the day . . . We are somewhat more than our selves in our sleepes, and the slumber of the body seemes to bee but the waking of the soule. It is the ligation of sense, but the liberty of reason . . . *Noctambuloes* [or] night-walkers, though in their sleepe, doe yet enjoy the action of their senses; wee must therefore say that there is something in us that is not in the jurisdiction of *Morpheus*; and that those abstracted and ecstaticke soules doe walk about in their owne corps, as spirits in the bodies they assume . . . [T]he soule beginning to be freed from the ligaments of the body, begins to reason like her selfe, and to discourse in a straine above mortality. (*RM* 11.11)

Section 11.11 as a whole considers 'the Microcosme of mine owne frame', and dreams are only one example of the way in which he contains all within himself. For example, in dreams he claims to compose, view, and laugh at complete comedies, even though in waking life he is indisposed for mirth. That we are not at all like ourselves in sleep is a conclusion generated in 'On Dreams', but there he uses it to propose the deception of dreams, 'wherin the soberest heads have acted all the monstrosities of melancholy' (*MT*, 230). In *Religio*, by contrast, he less clinically uses that disjunction between our sleeping and waking selves to offer a surprisingly modern theory of personality – that dreams show us another (and, for Browne, semi-divine) part of ourselves which has no ready expression in waking. This discussion in *Religio Medici* is more free, more contingent, with the topics of happiness and the experience of happiness, the microcosmic plenitude of the individual, and the nature of self all loosely bound up with a theory of dreams which is generous and undogmatic, which can move among Browne's worlds of experience without demanding finality or certainty from them, and move without the compilation of evidence offered in 'On Dreams' to a highly speculative conclusion about the nature of the soul.

Sometimes the thematic and logical transitions of *Religio Medici* are straightforward, or at least obliquely linked within a discrete section, as in the passage on dreams, but often they can be accounted for only in an ample overview. In Part 1, for example, sections 20 to 26 form a semi-contingent progression, with section 23 the final instalment of a set of four sections (20–3) which jointly deal with the credit and interpretation of Scripture. Section 23 considers the mere longevity of the Bible as a validation of its authority – the law of Moses and the Gospels have lasted without alteration since their composition, he says, and even pagans like Ptolemy admired the Septuagint. This brief discussion ends with the observation that unlike almost all other antique writings the Bible is 'a Worke too hard for the teeth of time'. Sections 25 and 26 examine sectarianism and its compulsion to insist on certain absolutes which are really only points of indifferency. This discussion has a contingent relationship with that of sections 20–3, the nature of Biblical authority being seen as on the one hand secure grounding for belief, and yet on the other hand one that has been improperly multiplied into antagonistic, competing claims of authority by various ancient and modern religions and sects obstinately adhering to subsequent documentary law. Full of references to the varieties of belief – rabbinical, Samaritan, Roman, Egyptian, Muslim, and so on – as if by enumeration reminding us of the disarray of the human condition, sections 25–6 end in an examination of the fruitlessness of persecution as a method of spreading religion.

The contingent connexion between these two sectional groupings is not only never stated; it is actively occluded and disrupted by the intervention of section 24, an extremely brief, apparently unrelated digression on lost writings and superabundant ones. Here Browne dismisses the nostalgia for what we lack of Cicero's works, and extravagantly wishes the Vatican and its archives burnt: he thinks a few Solomonic leaves reclaimed would make up for this destruction. Disparaging those who cite thousands of writers either inconsequential or positively confusing to 'weaker judgements', he calls for a synod to cleanse the world of all but 'a few and solid Authours'. The invention of printing itself, he remarks, is 'not without . . . incommodit[y]' and its profuse output appears only to benefit typographers (*RM* 1.24).

Now, this uncharacteristically splenetic outburst feels like a swerve in the contingent progression of this part of *Religio Medici*, with section 23, on the excellence of the Bible as document, and section 25, on the harmful prolif-eration of inflexible readings of it, exhibiting an identifiable if free cohesion and logic. Section 24 – brief, waspish, exaggerated – comes as a surprise (see diagram). Yet Browne's outburst *is* seemly in the terms of the surrounding argument: the proliferation of 'authorities' (one of his great themes, after all, in *Pseudodoxia*) cannot enhance the credit of divine authority and is the seat of religious dispute, and by extension religious persecution.

SECTIONS 20–3	→	SECTION 24	→	SECTIONS 25–6
Validity of		Disposability		Sectarian interpretation
Scripture		of learning		of Scripture

Besides functioning as an emphatic punctuation within a broader discussion of 20–6, section 24 has its own binary structure, the first part an exordium of diverse exempla in the mode of *Urne-Buriall*, the second the consequences arising from them. I reproduce the section:[48]

I have heard some with deepe sighs lament the lost lines of *Cicero*; others with as many groanes deplore the combustion of the Library of *Alexandria*; for my owne part, I think there be too many in the world, and could with patience behold the urne and ashes of the *Vatican*, could I with a few others, recover the perished leaves of *Solomon*. I would not omit a Copy of *Enochs* Pillars, had they many neerer Authors than *Josephus*, or did not relish somewhat of the Fable.

Some men have written more than others have spoken; *Pineda* quotes more Authors in one worke than are necessary in a whole world. Of those three great inventions in *Germany*, there are two which are not without their incommodities; and 'tis disputable whether they exceed not their use and commodities. 'Tis not a melancholy *Utinam* of mine owne, but the desire of better heads, that there were a generall Synod; not to unite the incompatible differences of Religion, but for the benefit of learning, to reduce it as it lay at first in a few and solid Authours; and to condemne to the fire those swarms and millions of *Rhapsodies*, begotten onely to distract and abuse the weaker judgements of Scholars, and to maintaine the Trade and Mystery of Typographers. (*RM* 1.24)

The first part feels provocatively histrionic, with groans and sighs competing with the trim and easy dismissal of their misapplied theatricality ('for my owne part, I thinke there be too many'). Even more provocative, however, is the sense that the modern equivalent of the Alexandrian library could be burnt without disadvantage, and that the indestructible record of Enoch's pillars could with almost as little loss be forfeited. The entire thrust of his subsequent work, especially *Musæum Clausum* (which particularly alludes to lost books and libraries), would seem to contradict these sentiments utterly. The destruction of works is intellectual effrontery, a reckless and hubristic 'solution' offered from the vantage of seemingly callow conviction.

---

[48] The 1643 *Religio Medici* does not divide 1.24 or any other section into distinct paragraphs, but most modern editions very reasonably do.

The shock of the first paragraph is not much mitigated by the second, which moves on to what seem to be more general concerns but are in fact merely the consequences of the former. Quite apart from the extraordinary insult to Pineda (an author Browne would later cite approvingly four times in *Pseudodoxia*, itself a massive work citing hundreds of authors), the great intellectual technology of the early-modern period is utterly disdained as more troublesome than worthwhile. Perhaps it is not altogether astonishing to find the author of the 1643 preface to *Religio Medici* inveighing against printing – his crack at typographers, although written in the originating period in the mid-1630s, could almost foreshadow his fury at the pirated 1642 editions of the work. But that 'better heads' should wish to reduce knowledge to a few works is precisely the kind of bias he deplores in the strait-laced sects who believe only what Luther affirmed or disbelieve only what Calvin disavouched.

This section is so astonishingly un-Brownean, so like a *reductio ad absurdum*, that we are obliged to pause. His thoughts on the excellence of the Bible seem to have led him into a kind of thought-experiment – possibly spontaneous and unplanned when first enunciated – which he retains not because he seriously believes in the suppression of books or the reduction of antique sources, but because the problem of false authority, so eloquently expressed in the first book of *Pseudodoxia* a few years later, is a serious difficulty for the republic of learning. A thought-experiment, in other words, leads unexpectedly to severe conclusions which are not offered as *probable*, but as usefully illustrative of a problem and its solution, the extreme conclusion which might be drawn from the Baconian project to clear out the dead wood of misunderstanding.

What we see in these sections is a sort of order which is likely to be adventitious but none the less rational: the grouping of sections 20–6 obliquely makes a point about the uses and abuses of authority and the consequences of such abuse in the current intellectual climate. Section 24, with its own compositional balancing act, is both internally ordered and externally significant in the ongoing structure of this larger section, an example of what Frank Warnke calls 'cosmic play'.[49] The more ambitious, macrocosmic design of 20–6 and the miniaturist, microcosmic one of section 24 suggests an orderly mind at work but not necessarily an orderly composer. That sort of order would come afterwards, in the huge framework of *Pseudodoxia* and in the concise ones of *Urne-Buriall* and *The Garden of Cyrus*.

---

[49] Warnke, 54. Warnke argues that Browne's playfulness has merit in its own right and need not, as Fish insists, have moral designs on the reader. 1.24, it seems to me, needs neither excuse: it is *both* playful and instructive.

Other parts of *Religio Medici* also show signs of associative thought-patterns. Part 1, section 15 commences with an 'indisputable axiome' of Aristotle's: '*Natura nihil agit frustra . . .* there are no *Grotesques* in nature' (*RM* 1.15).[50] Although the previous section ended with a criticism of Aristotle's 'imperfect piece of Philosophy' (*RM* 1.14), here Browne takes up this axiom and pursues its implications. If nothing has been uselessly or frivolously created by God, even the so-called 'imperfect' creatures – mainly insects which Noah excluded from the Ark – must be examples of His providence and wisdom, creatures He has placed everywhere, to reproduce abiogenically from mud and feculence. Browne's continuing interest in the moral emblematics of insects, particularly bees, is very striking. Here, by citing Solomon's injunction to learn from the social insects, he positively denies their imperfection by pitching one Biblical authority (Solomon) against another (Noah). Until this point, the rhythm of the section follows a standard exemplary format, with a general principle instantiated by recourse to the best authorities. But, this point made, Browne's attention seems to wander slightly toward, or to become distracted by, a contingent set of ideas which arise not from his Biblical reading but from his natural-historical expertise: the bees are suddenly compared with the 'Colossus and Majestick pieces', whales, dromedaries, elephants, and camels.[51] The homely and Scriptural example of bees gives way for a moment to the exotic and learned vision of these other creatures, creatures moreover which might come under the category of 'monsters'. But they are dismissed immediately as merely ordinary miracles likely to impress only the vulgar; the bee is reinstated, though learnedly, as a 'narrow Engine' full of 'curious Mathematicks'. The civility of bees, the Solomonic commonplace, sits next to Browne's rhetorical question to the scientifically and theologically learned, 'Who admires not *Regio-Montanus* his Fly beyond his Eagle, or wonders not more at the operation of two soules in those little bodies?' In this passage we observe Browne oscillating between the homilist and the scientist, between the common and the elite example.

The remainder of the section shows that the elite scientist has triumphed: a series of natural wonders – magnetic north, the tides, the flooding of the Nile – do not, he claims somewhat airily, impress him as much as 'obvious and neglected pieces of Nature', and we expect him to return, as he did earlier, to his bees. However, it is not bees which claim his attention but humankind, and more particularly *himself*. The microcosmography of a single

---

50   The literal translation is 'nature does nothing in vain'.

51   Of these, Browne had seen whales and an elephant in the flesh; the comparison, however, is a standard one in the period.

individual contains 'all *Africa*, and her prodigies', and he accounts self-study a convenient and efficient method of perusing a large compendium rather than multiple volumes. Thus the oscillation between common and elite is accompanied by a movement from the macrocosmic and prodigious to the microscopic and microcosmic in the form of bees and humans. The containment of curiosity within the bounds of the self is both confining and liberating, with the Pauline injunction 'man know thyself' implicit in the conclusion of the section. The patterns of thought which characterise *Religio Medici* are thus often binarisms, not formal, but cognitive and thematic: textual and artefactual (or textual and observational), factual and speculative, declarative and qualifying, informational and interpretive, physical and metaphysical, enumerative and associative, direct and digressive, elite and common. Such pairings, which function as competing views or voices, reinforce the dramatic qualities of *Religio Medici* as a whole.

STOIC YOUTH

The ethic of civility invoked by Browne in the preface to *Religio Medici* has much in common with humanist or neo- (or Christian) Stoicism, the fashion of Browne's youth and middle age, a set of ideas wittily described by Peter Miller as a 'lifestyle that aspired to the status of philosophy'.[52] The characteristic neo-Stoic project is the cultivation of virtues that make one 'philosophical', a term specifically alluding, at least in England, to learning. In *Christian Morals*, Browne argues that 'Bright Thoughts, clear Deeds, Constancy, Fidelity, Bounty and generous Honesty are the Gems of noble Minds; wherein . . . the true heroick England Gentleman hath no Peer' (*CM* 1.36). These selfless and tolerant virtues promote friendship, self-control, and conversation. The practice of the Senecan Stoic virtues was originally posed as a defence against Imperial Roman moral exactions through retirement from a public life of compromise and moral ambiguity.[53] It was to inculcate a heroic resistance, through indifference, to the petty demands of worldliness, by promoting participation in a society of internal émigrés of like mind who tended a private network of friends. As a response to political and social turmoil, Stoic seclusion had a clear attraction for late-humanist culture, embroiled unavoidably in the century of upheavals throughout Europe between about 1560 and 1660, yet attempting to reserve an intellectual territory where flourished that phantom nation, the republic

---

[52] Peter Miller, 134.
[53] Seneca, who was never a true practitioner of his own philosophy, in fact accepted retirement when he fell out of favour with the young Emperor Nero.

of letters. The English brand of this disposition, which was not always clearly distinguished from Epicureanism, was highly developed before and during Browne's lifetime.[54] Although it can be traced at least back to Wyatt, Ben Jonson represents the immediately prior and perhaps most integrated version of English neo-Stoicism, with the poet presenting himself as a semi-retired and removed counsellor and disinterested moral guide to those of standing in public life; and at the other extreme, Andrew Marvell's retreat into a retrograde, Petrarchan or Horatian solitude of gardens and greenery is a total rejection of the tumultuous political world of tenuousness and disappointment. The neo-Stoic emphasis on friendship and learned sociability, and through these the collaborative, selfless advancement of learning, is a form of charity which is alluded to in *Religio Medici* and would be further implied and insisted upon in the prefaces to *Urne-Buriall* and *The Garden of Cyrus*, and in Browne's opening remarks in *Pseudodoxia Epidemica*.[55]

Aside from his grounding in the writings of Seneca, Cicero, Tacitus, and Lucan within the traditional school and university syllabuses in England, Browne had access in original and translated versions to Marcus Aurelius, Plutarch, and Epictetus, and would also have read Epicurus, Sextus Empiricus, and Diogenes Laertius. Moreover, he travelled in France and Italy at exactly the period when neo-Stoicism flourished with particular force among the Continental intelligentsia, the heroic age of eirenic anti-quarian projects especially strong in the Continental centres of learning – Montpellier and Leiden – where Browne was being medically trained in 1630–3. Montpellier was the *alma mater* of Nicholas Peiresc, who in those years was at the height of his fame and activity in nearby Aix and Marseilles, and Pierre Gassendi was teaching at Aix. The great Stoic scholar Justus Lipsius had taught at Leiden in the generation before Browne's birth, and his inheritor, the Stoic theologian Hugo Grotius, a professor there in Browne's time, extended his legacy. Joseph Hall ('the English Seneca'), Calvinist Bishop of Norwich in the 1640s and 50s, and Browne's friend and patient, was already an influential English adherent of neo-Stoicism in Browne's youth.[56] The names of Lipsius, Grotius, and Hall recur often in Browne's

---

[54] On the Stuart mingling of the Stoic and the Epicurean, see Barbour, 13. On the development of its European antecedants, see R. J. W. Evans, *Rudolf II and His World: A Study in Intellectual History 1576–1612* (Oxford: Clarendon Press, 1973), 92–3.

[55] For a discussion of this aspect of neo-Stoicism, see Peter Miller, 17 and 46–9. For further discussion of Browne's practice of learned sociability, see Chapters Three to Five, below.

[56] It is worth noting that Browne was close to this distinguished Calvinist despite his dislike of Calvinist certainty. He described Hall as 'a person of singular humility, patience, and pietie' (Thomas Browne, *Repertorium: Tombs of Norwich* in Keynes III, 134).

writing; and he mentions Peiresc approvingly, of whom he would probably have been well aware even as a student.[57] Despite the maddening absence of information about Browne's experiences and movements during his years on the Continent, we can at least plausibly imagine the kinds of people and ideas to which he could have been exposed. It is not unlikely that he met Grotius or at least heard his lectures in Leiden, and it is even conceivable that he encountered Peiresc or members of his circle in the south of France. There is much, in other words, to urge *Religio Medici*, the product of the years immediately following his travels and education, as a product of this experience, partly meant as a neo-Stoic exercise in restraint, and a demonstration of neo-Stoic sociability or civil conversation, in a semi-private and essentially apolitical world of friendships rather than alliances, beneficence rather than strategy.[58] Yet for all this Stoic influence, we cannot easily enlist Browne in that school. For one thing, Stoicism with its cultivation of an interior and private state of tranquillity, possibly in the form of indifference or resistance, was perceived as dangerous to the autocratic monarch and to the state: Stoicism was linked with republicanism in England, and Browne himself notices the dangers of a creed which had produced extremes like the 'philosophical' suicides of Cato, Curtius, and Codrus (*RM* 1.44), urging us to 'look beyond Marcus Antoninus, and terminate not thy Morals in Seneca or Epictetus' (*CM* III.21).[59]

Yet the Senecan concentration on measured intellectual fortitude was also a favourite Cavalier position, especially during the Protectorate.[60] The voice of Browne's preface in *Religio Medici* alludes to Stoic reason and endurance, with the invulnerable self ceding to the helpless, retiring, but constant self which endures the affronts of the press; yet he is, if anything, articulating an unwilling shift from what is presented as the retired life of the Epicurean, moving among friends and well away from political involvement and civil turmoil. Stoicism and Epicureanism, as Reid Barbour has shown, are linked but essentially incommensurable doctrines in the first half of the Stuart era, and Browne is a good example of the bivocal nature of Stuart approaches to those two discourses: Browne, Barbour observes, is fascinated by Stoic

---

[57] Gassendi's important and influential biography of Peiresc did not appear until 1641, after *RM* was written, and Peiresc is not mentioned by name in the essay. Browne's library contained the 1655 edition of Gassendi's life of Peiresc, and Browne's 1658 revisions of *PE* included reference to Peiresc's observations of the chameleon.

[58] Peter Miller, 60.

[59] For a detailed analysis of Stuart Stoicism, see Barbour, 1–19, 145–266.

[60] This strand of Stoicism is more precisely 'Senecanism'. See Adriana McCrea, *Constant Minds: Political Virtue and the Lipsian Paradigm in England, 1584–1650* (Toronto: University of Toronto Press, 1997), 183.

individualism and also deeply critical of it, a position which becomes even clearer in *Pseudodoxia Epidemica*.[61]

Analysis of voice and tone in *Religio Medici* might, therefore, be made by reference to this apparently neo-Stoic element, which sorts with the assumptions of civility and privacy underlying the 1643 preface. But let us examine that element in *Religio Medici*. Although Seneca and Roman Stoic writing in the essay are strongly represented – besides the Bible and Aristotle, the only philosophical/theological authorities more frequently cited than the Stoics are Plato and St Paul – Browne claims that he has 'runne through all sects, yet finde[s] no rest in any; though our first studies & *junior* endeavors may stile us Peripateticks [Aristotelians], Stoicks, or Academicks [neo-Platonists], yet I perceive the wisest heads prove at last, almost all Scepticks' (*RM* 11.8). These sceptical 'wisest heads' represent not a set of beliefs, however, but a mode of thinking about belief, a habit of avoiding easy certainty or intellectual pride. Its extreme mode is Pyrrhonism, a scepticism which doubts certainty has been achieved but hopes it may be achievable.[62] This late admission by Browne tempers that agreeable quality of Stoic condescension (to which Browne was sometimes inclined) with the recognition that it was potentially a danger, a form of pride needing the curb of what he called 'wise and pious discretion', a way of keeping an open mind which was, as Huntley puts it, neither 'the jaunty skepticism of Montaigne [nor] the hard-boiled skepticism of Hobbes'.[63] The deliberative (if not always absolute), declarative, sententious mannerisms of *Religio Medici*, the air of philosophical conclusion (rather than intellectual uncertainty), the programmatic if easy-going movement through the major doctrinal areas almost as if each section might have been more magisterially entitled *de resurrectione*, *de virtute*, and so on, look like an impressive but peculiar self-styling by Browne as another English Seneca. Except for *Religio Medici*'s prefatory paraphrase of *Thyestes*, all his other Senecan or explicitly Stoic references belong to the voice of his younger self of the mid-1630s. He devotes a chapter to a discussion of death which is framed in Stoic terms – Lucan, Zeno, Cato, Curtius, Scaevola, and Codrus are all invoked to demonstrate the happiness of death compared to the misery of life (a standard Stoic truism) and to show that 'wee are in the power of no calamitie, while death is in our owne' – but at the same time he moderates his regard for various noble Roman suicides by preferring the

[61] Barbour, 3–4, 9, 13.
[62] Basil Willey, *The Seventeenth-Century Background* (New York: Columbia University Press, 1934), 55–9.
[63] Huntley, *Sir Thomas Browne*, 182.

Stoic endurance of Job, the *ur*-Christian Stoic icon, who showed that in abiding life 'it is . . . the truest valour to dare to live' (*RM* 1.44).

Everything in Browne's writing reminds us to beware moral and intellectual certainty, and scepticism is the leavening element in what he normally frames as a neo-Stoic social and behavioural ideal. *Religio Medici* shows a writer whose social attitudes are broadly Stoic (or Stoic-Epicurean) but whose intellectual philosophy is Pyrrhonist. The instability of the young authorial voice – alternately approving and disparaging his examples almost as in an interior monologue – is shown in the way he introduces the standard Stoic social themes but is not quite happy about them without the sceptical inflection of Christian humility and containment of pride through admission of uncertainty. By making Job into the perfected Stoic he can comfortably admire the later positions of his Roman heroes, while celebrating Job's endurance above the noble refusal of the pagan suicides (*RM* 1.44). In a chapter about the resurrection of the dead he tries out a Senecan thought-experiment – he imagines himself when alone to be in the presence of friends 'to detaine me from the foulnesse of vice'.[64] This deterrent, however, Browne finds to be 'nought but morall honesty' because it is done without reference to Him 'who must reward us at the last'. The day of judgement is the 'onely power to make us honest in the darke, to be vertuous without a witnesse' (*RM* 1.47). As in the earlier section on Roman suicides, the Stoic position is not dismissed (it is an 'honest artifice'), but it is modified in keeping with Christian eschatology. Browne's scepticism is intimately connected to his faith. In a late section he observes that Seneca and Lucan, who could choose their method of self-slaughter, might best have elected to be murdered in their sleep. That sleep is a milder version of death is for Browne a 'dormitive' which assures him of his end in resurrection (*RM* 11.12). Here the Stoic position is enhanced by attaching a Christian, eschatological moral to exemplary historical episodes, a common strategy also in the work of his friend Bishop Hall.[65] Browne was deeply immersed in an inflected neo-Stoicism, that hybrid of *modus vivendi* and moral theology so attractive to those latitudinarians and members of the learned Latin Republic averse to imbroglios. If, as Peter Miller has observed, neo-Stoicism like all eclectic philosophies is imperial in tendency, willing and able to encompass everything, it offered Browne his natural intellectual home, where the variety of his attitudes in *Religio Medici* and the variety

---

[64] See Seneca, *Epistulae Morales*, 11.8, 25.5–6.
[65] See, for example, Joseph Hall, *Occasional Meditations* (1630) in *The Works of the Right Reverend Joseph Hall*, ed. P. Wynter, 10 vols. (Oxford, 1863), x, 119–87. See also Harold Fisch, 'The Scientist as Priest: A Note on Robert Boyle's Natural Theology', *Isis* 44 (1953), 256.

of his investigations in *Pseudodoxia* and subsequent scholarly works could freely cohabit.[66]

Browne's neo-Stoic positions in the 1635 *Religio Medici* – intellectual and spiritual tranquillity, the apparently hard-won tokens of vital self-knowledge – further assist his ventriloquizing of age: the Stoic voice is by tradition and temperament the voice of experience. Seneca's own characteristic rhetorical position is one of advice, of epistolary condescension to a younger man as in *Epistulae Morales*. But in this tradition Browne would more naturally be Lucilius, receiving rather than delivering Stoic (let alone corrected-Stoic) certitudes. So when he reiterates the Stoic maxim that 'no man can judge another, because no man knows himself' (*RM* ii.4), we recognise that, Stoic humility aside, he is simply too junior in self-knowledge to know himself fully.

NATURAL THEOLOGY AND THE CIVILITY OF INSECTS

Montaigne, paraphrasing Raymond Sebonde, wrote:

There is no parcell of this world, that either belyeth or shameth his Maker. It were a manifest wronging of Gods goodnesse, if all this universe did not consent and simpathize with our beleefe. Heaven, earth, the elements, our bodies, our soule; yea all things else, conspire and agree unto it.[67]

Echoing this idea in his famous declaration of the Bible and nature as his two texts in divinity, Browne notes that the heathens took the natural world as their Scripture and theology, that 'nature wrought more admiration in them, than in the other all his miracles; surely the Heathens knew better how to joyne and reade these mysticall letters than wee Christians, who cast a more carelesse eye on these common Hieroglyphicks' (*RM* i.16). The sense of the world as text, as legible, was especially attractive to seventeenth-century millenarian belief. It gave reassurance of order in the midst of chaos – not only in the midst of man-made confusion, but also within the confines of an apparently disordered natural world for which God's plan was often obscure. To know that instructions, meanings, messages, 'expressions hee hath left in his creatures' (*RM* i.13) lurk in the natural world and are communications which might aid the Christian in understanding his own task, but which might also direct the medic to discover remedies in

---

[66] Peter Miller, 115. My understanding of Browne's thinking in this area is very much indebted to Miller's excellent discussion of Peiresc's neo-Stoic heritage and practice in *Peiresc's Europe*, especially Chapters Two and Four.

[67] Michel de Montaigne, 'Apology for Raymond Sebond' in Montaigne, ii, 135–6.

the plant and mineral world, was a prompt to investigate and read those inscriptions. Browne's use of such signatures will be considered at greater length in Chapter Six, but it is important to note here his implication in *Religio Medici* of a natural theology whose objects and phenomena carry 'not in capitall letters, yet in stenography, and short Characters, something of Divinitie, which to wiser reasons serve as Luminaries in the abysse of knowledge' (*RM* 1.12), a theology in which even human countenances contain 'certaine characters which carry in them the motto of our Soules, wherein he that cannot read A.B.C. may read our natures'. These 'outward figures ... aptly joyned together make one word that doth expresse their natures', he explains; and such phytognomy is the remnant of innocence; its characters, 'aptly joined together', would restore Adamic, perfect knowledge (*RM* 11.2). The ease with which Browne seems to entertain a reading of nature based on such signs even in the midst of purely natural-historical considerations is an important feature of his thought. In the essay on fishes, the Peterfish is casually noted as having the signature of Peter's fingers, which Browne dismisses as false only because of the provenance of the species; he mentions it also in his notes on the natural history of Norfolk, where its signature spots are mentioned together with what the naturalist notices as 'its disproportionable mouth & many hard prickles about other parts' (*NHN*, 420). The signaturist and the naturalist operate in tandem. Basil Willey long ago commented on the nearness of the 'many different worlds or countries of the mind' in the early-modern period, and on the 'inter-availability of all [Browne's] worlds of experience'.[68] Such contingent categories, or rather contingency itself, constitute part of the intellectual framework we lack in thinking about the work as a whole: *Religio Medici* is founded on a set of overlapping investigative categories which shape his understanding of his subject and form the structures of his writing.

In *Religio Medici* 1.48, Browne the natural theologian is to the fore:

I have often beheld as a miracle that artificiall resurrection and revivification of *Mercury*, how, being mortified into thousand shapes, it assumes againe its owne, and returns to its numericall selfe. Let us speake naturally, and like Philosophers: the formes of alterable bodies in these sensible corruptions perish not; nor, as wee imagine, wholly quit their mansions, but retire and contract themselves into their secret and unaccessible parts, where they may best protect themselves from the action of their Antagonist. A plant or vegetable consumed to ashes, to a contemplative and schoole Philosopher seemes utterly destroyed, and the forme to have taken his leave for ever: But to a sensible Artist the formes are not perished, but withdrawne into their incombustible part, where they lie secure from the action

[68] Willey, 42–4.

of that devouring element. This is made good by experience, which can from the ashes of a plant revive the plant, and from its cinders recall it into its stalk and leaves againe. What the Art of man can doe in these inferiour pieces, what blasphemy is it to affirme the finger of God cannot doe in these more perfect and sensible structures? This is that mysticall Philosophy, from whence no true Scholler becomes an Atheist, but from the visible effects of nature, growes up a reall Divine and beholds not in a dreame, as *Ezekiel*, but in an ocular and visible object the types of his resurrection.

Having opened the section with a brief consideration of inductive and experimental knowledge, of descriptive reasoning versus ocular demonstration 'to perswade a man to beleeve the conversion of the Needle to the North' (*RM* 1.48), he subsequently manipulates several key paradigms in his mental spectrum. The first phrase seems to mingle two such categories, the mystical and the rational or empirical, with the conglobulation of mercury seemingly 'miraculous' but in fact a 'natural' and ordinary property of this metal. Mercury as an anti-venereal in physic and as an antagonist of magnetic attraction are higher functions familiar to his professional practice and to his investigative projects.[69] However, that mercury in its liquid state behaves as it does, in a lower and quotidian 'miracle' familiar not only to doctors and natural philosophers, figures forth another kind of artifice: it is a signature of resurrection in a world full of tidings inscribed by God to remind us that 'the life therefore and spirit of all our actions, is the resurrection, and stable apprehension, that our ashes shall enjoy the fruit of our pious endeavours' (*RM* 1.47).[70] This elemental phenomenon, overlaid with a divine, mystical signature, is and is not a miracle.

The intermingling in Browne's writing of scientific observation, mystical readings of the book of nature, and play on the concept of the miracle in the Peterfish and mercury produces his natural theology – an essentially neo-Platonic rather than Baconian reading of natural phenomena which demonstrates a governing, providential design in all of creation and performs the act of worship – expansive enough to contain those many 'countries of the mind'.[71] Similarly, the discussion of the combustion and

---

[69] See, for example, *PE* 11.iii.101–2.

[70] I borrow the suggestive word 'tidings' from Gordon K. Chalmers, because it presumes messages from a communicating divinity ('That Universal and Publick Manuscript', *Virginia Quarterly Review* 26 (1950), 429. Early-modern signaturist works include Giovanni Battista della Porta, *Phytognomica* (Naples, 1588); Oswald Croll, *Tractatus de Signaturis Internis Rerum* in *Basilica Chymica* ([Frankfurt], 1647), 1–152; and Emanuele Tesauro, *Il Cannochiale Aristotelico* (Rome, 1664).

[71] I cannot agree with Andrew Cunningham when he claims that Browne's yoking of science and theology was *not* a form of 'natural theology' (Cunningham, 'Sir Thomas Browne', 50). My reasons for insisting that it was – based on Browne's practice of and belief in signaturism – are developed in Chapters Three and Six. I am aware, however, that the term 'natural theology' has usually been

revivification of plants derives from observation, but also alludes to the theology of resurrection, with the 'forms', like human souls, withdrawn but not destroyed, 'retire[d] . . . into their secret and unaccessible parts'. This apparent miracle of renewal, says Browne, would be merely incomprehensible to a 'contemplative and schoole Philosopher' because such a one is not a 'sensible Artist', not a practising scientist, and so cannot make good his conclusions by 'experience' (experiment). Science, he says, can apprise him of the miraculous and the divine; to 'speake naturally, and like Philosophers' is to allow his science to support his theology. The true scholar, he says, only 'growes up a reall Divine' by studying 'the visible effects of nature'. The burden of the title's playful oxymoron '*religio medici*' (alluding to the suspected atheism of doctors) is mitigated by the theology of the science Browne practises.[72]

As so often in his later works, Browne is here working as a kind of *bricoleur*, observing and selecting the possibly fortuitous similarity between the physical characteristics of unlike things to construct a coherent totality of meaning from odds and ends.[73] It is a completely reasonable response from a Baconian compiler dissatisfied with mere compilation. The behaviour of mercury and of burnt plants, the vision of Ezekiel, and the resurrection of bodies are forged into a pattern of resemblance which begins with the empirically observable but moves to the visionary and the mystical almost as if there were no difference in kind. These distinct intellectual positions demonstrate his willingness to seize on coincidental, happy structures and patterns which display them, since such patterns inhere in the material at hand to be co-opted by a virtuosic, interdisciplinary opportunism which open-mindedly remembers all available realms of experience and understanding. As naturalist he prizes experimentation and 'ocular and visible objects' which nevertheless function as mystical signatures of heavenly purpose, with the empirical and the divine working in concert. He questions the (Aristotelian) authority of Schoolmen and others who dare assert natural facts without observation, but applauds the useful Biblical metaphor of Ezekiel's dream. The signatures he derives from mercury and plant-ashes are resurrectionary and allude to the reacquisition of innocence by the damaged material of creation; and as symbols they are in themselves 'innocent', precious fragments of the Adamic purity of

applied to the work of a somewhat younger generation of scientists – Ray and Boyle in particular. I would argue that it is a phenomenon which must have developed earlier, and that Browne may be one of its transmitters.

[72] On the atheism of doctors, see Cunningham, 'Sir Thomas Browne', 12.

[73] I have borrowed this term from Claude Levi-Strauss, *The Savage Mind* (London: Weidenfeld and Nicolson, 1966), Chapter One.

conception lost at the Fall and only strenuously recovered by natural philosophy. These themes – authority, innocence, signaturism, resurrection,
and empirical investigation – are, I suggest, the themes of Browne's science
and of all his subsequent work, a natural theology fully proposed in *Religio
Medici*.

In one of *Religio Medici*'s poems Browne reminds himself to emulate
the bee, the natural Christian-Stoic emblem of selflessness. He wants to
be like 'that industrious flye' who gathers honey like knowledge and carries it home to the communal hive, there to 'buzz' the praises of God
(*RM* 1.13). The useful signature of bees is one to which Browne returns
near the end of *Religio Medici*, in a discussion which can stand, in its large
range of reference and its gathering of different categories of learning, for
the range of *Religio Medici* itself, and of the later works. Most significantly,
it links the virtue of charity – that complex idea to which Browne adds the
generosity or selflessness of the Stoic – to the standards of civility which
govern his intellectual and moral life.

One of Browne's favourite words – always connected with falseness or
confusion of one kind or another – is *swarm*: Greece 'swarmed' with fables
which we have somehow managed to elevate to the status of unimpeachable truth (*PE* 1.vi.35), and false authorities and misguided writings buzz in
our heads like 'swarms' (*PE* 1.vii. 44).[74] It is even applied to the proliferation of diseases, with typical illnesses characterised as 'the common swarm'
(*LF*, 107). The metaphoric meaning of 'swarm' as crowd or multitude places
the word within the array of derogatory ideas about the masses versus the
individual, the rude versus the gentle, and so on, which is so pronounced
a feature of the Royalist lexicon.[75] The insect allusion is also unmistakably
devilish: the Satanic soubriquet Beelzebub is the Akkadian for 'prince of
flies', and the hordes of Hell, as Milton would personify them, are traditionally allegorised as 'a pitchy cloud of locusts', worship of whom was
said to have been the prompt for false belief and general error in the pre-
Christian period.[76] The rebellious angels became, in their uncivility, no
more than an unruly insect crowd, and Satan is reckoned by Browne as the
gadfly in the 'Empire of Truth' (*PE* 1.ix.72), that empire a civic metaphor
in which the post-lapsarian 'obscurity' in our understanding is to be auda-
ciously, and civilly by 'the conjunction of many heads', cleared and cleansed
(*PE.*Reader, 1).

[74] Browne cites what he characterises as a 'swarm of philosophers' in Dante's *Inferno* IV. 138–40 as
examples of unreliable antique sources, which include Plato and Socrates, but not Pythagoras (*U-B*
IV, 162).
[75] See, for example, Hobbes, *De Cive*, 76–7.
[76] John Milton, *Paradise Lost*, ed. Alastair Fowler (London: Longmans, 1968), Book 1, lines 340–1.

If Satan and his crew are flies and locusts, and if most insects were specifically excluded from Noah's Ark as anomalous because their copulation and parturition was abnormal, aurelian, remote, and seemed to early cataloguers of natural order to be schismatic and disobedient to the normative patterns of generation, how could these other, social insects – bees, ants, and spiders – provide Browne with such happy instruction?[77] Bees (and most insects) were thought to be corruptively engendered – they apparently arose out of putrefaction and were understood to be innate in mortal bodies, a signature of our own fallenness. Goodman explains insects as signatures of the total degeneracy of nature, not just of man:

Mixt imperfect creatures (the wormes, and the flies) . . . *generantur ex putri*, they are engendred of corruption; the baseness of their birth showes their condition; they are markes of corruption, more imperfect then the elements, worse then corruption itselfe, being indeed the fruites of corruption . . . If nature were sound and entire, either shee would not busie her selfe, to beget such base and contemptible wormes; rather she would first prevent the corruption it selfe, and give them a more noble birth. [78]

Bees, however, have another venerable anecdotal and analogical tradition quite separate from and antithetical to the theory of their imperfection. Hesiod, Varro, and Vergil – to name only a few – generated images of apian virtues and attributes which were quickly Christianised: in the thirteenth century, for example, bees were the image of scholarly clerics gathering in the honey of the ancients by diligently sampling many books and authors, an image peculiarly descriptive of Browne's own polymathic intellectual practice, especially as found in *Urne-Buriall* and *The Garden of Cyrus*. In the medieval tradition the bee was originally pure white; she had been the only creature to escape Eden without moral taint, only her stripes the marks of the angelic flaming swords which scored her as she fled its boundaries.[79] And bees as virginal and 'innocent' (because their reproduction seemed not

---

[77] Browne was reading Harvey's *De Generatione* in draft in 1638, some thirteen years before its publication. For his most extended discussion of 'imperfect' animals and their corruptive reproduction, see *PE* III. xii.207 and II.vii.144: 'So when the Oxe corrupteth into Bees, or the Horse into hornets, they come not forth in the image of their originalls. So the corrupt and excrementous humours in man are animated into lyce.' See also Thomas Moufett, *Insectorum sive minimorum animalium theatrum* in *The History of Fourfooted Beasts and Serpents . . . whereunto is now added The Theater of Insects*, by Edward Topsell (1658), Ffff5ʳ.

[78] Goodman, 19. Browne's speculations on the corruptive origins of many insects lead him to remark that 'the problem might have beene spared, Why wee love not our lice as well as our Children, Noah's Arke had been needlesse, the graves of animals would be the fruitfullest wombs; for death woud not destroy, but empeople the world againe' (*PE* III.xii.207). See Elizabeth Gasking, *Investigations into Generation, 1651–1828* (London: Hutchinson, 1967), 55.

[79] Hilda M. Ransome, *The Sacred Bee in Ancient Times and Folklore* (Burrowbridge: Bee Books Old and New, 1937), 253.

to be copulative) were regularly associated with the Virgin Mary and with the heaven-bound soul itself.[80] The virtue of bees was still a byword in the early-modern period and gained power especially among Royalists in mid-seventeenth-century England interested in civil monarchies.[81]

Like ants, bees cooperate like comrade-members of the same common-wealth, and bee-emblems of the Renaissance usually reiterate their com-munal selflessness – *non nobis* [not for us [but for others]], or *labor omnibus unus* [the one work for all] – or the power of the oppressed against the tyrant ('great persons shal not with their might oppresse the poorer, though they might').[82] Vergil's *Georgics* IV, the *locus classicus* of Renaissance bee-lore, has bees educating their young, exiling themselves in age from the hive, and making provision for the future of the state.[83] In *Insectis Theatrum*, Thomas Mouffett, the sixteenth-century French naturalist, says that their politic, ethic, and economic virtues make bees the most admirable of all creatures.[84] Like ants, bees demonstrate precisely those civic and civil qualities enjoined by the courtesy-writers and by the theorists of the commonwealth. James Harrington, in *A System of Politics* (*c.* 1661), likens the development of a civil government to that of the unhatched insect egg whose '*punctum saliens*, or first mover from the corruption of the former to the generation of the succeeding form' coalesces in either a monarch or a ruling coun-cil.[85] Shakespeare's 'Creatures that by a rule in nature teach / the act of order to a peopled kingdom'[86] coincides with Browne's inclination to find such signatures of very large ideas in very small things, one of the ways in

[80] H. Hawkins, *Parthenia Sacra* (1633), 74; Emanuele Tesauro says 'Esse Apibus partem Divinae Mentis' (*Il Cannochiale Aristotelico*, 94).

[81] For further writing on the virtue of bees, see Hesiod, *Theogony* in *Homeric Hymns and Homerica*, trans. Hugh G. Evelyn-White (London: Heinemann, and Cambridge, MA: Harvard University Press, 1967), 592-4; Aristotle, *Historia Animalium*, trans. A. L. Peck, 3 vols. (London: Heinemann, and Cambridge, MA: Harvard University Press, 1970), 11, v.i, and *De Generatione Animalium*, trans. A. Platt (Oxford: Clarendon Press, 1910), Books 111 and 1x; Isocrates, 'To Demonicus' in *Isocrates*, trans. George Norlin, 3 vols. (London: Heinemann, and Cambridge, MA: Harvard University Press, 1966), 1, lines 52-9; Dante, *Paradiso*, 21, lines 110-11; Thomas of Cantimpré, *Bonum universale de apibus* (1262-3); John Daye, *The Parliament of Bees* (*c.* 1607; published 1641); and Samuel Purchas, *A Theatre of Politicall Flying-Insects* (1657). For a later economic and social satire, see Bernard Mandeville, *The Fable of the Bees* (1714). A history of the bee as a cultural symbol is available in Claire Preston, *Bee* (London: Reaktion Press, 2005).

[82] Thomas Combe, *The Theater of Fine Devices* (London, 1614), xxxii, showing a swarm of bees chasing away an eagle.

[83] '[T]he grave experienced bee / . . . in the affairs of state / Employed at home, abides within the gate, / To fortify the combs, to build the wall, / To prop the ruins, lest the fabric fall' (Vergil, *Georgics* IV. 178–81). The just management of the state was the burden of the famous bees in the Barberini family escutcheon, where the virtuous insects legitimised huge power.

[84] Mouffett, 889.

[85] James Harrington, *The Commonwealth of Oceana and A System of Politics*, ed. J. G. A. Pocock (Cambridge: Cambridge University Press, 1992), 276.

[86] William Shakespeare, *Henry V* 1.ii.187–213.

which he maintains his grasp on a hidden but discernible structural order which has somehow survived the damage of the Fall. Like Moufett, he asks: 'where is nature more to be seen than in the smallest matters, where she is entirely all?'[87] Ants and bees possess proverbial virtues of domestic and economic efficiency, prudence, modesty, and foresight which regulate their social behaviour in civil patterns of community and mutuality.[88] The more 'prodigious' natural occurrences may amaze 'ruder heads'; but the tiny creatures Browne admires, 'imperfect . . . and such as were not preserved in the Arke' (*RM* 1.15), nevertheless inscribe in the wisdom of the pismire the wisdom of God.

These minor patterns of good order and civil behaviour are signatures to Browne of larger patterns of reliable hierarchy. In 'the first and primitive Commonwealths, and . . . yet in the integrity and Cradle of well-ordered polities' he discovers a 'naturall dignity' which governs rank and manners (*RM* 11.1). Indeed, bees and ants were regularly imagined as the citizens of commonwealths, with bees as monarchists and ants as democrats, and various apiarists – Charles Butler in *The Feminine Monarchie* (1609), Richard Remnant in *A Discourse or Historie of Bees* (1637), and John Levett in *The Ordering of Bees* (1634) – admire the altruistic public-spiritedness of these creatures.[89] George Wither chooses bees, as innocent victims of greed and selfish practice, silently to accuse wicked and uncivil booksellers who, like 'those cruell Bee-masters [who] burne the poore Athenian bees for their hony . . . usurp upon the labours of all writers'.[90] The well-behaved civic polity of bees under the careful rule of a monarch bee is always emphasised, as are their elaborate judicial procedures and strict attitude toward oath-giving and oath-breaking.[91] Bees are a natural signature of the political order which was falling apart and being reconstructed from 1630 to 1660.

It is, however, the selflessness of these insects which most interests Browne. Like the civil actors in the elaborate ceremonies of modesty, disclaimer, respect, and praise which govern the civil conversation observed in the Browne–Digby exchange and advocated by neo-Stoics, individual bees and ants retire from celebrity but not from society, and prefer the success of the common enterprise to the notoriety of single accomplishment.[92]

---

[87] Moufett, Ffff5[r].

[88] Moufett, 1066–71. Henry Thoreau, in *Walden*, resurrects this ancient byword in his famous account of the formicomachia between red and black ants (228–32).

[89] Charles Butler, *The Feminine Monarchie* (1609), A1[v]–A2[r]; Richard Remnant, *A Discourse or History of Bees* (1637), 3; John Levett, *The Ordering of Bees* (1634), [4*[v]]. See also Samuel Hartlib, *The Reformed Commonwealth of Bees* (1655), 4, 47.

[90] Wither, 5.

[91] For other aspects of their supposedly elaborate social and political structures, see Moufett 889–97.

[92] On the modesty of bees, see Moufett, 894; and Charles Butler, B7[v].

They seemed, in short, a natural signature of a modified Stoic civility, with common enterprise and mutual benefit forwarded by the individual virtues of modesty and selflessness. For Browne, the natural history of bees makes them additionally interesting. In spite of their corruptive origin, the best honey was judged by the apicultural writers to come from bees born in dead calves, and prudent bee-keepers were advised to place a carcass strategically near the waiting artificial hives.[93] This folk-belief was still deemed worthy at least of investigation in the seventeenth century: Hartlib considered this way of generation and reprinted the remarks of another investigator who claimed to confirm it.[94] Thus, although indisputably 'imperfect' and thus excluded from the ranks of proper animals in the Ark, the virtuous bee proved that life and death are commingled, that the death of one animal can sponsor virtuous and utile life in many others.

In the second part of *Religio Medici*, which deals with the virtue of charity, Browne reconciles the two competing strands of bee-lore, the corruptive and the virtuous, when he imagines wisdom itself. Learning, he thinks in his most civil mode, is to be given away – to do so, he says, is 'like the naturall charity of the Sunne, illuminat[ing] another without obscuring it selfe' (*RM* 11.3). Selfishness should have no part in the acquisition and distribution of knowledge:

> To be reserved and caitif in this part of goodnesse, is the sordidest piece of covetous-nesse, and more contemptible than pecuniary avarice. To this (as calling myself a Scholler) I am obliged by the duty of my condition, I make not therefore my head a grave, but a treasure of knowledge; I intend no Monopoly, but a Community in learning; I study not for my owne sake onely, but for theirs that study not for themselves. I envy no man that knowes more than my selfe, but pity them that know less. I instruct no man as an exercise of my knowledge, or with intent rather to nourish and keepe it alive in mine owne head, then beget and propagate it in his. (*RM* 11.3)

This vision of intellectual charity is specifically civil, specifically '*non nobis*', not for ourselves. Knowledge emerges from the ruins of his mortal body, like

---

[93] Vergil (*Georgics* IV) is the principal source of this belief, although it arose also with the Alexandrian Greek writers, who had it from the Egyptian myth of Apis, the bee-engendering ox; and it has an Old Testament use as well (Judges 14), which has survived into modern commercial culture in the Tate and Lyle Golden Syrup logo of a dead lion and swarming bees, with the motto 'Out of the strong came forth sweetness' (see Ransome, 112–18). The realisation that insects lay their eggs in rotting matter was not fully developed until the late 1660s by Jan Swammerdam (*Historia Insectorum Generalis* (1669)) and others (see A. J. Pyle, 'Animal Generation and the Mechanical Philosophy: Some Light on the Role of Biology in the Scientific Revolution', *History and Philosophy of Life Sciences* 9 (1987), 247).

[94] 'I did ever think that the generation of Bees out of the carcase of a dead calf...had been but a fiction, but am glad to find the contrary by your letter, which confirmed the same out of modern and English experience' (Hartlib, *The Reformed Commonwealth of Bees*, 23).

bees from dead calves, to enrich the 'community in learning'. It alludes, as the generation of bees alludes, back to the Pauline metaphor of the grave as *seminatio*, the place of resurrection into new life. If in the 'great autumne' of the last day men shall rise up from corruption, like those equivocal swarms, then the generation of bees and their good works, and the salvation of hard-won ideas by civil exchange between mortal minds, are in Browne's reckoning wonderful and cognate signatures of the divine purpose. Thomas Browne signals himself as a true citizen of the commonwealth of letters and learning, and we might therefore style his complete works *civilitas medici*.

CHAPTER 3

The civil monument: Pseudodoxia Epidemica and investigative culture

'Tis not only an ocular demonstration of our resurrection, but a notable illustration of that Psychopanuchy wch Antiquity so generally received; how these Formes of ours, may be lulled asleepe after the Separation, (closed up in their ubi's by a surer than Hermes his seale,) untill that great and generall Day, when by the helpe of that gentle heat, wch in six dayes hatch'd the world, by a higher chymistry it shall be resuscitated into its former selfe.

(Henry Power to Thomas Browne, 10 February 1647).[1]

A NATURAL HISTORY OF THE VULGAR

The vulgarisation, in epochal succession, of Hebrew, Greek, and Latin, and the subsequent early-modern dominion of the so-called vulgar European vernaculars in the West, remind us how slippery and indeterminate the word 'vulgar' is. From the medieval Latin 'vulgaris', meaning 'of the common people', the word had, like the understanding of vulgarity itself, become by the mid-seventeenth century a complex of social and intellectual designations, which Browne employs fully in *Pseudodoxia Epidemica* [*Vulgar Errors*]. Implicit in the designation of languages as 'vulgar' is the notion of decay and decline, language like all else in the sublunary post-Edenic world having sustained damage. To recognise Browne's sense of vulgarity is to recognise his civil conception of his intellectual project, a conception of regeneration from decay, or at least of the termination of the otherwise inevitable process of destruction. *Pseudodoxia*, an enormous project to catalogue and correct widely held but erroneous beliefs (which in its entirety spanned his active writing career) is, I argue, his formal rendition of the conduct of a lifelong investigative project which comprehended private and social mores, in which, indeed, the personal and the civil, the intellectual and the social, are commensurate, co-extensive, and retributive.

[1] British Library MS Sloane 1911–13, f. 78.

'The wisdom of God', he says in *Religio Medici*, 'receives small honour from those vulgar heads that rudely stare about, and with a gross rusticity admire his works.' His own 'humble speculations', he goes on to say, 'more highly magnify [H]im', and 'return the duty of a devout and learned admiration'. This activity he likens to the work of that civil animal, the bee, as 'almost all wherein a humble creature may endeavour to requite and someway to retribute unto his Creator' (*RM* 1.13).

Part of the appeal he makes in *Pseudodoxia*, it will emerge, is to the central civil virtue, modesty; and even if *Pseudodoxia* was recognised in its own day as magisterial and authoritative, this authority is established and maintained by couching the work in a civil framework which distinguishes the intellectually vulgar from the thoughtfully cautious and modest, and manages this distinction by insisting on his own non-vulgar incapability or insufficiency, one best expressed by *hoc tantum scio quid nihil scio* ['I know this much, that I know nothing'] (*PE* 1.iii.17). With his learning fully displayed in *Pseudodoxia*, he does not hide his knowledge; however, he is modest about the *way* in which he knows it, and this qualified position informs his writing of the science he performs and addresses.

The English adjective 'vulgar' and its cognate adverb are first assigned by the *OED* to Chaucer, who uses it simply to refer to ordinary, everyday (rather than elevated or learned) linguistic style.[2] By the mid-seventeenth century, however, it had acquired the additional senses of customary, general, vernacular, native, idiomatic, prevalent, rumoured, erroneous, prejudiced, commonly occurring, demotic, plebeian, of the world at large, commonplace, ignorant, undistinguished, low-bred, low-class, unrefined, simplified, offensive, mean, and coarse. With such variants available to him, it is important to understand Browne's particular range of the meanings of the word and the conception central to his sense of his learned enterprise. He is cited by the *OED* as the first user of 'vulgarity', a substantive meaning 'an ordinary sort' (*PE* 1.vii.41), conferred on the common people as a mocking title (*PE* 1.iii.19) and as 'the quality of being commonplace' (*PE* 1.iii.21).

Although he uses 'vulgar' more than eighty times in his major works (sixty-five of those occasions arise in *Pseudodoxia* together with three uses of 'vulgarity'),[3] and the book was entered in the Stationers' Register in April 1646 as 'Pseudo-Doxia epidemica or Enquiries into Vulgar & comon Errors', in none of the six editions that appeared in Browne's lifetime does

---

[2] *OED* 'vulgar', *a.* 1.1; 'vulgar', *a.* + —LY2.1.
[3] To search the Browne *oeuvre* I have used James Eason's Thomas Browne website http://penelope
.uchicago.edu.

the word 'vulgar' appear on the title-page.[4] The convenient conversion of the Greek title to the easier *Vulgar Errors* is itself an English-Latinate vulgarisation – one which Browne himself was using by the 1670s[5] – and, moreover, a somewhat free translation which insinuates this highly nuanced word into what might have been more neutrally rendered as 'popular misunderstanding', or even literally as 'mistaken beliefs prevalent among people'. '*Vulgar Errors*' is a reading of the title which pointedly discerns social nuance in the *demos* of 'epidemica'. In the work itself he does employ the word *vulgar* in its early senses – 'the vernacular', 'Latin', 'the Vulgate', and '[that which is / those who are] unlearned' – but it is more often burdened with more pejorative meanings: 'low-bred'(*PE* III.xxvii.279), 'inelegant' (*PE* I.x.60), 'unsubtle, slow-witted' (*PE* IV.xiii.366), 'ignorant, or unintelligent' (*PE* I.v.28), 'coarse, unrefined' (*PE* VI.xii.525), 'cheap' (*PE* II.iv.117), and 'senseless' (*PE* I.iv.24). The vulgar are consistently described as those who are deceived by rhetoric (*PE* I.vi.38), of small value (*PE* II.iv.117), persuaded by the mere weight of popular opinion (*PE* I.vi.38), credulous (*PE* I.ix.54), and literal-minded (*PE* I.x.59). These characteristics refer to judgement, wisdom, and discrimination, not explicitly to social categories.

It would, however, be uncharacteristic of his station and education if Browne were not firmly committed to a stable social hierarchy of which the 'vulgar' form a necessary base. Although he had already noted that the Last Judgement will 'reduce ... seeming inequalities and respective distributions in this world to an equality ... in the next' (*RM* I.47), he is no egalitarian on earth, and insists later that the wise are possessed of the 'privilege' of virtue which sets them above the ignorant. If not precisely a class-conscious view of learning, it nevertheless strongly mediates in favour of a social hierarchy of knowledge. Although there is nothing in Browne to suggest unusually marked social antagonisms, he does not go out of his way – as Sprat does a little later when he cites Charles's appointment to a Royal Society fellowship of John Graunt, a London haberdasher and author of *Natural and Political Observations ... Made upon the Bills of Mortality* (1661) – to make his commonwealth of wisdom socially inclusive.[6] 'The people', he says, 'are the most deceptible part of mankind', those whose 'uncultivated understandings' prevent them from making adequate judgements (*PE* I.iii.15). On the other hand, in *Religio Medici* he asserts that 'there is a rabble even amongst the gentry, ... men in the same level with mechanics, though their fortunes do somewhat gild their infirmities'

---

[4] It appears, however, in the running subtitles in all the editions of Browne's lifetime.
[5] Thomas Browne to John Aubrey [14 March 1672/3] (Keynes IV, 376).   [6] Sprat, 67.

(*RM* 11.1). The primary disability of the vulgar is poor understanding, which may be intensified by their numerousness, their disposition to think *en bloc*: as a multitude, they are capable of promoting errors amongst themselves with the greatest efficiency, and those errors, by relentless communication and repetition, are elevated as commonplaces, incorrect precisely because they are common (*PE* 1.iii.17; *PE* 1.vi.37). Browne is constantly at pains to distinguish the individual from the herd, the unitary from the multitude, and his lexical characterisation of the rabble – farraginous, democratical, swarming (*PE* 1.iii.17; *PE* 1.iii.21; *PE* 1.vii.44) – betrays his ongoing distaste for mixedness, or 'promiscuity'. '*Nos numerus sumus* ['we are but ciphers'] is the motto of the multitude', he says, quoting Horace,[7] 'for things as they recede from unity, the more they approach to imperfection and deformity' (*PE* 1.vii.31). This is a remark that can be read as emblematic of the pacific, tolerationist horror of disorder in the 1640s, but one which also derives its metaphor from Aristotle's *scala naturae*, the hierarchy of beings in natural history.[8]

Because their judgements are yoked to the 'sensible' rather than to the rational faculties, the vulgar repeatedly err by taking literally, physically, or 'manually' statements made tropically, figuratively, or speculatively, the lower and grosser forms of judgement overthrowing 'deuteroscopy' ('ulterior meaning') (*PE* 1.iii.16).[9] Foremost among the vulgar is the Devil, the 'unruly rebel' described in *Religio Medici*, the reckless individual whose pride or self-devotion and self-advancement ruined the world. Individuation in the form of pride or immodesty caused disorder, but this unitary sin has fostered the sins of the multitude, instanced in *Pseudodoxia* by vignettes of a disordered rabble – the near-fatal stoning of Paul, the wild Ephesian worship of Diana, the mutinous idolatry of the Israelites in the wilderness, and the mob roaring for Christ's crucifixion.[10] The dominion of the many irrational senses over the single rational intellectual faculty in human understanding is a subtler variety of rebellion (or tyranny) (*PE* 1.iii.17). Crude literalisation leads vulgar heads to expect truth in fables and reality in metaphors, foibles unexpectedly illustrated by Alexander Ross, Browne's most vociferous – and, incidentally, highly learned – detractor. The vulgar, it appears, are not after all confined to the rude, illiterate mob. Indeed, as we shall see, they are best understood as those whose intellectual vulgarity offends against canons of civil courtesy.

---

[7] Horace, *Epistles* 1.ii.27; trans. H. Rushton Fairclough, *Satires, Epistles, and Ars Poetica* (London: William Heinemann/Loeb, 1926).
[8] See E. S. Merton, 'Sir Thomas Browne as Zoologist', *Osiris* 9 (1950), 432.
[9] Literally, 'second look'.   [10] Acts 14:1–20; Acts 19:19–40; Exodus 32:1–8; Luke 23:21.

Browne repeatedly invokes the language of courtesy. In 'To the Reader' and in Book I of *Pseudodoxia* he offers a precise picture of vulgarity and its discontents and shows that vulgarity and incivility are inextricable from one another. His self-effacing remarks are partly designed to forestall social friction: he refuses to be 'magisteriall', or 'Dictator-like obtrud[e] our conceptions', but instead will humbly propose them; he announces that he will only invoke the authorities he honours, discreetly declining to mention those he cannot approve (although this is a rule he will break) (*PE*.Reader, 1). This is the language of humility, complaisance, and respect, the modest behaviour enjoined by de Courtin as 'the only Civility',[11] a language which cloaks the writer in forbearance but never injures the vigour of the ideas themselves. It is the prerequisite for participation in communal investigative enterprises, a hallmark of the English scientific project before its codification by the Royal Society. As Browne describes it, it is 'the conjunction of many heads . . . of . . . cooperating advancers' (*PE*.Reader, 1). Browne anticipates Robert Boyle, who later describes the writer attempting to construct an entire, coherent system as inherently immodest in ambition and self-confidence, in contrast to the experimental essayist, whose open-ended and tentative approach is 'sober, modest', evidently preferring the advance of natural philosophy to individual self-aggrandisement.[12]

The vulgar are, in their credulity, impolite: they fail to examine a world which is 'quodlibetically constituted' (i.e., put forward for discussion) (*NCB*, 291), and thereby insult God, 'who hath proposed the world unto our knowledge', a phrase heavy with the implication of social affront: God's courteous 'proposal' of creation to us, designed expressly for its inquisition, is spurned by interlocutors whose civil modesty ought to remind them that they know nothing. But the likeness between the self-effacing modesty of the civil participant, the altruistic retreat into a common (but not vulgar) intellectual cause, and the 'unindividualled' group mentality of the vulgar throng is potentially disturbing. 'A man should be something that men are not', Browne declares, 'and individuall in somewhat beside his proper nature. Thus, while it exceeds not the bonds of reason, and modesty, we cannot condemn singularity. *Nos numerus sumus* is the motto of the multitude, and for that reason are they fooles' (*PE* 1.v.31). Civil heads working in concert will produce results greater than the sum of their parts, but in the vulgar multitude great individual imperfections are only enlarged by congregation, and 'being erroneous in their single numbers, once hudled together, they will be errour it selfe' (*PE* 1.iii.17).

---

[11] de Courtin, 7.   [12] See Shapin, 'Pump and Circumstance', 494–5.

The confession of modesty by such a savant as Browne or Boyle emphatically does not preclude accomplishment and ambition: the stature of the undertaking is not compromised by authorial humility, but rather assisted by it, in inviting other judgements and further correction or extension. Thus, those who detect false modesty in Browne's preface to *Pseudodoxia* miss the point: modesty encourages cooperation, a cooperation which ensures authority. Browne's rhetorical and ethical position might be described as 'singular disindividuation': it is the office and the privilege of the learned person to disavow his particular attainment in favour of the corporate, anonymous project or common cause, even while promoting that cause as only the savant can, in his own respected name and learned reputation. His own modesty, his willingness to yield to 'maturer assertions', 'to bee swallowed in any worthy enlarger' (*PE* I.v.29),[13] is supported by an acknowledgement of his 'lapses' and his distress at having had to 'stand alone against the strength of opinion' (*PE*.Reader, 3); however, his very ability to make the attempt is based on individual and recognised attainment.

The rules of civility within which Browne presumes scientific discourse to be conducted extend further: to persist in error, especially in the face of reason and evidence, is to be discourteous to God himself, to fail in requiting and retributing the creator. If enquiries like his own have been rudely 'dismissed with censure, and obloquies of singularities' (*PE*.Reader, 2), how much more outrageous are 'perverted apprehensions, and conceptions of the world, derogatory unto God and the wisdom of his creation' (*PE* I.iii.15). Such discourtesy, he warns darkly, may ultimately be 'the inexcusable part of our ignorance, and may perhaps fill up the charge of the last day' (*PE* I.v.30). By transferring the canons and dictates of reciprocal courtesy from human intellectual conversation to our conversation with the creator, Browne endows scientific writing with a purpose far beyond the simple correction of error.

The grossness of common misunderstanding invites, for Browne, comparison with gross ingestion: 'farraginous', from 'farrago' (a mixed cattle fodder), indicates conglomeration and subtly indicts the 'confusion of knaves and fooles' as bovine, indiscriminately ruminant, bestial; indeed, these common herds 'promiscuously swallow anything' (*PE* I.v.31). The qualities of mob-mentality feature the usual Brownean watchwords: 'promiscuous', 'swarm', the imagery of gorging. Such wilful spiritual ignorance is summarised when he assesses the efforts of the Devil to disprove Scripture:

---

[13] See also I.viii.52 for his warnings about the danger of greedily swallowing the received opinions purveyed by the published authorities.

the attempt cannot succeed because 'this is a stone too bigge for Saturnes mouth, and a bit indeed oblivion cannot swallow' (*PE* 1.x.65) – the vulgarity of gourmandising, behaviour already attached to credulity and idolatry, is intensified as ineffective gobbling, and Scripture, the word of God, resists falsification by resisting mere ingestion.

For Browne, therefore, the people are relegated to a low station by their disposition to folly, confusion, gross appetite, and irrational behaviour, their vulgarity a form of delusion.[14] Social exclusion is based ultimately on the attainments of the mind. In *Religio Medici* he dismisses 'the multitude in their humours' because he knows that 'wisdom is not profaned unto the world' (*RM* 11.4); and this powerful sense of addressing an intellectual elite is reinforced throughout Book 1 of *Pseudodoxia*. Judgement, he says, like the 'slow and sober' annual orbit of the earth, reins in potential disorder and unreason, pictured as the 'swindge and rapt' of whirling diurnal revolution (*PE*.Reader, 1) – a sophisticated astronomical metaphor itself only available to the learned. Nevertheless, he emphatically addresses his work *not* to 'the Latine republike and equall judges of Europe', the group to whom any discussion of intellectual vulgarity might normally be offered; instead, he says, it is something 'owed' both as a 'service unto our Country', and to the group which best epitomises it, 'its ingenuous Gentry' (*PE*.Reader, 2).[15] 'Ingenuous', although frequently a variant spelling of 'ingenious' ('intelligent', 'discerning', 'sensible'), here signals its other sense: qualities of noble nature and disposition, liberality, high-mindedness, generosity, candour, and honour.[16] For this worthy group *Pseudodoxia* is thus not only written in English, but composed in what has been identified as Browne's 'low' style, a style lacking the mockable 'elegancie' of obscure Latinate English.[17] This pair of rhetorical-social decisions – to use English, and a

---

[14] It may be that *Pseudodoxia*'s pointed remarks about the vulgarity of literal-mindedness are partly aimed at the intemperate Alexander Ross, author of *Medicus Medicatus* (1645).

[15] Allusions to the superiority of English to learned tongues are familiar and plentiful in English literature from the 1580s onward.

[16] *OED* 'ingenuous', *a.* 1.–3.

[17] Austin Warren assigns the middle style to *Religio Medici* and *Christian Morals*, and the high to *The Garden of Cyrus* ('The Style of Sir Thomas Browne', *Kenyon Review* 13 (1951), 678). I have serious reservations about the utility of the various stylistic 'levels' and manners marked out by Warren and others; however, *Pseudodoxia* undoubtedly has a style distinct from Browne's more elevated works.

Robin Robbins notes that the superior marketability of English-language books from the late-1630s may also have played a part in Browne's decision (Robbins *PE* 11, 644). Although Browne was a fluent Latinist, there is no evidence (as there is, for example, for Descartes) that he ever considered publishing anything in Latin, so that commercial considerations may have been neither here nor there. The complaint against overly Latinate expression was, however, common: John Evelyn's *Sylva* (1664), it was claimed, insisted 'the countryman . . . go to learn Latin and the poets to understand our author' (Michael Hunter, *Science and Society in Restoration England* (Cambridge: Cambridge University Press, 1981), 100-1).

relatively unelevated English at that – alerts us to a particular audience and purpose: this group is certainly exclusive, but not as exclusive as we might imagine (not, for example, the audience of Primerose, or Aldrovandi, or of any other contemporary neo-Latin encyclopaedists), and its characteristic style is not Browne's most elaborate and elegant voice. The choice of the vernacular, moreover, is a thoroughly Baconian one: to revile secrecy in learning by expressing it in common languages was to oppose the subtle obscurities of Scholasticism and the extravagant occultism of alchemy; it was to promote the utility of learning for the common good.[18] The choice of English for *Pseudodoxia* was ultimately a civil act.

RECIPROCITY AND COLLABORATION

Was *Pseudodoxia* presented to a relatively learned audience, or was Browne genuinely attempting to correct the unfortunately vulgar opinions of the otherwise ingenious and ingenuous? Some have assumed that he was merely a populariser, that *Pseudodoxia* was written not for 'the profession', but for a curious, mainly uninformed, public.[19] His adversarial remarks about 'the people (whom Bookes doe not redresse, and are this way incapable of reduction)' (*PE*.Reader, 3) do not clearly designate his audience, only distinguishing his own readers from the unlatined and perhaps the illiterate. It seems clear, however, that *Pseudodoxia* was aimed at those who at least honoured and interested themselves in learning, rather than at the learned exclusively, a middle-class, book-buying audience which would have been variously informed on Browne's subjects. From this group issued the great majority of major and minor scientists in the years 1630–80. A statistical sketch of 'serious' scientists in the Restoration shows that about 80 per cent came from landed, clerical, professional, and mercantile families;[20] the so-called 'virtuosi' – admittedly a diffuse category of ancillary collectors, amateur experimenters, naturalists, and 'curious' persons who *en bloc* accounted for significant contributions to the Baconian project of observation and assembly – were self-evidently men of at least minor means. All of them would have had a notionally Latin formal education, and many would have been completely fluent and so quite capable of being addressed in the lingua franca of European learning. Although many major scientists of the day paid attention to *Pseudodoxia*, and responded to its assertions, a purely scientific audience could not have made it the bestseller it became in

---

[18] Hunter rightly describes this principle as Bacon's 'most critical message' (Hunter, *Science and Society*, 100).
[19] Huntley, *Sir Thomas Browne*, 147.   [20] Hunter, *Science and Society*, 60–2.

Browne's lifetime, which suggests a much broader readership. *Pseudodoxia* appears to be delivering a Baconian message to those intellectuals equipped to receive it, and a more general, homiletic one to the well-intending and open-minded.[21]

The first of these messages is very obvious. In the introductory chapters of *Pseudodoxia*, Browne makes a statement of what would become the ideological charter of the Royal Society and other late-seventeenth-century expressions of virtuous scientific behaviour. It is of course an ideology codified (if not actually inaugurated) by Francis Bacon in *The Advancement of Learning* and *New Atlantis*; and utopian fantasies of intellectual cooperation throughout the century such as Andreae's *Christianopolis* (1619), Samuel Hartlib's *Kingdome of Macaria* (1641), Abraham Cowley's *Proposition for the Advancement of Experimental Philosophy* (1661), Margaret Cavendish's *A Blazing World* (1666), and even Thomas Sprat's *History of the Royal Society* (1667) and Joseph Glanvill's *Plus Ultra* (1668) all argue that intellectual life (namely, natural philosophy) informs civil life, that the intellectual consensus so generated promotes social order, that scientific progress is too large to be other than an undertaking of many minds, and that theoretical diversity assisted by intellectual and theological toleration transcends sectarian and factional divisions.[22] Browne comments in *Religio Medici* that the 'forlorn person' of intellectual parts possesses 'nobility without heraldry', which was honoured and included in 'the first and primitive commonwealths and is yet in the integrity and cradle of well-ordered polities' (*RM* ii.1). 'Methinks', observes Sprat in a related vein, 'there is an Agreement, between the growth of *Learning*, and of *Civil Government*'; that growth, he says, is an enterprise in which

some must gather, some must bring, some separate, some examine; and to use a similitude . . . it is in *Philosophy*, as in *Husbandry*; wherein we see, that a few Hands will serve to measure out, and fill into Sacks, that Corn, which requires very many more Labourers, to sow, and reap, and bind, and bring it into the Barn.[23]

Scientific progress was likely to heap benefits on the commonwealth, and the impulse to create social and political order during and after the tumults of mid-century informed the attempts to use natural philosophy and its ancillary disciplines as the occasion of communal, cooperative enterprises

---

[21] One cannot, therefore, second Huntley and others who regard Browne as a *haute vulgarisateur*.

[22] On these ideas, see Hunter, *Science and Society*, 18–28. See also Margaret Jacob, *The Cultural Meaning of the Scientific Revolution* (Philadelphia: Temple University Press, 1988), 78. Harold Cook very appropriately describes the large network of contributing virtuosi – natural historians and chemists in the main – as the 'big science' of the early-modern period, in terms of numbers and of expenditure (Harold Cook, 'The Cutting Edge', 58).

[23] Sprat, 29, 21.

spacious enough to house what had been competing, sectarian interests. The scientists of the 1640s, for example, remained politically and theologically neutral in their scientific pronouncements, craving, as Sprat puts it, 'the satisfaction of breathing a freer air, and of conversing in quiet with one another, without being ingag'd in the passions, and madness of the dismal Age'.[24] They treated their ideas as common property.[25] The '1645 Group' in London, according to Wallis, excluded 'all Discourses of Divinity, of State-Affairs, and of News'.[26] If mid-seventeenth-century natural philosophy was sometimes posed, almost theologically, as a return to primitive truth, and the cooperative scientific enterprise as communal and levelling, it was being pitched as an equal but opposite response to the world turned upside down by some of the more extreme religious elements – 'Atomist or Familist', 'sub-reformists and sectaries' (*RM* 1.56). The Baconian direction to enact corporate, cooperative philosophical enquiry came into its own as a vital *modus operandi* for mid-century science, insisting on intellectual generosity, theological latitude, and above all social quiet and economic prosperity. In short, ideological civility intersected with intellectual pragmatism. The Royal Society was only a late instalment of the Baconian argument for organised, institutionalised learned and technological advancement, but the nation's intellectual fabric was already knitting together along those lines much earlier in what Flamsteed called 'the seminary of wit', the networks of local investigators working sometimes in small groups, and of isolated corresponding provincial naturalists, men like Browne, of at least a certain substance and authority within their own districts.[27] Many other minor contributors, often provincial, offered small, often local, but ultimately vital parcels of descriptive and collective expertise to central bodies such as the Royal Society's treasure-house, to its *Philosophical Transactions*, to the Royal College of Physicians' collections and stored expertise, to the Bodleian and later to the Ashmolean at Oxford, and to the collections and 'databases' (so to speak) of celebrated local savants like Browne himself. Although there has been some debate about the sectarian origins of post-Baconian English science, it was mainly eirenic and self-consciously apolitical from Bacon onward, whatever the private allegiances of its practitioners, with experimental philosophy imagined as a moderating discipline which promoted laborious consensual undertakings in inductive thinking

---

[24] Sprat, 53.   [25] Frank, *Harvey*, 216; see also Sprat, 55.

[26] John Wallis, *Dr Wallis's Account of Some Passages of His Own Life*, quoted in Robert G. Frank, Jr, 'The Physician as Virtuoso in Seventeenth-Century England' in *Papers Read at a Clark Library Seminar*, 5 February 1977 (Los Angeles: William Andrews Clark Memorial Library, 1979), 80.

[27] An example was the Townely group in Yorkshire, which included among others Henry Power and members of the wealthy Townely family.

and observation.[28] The contemplation of nature, Sprat informs us, 'never separates us into moral Factions; . . . gives us room to differ without Animosity; and permits us to raise contrary Imaginations upon it, without any Danger of a *Civil War*'.[29]

The expressed aims of intellectual groups were naturally not always consonant with the reality of scientific behaviour – as Michael Hunter notes, Sprat's 'history' of the Royal Society was substantially idealised.[30] Nevertheless, Browne's remarks and assumptions are interestingly early expressions of Baconian ideals which, in the early 1640s, had hardly received an organised trial in the form of an instituted, self-conscious attempt at cooperative scientific progress,[31] and seem to second the Cartesian aim of 'proper behaviour'.[32]

Continental thinking urged science as socially utile: Descartes believed the progress of science was a source of social power, which, maintained as private property, would enhance the social hierarchy and contain potential disorder from below.[33] The practices of science could also, according to some of the Italian theorists, contain the lower orders by occupying and distracting them from potential uprisings: Campanella went so far as to suggest that the study of nature would promote obedience to authority.[34] English science, however, was never so precisely imagined as socially functional or authoritarian, and was never as hierarchical in its self-scrutiny, even though Sprat and others adopted the social utility argument after the Restoration. Rather, the Baconian reticulation of society through intellectual exchange, an almost Paracelsian model of an interconnected knowledge-economy, was envisaged as an ever-expanding network of mutual obligation and support

[28] Margaret Jacob has argued that English science of the early-seventeenth century was essentially Puritan in origin; Michael Hunter suggests that it was latitudinarian Anglican from the outset. Browne's own position, given his apparently early (i.e., 1630s and 40s) latitudinarianism and his rejection of Puritan positions of all kinds, supports the latter view. (See Jacob, 84–5; Hunter, *Science and Society*, 113–14; and Michael Hunter, 'The Conscience of Robert Boyle: Functionalism, "Dysfunctionalism", and the Task of Historical Understanding' in *Renaissance and Revolution: Humanists, Scholars, Craftsmen, and Natural Philosophers in Early Modern Europe*, ed. J. V. Field and Frank A. J. L. James (Cambridge: Cambridge University Press, 1993), 147–53).

[29] Sprat, 56.   [30] Hunter, *Science and Society*, 28.

[31] The Oxford scientists of the late 1640s and early 1650s, led by John Wilkins, did not formally convene as the Philosophical Society of Oxford until 1651, a formation which was to become, a decade later, the Royal Society (see R. T. Gunther, *Early Science in Oxford*, 2nd edn, vol. IV: *The Philosophical Society* (London: Dawsons, 1968), 1–3).

[32] Peter Dear, 'A Mechanical Microcosm: Bodily Passions, Good Manners, and Cartesian Mechanism' in *Science Incarnate: Historical Embodiments of Natural Knowledge*, ed. Christopher Lawrence and Steven Shapin (Chicago: University of Chicago Press, 1998), 61; on the Cartesian model of cooperation, see Dunn, 98–9.

[33] Kevin Dunn has described this Cartesian attitude as 'suburban' in its reliance on 'a model of the public realm subdivided in small private holdings' (Dunn, 100).

[34] See Jacob, 29–30.

which would bind diversity into civil unity.[35] Even if the English model of social utility was not precisely that of Europe, nevertheless the recuperative, eirenic impulses of English science were pitted against the restless motions of the vulgar populace. Science itself was to be a correction of vulgarity.

Almost nothing of Browne's correspondence before 1660 survives, and the great bulk of the post-1660 material consists of letters to and from his son Edward,[36] himself a doctor and a natural historian, letters with much in them of Thomas Browne's scientific and medical concerns, but necessarily (because family documents) less helpful in identifying the formal civil practices of scientific exchange. What does survive of his formal correspondence is, by contrast, highly revealing, and demonstrates precisely the self-consciously civil, cooperative, careful, deferential, contributory effort which contains vulgar disorder. To John Evelyn, in their exchange of 1664, Browne marks out these two antagonistic constituencies according to their reception of Evelyn's *Sylva* (1664): 'the ingenious world' which will honour its excellent delivery, and 'the lower minded world whom profitt at least will rayse up to such attempts'.[37] Browne himself had approached Evelyn in 1660 to offer information about trees, knowing of Evelyn's work-in-progress. For this kindness, Evelyn floridly proposed to include Browne in the roster of his imagined '*Paradisi Cultores* . . . and hortulan saints'.[38] In the previous year Browne had responded to Elias Ashmole's request for help in the matter of John Dee's astrology by sending a list of tracts in his possession which he was ready to lend.[39] To Christopher Merrett, the author of a distinguished natural history of the British Isles, Browne made the unsolicited offer of identification and specimens of birds, marine creatures, and fungi for Merrett's proposed second edition. Merrett thanks Browne for his letters, 'as full of learning in discovering so many curiosities as kindness in communicating them to mee & promising your farther assistance'. Merrett signs off by pleading 'the publique interest & your own good genius' as his excuse for desiring more information.[40] In such exchanges the active broadcasting of material is posed as a social benefit and is couched in the elaborate, substantive courtesies of civil conversation.

---

[35] For a discussion of the intellectual exchange associated with the Continental academies and with humanist conceptions of friendship, see Peter Miller, 64–5.

[36] The reason for this is not known. Simon Wilkin thinks Browne destroyed those of his letters that contained political opinions, not being confident of the judgement of either Anglican or sectarian (Wilkin I, lvi).

[37] Thomas Browne to John Evelyn, 26 March 1664 (Keynes IV, 281).

[38] John Evelyn to Thomas Browne, 28 January 1659/60 (Keynes IV, 275).

[39] Thomas Browne to Elias Ashmole, 25 January 1658 (Keynes IV, 293–4). Browne had known Dee's son, Dr Arthur Dee, well.

[40] Christopher Merrett to Thomas Browne, [29 August 1668] (Keynes IV, 347).

The liveliest remains of civility are represented by Browne's exchanges with Dr Henry Power, a Fellow of the Royal Society and author of the first English book on microscopy.[41] Power first sought guidance in training and reading matter from his father's old friend when he was still a Cambridge medical student, and Browne had urged him to 'lay your foundation in Anatomy, wherein αὐτοψία [autopsia] must be your *fidus Achates*',[42] advice the young man clearly heeded. Power's breathlessly reverent letters of subsequent years on his adventures in simpling ('have brought home with mee 2 or 3 Hundred Hearbs');[43] the hibernation of toads, swallows, and snails; the respiration of fishes; the anatomy of the viper's head, the cure for rickets;[44] the treatment of the tertian ague;[45] and the anatomy of seeds[46] show a conversation of some years between the two men about problems of mutual interest in natural history and medicine. The conversation is conducted, even after Power himself became a practising and established physician and despite the longstanding connexion and Power's visits to Browne in Norwich, in the terms of extreme courtesy and reciprocal deference, terms strikingly like those employed by Browne and Digby, strangers communicating in 1643. These elaborate rehearsals of courtesy remind us that the disinterested exchange economy of knowledge was viewed as a civil exercise which could flourish even between well-acquainted individuals and good friends. Their relationship as equals in enthusiasm and deference in civil intellectual exchange is replicated by Browne's own address to the reader in *Pseudodoxia*.

Browne is listed by the *OED* as the first user of the adjective 'individual' to mean 'distinguished from others; peculiar or striking'.[47] Although it is not noted by the *OED*, 'individual' was also used as a verb. 'To individual' seems to refer primarily to the constituting of discrete objects or persons – thus God's summons to the dead on the Last Day will 'call them out by their single individuals' in a general resurrection of whole bodies (*RM* 1.48), and Henry Power uses it in this way when he discusses palingenesis, the conjuring of a ghostly plant in its 'very form and *idæa*' from its ashes. One of Power's student letters to Browne discusses the resuscitation of plants from their ashes, 'so high, & noble a piece of chymistry, viz. the

---

41 Henry Power, *Experimental Philosophy* ([1663] 1664).
42 Thomas Browne to Henry Power [1646] (Keynes iv, 255). It is likely that *Religio Medici* was addressed to the father, John Power of Halifax (see Huntley, *Sir Thomas Browne*, 97).
43 Henry Power to Thomas Browne, 15 September 1648 (Keynes iv, 260).
44 Henry Power to Thomas Browne, 28 August 1649 (Keynes iv, 261–4).
45 Henry Power to Thomas Browne, 9 November 1658 (Keynes iv, 265).
46 Henry Power to Thomas Browne, 10 May 1659 (Keynes iv, 265–7).
47 *OED* 'individual', *a.* 4.

re-individualling of an incinerated plant',[48] a kind of Platonic magic believed in by Kenelm Digby, Walter Charleton, and others.[49] He seems to
have heard of it from Browne either in an earlier communication, or simply
from having read *Religio Medici* 1.48, where this phenomenon is perhaps
referred to. In his own papers, Power describes an elaborate chemical preparation which yields a vision of the plant in the smoke produced from its
residue;[50] but Browne's own recipe, which survives in his papers, merely
shows how to make colourful displays in liquid with herb-roots and nitre
(saltpetre) or sal amoniac.[51] In *Religio Medici*, on the other hand, he may
be writing neither of his own nor of Power's recipe, but of the well-known
and much simpler ability, apparently palingenical, of some plants to re-
grow from the unburnt root, or of the pyrogenous germination of seeds,
phenomena he assures us he 'make[s] good by experience' (*RM* 1.48).[52]
As an embryologist, he thinks of seeds as containing 'the perfect leaves,
flowers, and fruit' of the mature plant (*RM* 1.50),[53] so that the notion of
resurrectionary reconstitution – so persistently adverted to by Browne and
other scientists – was an almost literal account of the scientific enterprise's
reconfiguration of a fragmented, innocent creation. It was also a way of
thinking about scientific exchange itself: the competitive, factioned enmity
between species originating in the Fall is itself recuperated and salved by
the eirenic, collaborative impulses on display in Browne's correspondence.
From the ashes of innocence, the cooperating advancers re-summon that
'paradise and unthorny place of knowledge'. John Evelyn looks for

a noble, princely, and universall Elysium . . . I would have . . . a society of the
Paradisi Cultores, persons of antient simplicity, paradisean and hortulan saints,
to be a society of learned and ingenuous men, such as Dr Browne, by whome
we might hope to redeeme the tyme that has bin lost, in pursuing vulgar
errours.[54]

---

[48] Henry Power to Thomas Browne, 10 February, 1647 (BL MS Sloane 1911–13, f. 78).
[49] See Wilkin's note on this matter (Wilkin 11, 70). Jorge Luis Borges has written a story featuring the
elderly Paracelsus undertaking this feat ('The Rose of Paracelsus' (1983) in *The Book of Sand and
Shakespeare's Memory* (Harmondsworth: Penguin, 1998), 504–7.
[50] BL MS Sloane 1334, f. 33.
[51] Cited in Wilkin, 11, 70. I am unable to locate this letter under the British Library classmark Wilkin
gives.
[52] Coleridge later described this section of *RM* as 'a series of ingenious paralogisms [unreasonable
claims]' (*Marginalia*, 785).
[53] Despite Merton's claim that Browne 'favoured epigenesis', his observations in embryology and
generation are equally favourable to the theory of preformation, to which this passage refers (Egon
Stephen Merton, 'The Botany of Sir Thomas Browne', *Isis* 47 (1956), 164).
[54] John Evelyn to Thomas Browne, 28 January 1659/60 (Keynes IV, 275).

Of the millenarian tendency to invoke resurrectionary imagery in discussing the scientific project, Jacob observes: 'Almost every important seventeenth-century English scientist or promoter of science . . . believed in the approaching millennium.'[55] In addition, as Michael Hunter notes, the advancement of science became 'a secular counterpart to millenarianism', with intellectual enlightenment achieved as a parallel with mystical revelation, both working as signs of the approaching end of days.[56] Browne's own practice locates him somewhere between these explanations, namely with the 'natural' theologians. Plants might be resurrected by science; scientists themselves, in forming cooperative networks of intellectual exchange, disposed themselves in orderly behaviour-patterns which seemed to resurrect a prelapsarian *pax*, and the knowledge they were working to renew was an instauration of the world as it might have existed on the sixth day.

Through this resurrectionary theme we can understand the task and organisation of *Pseudodoxia*: scientific enquiry is an act of devotion; it attempts to repair original sin by reconstructing the fractured body of knowledge within which we labour; the enterprise of that enquiry is civil, joint, selfless, cooperative, a re-enactment of that blessed prelapsarian state in which man and the natural world were innately civil; and the projects and outcomes of these enterprises – in Browne's case, specifically the printed record of enquiry – should themselves simulate the intellectual order they seek to restore. It is from this last principle that we can derive a sense of *Pseudodoxia* as a literary artefact.

IN THE WILDERNESS OF FORMS: A NATURAL HISTORY OF ORDER

There is nothing quaint about *Pseudodoxia Epidemica*. That charge has been carelessly levelled against most of Browne's works for at least the past 200 years; for none of them is it less apt than for his bestselling encyclopaedia. That many of the problems and errors he discusses are now inconsequential has often distracted attention from the fact that *Pseudodoxia* responds to, and stimulates, projects abroad in the scientific climate of the mid-century. Bacon had envisaged a calendar of errors,[57]

---

[55] Jacob, 75. This claim, however, intended to support her contention that English scientific innovation was Puritan in origin, will not sort with the religious profiles of many of these same scientists.

[56] Michael Hunter, *John Aubrey and the Realm of Learning* (London: Duckworth, 1975), 19.

[57] Francis Bacon, *Parasceve* in *The Philosophical Works of Francis Bacon*, ed. and trans. James Spedding and John M. Robertson (London: George Routledge and Sons, 1905), 4th aphorism, 404. See also Gordon Keith Chalmers, 'Thomas Browne, True Scientist', *Osiris* 2 (1936), 40.

and Hartlib had imagined an information bureau.[58] These assemblages, together with many donations and designs for repositories, such as those by Harvey to the Royal College of Physicians and by Hooke for the Royal Society, were impelled by this notion of an informational conclave.[59] For Browne and his peers, the project of banishing misapprehension, particularly though not exclusively about the natural world, of reconstructing on solid experimental and logical principles the foundations of intellectual architecture, was work than which nothing under heaven could have more priority.

This work is, of course, endless: in *Pseudodoxia*, Browne admits that 'as his wisdome is infinit, so cannot the due expressions thereof be finite, and if the world comprise him not, neither can it comprehend the story of him' (*PE* vi.v.468). Thus, anything ventured by the empiricist must be heavily qualified by *quod aiunt, fortasse, saepe aut numquam*, and *aliquando* ('as they say', 'probably', 'often or never', and 'sometimes').[60] 'In this strict enquirie of things', he warns, '. . . for the most part, *probably* and *perhaps* will hardly serve the turne or mollifie the spirits of positive contradictors' (*NCB*, 291).[61] But such disclaimers and qualifiers (both intellectually cautious and civilly modest) contend in tone with what feel like the much more magisterial procedures by which he organises each chapter. Authority, though courteously noted in every case, as if in keeping with the tenets of civility, is in fact summarily dismissed almost from the outset of the book: Browne remarks that 'it hath no place in some Sciences, small in others, and suffereth many restrictions, even where it is most admitted' (*PE* i.vii.40), echoing Bacon's remark in *Parasceve*.[62] Almost every error addressed after Book i begins with a précis of 'authoritative' opinions whose justice Browne then analyses rationally, and with his own 'exantlation' (*PE* i.v.30) or with the 'honourable'

---

[58] Samuel Hartlib, *Considerations Tending to the Happy Accomplishment of England's Reformation* (1647) in *Samuel Hartlib and the Advancement of Learning*, ed. Charles Webster (Cambridge: Cambridge University Press, 1970), 126–39. See also G. H. Turnbull, *Samuel Hartlib: A Sketch of his Life and his Relations to J. A. 'Comenius'* (Oxford: Oxford University Press, 1920), 16–17.

[59] Frank, 'Physician', 89; Zakin, 4.

[60] These words, like a number of other Brownean phrases, were picked up by Boyle: 'in almost every one of the following essays I [speak] so doubtingly, and use so often, *perhaps, it seems, it is not improbable*; and such other expressions, as argue a difference of the truth of the opinions I incline to, and that I should be so shy of laying down principles, and sometimes of so much as venturing at explications'. Quoted [imprecisely] in Shapin, 'Pump and Circumstance', 495. The influence of Browne on Boyle has yet to be thoroughly explicated.

[61] Indeed, Jonathan Post has observed that 'probably' and 'perhaps' were among Browne's favourite words (Post, 61). Douglas Lane Patey translates Browne's use of 'probably' as 'with authority' (*Probability and Literary Form: Philosophic Theory and Literary Practice in the Augustan Age* (Cambridge: Cambridge University Press, 1984), 6.)

[62] Bacon, *Parasceve*, 3rd aphorism, 403.

testimony of contemporaries adduced finally either to settle the issue or to leave the question open and unresolved (*PE* vi.viii.501). Frank Huntley has described this process as one of cause and cure (he reads the 'epidemica' of the title in its medical sense), with error diagnosed and banished by rational medicament.[63] That is a highly attractive and appropriate metaphor for the structure and purpose of *Pseudodoxia*, and for Browne's own professional practice, but there are also other paradigms governing this complex work.

Augustine had argued that reason was granted to mankind to bring us closer to salvation. Learning or *scientia* – the burden of reason – is a required adoration of the divine, the approach to the wisdom which in death and resurrection, in Donne's phrase, will 'create us all Doctors in a minute'.[64] An important type of seventeenth-century investigation, including the cor-puscularian procedures of Boyle and the mechanistic ones of Newton, was imagined as natural theology, study either specifically recovering provi-dential messages inscribed in nature or discovering a poetics of nature, 'to understand the *Artifice* of the *Omniscient Architect* in the composure of the *great* World'.[65] The collecting natural historians followed Pliny in gathering up fragments as tokens of a greater, lost whole, a convening of available information which Bacon had more recently proposed as interpo-lations in the gaps in our 'knowledge broken' of the world.[66] This project, I have been suggesting, is at least metaphorically, if not for some literally, resurrectionary, the reindividualling out of the wilderness of forms items of lost understanding. Another important result of such convening was the early-modern encyclopaedic collection, the tradition in which Browne is most clearly working in *Pseudodoxia*.[67] Whether a compilation of objects,

---

[63] Huntley, *Sir Thomas Browne*, 149.

[64] See Leonard Nathanson, 'Sir Thomas Browne and the Ethics of Knowledge' in Patrides *Approaches*, 14.

[65] Joseph Glanvill, *Plus Ultra* (1668), quoted in Hunter, *Science and Society*, 9. See also John Ray, *The Wisdom of God Manifested in the Works of Creation* (1691) for another expression of this idea. Olmi notes that in making their collections as metaphors of the world, the later Italian museum cataloguers used the examples of Tesauro and his contemporary, Marino (G. Olmi, 'Science–Honour Metaphor: Italian Cabinets of the Sixteenth and Seventeenth Centuries' in *The Origins of Museums: The Cabinet of Curiosities in Sixteenth- and Seventeenth-Century Europe*, ed. Oliver Impey and A. MacGregor (Oxford: Oxford University Press, 1985), 13.

[66] Francis Bacon, *The Advancement of Learning* (1605), ed. Brian Vickers (Oxford: Oxford University Press, 1996), 125. Harold Cook notes that the ancient encyclopaedic tradition of Pliny and Dioscorides transmitted a structure (from cosmology to customs) 'virtually identical to the [early-modern] en-cyclopaedic tradition', a structure reflected in *Pseudodoxia Epidemica* (Harold Cook, 'The Cutting Edge', 48).

[67] It is important to establish that such self-conscious convening is a feature of the *serious* (by which I mean 'scholarly', 'scientific', or even 'Baconian') collection. Cabinets of curiosity were a vogue among many who simply enjoyed the pleasures of accumulation and expenditure, and followed various cultural fashions remote from or entirely unconnected to science or learning.

ideas, or errors, such collections attempted to stabilise our understanding which, like the vulgar themselves, must be kept in check, corrected, and enlightened.[68] The recursive quality of the collection – itself a tamed order but designed also to tame the disordered understanding of the spectator – is one of the organising principles of *Pseudodoxia Epidemica*. The collection, moreover, is a type of incomplete database whose retrieval system had to be founded on notions of connexion and likeness which were perilously unstable on account of those Baconian gaps.[69] Browne, both a collector and an encyclopaedist, knowing that the patterned world-puzzle still lacked many of its most important pieces, produces his encyclopaedia as an act of amendment to remind us of all that we know and, more significantly, all that we don't.

Noah was the first collector, a proto-Baconian compiler. What Nathaniel Fairfax called 'the whole bulky throng of the world'[70] (or at least its thronged fauna) was in the Ark collected systematically in sexed pairs for the express purpose of salvaging and reimposing a creational order about to be effaced by the deluge. The likeness of the Ark to contemporary cabinets of cu-riosities and natural history displays was implicitly recognised by the Jesuit collector and polymath Athanasius Kircher (whose own museum was one of the wonders of Rome) in *Arca Noë* (1675) (see Illustration 1). The serried tiers of animals and supplies distinctly resemble the vertical and horizon-tal patterns of contemporary curiosity cabinets. Birds, along with Noah's family, are in the top deck of the Ark, as if to suggest their near relation to the heavens; quadrupeds and creeping things live far below, apparently organised by weight; and snakes, preserved to remind mankind of his orig-inal sin, are consigned to the bilge, where they are shown swimming about freely. Except for a pair of horses who seem to be copulating, all the an-imals appear to be very well behaved. Noah was obedient to God, and was saved by his obedience; and good behaviour is the concept underlying encyclopaedic collections of things: the theology of their arrangements is, like orderly scientific discovery, that of restoration or recuperation of the lost or submerged order which the world has lacked since Adam disobeyed.

---

[68] Paracelsus's theory of the decay of nature via the infection of man's Fall, supported by Godfrey Goodman, Gerrard Winstanley, and others, was disputed by those like Hakewill who argued that nature itself had not been disturbed by the Fall of man. John Rogers winningly describes the Goodmanian mechanism as 'lapsarian effluvia' (*The Matter of Revolution: Science, Poetry, and Politics in the Age of Milton* (Ithaca, NY: Cornell University Press, 1996), 149).

[69] See also John Hoskyns, who commended the catalogue of the Royal Society's collection of rarities as a tool 'to find likenesse and unlikenesse of things upon a suddaine' (letter to John Aubrey, 25 March 1674) (quoted in Hunter, *John Aubrey*, 67).

[70] Nathaniel Fairfax, *A Treatise of the Bulk and Selvedge of the World* (London, 1674), 1.

Illustration 1 A view of the interior of the Ark from Athanasius Kircher, *Arca Noë* (Amsterdam, 1675). Reproduced by permission of the British Library.

John Tradescant the Younger compares learned collecting to the arts 'which Adam studied, ere he did transgresse'.[71]

The order of things generates human obedience, and good behaviour arises initially in the act of assemblage, in orderly presentation, and in preservation. Eulogised for their energetic efforts in conservation (John Weever called Robert Cotton a 'Philadelphus . . . magazin . . . Treasurie . . . [and] store-house of Antiquities'),[72] the collectors are virtuous preservers of the prelapsarian clarity that their collections replicate, imposing 'right' behaviour on the unmarshalled bulk and selvedge of the world. To promote their orderly patterns and categories, the collectors insisted on binding their materials to one or another domain, episteme, or paradigm, which either excluded or anarchised those items which resisted classification.

[71] John Tradescant, *Musaeum Tradescantium: or, a Collection of Rarities Preserved at South-London . . .* (London, 1656), A4^r.
[72] John Weever, *Ancient Funerall Monuments* (London, 1631), a3^v–a4^r.

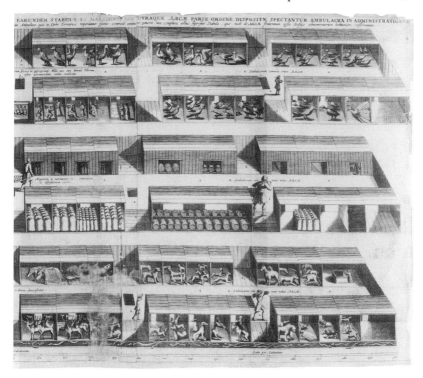

Illustration 1 (*Continued*)

Noah admitted the snakes to remind us of original sin, but other 'in-sects' – frogs, scorpions, mice, and bugs – were denied room because their reproduction was apparently 'imperfect' (spontaneous, or corrup-tive). By excluding them, Noah therefore consigned them to some specif-ically refractory and anomalous sector; similarly, in some natural history and curiosity collections the mule, the camelopard or giraffe, the hippar-dium (a horse-panther cross), the armadillo (a hedgehog-tortoise), and the allopecopithicum (a fox-monkey) were delinquent because they trans-gressed between species.[73] Certain inanimate items in the natural history cabinets also seemed to misbehave. 'Metallophytes' (fossils) appeared to be both mineral and either animal or vegetable; coral, a zoöphyte, was some sort of vegetable-mineral; and mercury's 'subtility' or thinness made it separable, like solids, yet strangely able, like 'liquors', 'to clap into a

---

[73] See Joscelyn Godwin, *Athanasius Kircher: A Renaissance Man and the Quest for Lost Knowledge* (London: Thames and Hudson, 1979), 26

Illustration 2 The Calceolari Museum in Verona from Benedetto Ceruti and Andrea Chiocco, *Musaeum Francisci Calceolari Veronensis* (Verona, 1622). Reproduced by permission of the Syndics of Cambridge University Library.

roundnesse'[74] like water droplets. The indeterminacy of these transgressors of categories could be signalled in the cabinets by the placement *between* kinds of things – thus coral and armadilloes were often interstitially mounted, as in the Calceolari Museum, between shelves (see Illustration 2). Printed compendia also signify the ruly and unruly in spatial practice: Aldrovandi's *Monstrorum Historia* (1642) is organised around a central section on normal human development, with monsters and prodigies (a centaur, a shower of crucifixes, a woman who vomited ears of wheat) framing it, a structure which decentres the peculiar and unnatural.[75] Although the 'misbehaviour' of certain species was

---

[74] Robert Basset, *Curiosities: or, the Cabinet of Nature* (London, 1637), 28–9.
[75] Bacon's assignment of phenomena to the three discrete sectors – nature, 'monsters', and arts – by contrast centralises the unnatural (*Parasceve*, 1st aphorism, 403).

sometimes described as *lusus naturae*, a joke inscribed in the text of nature by the hand of God,[76] the infraction of our first parents had more
solemn consequences for the order of things: the result of the Fall was
to distemper the natural world with 'the poyson of mans unrighteous
body' (to quote Winstanley).[77] Patterns of similitude and adherence to
categories of fitness had become dangerously fractured, confused, and neglected, and it remained to man to 'repair [his] primary ruins' (*PE* 1.v.37–9).

EARLY-MODERN CABINETS AND MUSEUMS

Although there flourished a large and popular category of printed
'marvels',[78] a thorough survey of the serious and often rigorously organised
cabinets would distinguish between the princely, the gentlemanly, the specialist, and the encyclopaedic collection. These definitions are partly social
and partly functional, but they are usually indicative of content: princely
collecting tended to emphasise dynastic wealth or the trappings of power in
expensive artificial trifles and royal regalia.[79] Specialist collections, such as
Francesco Buonanni's of seashells, and gentlemanly ones, such as Browne's
of ancient coins and medals, could contain almost anything but were determined by the particular enthusiasms and by the purse of the individual.
Prince Henry's huge collection of 10,000 seals was both princely in its
magnitude and specialist in its focus.[80] The encyclopaedic collection, like
the one assembled by the Royal Society or by individuals like Aldrovandi,
attempted a huge range but did not usually achieve the completed domains
of specimens it aimed at. Although it is the encyclopaedic collection which
is most consonant with his literary assemblages, we must understand something of each of these to situate Thomas Browne's work within the culture
of collecting. Their rubrics influence that of *Pseudodoxia*.

Imagined not only as an Ark, but also as *aemula naturae*, as *theatrum
mundi*, as the world in miniature,[81] as a memory theatre,[82] and as a

[76] See Paula Findlen, 'Jokes of Nature and Jokes of Knowledge: The Playfulness of Scientific Discourse
in Early Modern Europe', *Renaissance Quarterly* 43 (1990), 292–331.

[77] Winstanley quoted by Rogers, 149.

[78] Basset's *Curiosities* is organised under the undemanding rubric of 'strangeness', his marvels and *quaeres*
(such as the elephant's fear of its reflection and the constancy of women) having no other obvious
similarity to each other. Other marvel-books include James Gaffarel's *Unheard-Of Curiosities*, trans.
Edmund Chilmead (1650); and John Jonston's *An History of the Wonderful Things of Nature* (1657).

[79] See Hunter, *Science and Society*, 66; and Paula Findlen, *Possessing Nature: Museums, Collecting, and
Scientific Culture in Early Modern Italy* (Berkeley: University of California Press, 1994), 41–2, 47.

[80] Walter E. Houghton, 'The English Virtuoso in the Seventeenth Century', *Journal of the History of
Ideas* 3 (1942), 66.

[81] See L. Seelig, 'The Munich Künstkammer, 1565–1807' in *The Origins of Museums*, ed. Impey and
MacGregor, 85.

[82] Frances Yates, *The Art of Memory*, 2nd edn (London: Ark, 1984), 371.

supralinguistic assembly of denotative Adamic signs, the serious cabinet and collection were designed, in the era before animals and vegetables were reduced to method by the Linnaean descriptive system, to recreate by spatial analogies the supposed likeness between things. The openness of taxonomic systems was both liberating and disturbing to natural historians. Early scientific culture was perfectly capable of entertaining diverse, not necessarily competing, classifications based on observable physical evidence such as colour, location, parturition, and size, as well as designations derived from emblematic, mythological, and hermetic signification. The epistemes by which things were arrayed in cabinets as like or unlike, or as ruly or unruly, by which they were arranged on walls and in drawers and cupboards, were often expressed as antitheses: natural/artificial, normal/abnormal (or natural/monstrous), ordinary/extraordinary, valuable/valueless; they might be arranged by material, by use, by kingdom, by size, by weight, by probability, or by ability to astonish.

The Imperial collection of artificials at Vienna in the 1670s, a standard princely collection described by Edward Browne, moves simultaneously between the relative value of wrought substances and the rarity of the craftsmanship. So, for example, things made of ivory come 'lower' than, or before, things made of semi-precious stone, and crystal comes lower than gold, a hierarchy not reproduced by Edward Browne, who favours remarkable craftsmanship over mere material – Turkish saddles, carved rhinoceros horn, inlaid wood, works by Dürer, and so on – as well as historical souvenirs (a knife swallowed by a Czech peasant, the coat in which Gustavus Adolphus was killed, a cup from the temple of Solomon).[83] Michele Mercati's specialist mineral collection in the Vatican was organised by 'invariateness', a quality associated with the four Aristotelian elements (see Illustration 3). His *metalloteca* divided specimen presses into METALLEUTA, or elemental mineral ores like gold, silver, copper, lead, and iron, all requiring refinement, and the much larger category ORUKTA, or what the natural historian Robert Plot called 'formed stones', apparently self-generated, discrete entities such as quartz crystal, lime, chalk, salts, and coal as well as fossils, lodestone, asbestos, and amber.[84] The Elector Augustus's specialist *künstkammer* at Dresden was, unlike many of the German and Austrian princely collections, almost entirely made of tools, an early technology collection of implements and their products in mining, geodesy, navigation, arms, agriculture, joinery, measurement, and so on, wholly appropriate

[83] Edward Browne, *An Account of Several Travels through a Great Part of Germany: In Four Journeys* (1677), 95–100.
[84] Robert Plot, *The Natural History of Staffordshire* (London, 1686); see also Findlen, *Possessing Nature*, 61.

Illustration 3 The Mercati Museum in the Vatican from Michele Mercati, *Metallotheca* (Rome, 1719). Reproduced by permission of the Syndics of Cambridge University Library.

to the ruler of industrial Saxony. Although most famous for its specialist plant collection, the Tradescant museum in south London held some true oddities (the phoenix's tailfeather, a roc, Amerindian items and other New World treasures) but it was mainly geared (like a number of the English collections) to utility and accessibility ('a benefit to such ingenious persons as would become further enquirers into the various modes of Natures admirable works').[85] John Bargrave's seventeenth-century collection reflected no special mystical, scientific, or aesthetic design; he was a private gentleman and a Canon of Canterbury Cathedral whose acquisitions were determined by his historical interests, his travels, and his relatively slender means. He favoured chips of Greek and Roman antiquities, tourist pickings such as pumice from Mt Ætna and ashes from Vesuvius, Tiber gravel, a bit of Cicero's house at Tusculum; he also collected devotional items from shrines, and fossils, optick glasses, shells, a North African chameleon, ethnographical items, and the finger of a Frenchman.[86] Likewise, Thomas Browne's own collection, strongly but not exclusively natural-historical, included

[85] Tradescant, a1r.
[86] Arthur MacGregor, 'The Cabinet of Curiosities in Seventeenth-Century Britain' in *The Origins of Museums*, ed. Impey and MacGregor, 154; and David Sturdy and Martin Henig, *The Gentle Traveller: John Bargrave and His Collection* [Abingdon: Abbey Press, 1983], [no page numbers].

many animal and plant specimens, eggs, seeds, drawings of creatures, and sperm-oil, as well as coins, medals, urns, and archaeological fragments. The sixteenth-century Giganti collection at Bologna aimed less at an intellectual rubric than at a kind of visual harmony between the natural and the artificial in a rhythmic juxtaposition of objects.[87] The seventeenth-century Cospi collection, also in Bologna, consisted almost entirely of 'monsters', or abnormal phenomena, and was explicitly designed to provoke wonder and aesthetic delight in its patterned arrangements (see Illustration 4). The Neapolitan Imperato collection was organised by 'animal semantics', a paradigm which featured the symbolic history and meaning of each creature (see Illustration 5).[88]

The cabinet of Ole Worm, the seventeenth-century Danish antiquarian and professor of medicine, has the typical structural patterns in encyclopaedic collecting and array (see Illustration 6). The printed catalogue of the museum (produced after his death) neatly divides his holdings ascendingly into earths, rocks, metals, plants, animals, and artificial objects, designations apparently maintained more or less vigorously in the museum. Each printed category contains corollary and potentially problematic classes: the earths, for example, include medically useful minerals, as well as amber and spermaceti; in plants we find funguses, saps, and zoöphytes; animals, from insects to ungulates, extend also to 'monsters'. The catalogue's Aristotelian progression upward from earths through plants and animals is also preserved within the category of artificials, so that things made of earth precede those made of wood and animal remains. This hierarchical organisation is perceptible in the engraving of his cabinet, where in general the lower substances and lower animals are collected in labelled boxes on the lower shelves, with higher animals and man-made objects on the higher ones and on the walls, and the usual transgressive, equivocal items like the 'false' basilisk and coral placed between.

Worm's artificials, as in most cabinets, are the most varied and apparently disorganised group: he collects things which are made of the previous categories of materials – a gypsum statue of the rape of the Sabine women stands in its correct position in the hierarchy of earths, but is noted in the catalogue as a comparison with Livy's description of the event. Because he collects animal bones, he possesses a chair made of whale spondiles; his minerals include a naturally occurring map of the world in a globe of Florentine

---

[87] Laura Laurencich-Minelli has developed the suggestive terms 'alternate microsymmetry' and 'repeating macrosymmetry' to identify certain spatial patterns ('Museography and Ethnographical Collections in Bologna during the Sixteenth and Seventeenth Centuries' in *The Origins of Museums*, ed. Impey and MacGregor, 19).
[88] Olmi, 9–10.

marble. This same junction of material and use extends to ethnographical objects, and thus a Greenland kayak (made from sealskin) hangs from the ceiling next to a polar-bear cub and other environmentally contiguous 'marine' creatures. The collection of reindeer and moose antlers and cow horns includes carved hunting and drinking horns, eliding the material and its utility. The basic structure of Worm's cabinet was fairly common, but not universal. Each cabinet illustrated a rubric in some respect unique to itself. The catalogue of the sixteenth-century physick-based Calceolari museum in Verona, for example, moves through the terraqueous globe from the oceans (including marine plants, sea-creatures, amphibians, and the kingfisher), to dry land (earths, gems, and metals), and finally to terrestrial plants and animals;[89] but the pictured layout of the museum itself seems, unlike Worm's, inconsistent with the catalogue.

What Browne styled 'the compage of things' (*NCB*, 291)[90] – the inherent, natural syntax of creation long since occluded by error, which has become a ruined coherence, the 'remains of a greater whole' – the collectors were attempting to read by transforming it into a 'sober and well collected heap'.[91] Sometimes a collection, especially in printed form, was suggestively called a 'thesaurus' ('treasure-house'), either of things or of ideas, a word which was gradually acquiring the additional sense of semantic synonymy. In a world which seemed to present itself as a wilderness of forms, a variety of analogous or synonymous systems could provide the equivalent of a visual search-engine, much as we search a modern electronic database by finding an exact alphabetic or ASCII match for a flagged semantic item. The arrangements of ideas through contiguous things in the cabinets and the printed encyclopaedias were to act as a 'promptuarium'[92] where contingency would discover the 'answerings or analogies of beings'.[93]

Dominique du Cange, the sixteenth-century French philologist, suggested (incorrectly) that the words 'musæum' and 'mosaic' were cognate;[94] backed by the hermetic belief in *signaturae rerum* and reassuringly endorsed by etymology, the notion of a collection as a tessellated demonstration of such likenesses was deeply attractive. Signatures – occult likenesses between macro- and microcosmic objects – are manifest in earthly objects through graphic, behavioural, or gestural signs which obliquely or secretly

---

[89] See A. Chiocco and B. Ceruti, *Musaeum Francisci Calceolari Veronensis* (Verona, 1622).
[90] Michel Foucault more recently describes this compage felicitously as 'the prose of the world' (*The Order of Things: An Archaeology of the Human Sciences* (London: Tavistock, 1982), 17–45).
[91] Hooke, *Micrographia*, b2r.
[92] This is the term of Samuel Quicchelberg (1529–67), adviser to Albrecht V of Bavaria and author of the earliest known museological treatise. See E. Schultz, 'Notes on the History of Collecting and of Museums' in *Interpreting Objects and Collections*, ed. S. M. Pearce (London: Routledge, 1994), 178; and Seelig, 87.
[93] Fairfax, 2.   [94] Findlen, *Possessing Nature*, 50.

Illustration 4 The Cospi Museum in Bologna from Lorenzo Legati, *Museo Cospi* (Bologna, 1677). Reproduced by permission of the Whipple Library, Cambridge University.

indicate their connexion to cosmic or to heavenly things. Samuel Purchas describes signatures as 'most excellent admonitions and instructions'.[95] The signaturist Oswald Croll thought gallstones would be cured by saxifrage or stonecrop; Battista della Porta read portents in facial features. Emanuele Tesauro proposed 'the universal and public manuscript' of Browne's famous formulation as a text embodying *argutezza della natura*, a wittiness akin to natural jokes awaiting explication by man, and the talk of the learned to 'crack the hidden mysteries from the rind of letters'.[96] Browne notes routine correspondences in the figures of nails and other implements of Christ's crucifixion in the passionflower (*GC* III, 207–8), in the 'natural signature of the venereal organs' in beans (*PE* I.iii.23), in the Greek αιαι in the iris (signature of Apollo's grief at the death of Hyacinth), and in 'fatell mouls' in the face which make a model of the whole body (*GC* III, 206–7).[97] The system of occult resemblance through signature seemed to duplicate that covert, super-subtle coherence originally plain in the creation. Minerals and plants can be assigned 'reasons' from their figures, and although these are sometimes judged by Browne to be 'catechresticall and farre derived similtude[s]' (*PE* II.vi.141), he agrees that 'the finger of God hath set an inscription upon all his works … [B]y this alphabet Adam assigned to every creature a name peculiar to its nature' (*RM* II.2). The signaturist tendency – the insistence on hidden and idiosyncratically selected likenesses which Browne refers to as 'the Syntaxis of their natures (*PE* V.xx.419) – is a feature of nearly all the cabinets and their encyclopaedias. It is a syntax of resemblance or identity, patterns to be read as comparative contingencies or juxtapositions, as a system of potential *matches*. Indeed, the relation between spatial arrangement and meaning is so deeply embedded in early museums that our sense of it can sometimes mislead: Robert Cotton's enigmatic designation of his manuscripts under the twelve Caesars and two empresses whose busts adorned his bookpresses was no more than a whim: there is, for once, no rationale; the joke is on us.

No cabinet or museum survives completely intact from the early-modern period, so our knowledge of the structure of collections depends on their resemblance to their catalogues, and to surviving illustrations of their physical appearance. Because catalogues and illustrations very probably idealised or tidied up such structures by imposing graphic or typographic pattern on assemblages which in reality obeyed no such rule so consistently, the

---

[95] Purchas, A2v.
[96] Oswald Croll, 27; Porta, *De Humana Physiognomia* (Naples, 1598); '*ci sappiano dalla buccia della lettera snoccolare i misteri ascosi*', Tesauro, 87.
[97] See also *NE*, 366.

Illustration 5 The Imperato Museum in Naples from Ferdinandus Imperatus, *Dell'Historia Naturale* (Rome, 1599). Reproduced by permission of the Syndics of Cambridge University Library.

relationship between these different kinds of evidence is complex and often only speculative. But printed encyclopaedias and cabinets are functionally alike. Many cabinets contained libraries as well as objects: a significant part of the Aldrovandi museum, for example, comprised 8,000 illustrations, a huge collection of woodblocks for printing them, and 7,000 dried plants pasted into fifteen volumes, converting part of the cabinet into a library or a printing workshop, and the books themselves into museum-like aggregations of things. Buonanni presents his own printed encyclopaedia of shells richly illustrated as if to demonstrate that with natural miracles, *res ipsa loquitur*.[98] Likewise, although Robert Hooke devotes his *Micrographia* (1665) to painstaking descriptions of substances and objects through a microscope, the full-page and fold-out engravings of animal hairs, seeds, moulds, ices, snowflakes, insects, and parts of insects (especially eyes) give the quality of a specimen cabinet to a densely descriptive book. In the cabinets things become books and books contain things.[99]

'THE ABYSS OF KNOWLEDGE': *PSEUDODOXIA
EPIDEMICA* AND CABINET STRUCTURE

The notebooks and correspondence allow us to imagine the sort of cabinet Thomas Browne might have assembled. In *Religio Medici* he has already bequeathed his learning, like a thesaurus, to the republic of letters when he announces 'I make not therefore my head a grave, but a treasure of knowledge' (*RM* 11.3). This gesture, reminiscent of the bequests of the great collections to municipal or royal repositories, designates his literary remains as equivalent in purpose and use to those physical collections of artefacts donated to posterity by Harvey to the Royal College of Physicians, by the Amerbachs to Basel, by Kircher to the Roman College, by Worm to the Danish royal house, and by Ashmole and Aubrey to Oxford University.[100] Like real cabinets and catalogues, Browne's works compel us to analogise: he makes up centoes, collections of astonishing variety (of graves, of errors, of signatures in nature) whose hidden patterns of contiguity have to be recomposed in a re-enactment of the great primitive order. In each undertaking Browne, like the cabinet-collector, imitates God, whose voice shall return 'the parts

---

[98] F. Buonanni, *Ricreatione dell'occhio e della mente nell'osservation' delle Chicciole* (Rome, 1681), 127–8. S. M. Pearce notes that 'collections . . . do not merely demonstrate knowledge; they are knowledge' (*On Collecting: An Investigation into Collecting in the European Tradition* (London: Routledge, 1995), 111).

[99] Olmi, 8.

[100] Browne did, in fact, send some of his own curiosities – a petrified bone, an egg within an egg, a sealed bottle from which the wine had evaporated – to the Royal Society in 1668 (M. B. Hall, 184).

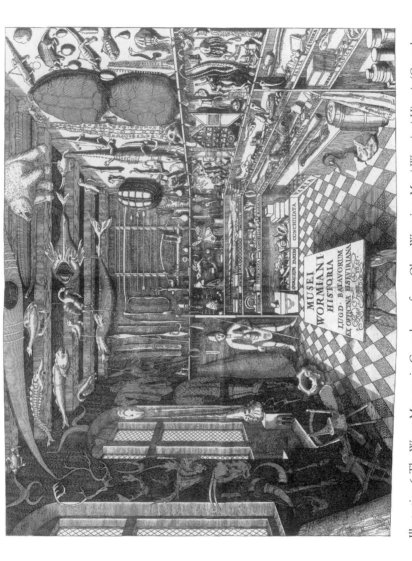

Illustration 6 The Worm Museum in Copenhagen from Olaus Wormius, *Musei Wormiani Historia* (Copenhagen, 1655). Reproduced by permission of the Syndics of Cambridge University Library.

of minerals, plants, animals, elements . . . and corrupted relics . . . scattered in the wilderness of forms'.

There are striking structural connexions between *Pseudodoxia Epidemica* and the culture of collecting. As a collecting naturalist Browne refers often in his letters to specimens brought to him by local hunters and fishermen, and he seems to have kept animals at various times for observation and eventual dissection. In his natural history notes we read of an eagle brought from Ireland which he kept for two years before giving it to the Royal College of Physicians (where it eventually perished in the catastrophic fire of 1666); he also kept various live animals to feed it on. He regrets the destruction of forty unusual local animals (including among other things a stuffed pelican), which were hanging in his house until the plague year of 1666, when 'the person intrusted in my house burnt or threwe [them] away', apparently to ward off contagion.[101] He had a bittern, curlews, and various other birds, as well as spiders, a frog, female vipers, dogs, toads, worms, flies and other insects, and a box of death-watches. He even acquired an ostrich,[102] and it is tempting to imagine his extensive range of shells, eggs, dried marine specimens (including two whale's heads), coins, medals, archaeological fragments, and insects as a formal cabinet, the physical counterpart of *Pseudodoxia*. John Evelyn described Browne's house (perhaps poetically) as 'a cabinet and paradise of rarities',[103] but the evidence of his notes and letters suggests that as a practical naturalist he was most often focused on whatever came to hand, that his assemblages were more opportunistic than otherwise. In every respect, Browne was the ideal candidate for possession of a gentleman's collection on the pattern of Ralph Thoresby and Walter Cope.[104] However, apart from Evelyn's casual remark, there is no evidence of anything so spatially or even categorically organised: Browne's interests were so thoroughly investigative that he may never have succumbed to the delights of studied collecting and instead acquired objects as his studies led him. If we wish to view the formal cabinet of Dr Browne we must look rather to his literary productions.

The four substantively distinct editions of *Pseudodoxia* supervised by Browne (of 1646, 1650, 1658 (the first of two in this year), and 1672), preceded by the questions and authorities cited in *Religio Medici*, form a combined record, Robin Robbins has suggested, of a pattern of continuous collection and addition to an original corpus of learning which in *Religio Medici*

---

[101] Thomas Browne to Christopher Merrett, [no date], 1669 (Keynes IV, 362).
[102] *NE*, 354–6; and Thomas Browne to Edward Browne, 13 January, 3 February, 5 February, 10 February, and 13 February 1681/2 (Keynes IV, 204–11). See my discussion of Browne's ostrich in Chapter Six.
[103] John Evelyn, *Diary*, ed. W. Bray (London: Everyman, 1907), II, 69 (17 October 1671).
[104] On these collections, see MacGregor, 'The Cabinet of Curiosities', 48–9; 154.

Browne imagines as a mental thesaurus or treasury.[105]   The 1650 (2nd) edition of *Pseudodoxia* incorporates a large quantity of further reading, some of it of very recent publications or reprints by, for example, Johannes van Helmont, Aldrovandi, Gassendi, and Kircher. The 1658 (3rd) edition is less extensively enlarged, but nevertheless is abreast of still more recent work, as for example Jonston on whales, and catches up on earlier work by important scientists like Harvey. By the time of the 1672 (4th) edition, *Pseudodoxia* was near saturation point, and relatively little was added; nevertheless, Power's experiments in microscopy find their way in.[106]

The character of Browne's presentation and explication of 'error' varies within *Pseudodoxia*, and partly accounts for some of its other structural features. The greater portion of the chapters are simply corrective: a well-known and often indefensible misapprehension is selected and demolished with arguments from experience and reason taking the lead. But a significant minority are what might be described as 'establishing' items in this encyclopaedia: often following his own investigations in physics and biology, he presents results and information from which he is usually able to make conclusive judgements; these 'establishing' sequences are not proposed as corrections of foregoing errors but are offered as presentations of new knowledge, or at least as confirming evidence to support new developments elsewhere. Thus, 'That a Beare brings forth her cubs informous or unshaped' is a corrective essay which proves the fallacy by various kinds of evidence, whereas 'Of Bodies Electricall' is an account of the ability of different substances, from gems to wood to elk's hoof, to generate and maintain a static charge – a project arising from Browne's reading of William Gilbert. The difference between these two kinds of sections is usually signalled by their titles: those posed as formal propositions ('That the roote of Mandrakes resembleth the shape of man') are usually straightforward refutations of errors; titles posed in the ancient locution '*de . . .*' ('Of the Dead-Watch', 'Of the Tainct or Small Red Spider') are more neutral and likelier to be establishing essays. Many chapters – 'Concerning the Lodestone', for example – are a mixture, both correcting errors and establishing information.

Browne's theoretical understanding of 'this strict enquirie of things' in *Pseudodoxia* is based on his understanding of the nature of scientific truth, whose character, Steven Shapin reminds us, was not yet monolithic and certainly not exclusively Cartesian or possessed of certainty. Probability in natural philosophy included a range of styles of proof, all, perhaps,

[105] Robbins *PE*, xxvii–xxviii.   [106] Robbins *PE*, xxv–xxvi.

increasingly grounded in an appreciation of empirical evidence, but not always – as with Browne's own asseverations about the chameleon based on the recent findings of Peiresc – demanding direct experience.[107] We might describe this form of early-modern probability as 'appropriate validation' in order to indicate the range of truth-claims available as evidence to someone like Browne. And he is perfectly aware, I think, of the nature of this range, as is obvious from his careful use of expressions of authority, evidence, and probability, in which he always differentiates, as part of the structure and reliability of his argument, between kinds of evidence and kinds of proof.

The primary disposition of the natural philosopher – as opposed to the naturalist – is toward an active and guiding interest in method.[108] A Baconian inductionist, though one with some sympathy for Cartesian deduction, arguing from observable fact to theoretical explanation, Browne refers constantly to the primacy of experimental and ocular proof in *Pseudodoxia*: 'those principles (though seeming monstrous) may with advantage be embraced, which best confirme experiment, and afford the readiest reason of observation' (*PE* 11.i.88); in other words, the explanation which derives from, and most simply and straightforwardly accounts for, experimental results is likely to be correct. He is, however, appropriately wary of gross ocular evidence: 'most things are knowne as many are seen, that is by parallaxis & in some difference from their true & proper beings; the superficiall regard of things being of different aspect from their centrall natures, wch long search and deepe enquirie is only able to discover' (*NCB*, 287). By itself, simple observation of phenomena is an insufficiently reasoned activity, and is, moreover, one which is likely to yield error; the search for 'centrall natures' beneath the 'superficiall regard of things' is also deeply Baconian.[109]

His attitude to probability – perhaps the most important epistemological concern of the period, the means of designation of what was worthy of credit – is essential, therefore, to our understanding of Browne's science. Probability could be established authoritatively or socially: either antique, or modern testimony, if from 'reliable' sources, rendered assertions probable; and even if classical authority was being steadily undermined as probable evidence throughout the seventeenth century, social probability was still viable in what Locke, in his *Essay concerning Human Understanding* (1690), could schematise as 'degrees of assent' – probability based on what was

[107] Shapin, *A Social History of Truth*, 120–1.
[108] Browne had likely read Descartes's *Discourse on Method* in the late 1630s, shortly after its publication in 1637.
[109] See Lorraine Daston, *Classical Probability in the Enlightenment* (Princeton: Princeton University Press, 1988), 241.

testified to as true by all, by most, by all the wise, by most of the wise, or by the best of the wise.[110] The debate about probability is also intimately connected with the conditions of proof associated with the 'ancients and moderns' controversy, and Browne is without doubt very aware of it, not only in his more standard complaint against the credulous adherence to antiquity and classical sources, but even in his expressions and management of various kinds of testimony in *Pseudodoxia*, where, for example, the discoveries and theories of Gilbert, Cabeus, Digby, and Descartes on magnetical bodies are deemed more probable than those given by Anaxagoras, Socrates, Democritus, Xenophanes, or Thales Milesius (*PE* 11.ii.86–7). In Book 1 of *Pseudodoxia* he discusses the issue at some length in his consideration of authority: 'dictates' and 'testimoniall engagements', he says, are 'but a weaker kinde of proofe', and in the 'harder' sciences have no place at all. 'Probable inducements of truth' – experimental, observable, and ocular, to use some of Browne's own terms – are 'a surer base of reason' (*PE* 1.vii.40). The analogously probable, entirely grounded on the observable in other, nearer creatures, governs his conclusions about the digestion of the chameleon, which he has not seen, and the truth of which is delivered only testimonially by ancient authors whose 'naked asseverations' seem flatly contradicted by those of experimenters and observers of his own time whose word he has no reason to doubt. Probability, rather than certainty, was ultimately an expression of a wise modesty, a rejection, in Shapin's words, of 'failed dogmatism'.[111] Probabilism in *Pseudodoxia* is for Browne the rhetorical position and trope which expresses both proper intellectual ambition and spiritual deference. At the same time, probabilism promotes a cabinet of ideas, a *musæum Browneanum*, in which all options are open and many explanatory paradigms are available.[112]

The encyclopaedic character of *Pseudodoxia* is partly assembled from its multiplicity of a certain category of thing (in this case, specific human errors), giving it affinity with the specialist compendium. It is partly, however, generated from the overarching and inclusive structure of its categories, which, like the truly encyclopaedic collection, comprehends heaven and earth, naturals and artificials, man and God. And it partly arises from the transgression of its own self-imposed boundaries: the occasion of the error-catalogue permits latitude for other related discussions – the 'establishing' essays – which are not themselves founded on error but on the learning

[110] See Patey, 4–7; see also Daston, Chapter Five.
[111] Shapin, 'Pump and Circumstance', 483. 'The quest for necessary and universal assent to physical propositions was seen as improper and impolitic', Shapin argues.
[112] For an example of this openness, see my discussion in Chapter Four of Browne's exchange with William Dugdale on the subject of a fossil bone.

acquired in the eradication of error. After the Baconian introductory essay of Book I on the genesis of error and of 'obstinate adherence unto Antiquity' and Authority, Books II through IV address, respectively, erroneous beliefs in the natural history of minerals and vegetables, of animals, and of mankind. After this, Browne abandons the natural world for a discussion, almost anthropological in tenor, of human belief and the man-made: thus Book V covers 'many things questionable as they are described in pictures'; and Books VI and VII consider errors in geography and historiography, and in Scripture and ancient and medieval history. Robbins points out that the bipartite division of natural and human history corresponds to Bacon's partition of *The Advancement of Learning* into 'Naturall' and 'Civile' history.[113] But it is equally clear that Browne is following the characteristic division of the cabinets and cabinet-catalogues into 'naturals' and 'artificials', with pictures and the history of ideas standing in *Pseudodoxia* for the latter. Within his *naturalia*, Books II through IV progress from 'lower' things to the higher animals, and thence to the human summit of the three kingdoms, man the microcosm. Book V, with discussions of pictures of folk-wisdom, considers man in his works and beliefs. Book VI concerns the cosmos of which man is the signature. Book VII is a kind of coda, with false tenets from Scripture, classical antiquity, and anecdote all under scrutiny. With the human animal the subject of Book IV, the central book of the seven, Browne situates 'that great amphibium', the ultimate anomaly, symbolically between the natural world and the world of ideas, just as Aldrovandi organises his book of monstrosities around an axis of normality.

Despite Browne's emendations and additions, which were continual and sometimes substantive, the overall structure of the work remained unchanged. The hierarchical arrangement of *Pseudodoxia*, like an encyclopaedic museum, could allow for additions and intercollations in its perpetually more-dense tessellation. 'Of the Cameleon' (*PE* III.xxi), for example, shows Browne in action as a collector and organiser of information. The chapter initially addresses the erroneous belief, of ancient ancestry, that the chameleon lives only on air,[114] but the closely argued discussion ranges among theories of animal digestion and respiration, particularly those of van Helmont, anatomical evidence from dissections, speculations on stored energy in solid matter, and the composition of air itself. In the

---

[113] Robbins *PE*, xxxi.
[114] For an account of emblematic and scientific illustrations of the chameleon, see William Ashworth, 'Marcus Gheeraerts and the Aesopic Connection in Seventeenth-Century Scientific Illustration', *Art Journal* 44 (1984), 134–7. Aldrovandi correctly shows a chameleon catching a fly with its tongue in *De Quadrupedibus digitatis* (Bologna, 1645).

subsequent editions of *Pseudodoxia*, Browne inserted information from his further reading in the field, especially on ingestion and excretion.[115] In 1650 he added items from Etienne de Clave on the composition of air, and a note on the etymology of the word 'chameleon' from Aldrovandi. The 1658 version was enlarged with recent reports from Peiresc and Vizzanius of direct observation of the chameleon and its nourishment, and with an opinion of Hippocrates on the non-nutritive property of air. Then, more than a quarter-century after first producing his consideration of the chameleon, Browne made his most substantial emendations and additions to it: the 1672 version adds further observations on excretion, on the commixture of air into the blood during the pulmonary transit (following Richard Lower in *De Corde* (1670)), and on the vitrification of combustible elements in solids (probably alluding to experiments by Power and Hooke in the mid-1660s), and also adds information on the physiology of the sea-tortoise (from Johannes Faber on South American animals in 1651). He also deleted a passage on the expulsion of liquid through the gills in fish, because of new work by Severinus in 1661. This process of ever-denser instantiation of a topic, the interpolation of more refined connective information into a broader, aphoristic framework, is the process of filling in the gaps in broken knowledge, an intellectual and almost spatial infilling or inspissation.

Although many sections of *Pseudodoxia* are based on Browne's own experience and observation, the discussion of the exotic chameleon necessarily draws on the authority and observation of others, and he is careful to point this out. Further evidence is carefully gleaned from contingent topics, and integrated into an already precisely structured, tessellated discussion. The first half of the chapter divides the evidence for and against the error that chameleons live on air into the 'three inducements to belief': authority, probability or experience, and possibility or reason.[116] The first of these rehearses the pronouncements of various writers; the second discusses anatomical teleology (if an animal possesses digestive organs, it must be because it eats); the third speculates about the nature of air and its possible nutritional character.[117] This discussion extends to the interaction

---

[115] See E. S. Merton, 'Old and New Physiology in Sir Thomas Browne: Digestion and Some Other Functions', *Isis* 57 (1966), 253–5.

[116] This tripartite appeal is another example of the echoic relationship between Browne and Boyle: Boyle presents 'Sense, Reason, Authority Human or Divine' as the standards (in that order) of judgement (quoted by Zakin, 67).

[117] He is clearly drawing on speculations and experiments on air ongoing during his lifetime by Galileo, Harvey, Hartlib, Stubbe, Mayow, and of course Boyle and Hooke. The chameleon, as Merton notes, interests Browne also as a problem in the related theory of digestion ('Sir Thomas Browne as Zoologist', 415).

of air (an 'element') with other bodies, and is essentially a list of combustible materials and their properties. The consideration of elemental air directs him on to elemental water, and its capacity to contain minerals and microscopic life, which may qualify it as an aliment. After this contingent digression, Browne returns to the chameleon and offers observable reasons for the original misapprehension: it inflates visibly with inhalation (as if eating air), it keeps its mouth open, it hasn't much circulating blood, and it is 'abstemious' for long periods, especially in winter. The section ends with a few speculations on such abstemiousness in animals and humans, but Browne admits that this is a matter outside the range of his enquiry. This initially tripartite division – received opinions, empirical facts, speculative explanation – allows Browne to migrate between various categories of evidence, and between the original premiss-conclusion structure and certain potentially helpful digressions, and in later editions of *Pseudodoxia* to tessellate further and later information.

The books of *Pseudodoxia* all follow some fairly precise and significant internal pattern of organisation, even the apparently miscellaneous Book VII. Book II ('Of mineral and vegetable bodies') was, for example, enlarged and improved in the second revision by Browne's readings in mineralogy, meteorology, and magnetism. In its final form its starts with inquiries into the electro-magnetic properties of 'equivocal' fossil bodies – magnets, amber, and jet; it continues with various qualities of manufactured mineral substances (glass, gunpowder, porcelain); and moves on to consider coral (which hardens into a rock-like substance out of water), eagle-stones (geodes), fairy-stones and elves' spurs (echinites, belemnites, and other true fossils), the solar sponge, and the significations of the twelve semi-precious gems (see diagram).

     natural minerals $\longrightarrow$
       manufactured minerals $\longrightarrow$
         equivocal mineral-animal-vegetables (coral) $\longrightarrow$
           curious/equivocal minerals (eagle-stones and fossils),
           and mineral symbolics

If we take Aldrovandi's model, which proposed much of his museum in the form of scrapbook volumes of dried flora, we might by analogy regard *Pseudodoxia* as an album of a similar sort, to which Browne added subsequently collected items. Its contiguous hierarchical arrangement, like that of museum catalogues, alludes to the visual patterns of the museums themselves, so that the categorical distinction between a spatially arranged cabinet and a printed encyclopaedia or catalogue – the distinction in other words between words and things – becomes almost irrelevant.

'NATURALL DESOLATIONS': ENDING *PSEUDODOXIA EPIDEMICA*

The penultimate book of *Pseudodoxia Epidemica* dwells on the subject of time. The much-disputed age of the world generates considerations of the millennium and the second coming, of national origin myths, of Copernican cosmology, and of 'the arithmetic of the Last Day' (*PE* vi.vi.483). It also prompts lesser contemplations: calendrical superstitions in various cultures fill a chapter. Even the crucial qualifying phrases of testimonial report – 'Always or never, for the most part or Sometimes, Oftimes or Seldome' (*PE* vi.viii.502) – are temporal. The tone of the work is clearly changing: although most of Browne's jokes are in the last book, these die out, as if inappropriate, half-way through the penultimate chapter of Book vii, and *Pseudodoxia Epidemica* ends, as it began, with an account of Satan's primary part in the generation of error.[118] Although it feels like a miscellaneous collection of further errors perhaps not easily assimilable into the themed earlier books, the change in tone in fact signals purposeful design. For the first half of the penultimate chapter (vii.xviii), each numbered error is managed in Browne's usual style, where a proposition ('That the *Pamphilian* Sea gave way unto Alexander in his intended March toward *Persia*, many have been apt to credit ...') is made and then subjected to various authoritative opinions and ocular observations (*PE* vii.xviii.603). But error 11 in this chapter, on the subject of evidence itself, ocular and received, is proposed quite differently: 'If any man shall content his beliefe ... or desires before beliefe, to behold ... for my part I shall not be angry with his incredulity.' The remaining two errors in this chapter carry on similarly, without the initial categorical statement but instead with a more hesitant, ambiguous construction ('If any man', 'If any one'); they then conclude with an almost helpless deferral of certainty ('I shall not be angry', 'he shall not want some reason', 'I shall not much dispute with

---

[118] His humour is subtle, to say the least. Gravely considering the account of Jephthah's sacrifice of his daughter (which he considers to be improbable), he notes that the father might easily have commuted the sacrifice by paying between ten and thirty shekels, 'a sum that could never discourage an indulgent Parent, ... and will make no greater noise then three pound fifteen shillings with us' (*PE* v.xiv.405). The death of Aeschylus, who was killed by an eagle who mistook his bald head for a rock and dropped a tortoise on it, is dismissed as 'a very great mistake in the perspicacity of that Animall' (*PE* vii.xviii.602). Huntley regards *PE* as 'consciously a vast ironic comedy' (*Sir Thomas Browne*, 170–1).

their suspicions') which leaves judgement to the disposition of the reader. The failure of Browne's more typical imperatives ('That men weigh heavier dead than alive . . . we cannot reasonably grant' (*PE* iv.vii.315)) ushers in the final chapter of the work, darkly entitled 'Of some relations whose truths we feare'. In a work which until this point has insisted on promulgating truths, despite the authorities they topple, to conclude with fearful truths seems a contradiction of the work's very purpose. The errors contained in this chapter introduce themselves with trepidation: 'wee cannot but feare it may bee true'; 'I am heartily sorry and wish it were not true'. The topics of the last chapter are, indeed, not errors in the usual sense, but grave sins and heinous crimes of which Browne would desire no record, and for which 'there must never rise a Pancirollus, nor remaine any Register but that of hell' (*PE* vii.xix.608). As he commands us in the opening letter to the reader to 'forget and part with much we know', so, like Galen who refused to write a history of poisons lest such a work prompt malefactors, he argues that we ought to consign certain truths to oblivion.

Indeed, almost all the sins of the final chapter deal in a sinister mortality, with circular ironies encompassing life and death. Queen Rosimund poisoned her father and celebrated with his skull as a flagon; some Egyptian embalmers, according to Herodotus, were necrophiliacs; a monk gave a Holy Roman Emperor tainted Eucharist wine – each of these, in the consumption of the progenitor or first condition, as with the communicant who 'received his bane in a draught of his salvation' (*PE* vii.xix.607), concerns opposites or contingencies like damnation and salvation or generation and degeneration which meet and imitate the circular structure of *Pseudodoxia* itself, whose first and final injunctions are to forget, and whose initial and concluding image is that of Satan himself, father of error. The subtle deceiver of the Garden of Eden is invoked in the first chapter as the first cause of our infirmity; he reappears in the last as the serpent to which the souls of the wicked must finally transmigrate. 'The vicious examples of Ages past, poyson the curiosity of these present' (*PE* vii.xix.608), Browne says, reminding us of the irony that, even if curiosity was the original taint in human nature, only reciprocal, devotional intellectual curiosity can repair its mortal damage.

The change in tone of this final section sorts with a different and much earlier such shift, in i.x, where the enumeration of Satan's own peculiar heresies in us converts Browne's usually long periods into choppy partial sentences: 'That there is no God. That there are many. That he himselfe is God. That he is lesse then Angels or Men. That he is nothing at all' (*PE* i.x.65). The paragraph following this one continues to list the crimes as abrupt, unelaborated propositions, almost as if he wished to be rid of them as soon as possible, as if the 'quodlibetical' nature of enquiry must be suspended in the face of these peremptory, Satanically inspired heresies. In the final chapter, the otherwise ebulliently neologising Browne is silent on the subject of carnal congress with the dead ('we require a name for this' is all he will venture). It would almost seem that Satan as a subject of scrupulous contemplation disrupts normal linguistic patterns and investigative habits, a disruption Browne has already intimated in Book 1 where he warns against precipitate and audacious enquiries which 'come within command of the flaming swords . . . in attempts above humanity' (*PE* 1.v.30).

Milton says in *Of Education* that 'the end of learning is to repair the ruins of our first parents'.[119] The serious, learned, and utile cabinet or naturalist's collection was displayed as an amending template for a regainable innocence, as a devotional attempt to put the fragments of creation in order. Yet *Pseudodoxia Epidemica*, although its structure unmistakably alludes to contemporary cabinets and collections, is none the less a troubling assemblage of human ignorance and credulity rather than a coherent display of patterned order. Browne is collecting and expunging, by his learned attention, a great raft of errors which clutter and demean our understanding, and he certainly wishes to be understood as participating in that particular laundering exercise. By structuring the work as he does, he integrates it into the *kind* of work that cabinets do; yet in the terms of learned assemblage errors are a negative category, the obverse of those actual items in real cabinets which can be spatially represented as having connexions with each other, and which together attempt a coherent version of creation. Browne's cabinet of errors, beyond having the broad categorical similarities that allow him to place them in headings such as 'errors associated with minerals' or 'errors in pictures', have no ligature other than their mere incorrectness. In the next two chapters, on *Urne-Buriall* and *Musæum Clausum*, the magnitude of Browne's sense of investigative helplessness, the sense of futility suggested by the accumulation of errors themselves and by *Pseudodoxia's* final chapters, is fully developed.

---

[119] John Milton, *Of Education* in *The Prose Works of Milton* II, 366–7. The repair of fragments is an image found in *Paradise Lost*; dismemberment and reconstitution occur in *Areopagitica* and *The Doctrine and Discipline of Divorce*.

CHAPTER 4

The laureate of the grave: Urne-Buriall and the failure of memory

A monument is a thing erected, made, or written, for a memoriall of some remarkable action, fit to bee transferred to future posterities. And thus generally taken, all religious Foundations, all sumptuous and magnificent Structures, Cities, Townes, Towers, Castles, Pillars, Pyramides, Crosses, Obeliskes, Amphitheaters, Statues, and the like, as well as Tombes and Sepulchres, are called Monuments. Now above all remembrances (by which men have endeavoured, even in despight of death to give unto their Fames eternitie) for worthinesse and continuance, bookes, or writings, have ever had the preheminence.

(John Weever, *Ancient Funerall Monuments* (1631))

Now these Shells and other Bodies are the Medals, Urnes, or Monuments of Nature, whose Relievoes, Impressions, Characters, Forms, Substances, &c ... are the greatest and most lasting Monuments of Antiquity, which, in all probability, will far antidate all the most ancient Monuments of the World, even the very Pyramids, Obelisks, Mummys, Hieroglyphicks, and Coins[.]

(Robert Hooke, *A Discourse of Earthquakes* (*in The Posthumous Works of Robert Hooke*, 1705))

OF BONES AND BARROWS: THE BROWNE-DUGDALE CORRESPONDENCE

In 1658, not long after the publication of *Urne-Buriall*, Thomas Browne and William Dugdale were conferring on the subject of bones. Browne's dedicatory letter in *Urne-Buriall* had referred approvingly to Dugdale's earlier antiquarian work on English monasteries and to his chorography of Warwickshire (*U-B*.LeGros, 132); by 1658, as the associate of a consortium of speculators aiming to reclaim the East Anglian fenlands in the 1650s, Dugdale was working on his *History of Imbanking and Drayning* (1662), a kind of chorographical survey of the background of such attempts, from the Romans onward. This project would have been peculiarly interesting to Browne: although primarily an assemblage of documentary evidence of local legal undertakings in flood-control, it occasionally involved consideration (but not usually physical examination) of the subterraneous world of remains, the sub-stratum of history by which Dugdale partly established a map of the originally drowned lands of the Great Level of eastern England. Although Dugdale's preferred excavational sites were libraries, the earth itself divulged records, natural and artificial; and in thinking about the bones among them in relation to the topographical history of the east of England, Dugdale made enquiries of Browne which illuminate early-modern conceptions of relics and remains as remnants of a scattered, corrupt creation. At the same time, they demonstrate the civil exchange of learning which was itself both an emblematic and a practical foray against the forces of dispersion which investigation attempted to repair. Browne's own attitude to investigation, to evidence, and to the assemblage of relics (both natural and artificial) in this exchange with Dugdale, carried out almost simultaneously with his writing of *Urne-Buriall*, frames the far more remarkable manipulation of evidence in that antiquarian masterpiece of assemblage and array.

The difference between documentary and artefactual evidence will much concern the argument of this chapter – the difference, that is, between the library and the laboratory, the archive and the archaeological specimen, between words and things. Notions of the import and analysis of material remains, especially those retrieved from underground and other hidden places, were far from any modern concept of 'archaeology': the word itself, although in use in the early seventeenth century, was roughly synonymous with ancient history, or the documentary records thereof, rather than with the study of material remains.[1] And it was a library, interestingly, which prompted Dugdale to think about bones in the first place. Much earlier, during the Civil War, Dugdale had helped John Selden with the sorting and binding of the manuscripts in Robert Cotton's celebrated archive.[2] Like many such collections, Cotton's included along with documents a splendid array of curiosities, ranging from medals and coins to Roman tombstones.[3]

---

[1] *OED* 'archaeology', 1. The modern use of the word was not available until the mid-nineteenth century.

[2] Kevin Sharpe, *Sir Robert Cotton, 1586–1631: History and Politics in Early Modern England* (Oxford: Oxford University Press, 1979), 82.

[3] This collection of curiosities is, like most of its kind and date, now scattered and lost. The tombstones are in Cambridge (see David Howarth, 'Sir Robert Cotton and the Commemoration of Famous Men', *British Library Journal* 18 (1992)). Ulisse Aldrovandi's collections of books and things in Bologna, and of books with natural specimens pasted in them, are the best-known examples of the way such collections could mingle the textual and the artefactual. See my own discussion of this phenomenon in Chapter Three; and Kate Bennett, 'John Aubrey's Collections and the Early Modern Museum', *Bodleian Library Record* 17 (2001), 213–45.

Among these was one of Cotton's most remarkable treasures, the skeleton (perhaps only partial) of a great fossil fish unearthed at Conington Down, in Cotton's country estate in Huntingdonshire.[4]

Dugdale asked in 1658 to send Browne a bone from this fish, originally taken up by Cotton himself while digging a pond, 'desir[ing Browne's] opinion thereof and of what magnitude you thinke it was'.[5] The series of letters between them which allude to these landlocked fishbones embeds the discussion of the fossil within a more wide-ranging and ongoing set of queries and responses about the history and pre-history of the draining of the East Anglian fens. Dugdale is especially interested in a common fenland phenomenon: the firm subsoil of the region is found to be covered with a sea-borne layer of silt; above the sea-silt lies a layer of freshwater-borne fen soil. Beneath the sea-silt, on the subsoil level, well-preserved vegetation such as nut-trees and fir (which no longer grow in that district) is often found. The fossil fish from Conington is an anomaly in this respect, since it could not have been native to the dry land of the subsoil in which it lay, and Dugdale wants to know when and by what means the ocean waters inundated this region. He has plenty of recent historical evidence to show that some towns were once freshwater fen-islands – the name of Eye in Suffolk, for example, gives itself away as a place once surrounded by water since the suffixes '-ea', '-ey', and '-y' are Saxon for 'island', as in 'Ely' – and so can account for the fenny topsoil. He notes, too, that the dredging of the river at Wisbech uncovered, below the silt of the contemporary river-bed, a stony bottom eight feet further down with boats resting on it; when the Skybeck Sluice was dug near Boston in Lincolnshire, a smith's forge complete with horseshoes and other implements was found sixteen feet below the surface: these phenomena are easily explained by coastal siltation.[6] He theorises that the watery Great Level was formed when the sands in the Wash blocked the outflow of various East Anglian rivers, causing them to

---

[4] Hope Mirrlees contends that this was 'the fossilized skeleton of a colossal sea-fish'; however, as Dugdale's correspondence with Browne makes clear, it was not immediately obvious to the untrained eye what sort of creature the bones belonged to; and although Browne knew that the bones had been found with 'diverse others', he asks if ribs or skull were among them in order to make a surer identification (letter of 17 November 1660 (Keynes IV, 324). Mirrlees does not document her source for the claim that it was a whole skeleton, and little information exists about Cotton's rarities (Hope Mirrlees, *A Fly in Amber: Being an Extravagant Biography of the Romantic Antiquary Sir Robert Bruce Cotton* (London: Faber, 1962), 76. I am indebted to Dr Colin Tite for information about Cotton's collection of curiosities (private communication)). Dugdale himself describes this fossil in *The History of Imbanking and Drayning* (1662): 'the skeliton of a large sea-fish (neere xx foot long, as was then conjecture) lying in perfect silt, above six foot below the superficies of the ground' (172).

[5] Dugdale to Browne, 17 November 1658 (Keynes IV, 309). This query indicates that Dugdale had not seen an entire skeleton.

[6] Dugdale, *History of Imbanking and Drayning*, 178.

flood the land behind, and this, together with early draining and diking projects, must obviously have produced such effects as are discovered in Boston and Wisbech; but he is puzzled by this probably pelagian relic from Conington, well inland, embedded in the subsoil with both salt- and fresh-water silts layered above it. It would suggest that the fish swam through ocean waters to reach Conington, and that its remains were subsequently covered over by coastal and then inland siltation. '[T]herefore when, or on what occasion, it was that the sea flowed over all this . . . is a thing that I know not what to say to, desiring your opinion thereof.'[7] Although the fossil evidence supports it, nothing in Dugdale's extensive researches into the history of drainage had indicated that the sea, or even the fen, ever came so far inland as Conington, and only the sea, apparently, can account for such bones.[8]

Floods and inundations were imperfectly understood in the seventeenth century, although Browne is able to give a carefully reasoned and plausible logistical explanation of the tripartite layers of 'ancient & proper soyle' [subsoil], 'siltie soile' [saltwater-borne silt], and 'fenny soile' [freshwater-borne silt] to Dugdale.[9] Neither was the explanation or concept of fossils ('formed' or 'figured' stones) fully worked out or stable. Until the late-seventeenth century, fossils were thought to be stones made by nature to resemble animals and vegetables; the Vitalists argued that the 'seeds' of some organisms could prompt inorganic stone to propagate stony versions of the original organic one, so that marine fossils were explained as a result of the land's rivalry with the sea in attempting to produce similar creatures.[10] Later naturalists could accept that they were petrified remains of creatures and plants overcome by the Flood; and Robert Hooke in the late 1660s was one of the first to hypothesise that fossils were the remains of ancient extinct

---

[7] Dugdale to Browne, 24 February 1658/9 (Keynes IV, 317).

[8] *The History of Imbanking and Drayning* is principally concerned with the drainage of the 'Great Level', the watershed which extends from Lincolnshire to Norfolk, Suffolk, Cambridgeshire, Northamptonshire, and Huntingdonshire. Cotton's Conington (rather than the one near Peterborough) in the southwest of modern Cambridgeshire lies a few miles beyond the westernmost edge of the Great Level.

[9] Browne to Dugdale, 16 November 1659 (Keynes IV, 320). Robert Hooke believed that geological phenomena like the Great Level had been caused by ancient earthquakes which burst the natural banks holding the sea back from the land (Hooke, *A Discourse of Earthquakes* in *The Posthumous Works of Robert Hooke*, ed. Richard Waller (1705), 290–1, 299).

[10] Browne, in Vitalist mode, thinks of a formed stone like crystal, and by extension the various organic fossil remains, as having been produced by 'a lenteous percolation of earth, drawne from the most pure and limpid juyce thereof . . . [and] wrought by the hand of its concretive spirit', and remarks 'yet is there unquestionably, a very large Classis of creatures in the earth farre above the condition of elementarity . . . created and defined seeds committed unto the earth from the beginning'. (*PE* II.i.83). For a discussion of Vitalism, see Rogers, 6–149. On the shift in thinking about fossils in the seventeenth century, see Findlen, *Possessing Nature*, 232–7.

creatures overwhelmed by various natural catastrophes.[11] At the same time, however, Browne was questioning his son in Austria about a lake where 'scheyffersteyn' (slate) is common, in which 'the *shape* of fishes & froggs are found in stones' [my italics];[12] he had already compared the patterns of ammonites, echinites, and belemnites (which he describes as 'stones') to those in crystal and snow (*PE* 11.i.80–1). Browne thinks that these are all figured and shaped rocks. The organic origin of fossils was far from obvious, and the conclusion that they had been life-forms at all, and not occultly analogous sports of nature mimicking known species, was hedged with difficulties: how could marine creatures have got to the mountaintops where they were so often discovered; how did they become embedded in rock; and what could explain the apparent conversion of organic remains into mineral deposits?[13] Browne had once encountered a fossil fish in a cliff near the sea;[14] when he presented a bone from this large find to the Royal Society, Robert Hooke speculated that it 'seems to have been the Leg-bone of some Elephant, if it be not the fore Fin of some Whale', showing that the identity of such an object could be uncertain even to a trained naturalist.[15]

The attempt to explain fossil remains provoked naturalists and theologians alike. Marine fossils discovered very far from the sea could only be explained in terms of geological changes which were more profound than most investigators could readily credit without discounting the received Scriptural account of creation. Correct understanding of sedimentary rock-formation as propounded by Steno in 1660 was still a few years in the offing, as were Hooke's explanation of the organic micro-structure of fossils in 1663[16] and his proposal of earthquakes as the cause of anomalous fossil placement in 1667–8. Although Dugdale seems to accept the organic nature

[11] Although Hooke recognised the need for a chronology of shells in order to study alterations over time, he did not suggest any kind of evolutionary process as the explanation for the disappearance of fossil life-forms. See Paolo Rossi, *The Dark Abyss of Time: The History of the Earth and the History of Nations from Hooke to Vico*, trans. L. G. Cochrane (Chicago: University of Chicago Press, 1984), 13.

[12] Thomas Browne to Edward Browne, 1 March (*styl.vet.*)[1668/9] (Keynes IV, 42). See Stanley E. A. Mendyk, *'Speculum Britanniae': Regional Study, Antiquarianism, and Science in Britain to 1700* (Toronto: University of Toronto Press, 1989), 27–30.

[13] The best discussions of these matters are Martin J. S. Rudwick, *The Meaning of Fossils: Episodes in the History of Palaeontology*, 2nd edn (New York: Neale Watson Academic Publications, 1976); and Rossi. Rudwick notes that some fossil remains were relatively easy to identify and explain because they were found near the sea, where erosion and siltation had been observed. The 'harder' fossils were those with little or no likeness to known species, and any fossil discovered far from the seacoast in areas not apparently subject to movement and change (Rudwick, 49–100). Browne demonstrates these features of the debate over fossils in his description in his natural history notes of fossil finds in Norfolk (*NE*, 350–1).

[14] Browne to Dugdale, 17 March 1660 (Keynes IV, 325). [15] Hooke, *Discourse of Earthquakes*, 439.

[16] Hooke was studying petrified wood for the Royal Society in 1663, observations which he published in *Micrographia*, 107–12.

of this specimen – he refers to it as a bone and as part of an animal – his queries show that he was having difficulty explaining its location.

With geomorphological and palaeontological theory in flux, the Dugdale–Browne correspondence highlights with peculiar clarity the different intellectual temperaments of the absolutist and the 'possibilist'. Browne responds to Dugdale's queries with the observation that 'in points of such obscuritie, probable possibilities must suffice for truth';[17] and, instead of saying directly what is most likely, he offers a spectrum of answers. It is not, he begins, impossible that 'in large flowes, & great drifts of elder time' silt might have been washed to Conington naturally by rivers and inlets rather than by oceanic inundation, since bays and estuaries, before they themselves were 'cloyed' up, might have existed in the region and freely carried silt to parts of East Anglia now apparently remote from large bodies of salt water. Moreover, local floods regularly deposit silt even now, as then. More distantly, Aristotle's $\mu\varepsilon\gamma\alpha\varsigma$ $\chi\varepsilon\iota\mu\acute{\omega}\nu$ or cyclical great winter, caused by planetary alignments, would also promote large-scale flooding and re-configurations of the land, even if such deluges 'be too old for our records'.[18] Such large fossils may be remains of the Deluge, a standard explanation of dinosaur and other huge remains of creatures thought since to have given way to decadent smaller versions of themselves in the post-Noachic period. He meditates on so-called giants' bones found in Flanders and elsewhere, which are, he says, the remains of elephants brought originally by Claudius and Hadrian to northern Europe.[19] But he doesn't think that the sea has covered all areas where such 'reliques' are found; some parts of the earth 'rise and swell somewhat', he believes, gradually moving and engulfing surface items like trees, a suggestion of terrestrial shift.[20] He finally suggests, however, that unless the bone was found in isolation, in which case it might be a spondylite (a stone naturally occurring in the shape of a vertebra), the sea did indeed come so high as Conington, which itself must have been on lower and more vulnerable ground of old than now; and it must have receded naturally by seismic shifts of some kind, long before there were humans to undertake drainage projects. The Cottonian fish out of water seems to swim through this discussion of a landscape in which, by human as well as by natural agency, the waters have intruded and receded.

[17] Browne to Dugdale, 16 November 1659 (Keynes IV, 320–1).
[18] Browne refers to Aristotle's *Meteorology*.
[19] In fact such huge skeletons were Pleistocene elephant relics, not Roman remains at all. Graham Parry notes with some exasperation the insistence of antiquarians throughout this period on the Roman introduction of elephants to any part of Europe in which such discoveries were made (Graham Parry, *The Trophies of Time: English Antiquaries of the Seventeenth Century* (Oxford: Oxford University Press, 1995), 33). See also Rudwick, 72.
[20] Browne to Dugdale, [October 1660] (Keynes IV, 324).

In an earlier letter he had observed, however, that 'manie things prove obscure in subterraneous discoverie':[21] bones and other fragments are brought to their resting places by human agency, and this will be one of Browne's preferred themes in *Urne-Buriall*: sea shells in the high Alps and the fishbone houses of the Ichthyophagi and of the northern nations, 'where mortars were made of the backbones of whales, doores of their jawes, & Arches of their ribbes',[22] all testify – as do local Norfolk uses of beached whale-bones[23] – to anomalous locations. Not only have petrified stags' horns turned up in Norwich chalk pits; but

in a church yard of this citye an oaken billet was found in a coffin. About 5 yeares agoe an humerous man of this countrie, after his death and according to his owne desire, was wrap't up in the horned hide of an oxe, & so buried. Now when the memorie hereof is past, how this may hereafter confound the discoverers, & what conjectures may arise thereof, it is not easie to conjecture.[24]

What is striking is Browne's obvious ease in the midst of such reliquary confusion or 'points of obscurity'. In this long letter we see him engaging first in a naturalist's speculation about the bone:

the petrified bone . . . seemes to be the vertebra, spondyle, or rackbone of some large fish, & noe terrestrious animal, . . . ffor it is not perforated & hollowe, but solid, according to the spine of fishes . . . too bigge for the largest Dolphins, porposes, or swordfishes . . . but may be the bone of some bigg cetaceous animal.[25]

In succession he offers an archaeologist's observation of geological history, a classicist's reading of Aristotle on the weather, a Biblicist's interpretation of the Flood, an anthropologist's knowledge of the architectural remains of remote peoples who use animal bones for domestic purposes, an antiquarian's identification of imperial Roman elephant remains, and finally a digression on curious burials and the likelihood of ensuing perplexity among 'after-discoverers'. Such a range is habitual with Browne, whose spectrum of intellectual disciplines is not only potentially bewildering, but also enacts the bewilderment of the scattered and confused relics which are his subject.

For Browne reliquary confusion is always exhilarating. In his commonplace book he describes the demolition of the old charnel-house of St Paul's in 1549; the bones taken away from the site amounted to over a thousand cartloads which were put in a pile in Finsbury Fields and covered over with earth to make the foundations for three new windmills. Browne added a

[21] *Ibid.*   [22] *Ibid.*, 323.
[23] See Browne's account of a whale beached near Wells in Norfolk, in *PE* 11.xxvi.272–4.
[24] Browne to Dugdale, [October 1660] (Keynes IV, 325).   [25] *Ibid.*, 323.

memorandum in a 'To Do' list: 'To make an epigramme or a fewe verses upon this subject . . . of a windmill upon a mount of bones'.[26] The removal, mixture, or scattering of remains can be deliberate and meditated, not just accidental and opportunistic, and the civic necessity of removal and relocation of these bones, with the economic advantages of turning them into foundations for windmills, is not at all distressing or even melancholy; instead, it provides Browne with the occasion of meditation. Here, the ingenious recycling of bones, like many images in *Urne-Buriall* and other works, alludes to a regenerative, resurrectionary process by which even the most ordinary municipal and domestic economies become signatures of the afterlife.

This characteristic survey – an essentially empirical, categorical open-mindedness typical also of some other early-modern investigative and meditative writing – pervades most of his major works and has consequences for the texture and surface of his expression. By contrast, Dugdale – cataloguer, historian of ruined monasteries, archivist of local government transactions, and expert in Roman civil engineering – is not easy with so many compelling possibilities. Indeed, he seems to have misunderstood Browne's peregrination among the potential histories of the fishbone as an implication of inaccurate data, for Browne's next letter seems a trifle impatient with what must have been Dugdale's plaintive defence. 'I did not make any doubt of the *truth* of the fishbones', Browne testily explains, 'butt cast in some doubts more proper to some other things of the like nature then this, wch is soe authentically testified by all circumstances' [my emphasis].[27]

This correspondence neatly epitomises Browne's generous intellectual habits. He is willing to revolve a great variety of possibilities and to entertain various conclusions without apparent bias, drawing this variety from very distinct intellectual and investigative disciplines – natural-philosophical, etymological, theological, historical, and archaeological or anthropological – and moving easily within and especially *between* these fields. His mode is comparatist: he invokes other silt-fields, other burials, other fossil-discoveries in judging the Conington bone, and he has an almost unexamined sense of the likeness between the natural occurrence which buried the

---

[26] *NCB*, 275. These events are recounted in John Stowe's *Survey of London* (1635), 356; William Dugdale in his *History of St Paul's Cathedral* (1658) also notes the episode (130). Browne later referred to it again in *Repertorium* (Keynes III, 140). The charnel-house of Norwich Cathedral was also cleared, but the fate of these bones was unknown to Browne.

[27] Browne to William Dugdale, 17 November 1660 (Keynes IV, 325). This interest in such anomalies reappears in his tract 'Of Artificial Hills', a later composition based on this exchange of letters, in which he talks about the difficulties of knowing whether barrows, which he suspects are burial mounds, are Roman, Saxon, or Danish (*MT*, 84–7).

fish in Conington and the wholly artificial occurrences which placed planks and ox-hides underground in Norwich and made windmills of bones. His intellectual paradigms, in this sense, seem to overlap; or, more precisely, the parameter of the fossil – a 'thing buried' – comprehends a huge range of items and circumstances. In *Urne-Buriall*, a treatise on cremation and burial, knowledge itself is a fossil, imperfect or lost, and has to be excavated, unearthed, like various bones and burials, from the sepulchral oblivion of time.

'KNOWLEDGE BROKEN' AND FRAGMENTARY STYLE IN *URNE-BURIALL*

In the field of human monuments, Dugdale actively tried to preserve – as Browne never did – whatever he could. Where in *Pseudodoxia Epidemica* Browne is in effect destroying received ideas and traditions, Dugdale's efforts to save what was even before his eyes being destroyed or defaced were heroic. He was, after all, a man whose response to the political crisis of 1641 was to visit every cathedral from London to York (taking in the lesser churches of East Anglia, the Midlands, and the Marches) with a painter in tow to make 'exact draughts' of arms, monuments, and tombs, 'to the end that the memory of them (in case if that ruin then imminent might come to pass) ought to be preserved for future and better times'.[28] Some of his work preserves the folkloric as well as the historic, such as anecdotes and local traditions about early saints and their miracles. The densely instantiated *History of Imbanking and Drayning*, together with its scrupulous transcriptions of legal records, also contains lengthy hagiographies of Etheldreda and others, for Dugdale regards the undrained fens of early Saxon times as a kind of British desert in which the mettle of the holy man or woman could be assayed. But this is the limit of the extent to which he will venture into the conjectural territory which is familiar to Browne. Dugdale, like his model, Cotton, is primarily a '*Philadelphus* in preserving old monuments, and ancient records',[29] and his sole aim is to save what exists from oblivion. His antiquarian fame residing in an almost supernatural ability to record and marshal old documents and charters to make rational and orderly 'true' histories, Dugdale would almost certainly not have regarded his investigation of drainage as an archaeological project. His bent is for textual, not artefactual, evidence, his history of drainage 'extracted from Records, Manuscripts, and other Authentick Testimonies' rather than from material remains.[30] Browne suggested that the two of them

---

[28] Wood v, 695 (also quoted in Parry, 221).   [29] Weever, a7v–8r.
[30] Dugdale, *History of Imbanking and Drayning*, title-page.

excavate a barrow together; this, though, in spite of his minor concern with buried fossils, would have been a project more or less alien to Dugdale, and was never undertaken. Unlike Dugdale's, Browne's approach to the past is speculatively artefactual, as well as, or rather than, purely textual.

The contemplation of the fragmentary and the incomplete, specifically where the agent of incompleteness is time, contributes, as Leonard Barkan argues of the broken antiquities of Rome, 'to a living text of epic sim- iles whereby that which is seen becomes aggrandized through a ratio of comparisons to that which cannot be seen'.[31] The aggrandising tendency of English antiquarianism yields attempted preservation and reconstruc- tions; but Browne, unlike Camden and Dugdale, writes no annals, ge- nealogies, chronicles, or chorographies. 'We drive not at ancient Families,' he announces curtly (*U-B*.LeGros, 133). Instead, the aesthetic of loss, of incompleteness, occupies his thought on its own terms, and is itself the aggrandised feature of recovery and investigation: the deficit in creation and knowledge – together with the pervasive nostalgia of the humanists – prompts the recuperation and reminiscence promised by the prophets. However, as *Urne-Buriall* reminds us, the amplification of loss is the best that antiquarian research can offer.[32] In this sense, too, Browne is temper- amentally entirely unlike Dugdale: he is specifically interested in oblivion and its effects rather than in re-collecting the past from the grave of time for the benefit of the future, by recourse to the survivals of the present day. Browne's past, which compels him to look into a truncated future, is entirely more hypothetical, more conjectural than Dugdale's. In sensibility he is less akin to the English antiquarians and closer to the Italians: like Bosio, he dwells on '*occultati, dispersi, mescolati* '[33] [things hidden, scattered, mixed]. He is as moved by the obscurities of ruin as he is by the specificities of rediscovery.

---

[31] Leonard Barkan, *Unearthing the Past: Archaeology and Aesthetics in the Making of Renaissance Culture* (New Haven: Yale University Press, 1999), 72.

[32] Browne recognises this incompleteness as in itself worthy of philosophical consideration, in the same way that fragmentary classical sculptures were recognised as 'beautiful despite the carefully catalogued missing parts that under other circumstances might cause them to be considered monstrosities' (Barkan, 121).

[33] Antonio Bosio, *Roma sotterranea* (Rome, 1632), 6. Bosio, who is not interested in classical Rome so much as in the offences of the heathens against the bodies of the Christian martyrs, describes saints' bones mixed with those of asses and camels, dispersed in many pieces, or buried without identification. Bosio attributes the miraculous preservation of some saints' bodies to God's providence rather than to the forces of chance invoked by Browne. He approves, too, of pious Christian regathering of the thousands of pieces of saints' bodies, a practice open, as contemporaries were well aware, to abuse and fraud. Browne himself guys the practice with the body of Father Crispin in *Musæum Clausum* (see my discussion in Chapter Five). It is difficult to ignore the similarity of Browne's thinking about dispersal and erasure to Montaigne's in 'Of Glorie' (in Montaigne II, 340–55).

Browne's rhetorical habits themselves are inflected by this speculative adventurousness: just as the sorts of recording exercise engaged in by Dugdale are not really Browne's, so Dugdale's declarative histories are quite unlike Browne's open-ended and contingent syntactical rhythms, which are subject to reinterpretation and extension.[34] Various analysts of Browne's style have described this in terms of the baroque or 'Asiatic' on the one hand, or the anti-Ciceronian or 'libertine' on the other.[35] Browne is occasionally given to aphorism ('the long habit of living indisposeth us for dying' (*U-B* v, 165)), but these tend to occur in summary statements such as the last chapter of *Urne-Buriall* rather than in the more discursive considerations of his essentially investigative prose. His more characteristic manner consists of rhythms rather than shapes, of a developing, evolving narrative of contemplation rather than syntactically highlighted *aperçus* or adages.[36] It is a style notable especially for mutually contradictory, or completely absent, connectives which would normally guide our sense of the relationship between one claim and the next, an absence which, like Bacon's in the *Essays*, or like Montaigne's, leaves the strenuous consideration of fragmentary evidence to the reader.[37] We can observe these omissions, and consequently the almost tidal ebb and flow of Browne's undogmatic considerations, in a passage from *Urne-Buriall*:

Severe contemplators observing these lasting reliques, may think them good monuments of persons past, little advantage to future beings; and, considering that power which subdueth all things unto it self, that can resume the scattered Atomes, or identifie out of any thing, conceive it superfluous to expect a resurrection out of Reliques. But the soul subsisting, other matter clothed with due accidents may salve the individuality: Yet the Saints we observe arose from graves and monuments, about the holy City. Some think the ancient Patriarchs so earnestly desired to lay their bones in *Canaan*, as hoping to make a part of that Resurrection, and though thirty miles from Mount *Calvary*, at least to lie in that Region, which should produce the first-fruits of the dead. And if according to learned conjecture,

[34] The single exception in Browne's work is the late *Repertorium* (*c.* 1680), a pedestrian rehearsal of the monuments in Norwich Cathedral, which he had seen sacked in the early 1640s (see Chapter Two). It is a measure of the difference between Dugdale's thought and Browne's that, when Browne tries to do what Dugdale does, the result is flat and lifeless.

[35] See Morris Croll, 'Attic Prose', 69; R. F. Jones calls Browne's style 'swelling' and 'exotic' ('Science and English Prose Style, 1650–1675' in *Seventeenth-Century Prose: Modern Essays in Criticism*, ed. Stanley E. Fish (New York: Oxford University Press), 67–71); the longstanding but quite groundless contention that Browne was denied membership of the Royal Society for stylistic reasons is also supported by Jones. See also Warren, 674–87; and Robert Adolph, *The Rise of Modern Prose Style* (Cambridge, MA: Harvard University Press, 1968), 153.

[36] On Bacon's aphoristic style, see Anne Righter, 'Francis Bacon', reprinted in *Essential Articles for the Study of Francis Bacon*, ed. Brian Vickers (Hamden, CT: Archon Books, 1968), 300–21.

[37] Daniela Havenstein regards this feature of Browne's writing as 'the perfect frame' for his 'predilection for analogies . . . one of the cornerstones of his conception of the world' (110).

the bodies of men shall rise where their greatest Reliques remain, many are not like to erre in the Topography of their Resurrection, though their bones or bodies be after translated by Angels into the field of *Ezechiels* vision, or as some will order it, into the Valley of Judgement, or *Jehosaphat*. (*U-B* III, 157)

This passage is governed by conceptions of the past and the future as they were manipulated and understood by Biblical individuals concerned with the post-mortem fate of the body and the soul; and these conceptions are taken up and rejected in equal measure by the enquiring Browne, whose rhythm of thought is fluid and conjectural rather than fixed and unqualified. The theologically rigorous ('severe contemplators'), he begins, only honour remains as monuments of what has been, deeming any merely human conception of the futurity of corporeal remains in partial, full, or figurative resurrection to be unprofitable – a 'folly of diuturnity', as Browne might have put it, since God arranges the afterlife of relics wholly mysteriously and as He pleases. Reliquary arrangements, he admits under these terms, can have no reference to anything but human record. One imagines Dugdale himself to have been the type of this attitude, eager to honour – and to retain – what exists rather than to imagine what is lost or to come.

But, Browne observes contradictorily (and almost digressively) in the next part of the passage, bones – especially skulls – can preserve physiognomy; they may 'salve the individuality', a comment arising almost certainly from his naturalist's and physician's experience (*U-B* III, 157). Not exactly a refutation of the severe contemplators, such countenances are nevertheless not the kind of 'monument' they would have been thinking of. And in the next remark, beginning with 'yet', the rhetorical energy changes direction suddenly: the Bible (Matthew 27:52–3) gives a very explicit account of bodily resurrection when 'the saints' (the ancient patriarchs to be mentioned shortly afterwards) rose up out of their graves at the resurrection of Christ. With this evidence, Browne seems abruptly to deny the view of the severe contemplators in the first sentence by exemplifying bodily resurrection from the most reliable of all sources. Indeed, he adds, so persuaded of the likelihood of this particular futurity of the body and soul were the patriarchs that they insisted on being buried in a particular spot in Hebron, thirty miles from Mount Calvary, 'to lie in that Region, which should produce the first-fruits of the dead',[38] as if apprised of the salvationary event some day to take place there. The resurrection of entire bodies, Browne asserts,

---

[38] Dugdale uses the burials of Abraham's family, and indeed of many of the antique personages cited by Browne, for exactly the opposite purpose: to 'prove' the 'high regard, which the Ancients have had to decent and honourable sepulture'. Indeed, publishing in the same year as *Urne-Buriall*, Dugdale's account of funerary tradition could not be more unlike Browne's: the commemorands of pyramids and other monuments, though 'of this life they make small account . . . but that which after death is joyned with a glorious memory of virtue, they highly value' (*History of St Paul's*, 42, 44).

is likely to occur 'where their greatest Reliques remain', a suggestion wholly at odds by this point with the tenor of the original sentence. But then he observes that bones do not usually wander ('erre') from their place of burial anyway, and so remain intact at the site of their eventual resurrection. This proposition – that relics are fixed and coherent – entirely contradicts his own remarks to Le Gros in the dedication, that many relics 'seem to have wandred far' (*U-B*.LeGros, 131), and is an unexpected conclusion from an essayist centrally concerned with the inefficacy of sepulture, our *in*ability to guarantee the quiet of our bones. But this is, of course, *not* a conclusion, for he then changes tack again, allowing that some bones may after all be 'translated by Angels' to 'the field of *Ezechiels* vision, or . . . the Valley of Judgement, or *Jehosaphat*'. What such a figurative translation might be is difficult to say. Ezekiel's vision and Joel's prophecy (the Valleys of Bones and of Jehosaphat or Judgement) are predictive, spectral, not (yet) actual or real, epistemically different both from the actual decays of the grave and from the promised resumption of the dead into heaven. These two valleys are metaphorical renditions of an unimaginable event (the resurrection of the dead leading to the Last Judgement), itself unactualised. Although the Valley of Judgement is in fact at the northern tip of the Dead Sea, in Joel's prophecy this real place becomes a fantastic arena of genocide against the Canaanites, of Israelite reconvening, and of a paradisial landscape of milk and wine. Ezekiel's valley of bones, on the other hand, is never geographically specified, because it doesn't exist except in metaphor. Whatever this translation amounts to, Browne has moved away from notions of physical relocation of relics and into a territory of imagined, prophesied, and wholly fictive geography.

The passage doesn't, therefore, read as a coherent statement, nor is it designed to be one. The allusion to 'severe' contemplators seems deliberately emphatic, but the assurance of such opinion is instantly gainsaid by the to-and-fro of the passage itself. This rhythm is achieved by following its initial proposal with competitive or qualifying conjunctions: 'and . . . But . . . Yet . . . And . . . though . . . or'.[39] There is a difficulty with received authority, too: the allusion to 'severe contemplators', 'learned conjecture', and two separate opinions held by the anonymous 'some', together with Matthew and the editorial opinion of 'we [observe]', make it impossible to assign relative weight to any remark other than the Scriptural one. Instead, the passage presents its ideas as a turning over of often mutually opposed possibilities, equally promulgated and denied by an unspecified cast

---

[39] Morris Croll ('The Baroque Style in Prose' in *Style, Rhetoric, and Rhythm*, ed. J. Max Patrick *et al.* (Princeton: Princeton University Press, 1966), 221–2) identifies these as 'coordinating conjunctions', a feature of baroque prose; but see Havenstein's comments on Croll (Havenstein, 104–19).

of learned voices, almost re-enacting the errant history of relics in its shift-ing propositions, atomising our sense of certainty like death itself. That the disposition of remains should not concern us is a statement quickly coun-tered by evidence that it should, and that it *did* concern Biblical figures. That bones can at best indicate past history is contested by the thought that skulls actually show us the soul or inward nature of the individual. Whole bodily resurrection, as we know from Donne preaching in 1620, only partly relies on the stability of remains: 'Shall I imagine a difficulty in my body', he asks, 'because I have lost an arm in the east, and a leg in the north, and some bones in the south? . . . [He] that sits in heaven, and spans all the world, . . . reunites in an instant arms, and legs, blood, bones, in what corners so ever they be scattered.'[40] Bones can be gathered up by God, or, as Browne adds, they may be moved by angels to places entirely outside the epistemological framework of actual graves, to within unspecified and so far inexistent prophetic places. Browne doesn't even permit the vision-ary Valley of Bones its own stable purchase within the book of Ezekiel: he admits that it may in fact be merely an alternative description of the place and event in the book of Joel.[41]

The notion of an ascertainable or predictable – or even a contingent – future is here being toyed with, moved about back and forth. The apparent polemical confusion of this passage imitates the commixture of uniden-tified bones he discovers in the Walsingham urns and in human burial practices in general. Here we observe a Pyrrhonist Browne managing the conjectural open-endedness of intellectual and rhetorical positions as a cento of possibilities and instances, stitched together or convened under the heading of resurrection; moreover, the necessity imposed on his reader to put a position or an opinion together from the competing materials he offers bears an analogical resemblance to the act of reconvening attributed to God at the moment of resurrection, and imitated by the investigating antiquarian.

Although Browne does not regard himself as an antiquarian ('we are coldly drawn unto discourses of Antiquities', he insists), and would not have entered upon such a task were it not that he is eager to do civilly by the urns themselves, 'unwilling they should die again, and be buried twice

[40] John Donne, 'A Sermon Preached at Lincolns Inne', [?Easter Term, 1620] on the text 'And though after my skin worms destroy this body, yet in my flesh shall I see God' (Job 19:26) (*John Donne: Selected Prose*, ed. Neil Rhodes (Harmondsworth: Penguin, 1987), 166). For a more recent comic send-up of whole-body resurrection, see Mark Twain, *The Innocents Abroad* (New York: New American Library, 1966), 216.

[41] According to the 'learned conjecture' of Jacobus Tirinus's annotation of Ezekiel 37 in *Biblia Magna* (Paris, 1644), cited by Browne in a marginal note to this passage.

among us' (*U-B*.LeGros, 132), he speaks in *Urne-Buriall* as one antiquary to another, and the dedicatory letter to Le Gros is framed in the discourse of exchange, collection, and assemblage. To deliver the Walsingham urns by civil discourse to his friend is to fulfil the duties of the 'cooperative advancer' and perform the reparation of a shattered, buried truth. Le Gros, he acknowledges, a great collector in his own right, is unlikely to be especially excited by the unexceptional Walsingham urns; none the less, he goes on to say, they will prompt his thought to run upon 'the ancient of dayes, the Antiquaries truest object' (*U-B*.LeGros, 132). The discourse of urns will not promote these specimens in particular; instead, it will catalogue in a meaningful array the examples of obsequial practice in categories and ranges most apt to discover pattern. The Browne-Dugdale and the (implied) Browne–Le Gros exchanges are in this respect quite distinct. Although each exchange is civil, a part of the selfless exchange economy of the republic of letters, and each is concerned with the reliquary and the buried, the Conington fish *is* individually significant to Dugdale, who presents it to Browne as a marvel whose meaning and history (including the history of its discovery by Cotton) are likely to be remarkable; however, Browne's speculative response appears to dilute these qualities by running through so many possibilities of origin, all without hierarchical weight, and reducing the fishbone to a *type* of find. This is probably the source of Dugdale's anxiety about authenticity. The Walsingham urns which are Browne's nominal subject in *Urne-Buriall* are also a type, specifically demoted from singularity and wonder from the outset, even wearily derogated as 'sad and sepulchral Pitchers, which have no joyful voices' (*U-B*.LeGros, 131); and yet they stand as figures or types of resurrection, of whole bodies unearthed, risen from the grave. This subtly harmonised pair of readings of the urns – as dreary and sad and yet raised from the earth and pieced together – is prefigured by Browne in the address to Le Gros, in which the dedicatee is imagined as himself a 'Gemme of the Old Rock', a living piece of earth and a relic of older and better days (*U-B*.LeGros, 133).

Dr Browne notes that 'to preserve the living, and make the dead to live, ... is not impertinent unto our profession' (*U-B*.LeGros, 132). Making the dead to live, resurrection by physic, is analogised as the preserve, too, of the antiquarian, the restorer of moribund knowledge. In *Religio Medici*'s Augustinian account of the resurrection, God will call out the scattered dust of all created beings, the dilated sperm of Adam (*RM* 1.48, 51), and reconvene whole bodies from fragments. The resurrectionary vision of Ezekiel (twice specifically cited (*U-B* iii, 152 and 157) and at many other moments alluded to in *Urne-Buriall* (*U-B* ii, 140, and iii, 151) in which a valley of bones is reconstituted as entire bodies is, as I argued in Chapter One, an essentially orderly conception of the afterlife in which the theological notion of cleansing and purification produces its material analogue in the putting in order, and almost domestic economy, of systematic antiquarian array. God at the last trump, and the antiquarian imitating God, sort and rearrange the world's clutter; relics of all categories are put into their rightful places and systems. Browne considers 'two pounds of bones, distinguishable in skulls, ribs, jawes, thigh-bones, and teeth' (*U-B* 11, 140), and the 'suspected . . . mixture of bones' (*U-B* 111, 151) in the Walsingham urns, in the light of Ezekiel's 'hopefull draughts, and hinting imagery of the Resurrection' (*U-B* 111, 152).[42]

ENGLISH ANALECTA: CENTOS, REMAINS, AND ANTIQUARIES

If Browne's approach to the antiquarian project, the 'redemption of truth' (*PE*.Reader, 2), is primarily chaological and eschatological, that reassuring, housekeeperly vision of the Last Judgement has also a less cheering aspect. In an important passage of the dedicatory letter to Le Gros, Browne shows that such mustering of divided fragments is at best a sad post-lapsarian duty:

Tis opportune to look back upon old times, and contemplate our Forefathers. Great examples grow thin, and to be fetched from the passed world. Simplicity flies away, and iniquity comes at long strides upon us. We have enough to do to make up our selves from present and passed times, and the whole stage of things scarce serveth for our instruction. A compleat peece of vertue must be made up from the *Centos* of all ages, as all the beauties of *Greece* could make but one handsome Venus. (*U-B*.LeGros, 132)

The cento is an anthology or patchwork. Thinking back to the physical and typographical arrays of early-modern compiling discussed in the previous chapter – cabinets of curiosity, natural history collections, museums, encyclopaedias, and catalogues – the cento is the literary equivalent of those anthologies of things.[43] It is also thus an apt figure for Browne's abiding sense of the doubtful, necessary project of restoring decayed knowledge.

---

[42] Although the Old Testament writer of Ezekiel would have had no conception of resurrection, the Christian reading of the episode is quite clear from Browne's remarks. Bosio describes a pillar in the Vatican cemetery carved with Ezekiel's vision: '*S. Ambrosie . . . afferma parimente che quella visione fù mostrata al Profeta, acciò che facesse a noi testimonio certo della futura resurrettione*' (619) [St Ambrose . . . declares likewise that that vision was shown to the prophet so that he would make sure testimony of the future resurrection]. It may be this description to which Browne refers in *U-B* 111, 152.

[43] The cento, a late-classical form, was a jigsaw composition consisting of quotations from other works. 'Cento' became a more general term in English, where it means anything pieced together.

This metaphor of the cento, of risky reconstitution, although a governing idea in most of his work, is most extensively elaborated by Browne in *Urne-Buriall*, the work which is a cento about centos. A work which enacts its own subject, *Urne-Buriall* in arguing the fruitlessness of antiquarian enquiry offers a sparkling, finished array of recovered facts which only adds up to its own demolition. With its energetic hybridity, its imposition of orderly design on items distinctly foreign to each other and often incomplete in themselves, the cento is a work whose very structure betrays itself as fragmentary, much as an urn in shards pieced together by the restorer is the remarkable, but imperfect, type of the undamaged original. Browne notes that ancient brass items, retrieved from underground and 'exposed unto the piercing atoms of air, . . . begin to spot and betray their green entrails' (*U-B* III, 150), their decay and destruction beginning with their discovery. Curiosity, the primary human fault, paradoxically both repairs and ruins its objects, and in its mended productions calls attention to that damage. The antiquarian and the investigator are implicated in this curiosity. The darker regions of enquiry, where 'the attempts of some have been so precipitous, and their enquiries so audacious as to come within command of the flaming swords' (*PE* I.v.30), seem contiguous with those of Satan himself, the original of curiosity.

Browne reminds us that the Canaanitish woman, the good thief, the founder of the pyramids, and the architect of Diana's temple are unnamed, predicated, generically remembered, yet anonymous; likewise, the blessed ignorance of the past and its evils is in compensation 'a mercifull provision' by which 'our sorrows are not kept raw by the edge of repetitions' (*U-B* v, 168). In this respect the recuperation of the past may not be risk-free: if reminiscential evocation restores innocent knowledge, the mercy of forgetting is compromised by reminiscence. Browne's attitude here to the subject of investigation is thus highly equivocal. The penalty of curiosity is destruction; that of reminiscence, remorse. Like the oxidising brass, '[t]o be unknown was the means of their continuation', he says of the Walsingham urns, 'obscurity their protection' (*U-B* v, 164). 'Happy are they whom privacy makes innocent' (*U-B* v, 170). He frames his discourse of rediscovery as an examination of hazard.

To appreciate the unusually witty and imaginative quality of this position, we should be aware of how some of Browne's predecessors and contemporaries framed their own salvage efforts. Very few practitioners of the nascent disciplines on display in *Urne-Buriall* – proto-archaeology and proto-anthropology, etymology, genealogy, palaeontology – had quite Browne's relish for the uncertain, the heavily qualified. More typically, as promoters of the established order (especially when this was perceived

as threatened, as in the 1630s and 40s by Dugdale, but also during periods of national triumphalism, as in the late-Elizabethan era of Camden's
great works), antiquarian projects tended toward preservation of the status
quo, or of a glorious past concentrating on monuments, heritage, titles,
and so on; it is not coincidental that Camden, Weever, Dugdale, Ashmole,
and some of the other antiquarians were also heralds, preeminently the
chroniclers of apparently unimpeachable heritage. Others, however, also
contributed: Richard White still argued for the Galfridian Brutus-Arthur
myths in the late-sixteenth century; the Roman origin of Stonehenge was
being insisted upon by Inigo Jones in the 1620s, and its British origin
as Boadicea's burial place by Edmund Bolton in 1624; William of
Malmesbury's assertion of the introduction of Christianity into Britain
by Joseph of Arimathea was argued by Sir Henry Spelman in *Concilia*
(1639); and Aylett Sammes, in 1676, was promoting the early colonisation
of Britain by the Phoenicians and Greeks. Browne himself seems to credit
the myth of an early giant race in Britain when he refers to neolithic burial
mounds as the graves of giants (*U-B* 1, 135).

William Camden's *Britannia* (1586) and *Remaines concerning Britaine*
(1605) are the magisterial grandparents to much seventeenth-century antiquarian investigation; all seventeenth-century English antiquaries have
what seems like a genetic link to Camden either as his protégés or his
patrons.[44] Browne, like all the others, is much indebted: Camden's investigative methods, his participation in networks of intellectual exchange,
and his speculative disposition are all features imitated and referred to by
Browne. Camden is both an inter-cooperative and an *intra*-cooperative
polymath, generating and generous among his large circle of colleagues
and contacts, and one whose own many parts transgenerate to produce new understanding, a model of learning in which the branches of
knowledge, and the possessor of knowledge himself, behave like a civil
society.[45] Camden's personal qualities and his public works are in spirit a
template for Browne's in the next generation.

---

[44] Camden taught Robert Cotton at Westminster School; Cotton's friends included Henry Spelman,
John Selden, Thomas Bodley, and Thomas Coryate; Camden's friends on the Continent included
Peiresc and Jan Gruter. His protégé Augustine Vincent became in turn John Weever's mentor and
introduced him to Cotton. Vincent's papers were used by Dugdale, who helped the aged Selden to
organise some of the Cottonian manuscripts; Dugdale eventually became a herald whose son-in-law
was Elias Ashmole. Dugdale was acquainted with Browne and Aubrey, and Aubrey would encourage
the efforts of Thomas Tanner and his colleagues as they worked on the great revised edition of
Camden's *Britannia* (1695).

[45] D. R. Woolf describes this as the 'tendency in the Renaissance mind which allowed it to apply
insights borrowed from one sphere of knowledge to problems presented by another' (*The Idea
of History in Early Stuart England: Erudition, Ideology, and 'The Light of Truth' from the Accession
of James I to the Civil War* (Toronto: University of Toronto Press, 1990), 24).

In certain respects Camden also suggests the inherent fragility of the antiquarian, reconstructive project to which his own *Britannia* contributed so much. Although the nationalist antiquarian enterprise attempts to establish a credible and worthy past for England – 'to restore antiquity to Britaine, and Britaine to antiquity',[46] or, more precisely, an originary story which will explain and enhance contemporary British greatness – his dedication of *Remains* to Cotton describes this work as 'rude rubble and out-cast rubbish . . . of a greater and more serious work',[47] as if (as he reminds us in the epitaph *quavis terra sepulchram*) the world is itself a ruin, a grave, and so too man's works within it. *Britannia* itself had reconvened some of these fragments, but is still by his own reckoning no more than scraps, flotsam saved from shipwreck on the 'craggy rocks of antiquity'.[48] *Remains* is presented even more explicitly as a charnel-house of odds and ends apparently unassimilable within the attempted larger structure of the earlier and greater work. His excavational project is 'to seek, rake out, and free from darkness' the true history of Britain.[49]

Browne only faintly and peripherally engages with the patriotic project, but Camden anticipates Browne's relaxed approach to certainty, and this is, in antiquarian terms, a daring recognition of incompletion, of investigative failure. The discovery of fortuitous and potentially discomfiting evidence of an English history wholly unlike the prevalent received and preferred versions forced English antiquarianism into the sometimes unwilling recognition of a primitive British past, rather than a glorious Arthurian or Trojan one.[50] Camden is well aware that, even if according to Varro noble fictions like the Arthurian or the Brutus myths promote greatness in a people who claim such antecedants, the Galfridian story of a Trojan connexion for Britain is specious, and moreover that the true history of early Britain will be almost impossible to verify by ordinary documentary methods because those times were uncivil and unlettered, unable 'to preserve the memorie of things, and to make over the same to the succeeding ages'.[51] By a cagey rhetorical sleight-of-hand he manages to introduce the Brutus story in great detail while citing neutrally all its learned discreditors, thereby having his mythographic cake and eating it. '*Let* Brutus be taken for the father, and founder of the British nation', he declares with a wily jussive; 'I will not be of a contrarie minde' [my emphasis].[52] The

---

46 William Camden, *Britannia* (1586), trans. Philemon Holland (1610), *4ʳ.
47 Camden, *Remains*, 3. It is clear, however, that *Remains* is in fact a separate and coherent work and was so planned. See R. D. Dunn's comments in Camden, *Remains*, xvii–xviii.
48 Camden, *Britannia* [Scotland], 233.   49 Camden, *Britannia*, *5ʳ.
50 See Parry, 289–92; Stuart Piggott, *Ancient Britons and the Antiquarian Imagination: Ideas from the Renaissance to the Regency* (London: Thames and Hudson, 1989), 31, 58–86; and Woolf, 244.
51 Camden, *Britannia*, 4.   52 Camden, *Britannia*, 8.

glitter of Troy which gives competitive lustre to British origins on a par with Aeneas in Rome or Francio in Gaul is too politically attractive and useful a metaphor of Englishness to be wholly dispensed with, however unsound it may be according to antiquarian evidence and judgement. This is a case of partial antiquarian compliance with patriotic mythography, but also suggests an understanding of the merely anecdotal and folkloric as itself worthy of record, and of the historiography of Englishness, in English ideas about origins and nationhood, as itself part of English history. Although it had been proposed already by Polydore Vergil, Camden was the first English historian to acknowledge the vigour of Britain's pre-Roman aboriginals, eager as he is to establish imperial Roman credentials for his nation. This recognition is one at least partially adopted by Browne.

Camden, like Browne, is excavating in the darkness of British history by examination of material, as well as documentary, remains – graves, bones, and coins, as well as 'libraries, registers, memorials in churches . . . *Evidence*' [my emphasis][53] – and, of equal importance, by examination of the immaterial remains of language, philological fossils, so to speak, in the manner of Scaliger, his great French contemporary whose philological reconstruction of old texts and documents was a relatively new way of reclaiming the past for literary, philosophical, theological, and political purposes.[54] Like Scaliger, who copied out the inscriptions on fragmentary Roman ruins,[55] Camden records (often comical) English epitaphs from monuments and remains, but he is concerned also with speculative evidence when documents and material remains are not available, as in the case of the ancient Britons: '*Plato*, in his *Cratilus* commandeth that we recall the originalls of names to the barbarous tongues . . . as being most ancient. I thereupon in my Etymologies and my coniectures have made recourse to the British, or Welsh tongue . . . as being the same which the primitive and most ancient inhabitants of this land used, and to the English-Saxon tongue which our Progenitours the English spake.'[56] British and 'English-Saxon' have declined into a modern English with fragments of its originals atomised or buried within it. For Camden etymology is a kind of ghostly evidence, the sepulchral remains of a greater linguistic whole now decayed and scattered in modern usage and in place-names. Language itself is a ruin, an antiquity; epigraphy and speech – artefacts both – are Camden's evidentiary materials. Epigraphy, place-names, and the like are subjects,

[53] Camden, *Britannia*, *4^r.
[54] Anthony Grafton, *Joseph Scaliger: A Study in the History of Classical Scholarship*, 2 vols. (Oxford: Clarendon Press, 1983), 1, 37–42.
[55] Grafton 1, 119.   [56] Camden, *Britannia*, *4^v.

too, of Browne's writings.[57] His philological impulse, however, is elided, as Camden's is not, with 'natural' antiquarianism (to use Hooke's phrase): as Conrad Gesner and other naturalists prefaced their discussions with nomenclatural assessments of synonymy and etymology in their search for analogous phenomena in the classical writers, so Browne's ornithological correspondence with a fellow naturalist like Christopher Merrett is taken up with coining a correct Latin or Greek nomenclature.[58]

Not to be deflected by the 'mint-masters' who forge etymologies with their 'merry playing with words',[59] Camden, as Browne does later in laying out the ancient past of East Anglia, tries to establish relationships between the ancient 'primitive' languages of Britain and northern France, as well as the family relationship of 'English-Saxon' to various old Germanic tongues. This becomes a kind of linguistic archaeology which explains the name of Wandlebury, the Iron Age hillfort near Cambridge, and the origin of the tribal name 'Scot'.[60] Browne employs this strategy in *Urne-Buriall* when he somewhat desperately derives the ancient British tribal name 'Iceni' from the Greek '*iken*' or elbow ('*iken*' from, he says, the Biblical 'Anconia' (*U-B*11, 141–2)).[61] John Weever, who uses Camden's etymological technique energetically but less scrupulously, derives 'sepulchre' from 'semi-pulcher, half fair and beautiful; the external part or superficies thereof being gloriously beautified and adorned; and having nothing within but dreadful darkness, loathesome stink, and rottenness of bones'.[62] Browne is sincerely, if erroneously, straining after lexical origins; Weever, on the other hand, would certainly know that 'sepulchre' comes from the Latin *sepelire, sepultus*, 'to bury', which suggests a deliberate manipulation of etymological origins for rhetorical purposes.

Indeed, Weever is the typical, Camden-inspired but generally unimaginative English antiquarian against whom Browne must be judged. Like Camden's *Remains*, Weever's *Ancient Funerall Monuments* (1631) surveys epitaphs as a way of ascertaining reliable, stable reliquary fact. But where Camden seems to be charmed by the peculiar or the whimsical sepulchral

---

[57] Etymology, as Anthony Grafton notes, was one of the most fashionable of sixteenth-century studies, with Scaliger as the model and master in his conjectural reconstructions of ancient texts and of Latin and Greek linguistic history by reference to Near-Eastern philology (Grafton 1, 117).

[58] See Rudwick, 6.

[59] For example, *money* from 'my-honey'; *flatter* from 'fly-at-her'; and *maid* from 'my-aid' (Camden, *Remains*, 35).

[60] Camden, *Britannia*, 114 and 121. Spenser makes use of the interesting 'Scythian' etymology of 'Scot' in his *View of the Present State of Ireland* (*c.* 1598), where the Scythian (i.e., regrettably barbarian) heritage of the Irish is attributed to the Scottish/Scythian influence (Edmund Spenser, *A View of the State of Ireland*, ed. Andrew Hadfield and Willy Maley (Oxford: Blackwell, 1997), 45–6).

[61] The root is of course Celtic, not Greek. See Wilkin 111, 463.   [62] Weever, 9.

epigram, possibly to propose a peculiar genius of English expression, or to have an oblique scoff at obsequial pretensions, Weever ignores or censors the eccentric or the comic in his account.[63] He clearly expects monuments to function as serious and irrefutable social records, and he would not have been amused, as Browne is, by the survival of the tomb of Hadrian's horse. He is deeply (and humourlessly) exercised by the failure of record detectable in modern obsequies. Distinction of rank, for example, is not so nicely observed as it once was, with 'a rich quondam tradesman or griping usurer' entombed with more honour than potentates, one of many 'great errors . . . daily committed . . . and nothing will be left to continue the memory of the deceased to posterity'.[64] In monuments, Weever wants to repose not only corpses, but also the very fabric of society, whose desuetude antiquarian labour would forfend. Makers of inadequate monuments, like 'some varlet philosophers, as Diogenes, who desired to be devoured of fishes',[65] attract the derision of many antiquaries; for Weever, though, the failure of record is a pernicious outrage which beckons toward social anarchy. Like Dugdale, Weever is an efficient but plodding recorder rather than any kind of speculator, and he is dismayed by exactly the sorts of confusion Browne likes best. Thus there are, in studies of monuments, apparently two discrete teleologies: one type expects the monumental to preserve evidence, and seeks to assist that preservation; the other exercises reconstitutive speculation on the incomplete or illegible, and meditates on the obliterative properties of time itself. The first yields chronologies and surveys; the second does not.

The antiquarian closest in spirit to the more ample genetic line established between Camden and Browne, the line which honours and eagerly seeks out and records the eccentric, the whimsical, the imprecise, and the mysterious, is John Aubrey. Aubrey's well-known interest in neolithic stone circles and related structures, in combination with his energetic (and often far-fetched) etymologising, leads him into a snakes-and-ladders world of evidence. Visiting a number of barrows in France in 1664, Aubrey describes and draws them, aware that they are at least visually cognate: 'I have arranged these monuments together, for the near resemblance they have to

---

[63] Camden offers the following among many: 'One stone sufficeth (loe what death can doe)/ Her that in life was not content with two' (Camden, *Remains*, 358). With this honourable exception, a deficient sense of humour may be the occupational hazard of heralds. If, as has been waggishly observed, heraldry is the only *exact* science, it may explain the modern response of the 21st-century College of Arms, which, receiving the application for arms from a newly ennobled cinephile and Clint Eastwood *aficionado* who wanted his motto to be *Perge, scelus, mihi diem perficias* ('Go ahead, punk, make my day'), translated it in puzzlement as 'Proceed, varlet, and let the day be rendered perfect for my benefit' (private communication of Sir Christopher Frayling).

[64] Weever, 10, 17–18.   [65] Camden, *Remains*, 317.

one another.'[66] But a too-nimble ear and eye for likeness also yields completely uninformed conclusions: Slaughterford, near Bristol, he says, gets its names from a bloody battle with the Danes, and the vulnerary herb locally known as Dane's Blood 'sprang from the blood of the Danes shed there in battle'.[67] Dragon Hill, part of the site of the White Horse of Uffington, is so called because Uther Pendragon fought here against the Saxons and was perhaps slain.[68] All this folkloric supposition is based on over-reliance upon fortuitous but insignificant aural likenesses, a problem to which even Browne (a better philologist than Aubrey) is not always immune.

Where Aubrey is especially like Browne is in his attention to the contemporary, the observable, to physical and behavioural artefacts. Folk beliefs – corpse-candles, soul-cakes, anecdotal curses attached to certain great Wiltshire houses, and other country practices – occupy equal place with observations in natural history.[69] It is Aubrey, combining geology and philology, who notices that place-names with the Saxon phoneme *chilt* are always in chalky regions, and imagines 'a Mapp of England painted according to the Colours of the Earth, and marks of Mineralls'.[70] Like Browne, Aubrey is virtually unrestricted in the range of his enquiry, bringing to his studies of objects and natural history the investigative approach of his philological and textual expertise, and vice versa.[71] Antiquities, as Shakerley Marmion's antiquary declares, 'speak the truth of history better than a hundred of your printed commentaries',[72] and Browne must be understood as tending toward an Aubrey-like natural-historical antiquarianism from a solidly Camdenian base of classical and philological learning.

It will not do, on the other hand, to imagine Browne as purely, or even similarly, artefactual in the sense of the modern archaeologist, or even in the mode of Aubrey, who, only a generation younger, did excavate. It is enough to suggest that Browne is different from contemporary antiquarians not only in allowing the artefactual as the equivalent of the documentary into the realm of evidence, but also in accepting at times that objects

---

[66] John Aubrey, *Monumenta Britannica*, ed. John Fowles and Rodney Legg, 2 vols. (Sherborne: Dorset Publishing Co., 1982), II, 800.

[67] Aubrey, *Monumenta Britannica* II, 806. 'Slaughter', if from Old English *sleaht*, indicates the vicinity of an abattoir, but the name is even more likely to be derived from 'sloe-tree ford'.

[68] Aubrey, *Monumenta Britannica* II, 820.

[69] John Aubrey, *The Natural History of Wiltshire*, ed. John Britton (London: Wiltshire Topographical Society/ J. B. Nichols, 1848), [119]; and John Aubrey, *Remaines of Gentilisme and Judaisme* (1688?) in his *Three Works*, ed. John Buchanan-Brown (Fontwell: Centaur, 1972), 172, 181.

[70] Aubrey, 'Chorographia super et Subterranea Naturalis' in *Observations* in *Three Works*, 311–13.

[71] Aubrey's modern editor takes care to correlate Aubrey's books and objects as co-equal in his collection of 'reliques' (Kate Bennett, 215–16).

[72] Shakerley Marmion, *The Antiquary* in *Dodsley's Old English Plays*, ed. Carew Hazlitt, 15 vols. (London, 1875), XIII, 449 (Act 2 Scene 1).

outweigh texts in authority and authenticity. With his severely qualified reversion to textual authority – a qualification so robustly presented in the first chapters of *Pseudodoxia Epidemica* – Browne is concerned precisely with the failure of documentation, including the epigraphic, the incompleteness or incorrectness of surviving textual sources, both as an aesthetic of loss and as a project of reparation. This aesthetic is a developing antiquarian theme which Browne, of all his contemporaries, most completely adopts and colonises. He does this most elaborately in *Urne-Buriall*, and it is as artfully manipulated, as I shall propose in the next chapter, in *Musæum Clausum*.

OF URNS AND EPITAPHS: THE STRUCTURES OF *URNE-BURIALL*

In *Urne-Buriall*'s dedicatory letter to Thomas Le Gros, Browne mingles two of his favourite themes: after-discovery and reliquary dispersion. The buried plank and the corpse wrapped in an ox-hide of his own day remind us that men of ancient times little expected 'the curiosity of future ages should comment upon their ashes, and having no old experience of the duration of their Reliques, held no opinion of such after-considerations' (*U-B*.LeGros, 131). Such remains will give future investigators 'roome to guesse', in Aubrey's phrase.[73] Urns and bones lie in all parts of the earth, Browne says, and tend to scatter themselves, or be scattered, over time: Pompey's relics – his own remains and those of his sons – are spread over Asia, Europe, and Africa; Theseus died in Skyros but his bones were moved, generations later, back to Athens.[74] The anonymous individuals in the Walsingham urns are themselves far from Rome, their putative home;[75] many, it seems, are indeed 'like to erre in the Topography of their Resurrection' (*U-B* III, 157).

The essay's structure and texture seem at first to replicate the antiquarian project of after-discovery and reassembly, to mend that dispersion in the brisk marshalling of facts into categories packed with iterative evidence from Browne's vast reading. *Urne-Buriall*'s five chapters ostensibly organise

---

[73] Quoted in Hunter, *John Aubrey*, 178.
[74] See Plutarch, *The Lives of the Noble Grecians and Romans*, trans. John Dryden (New York: The Modern Library, [n.d.]), 23.
[75] The urns were in fact Saxon, something which Browne almost suggests midway through the essay (*U-B* II, 145–6), but does not seriously follow up. If the ancient Britons had left – apparently – too little artefactual or documentary evidence of themselves to make a serious impression on antiquarians of the early seventeenth century, the Anglo-Saxon heritage of England, though evident, was too lowly to satisfy those who hoped for a glorious Roman past. Browne, who must certainly have been capable of recognising the true provenance of these finds, might have assigned the urns correctly had he been predisposed to think in those terms, but he wants them to be Roman and effectively blinds himself.

obsequial data in a clear pattern ascending from the physical to the metaphysical. The first chapter considers burial and burning in various societies, and Chapter 11 makes a Camden-like survey of the Walsingham urns and their situation in order to authenticate them as Roman. These two chapters dwell in artefactual and documentary particularity, and the experience of reading them is not unlike viewing a museum of serried urns and gravegoods, with rites and beliefs arrayed in patterns of contiguity which reveal similarity and antithesis.

An index of the structure of Chapter 1 might be represented thus:

Sepulture as a function of resurrection

The modes and reasons of sepultures

A. **Modes:**

1.) *Water* (the oldest form); source: the Bible (OT)
    example: the Flood

2.) *Inhumation* (the second-oldest form); source: the Bible (OT/NT)
    examples: a.) Adam
               b.) The patriarchs
               c.) Christ
               d.) The saints

3.) *Burning* (the most recent form); source: Homer
    examples: a.) Greece
               b.) Persia
               c.) The Near East
               d.) Western Europe
               e.) Rome
               f.) Carthage
               g.) America

B. **Reasons:**

1.) *Water:* Bodies should return to their original element (Thales)

2.) a.) *Fire:*
       i.) Bodies should return to the master principle (Heraclitus)
       ii.) Avoidance of corruption and vermin (Greek)
       iii.) Purification and release of 'aetherial particles' (no source)
       iv.) In expectation of a fiery apocalypse, bodies should end in fire (no source)
       v.) Avoidance of mutilation by enemies (Roman)
       vi.) Fire immortalises (Indian Brahmins)

2.) b.) *Reasons against fire:*
       i.) Chaldeans would not pollute their deity ⎫
       ii.) Persians would not pollute their deity ⎬ (idolators of fire)
       iii.) Parsees would not pollute their deity ⎭

3.) *Embalming*:

  i.) Egyptians } (were afraid of fire and preferred embalming)
  ii.) Pythagoreans

4.) *Other means*:

  i.) Exposure to air among Scythians (who were idolators of air)

  ii.) Sea-burial among Ichthyophagi (fish-eaters) 'restores the debt of their bodies [to the fishes]'

  iii.) Urn-burial *without burning* among:

    a.) Balearians (bodies and wood forced into urns)

    b.) Chinese (burning of effigies and draughts of servants, chattels, and bodies, but not of the dead themselves)

5.) *Interment*:

  i.) Christians (who wish to be whole at resurrection) (but burn people alive)

  ii.) Muslims (who wish to enter Paradise whole)

  iii.) Jews (who wish to be whole at resurrection, but who sometimes burn to avoid pestilence) (and are remarkably free of Egyptian and Roman influence)

C. **Conclusion:** Nature itself supplies precedents for interment, particularly among civil insects.

Parsing or dissecting this chapter of *Urne-Buriall* uncovers a striking patterned structure. Examples are set out, to use a recently proposed set of terms to describe cabinet-arrangement, as a mixture of 'alternating microsymmetry' (where like and unlike items alternate) and 'repeating macrosymmetry' (where objects are contiguously placed in thematic or epistemic categories).[76] A real cabinet like Ole Worm's tends toward repeating macrosymmetry, with the morphological class 'antlers and horns', for example, physically grouping oxen, deer, antelope, moose, and narwhal, as well as hunting horns and drinking horns – source and use indiscriminately yoked – and all these alternating vertically with the legs and horny feet of bisulcous ungulates.[77]

Similarly, 'Modes' of sepulture in *Urne-Buriall*'s first chapter are arranged from oldest to youngest, from Biblical to classical and modern, and exempla within each mode also form strict chronological patterns. This thematic, chronological structure produces, like the grouping of antlers in Worm's cabinet, a repeating macrosymmetry, where the same rubric of progression or likeness governs each section. 'Reasons' of sepulture, however, although

---

[76] For these terms, see Laurencich-Minelli, 19.

[77] These animals are grouped in the catalogue of the museum, however, by hoof-structure, rather than by horns.

its modal sub-categories are repeating, contains an alternating microsymmetric rhythm of reasons for and against burning in the 'fire' subsection. This alternation may subtly indicate the relative importance of cremation (the subject, after all, of *Urne-Buriall*) over the other modes. And within the justifications for burning (B.2.a), items i–vi move back and forth from the metaphysical to the physical, another form of alternation. Similarly, 'interment' offers a small alternating rhythm in (ironically?) pointing out the Christian propensity to burn living bodies but not dead ones, and the pragmatic Jewish practice of abandoning inhumation in favour of burning in times of pestilence. This schedule of practices also includes what in a physical cabinet would be included under 'non-descripts' – practices neither entirely one thing nor another, such as Balearian urnal interment without burning, or Chinese cremation of draughts and effigies but not of bodies. The chapter further organises the variety of practical arrangements for dead bodies, together with the reasoning behind the practices, from the first records. Beginning with a general statement that all burials of whatever style are shallow (the deepest 'scarce below the roots of some vegetables') and likely to be discovered, the mystical conclusion of *Urne-Buriall* emerges from purely functional images of the resurrection of bodies and urns from underground by antiquarian activity. Resurrection and re-emergence govern Browne's discussion from the outset; and this restorative vision itself arises out of an apparently rigorous, if subtle, ordering practice in which confusion and diversity are reorganised and arranged in comprehensible classes.

Traditional antiquaries like Dugdale begin their considerations at the Beginning, with drainage, as it might be, traced from God's convocation of the waters.[78] Browne, too, introduces his subject by presenting the earliest example of each burial practice. Water is first (the Flood made a grave for 'almost mankind and the living creation'); inhumation is next in antiquity, with the patriarchs selecting this means; finally, burning, only slightly less ancient, has Homeric origins, its popularity spreading (like the refugees of Troy) over the whole of the hemisphere from Greece and the 'inward countries of Asia' to the ancient western European peoples, the Romans, the Carthaginians, and the Americans. He moves on to the reasoning behind various practices, with water, fire, embalming, exposure in air, interment, and other methods laid out in sequence, the fire section including counter-examples from belief-systems which could not countenance cremation, and the interment section giving equivocal examples in the practices of the

---

[78] The Egyptians, he goes on to say, contending annually with the flooding of the Nile, are 'the first [human] Masters in this Art of Drayning' (Dugdale, *History of Imbanking and Drayning*, 1).

Jews and the Christians. He concludes that the modes of sepulture may be attributable to custom and culture, but may also have precedents in the animal kingdom, notably in social insects such as ants and bees, 'which civill society carrieth out their dead, and hath exequies, if not interrments' (*U-B* 1, 140), a commonplace already noted in *Religio Medici*.

In its patterning evidence, the overall scheme of *Urne-Buriall* looks like this:

   i Burial vs. burning in various epochs and cultures (factual/evidentiary)
  ii A Camden-esque identification and discussion of the Walsingham urns (factual/evidentiary)
 iii Recollective nuances of the grave; particulars of the Walsingham urns (factual/evidentiary moving toward transcendental/speculative)
  iv The theology of obsequial ceremonies (transcendental/speculative)
   v The vanity of monuments (transcendental/speculative)

Beginning with two chapters of straightforward evidence, Browne then substantially abandons strictly antiquarian methods; the concrete yields to the speculative, the imaginary, the middle chapter displaying a commixture of the observed and the speculated, with the grand thematic notes of order versus confusion and the vision of Ezekiel beginning to dilate the purely factual and evidentiary. Chapters iv and v, on the theology of funerary practices and on the futility of commemoration respectively, are millenarian discourses from another realm entirely: ideas of futurity – indeed, the doubtful possibility of any significant future in the last age of the world – mingle to discredit the very idea of monuments and memory.

In Chapter iii, which considers the recollective nuances of graves and begins to enlarge upon the melancholy anonymity of the Walsingham burials, Browne starts to think about what is *not* in these urns, and to draw out the first of his astonishing mortuary conceits. The excavation has yielded none of the implements, bottled wines, aromatic oils, or lachrymatories typical of other Roman burials, omissions which might have led him to suspect their non-Roman identity; instead, the thought of mortuary liquors distracts him from a correct Saxon conclusion, and prompts him instead to imagine that

if any have tasted [them], they have farre exceeded the Palats of Antiquity: liquors not to be computed by years of annuall Magistrates, but by great conjunctions and fatall periods of Kingdomes. The draughts of Consulary date were but crude unto these, and *Opimian* Wine but in the must unto them. (*U-B* iii, 149)

These absent liquors (technically, he asserts, wearing his naturalist's cap, 'incrassated into gellies' when discovered intact) elicit from him a rhapsody on a timeless vintage, a draught not to be tasted by any man living or dead. Hard sepulchral facts about the fate of the body – this, after all, is the chapter in which we hear that certain bodies coagulate into hard soapy lumps consisting of nitrous earth and the body's 'lixivious liquor' (*U-B* III, 156)[79] – shift into a fantasy about the very flavour of mortality. From this point on in *Urne-Buriall* Browne oscillates between the material and transcendental, with the historical resurrection of Christ and the patriarchs giving way to imaginary and even metaphorical resurrections in the valleys of Ezekiel and Joel; so that the penultimate chapter, on the theology of obsequial ceremony, moves inexorably into the fifth, a meditation on forgetfulness and resurrection, a meditation at this point almost aerially unmoored from dust, ashes, and the fragmentary relict. The vision of Ezekiel, an established leitmotif of *Urne-Buriall*, becomes the signature or emblem not only for mingled and confused remains but for the mingled and varied categories of thought and of evidence by which he considers the next world. The recognisable antiquarian structure on which he builds his opening chapters is one from which he can launch altogether less orderly, more speculative, entirely immaterial conceits which positively disrupt the neatly patterned materiality of the collection and the evidentiary antiquarian survey.

The discovery of the Walsingham urns – at least partly – allows the antiquarian Browne to exercise his resurrectionary powers on their contents. What Lucan, in Camden's phrase, 'scoffingly termed camps and cottages of carcasses'[80] suggests the domestic and other homely arrangements of the grave which so interest Browne. The word 'obliterate' means, literally, 'loss of letters',[81] and although he cannot assign them the obliterated identity which would 'reindividual' them and let these monuments really speak, he can try to assign national and cultural identity to them, and so judges them to have been of the colonial Roman upper class of the period 60–350 AD.[82] Depending in good antiquarian fashion on etymological evidence, Browne decides that the proximity of the Walsingham urns to Brancaster in Norfolk (originally Roman Branodunum) makes them probable Roman remains, with the nearby remains of an *ustrina*, a Roman pyral oven, further evidence of the urns' origin (*U-B* II, 141).

---

[79] Adipocere, as this substance is known, was first explained by Browne, and this is probably the only original analytical scientific contribution he made.
[80] Camden, *Remains*, 319.   [81] Noted by Barkan, 72.
[82] These dates are hardly precise, covering almost the entire colonial period in Britain.

In the next chapter he describes the shape of the urns:

[M]ost imitate a circular figure, in a sphericall and round composure; whether from any mystery, best duration or capacity, were but a conjecture. But the common form with necks was a proper figure, making our last bed like our first; nor much unlike the Urnes of our Nativity, while we lay in the nether part of the Earth, and inward vault of our Microcosm. (*U-B* III, 148)

The uterine shape of these urns, with their fallopian handles and cervical openings, offers him another resurrectionary device in the form of an almost absurd signature: that the vessel of interment should remind him of the vessel of gestation, that the foetus and the corpse share a strange situational likeness, is a more elaborated form of the old womb–tomb rhyme, here literalised. Camden, after all, tells us that 'the place of buriall was called by Saint Paul, Seminatio, in the respect of the assured hope of resurrection'.[83] And that an urn should be uterine has, perhaps, an even more oblique form, already hinted at in the designation of the *ustrina*. For Browne, the place of turning bodies into particles, and that other place of turning particles into bodies, are cognate. By a subterranean bit of semantic excavation, it is no very difficult leap for the enterprising etymologist to lose a medial 's' and connect 'ustr-' and 'uter-'.[84] The artefactual evidence, moreover, in the relatively exact physical description of the urns and of the oven, yields another of the circular tropes of death-to-life with which *Urne-Buriall* abounds: if Thales, believing water to have been 'the orginall of all things, thought it most equall to submit unto the principle of putrefaction, and conclude in a moist relentment' (*U-B* I, 137), other cultures, on the same principle of the 'answerings and analogies of things', developed pyral interment to allude to the fire of the end of the world.[85]

Graves are good history – that, at least, is the contention of the mainstream antiquarians, for whom the sturdier monuments, especially, are helpfully time-resistant. Browne concurs: although the burial of coins so commonly performed 'as a Fee of the *Elysian Ferry-man*' was, he says, 'a practice full of folly', nevertheless, he concedes that this is a 'laudable' practice enabling after-discovery to assign 'actions, persons, Chronologies; and posterity will applaud them' (*U-B* IV, 160). At the same time, however, the figures of erasure and effacement in *Urne-Buriall* are more powerful than anything such recollective specimens can accomplish. Browne, an enthusiastic numismatist, expert in dates and inscriptions, discusses in *Urne-Buriall* the difficulties of using coinage as evidence. He suggests that, unlike

---

[83] Camden, *Remains*, 319.   [84] There is, of course, no such connexion between these two words.
[85] Fairfax, I.

plentiful Roman coins, British specie – often no more than iron rings and other pieces – is probably now mistaken for something else than money, and even at the arrival of the Romans British money was insignificant and easily overlooked. Saxon coinage is also hard to trace because it was reused, passing 'into other stamps, and the marks of after ages' (*U-B* ii, 143). This effacement of coinage is introduced by reference to the Spartans, who voluntarily ruined their copper money for other use by corroding it in vinegar. Coinage, one of the few other enduring artefacts besides funerary monuments to resist the defacements of time, is not proof against the ravages of deliberate human agency.

Other images of erasure are common in *Urne-Buriall*. British burial practices, like British coinage, are difficult to determine because they were so thoroughly Romanised (*U-B* ii, 146). Grave-robbery has indiscriminately destroyed the sepulchral records of many peoples, especially carnal interments, particularly vulnerable to 'desecrations which are escaped by cremation':

To be gnaw'd out of our graves, to have our sculs made drinking-bowls, and our bones turned into Pipes, to delight and sport our Enemies, are Tragicall abominations, escaped in burning Burials. (*U-B* iii, 155)

The word 'gnaw'd' in this passage is an editorial correction; it was first printed in 1658 as 'knaved'.[86] But to be knaved by pillagers or gnawed by worms is, in the end, a matter of indifferency, each agent an effective defacer of identity and history. Such semantic gaffes are well-known to the antiquarians, but known sometimes as fruitful misprisions. In *Pseudodoxia Epidemica* Browne points out that Moses is often depicted wearing horns 'upon the affinity of *kaeren* ["horn"] and *karan* ["to shine"]' in Hebrew: when he descended from Mount Sinai his face *shone*, a correct translation in the Chaldee paraphrase which was converted in the Vulgate to 'had horns' (*PE* v.ix.390). But Browne allows that the horns in fact do no injury to our conception of Moses 'because an horn is the Hieroglyphick of antiquity, power, and dignity' (*PE* v.ix.390–1). Aubrey pokes fun at this etymological scrambling after aural affinities when he mentions that in the ledger book in Malmesbury Abbey the name Avebury is spelt 'Aubery'; 'but here (methinkes) I see some Reader smile to himselfe, thinking how I have strained the place to be of my owne name: not heeding that there is

---

[86] The correction is a dubious one: 'knaved' means 'stolen'(*OED* 'knave', *v.* (c.)) and the passage refers to human desecration (in the translation of the skull and the bones to drinking-bowl and pipes) rather than to verminous corruption.

a letter's difference, which quite alters the signification of the words'.[87] So it is by a curious and ironic effect of 'after-discovery' that Browne's editors should deem it necessary to resurrect some hypothetical lexical intention by a kind of fortuitous aural likeness (gnaw/knave) which is as inventive as Aubrey and Avebury, as the oven and the womb. Although the passage is incontestably about *knavery*, knaving and gnawing are both discussed by Browne in *Urne-Buriall*. The antiquarian, the archaeologist, and the editor gnaw the past out of its grave, if only by reading the dead 'by bare inscriptions' (*U-B* v, 166). The circular argument of *Urne-Buriall* consists in this word gnawed/knaved: the very process which consigns the meaning and identity of relics to oblivion (depredations against burials by worms and knavery) is the same one that brings their purpose and identity to light by interpretive excavation of meaning. And Browne's final flourish on the antiquarian task is similarly equivocal:

> If in the decretory term of the world we shall not all dye but be changed, according to received translation, the last day will make but few graves; at least, quick Resurrections will anticipate lasting Sepultures; Some Graves will be opened before they be quite closed, and *Lazarus* be no wonder. (*U-B* v, 169–70)

Resurrection, the type and end of antiquarian re-collection, will itself frustrate memory by obviating graves. The carefully re-collective *Urne-Buriall* ends in an extravaganza on forgetfulness, on the coming obsolescence of record and of memory.

The nature of that obsolescence can only be understood in terms of the recording and ordering practices of the early-modern collector, antiquarian, and naturalist, which were partly addressed in Chapter Three. It is useful, however, to revisit those practices from a different angle to understand the difference between Browne's hopeful, optimistic cento in *Pseudodoxia Epidemica* and the darker and less sanguine one of *Urne-Buriall*. That aspect is provided for us by the tradition of sending up the collector, the antiquarian, and the naturalist, a tradition in which Browne himself participated. By digressing, in the next chapter, to one of Browne's late tracts, *Musæum Clausum*, it will be possible to extend our understanding of Browne's antiquarian limits, and even to reframe *Urne-Buriall* as an embryonic satire.

---

[87] Aubrey, *Monumenta Britannica* i, 41 (Bodleian MS Top. Gen.c.24, f37[r–v]). He believes 'Avebury/ Aubery' to derive from French *aube* because of 'the whiteness of the Soil about Aubury'.

CHAPTER 5

The jocund cabinet and the melancholy museum: a brief excursion into Brownean comedy

There is yet another conceit that hath sometimes made me shut my bookes, which tels me it is a vanity to waste our dayes in the blind pursuit of knowledge; it is but attending a little longer, and wee shall enjoy that by instinct and infusion, which we endeavour at here by labour and inquisition.

(RM 11.8)

A RUDE AND INDIGESTED CHAOS

'There are a bundle of curiosities', Thomas Browne writes in *Religio Medici* (1643), '... proposed and discussed by men of most *supposed* abilities, which indeed are not worthy our vacant houres, much lesse our serious studies; Pieces onely fit to be placed in *Pantagruels* Library, or bound up with *Tartaretus de Modo Cacandi'* (*RM* 1.21) [my emphasis]. Pieces suited only to such a collection as this – a library in Paris which Pantagruel visits during the period of his extraordinary education – include books, according to Rabelais, with titles like *On the Varieties of Soups,* a commentary on peas and bacon, and a receipt for purging doctors. If this huge catalogue of learned nonsense has a crackpot likeness to the carefully patterned arrays of information and things belonging to the early-modern curious collection and to encyclopædic works like *Pseudodoxia Epidemica* and the early chapters of *Urne-Buriall,* it is because the critical importance of restorative, regenerative compilation and investigation can be so easily abused by the inappropriate impulses behind certain kinds of collecting.

Rabelais's parodic library in part inspires a distinctive seventeenth-century English micro-genre based on this impropriety: this genre is the curiosity-spoof, either as the stinging caricature of the virtuoso and the curioso, or as the fanciful catalogue of absurd collections.[1] Although the great majority of these are squibs either comic or mildly satiric, *Musæum*

---

[1] Aside from those cited below, there existed a mock-auction-catalogue genre of poetic satire during the Restoration (Love, 235).

Clausum, a late work by Browne, tempers this spoof-tradition with serious, even discomfiting, provisos, ones which invest the practices and aims of collecting and investigation with distress and melancholy. To contemplate broken antiquities and fragments is for Browne to speculate on what is lost; this chapter considers, through the literary parodies of curiosity, collecting, and amateur natural philosophy, Browne's response to the remains of things which either cannot be seen whole, cannot be seen at all, or can at best be seen only imperfectly. By highlighting the more ridiculous consequences of fragmentation, the curiosity-spoofs help us to frame Browne's more sombre concerns in *Urne-Buriall* and *Musæum Clausum*, where the absurdity and the inefficiency of certain aspects of Baconian investigation and compilation and their associated practices stand in his thought as the emblem of failed enquiry, of the futility of recuperative assemblage.

The parodists and satirists mock the ludicrous elements in collecting, cataloguing, encyclopaedism, experimental philosophy, and souvenir- or trophy-hunting – the whole range of disciplines and practices connected with curiosity.[2] The reluctance of late-humanist culture to move away from textual, and authority made the antiquary's and the experimentalist's interest in things rather than in books or manuscripts difficult to assimilate into the prevailing model of learning;[3] thus, although the experimental philosopher's shelves of specimens and the gentleman's cases of souvenirs are distinct categories, because they are both material rather than textual, and because they seem and are cognate, the comic writers often detect little difference between the cockleshells of natural philosophy and the hodmadods of antiquity, the idiosyncratic zeal associated with each practically indistinguishable from the other.

'He's an enemy to wit, as all virtuosos are', says Thomas Shadwell; 'a sot who has broken his brains about the nature of maggots, . . . that has spent two thousand pounds in microscopes, to find out the nature of eels in vinegar, mites in cheese, and the blue of plums, which he has subtly found out to be living creatures'.[4] Butler has the natural philosopher ask:

> What is the nat'ral cause why fish,
> That always drink do never piss;

---

[2] Hunter notes that all the specifically scientific spoofs date from the period around 1670, the height of the 'ancients and moderns' debate triggered by the publications of Stubbe, the Casaubons, Sprat, and Glanvill (*Science and Society*, 148).

[3] Piggott, 25; and Hunter, *Science and Society*, 160.

[4] Thomas Shadwell, *The Virtuoso* (1675), ed. Marjorie Hope Nicolson and David Stuart Rodes (London: Edwin Arnold, 1966), 1.i.301–2 and 1.i.9–10. Houghton notes that Henry Peacham was the first user of the word 'virtuoso' in English (Houghton, 52).

Or whether in their home the deep
By night or day they ever sleep?[5]

Mary Astell accuses him of being one who values 'a camelion or salamander's egg above all the sugars and spices of the West or East-Indies, and wou'd give more for the shell of a star-fish or a sea-urchin entire, than for a whole Dutch herring-fleet'; moreover, '[h]e is a smatterer at Botany' whose interests range only among plants 'that are not accused of any vertue in medicine'.[6] The antiquaries, meanwhile, 'doat on decays with greater love than the self-lov'd Narcissus did on his beauty', according to Shakerley Marmion.[7] 'The ruins of wit, gutters of folly, amongst the rubbish of old writers', writes Robert Burton, '... is to them the most precious elaborate stuff, they admired for it, and as proud, as triumphant, in the meantime for this discovery, as if they had won a city or conquered a province.' The absurdity of natural philosophy and of antiquarianism becomes a byword for oddity, and Donne can characterise the unusual as 'stranger than seaven Antiquaries studies' in his *Fourth Satyre*.[8]

As Browne allows the accumulated sepulchral vainglories of *Urne-Buriall* to accuse themselves, so the caricaturists pile on the stuff – the sheer variety of items and projects and attitudes enumerated in the plays, poems, and essays – thrown up by the cults of collecting and of natural philosophy. But the parodies and spoofs are nevertheless orderly and even serious anatomies of a doubtful intellectual disposition which seems to encourage random, meaningless compilation and civil neglect: all this stuff, they insist, promotes social and moral debilitation in the collector and the naturalist, especially in the forms of isolation, domestic carelessness, and conceptual confusion. The non-dramatic mock-catalogue, unlike the plays, essays, and poems, can only imply a collecting persona, but it too appropriates the extreme specificity of collection and of enquiry, so that as the comic protagonist the items in the catalogued collection themselves characterise a sensibility, and indeed can maintain a wider and more suggestive field of ideas than is possible to establish for the extremely personalised virtuoso character. The catalogue converts its items into polemical, rhetorical energy

[5] Samuel Butler, 'Satyr upon the Royal Society' in *Satires and Miscellaneous Poetry and Prose*, ed. René Lamar (Cambridge: Cambridge University Press, 1928), 32, ll. 41–4.

[6] Mary Astell, 'The Character of a Vertuoso' in *An Essay in Defence of the Female Sex* (1696), 97. See also Ben Jonson, *The New Inn* in *The Complete Works of Ben Jonson*, ed. C. H. Herford, Percy Simpson, and Evelyn Simpson, vol. VI (Oxford: Clarendon Press, 1938), 1.i.24–40.

[7] Marmion, *The Antiquary*, 429 (Act I Scene I).

[8] Robert Burton, *The Anatomy of Melancholy*, ed. T. C. Faulkner, N. K. Kiessling, and R. L. Blair (Oxford: Clarendon Press, 1989) I, 102; John Donne, *Satyre* IIII, line 21, in *Donne: Poetical Works*, ed. Herbert Grierson, 2nd edn (Oxford: Oxford University Press, 1977), 141.

through extended bibliographical and artefactual enumeration; these lists, anonymous and in a sense vagrant, compel us to identify some meaning and purpose for the collection, as well as the disposition of the collector. Even if some of these mock-collections are deliberately decadent and conceptually vacant – they lack Baconian, recuperative frameworks – like the real cata-logues and collections they mimic, the spoofs themselves are thematically coherent, and transcend the sum of their extremely intricate parts.

The curiosity-spoof, associated with contemporary ideas of idleness and employment, has special significance for the developing culture of investiga-tion and assemblage in the early-modern period: some amateur naturalists and experimenters are suspected of economic and moral wastefulness, of diligence only 'to procure Triffles'.[9] Astell, Shadwell, and other Restora-tion voices explicitly criticise what were perceived to be the more eccentric experimental activities of the Royal Society, especially the indulgent intro-duction of outlandish and apparently impractical technologies. Shadwell's Sir Nicholas Gimcrack, for example, mimicking real experiments by Daniel Cox and Robert Hooke,[10] has transfused a sheep and a madman, a pro-cedure which made the madman 'wholly ovine or sheepish; he bleated perpetually, and chew'd the cud'.[11] Sir Nicholas's irascible uncle remarks that 'if the blood of an ass were transfused into a virtuoso, you would not know the emittant ass from the recipient philosopher'.[12] Later, Sir Nicholas is accused of inventing an engine-loom, but he is able to assure a mob of an-gry ribbon-weavers that they need have no fear of unemployment: 'I protest and vow . . . I have never invented anything of use in my life.'[13] And like that of Marmion's Veterano, and Suckdry and Sir Gudgeon Credulous in John Wilson's *The Projectors* (1665), Sir Nicholas's obsessional curiosity also results in various domestic embarrassments, including the misbehaviour of his headstrong wife and nieces.

Thomas Nashe, who says it 'argueth a very rusty wit, so to dote on worm-eaten eld', yokes antiquarian compiling to foolishness.[14] Donne, having elsewhere epigrammed the antiquary as a domestic liability, disparages his 'joy and complacency' in thinking he can 'resuscitate and bring to life again . . . mangled and lame fragmentary images and characters'.[15] John

[9] Astell, 97.   [10] Frank, *Harvey*, 173 and 202.
[11] Shadwell, 11.ii.191–2. The Fellows of the Royal Society did not take all this lying down. Henry Oldenburg referred to the spoofs as 'Ballets & Boufonries of these scoffing times'; John Evelyn disdained one spoof as 'some scurrilous interlude', no more than 'the Scoffs & Raillery, of the Bouffoones, & ignorant Fops of this abandoned age'. Quoted in Hunter, *Science and Society*, 177.
[12] Shadwell, 11.ii.197–9.   [13] Shadwell, v.ii.114–16.
[14] Thomas Nashe, 'The Commendation of Antiquaries' in *Pierce Penilesse his Supplication to the Devil* (Harmondsworth: Penguin, 1972), 80.
[15] John Donne, 'Antiquary' in *Poetical Works*; and his 'Variety in the Number' in *Essays in Divinity*, ed. Evelyn Simpson (Oxford: Clarendon Press, 1952), 56.

Evelyn doubts the taste of the antiquary who would 'spend his time in raking a Tinkers Shop for a *rusty* piece of Copper'.[16] For John Earle, the preservationist antiquarian who would 'goe you forty miles to see a saint's well or a ruined abbey, and if there be but a cross or a stone footstool in the way, hee'll be considering it so long, till he forget his journey' is suffering from a kind of derangement.[17] Evelyn argues that we should imitate God, who is 'always so full of *Employment*', and grouses that if God behaved like antiquaries, 'the whole *Universe* it self had been still but a *rude* and *indigested Cäos*'.[18] Chaos of one sort or another is the invariable situation of the spoof virtuoso and curioso, a mirror of the primary human intellectual condition that the serious collection is meant to redress. Like the obsessively experimental Sir Nicholas, whose household goes wild while he potters among his dissections and his swimming lessons, the antiquarian curioso is distracted from the essential business of life by the subject of his study.[19] The comic writers revel in his bizarre unworldliness, in the strangeness of the things he collects and investigates, in the mystical ordering of his collection, in his monomania (equivalent to a kind of humoral imbalance), and in the decadence of the times which permit such an out-of-control Baconianism to flourish.[20] They seem to forget that the real and threatening power of the 'cold causes' of the Society of Antiquaries (founded in 1572) were wound up by an uneasy King James early in his reign as potentially prejudicial to royal prerogatives, and that the 'rubbish' of Cotton's celebrated library was sequestered by a nervous Charles I in 1629.[21]

Shadwell's *The Virtuoso* is probably the most extended, informed, and zany portrait of experimental futility, an ongoing *donnée* in seventeenth-century literature. Sir Nicholas Gimcrack is an amateur experimenter but also a collector of curiosities. He keeps bottled air from various parts of the country and foregoes the inconvenience of travel or even of exercise by inhaling the country air of Newmarket, Bury, and Norwich in his own

---

[16] Evelyn, *Publick Employment*, 95.
[17] John Earle, 'The Antiquary' in *Microcosmography*, ed. Alfred S. West, 2nd edn (Cambridge: Cambridge University Press, 1951), 57–8.
[18] Evelyn, *Publick Employment*, 115.
[19] All the plays which figure an antiquarian or virtuoso are domestic farces in which worldly young people take advantage of scholarly distraction: these include Marmion's *The Antiquary* (1636), Wilson's *The Projectors* (1665), Shadwell's *The Virtuoso* (1676), Dryden's *Sir Martin Mar-All* (1668), Gay, Pope, and Arbuthnot's *Three Hours after Marriage* (1717), and Carlo Goldoni's *La famiglia dell' antiquario* (1750).
[20] Piggott notes that the antiquarian spoof was still being produced, somewhat wearisomely, as late as 1821 (18).
[21] Sharpe, 80, 36; and Parry, 44. Peter Miller suggests that the confiscation of Veterano's collection in Marmion's *The Antiquary* was an allusion to the closure of the Cotton library (78). If so, this notorious affront to sober antiquarianism is strangely converted into the material of comedy. Piggott (16) claims that Veterano is based on John Earle; however, since Earle himself derides antiquaries, this is not easy to credit.

house.[22] He is first seen learning to swim upon a trunk in his lab, a skill which he has no intention ever of trying out in the water. He is, he claims with pride, content with 'the *speculative* part of swimming; I care not for the practice. I seldom bring anything to use, 'tis not my way. Knowledge is my ultimate end.' He has managed to read the Geneva Bible by the light of a rotting leg of pork, an inspiration derived by him from 'a lucid sirloin of beef which shone in the Strand'.[23] Rotting foodstuff, normally a sign of faulty domestic economy, is for Sir Nicholas no crisis but an astonishing (if expensive) light-source; in his disarranged world even the proper use and valuation of basic commodities are turned on their heads. Curiosity and its practices, as Sir Nicholas's behaviour indicates, are also to a large extent dependent upon leisure and disposable income, and so the literary discourse of curiosity wavers between the turpitude of genteel idleness which leads to folly, and the noble ambition of disinterested learning which leads to improvements of one kind or another. When John Evelyn praises Robert Boyle, he is careful to link his scientific activities to selfless and world-improving employment: 'there lives not a *Person* in the *World*', says Evelyn, 'whose *moments* are more *employ'd* then Mr *Boyles* . . . there is nothing more *publick* than the *good* he's always *doing*'.[24]

The spoof genre obliquely attaches itself to the discussions of civility and civil discourse which govern the development of and attitudes toward scientific behaviour and cooperative endeavour, areas which were usually framed in the theological terms of admiration and moral duty to the Creator, or in political terms alluding to the public good and the flourishing of the commonwealth. The spoofs more directly introduce a hard-edged, socially exact, and personalised set of criticisms about utility, productiveness, and propriety in the individual, a set of allegations which reduce the sometimes grandiose claims of the Royal Society and its antecedent polemicists (who speak of the restoration of innocence, the advancement of learning, and the promulgation of a mighty nation) to domestic, familial examples in which the neglect of such aims by the silly 'curious' is immediately harmful to the micro-social practices (household economy, respect for elders, the

[22] This is an echo of one of Hooke's enquiries for Iceland, a project in which Browne participated. He asked for 'a bladder full of *English* air carried thither, and one of that island brought back' (Robert Hooke, *Enquiries for Is-Land* in *The Life and Work of Robert Hooke* in *Early Science in Oxford*, ed. R. T. Gunther, 2nd edn, 15 vols. (London: Dawsons, 1968), VI, 101); Hooke's queries appear to have been forwarded to Browne, who was in correspondence with an English Lutheran minister in Iceland and transmitted a collection of his observations back to the Society (*An Account of Island, alias Ice-land in the Yeare 1663* in Keynes III, 345–6).

[23] Shadwell, V.ii.27. This phenomenon was discussed by Boyle in 'Some Observations about Shining Flesh, Both of Veal and of Pullet' (1672) in Gunther, VI, 99–101.

[24] Evelyn, *Publick Employment*, 118–19.

governing of children, and so on) from which nations are built and on which they depend. The English spoofs consider the social penalty of curiosity when it is practised in the main by well-to-do persons who ought instead to be looking after their families and communities as landowners, justices, and professional men with substantial financial interest and political clout. The spoofs, in other words, portray the antiquarian and experimentalist as derelict, uncivil, and his curious matter as an image of incivility itself.[25]

MELANCHOLY CURIOSITY

Urne-Buriall, written almost twenty years before *Musæum Clausum*, is a kind of satire on antiquarianism, to the extent that it employs that same specificity and exhibits its relentlessly learned and ungainsayable accumulation of facts only to bring the laboriously constructed edifice of examples to dissolution in the final chapter, where Browne notifies the reader that just as urns and tombs cannot guarantee lasting memory, no amount of learning can secure what we have lost; and *Urne-Buriall* itself enacts that defeat, with the endlessly instantiated first four chapters going aground, so to speak, on the hard rock of the fifth. But *Urne-Buriall*, if it is a satire at all, is not of the same kind as the spoofs. For Browne, the labours of the antiquarian moralise the remoteness and loss of the past: the efforts of the scholar are not risible but instead a necessary and sadly instructive labour which teaches us about our own helplessness and mortality. His more typical contribution to the spoof genre is, by contrast, of a very different order, though no less thoughtful, no less melancholy.

The mood and messages of Browne's *Musæum Clausum* must therefore be judged in the light not only of the well-established spoof tradition, but also of his own enormous curiosity, and particularly the curiosity on display in *Urne-Buriall*. In the dedicatory letter of the earlier work, the doctor of medicine and practising general physician remarks that 'to preserve the living, and make the dead to live, . . . is not impertinent unto our profession' (*U-B*. Le Gros, 132). Although making the dead to live – resurrection by physic – is also, in his neat analogy, the preserve of the antiquarian as restorer of moribund knowledge, the Walsingham urns, he admits, 'arose as they lay', apparently without antiquarian aid. Some early-modern English curiosi, especially antiquaries like Camden, Weever, Dugdale, and Aubrey,

---

[25] The most extreme complaint of this kind is by John Norris, who asks: 'Is there anything more Absurd and Impertinent [than] a Man who has so great a concern upon his Hands as the Preparing for Eternity, all busy and taken up with *Quadrants*, and *Telescopes, Furnaces, Syphons*, and *Air-Pumps?*' (*Reflections upon the Conduct of Human Life* (1690)), quoted in Hunter, *Science and Society*, 175.

attempted such resurrections, reconstructions of fragmented remains, scattered histories, and decayed languages, by producing annals, genealogies, chronicles, chorographies, and surveys. Under a similar impulse, naturalists – notably the careful taxonomists like Ray, Lister, and Merrett – laboured to name, catalogue, and order the variety of flora and fauna in encyclopaedias and collections. Both antiquarians and naturalists were animated partly by a sense of intellectual disorder and ruin requiring learned ministration and reparation. For Browne, however, curiosity tries, and fails, to perform the work of reconstruction of a splintered reality. That the purposes of collecting and curiosity in seventeenth-century thought are sobering as well as (or rather than) purely enlivening, celebratory, or recuperative, is clear in *Urne-Buriall* where Browne betrays his Pyrrhonist sense of the whole project of enquiry, and in the more marginal *Musæum Clausum*, which harnesses to that doubt the comedic scepticism of the spoof by converting the despondency of the earlier work into a different kind of melancholy. In *Musæum Clausum* the recognition of self-defeat is transformed into the wry, sceptical acknowledgement of the merely equivocal and partial.

Religio Medici's expanded credo, in which Browne avers 'I beleeve that our estranged and divided ashes shall unite againe' (*RM* 1.48), epitomises his approach to the redemptive project of curiosity, specifically the 're-demption of truth'. Especially in his earlier works, this project is primarily a Baconian vision of the assembly of the world's analect. In his later work, however, the forces of decay, dispersal, and disorder always seem near at hand, and even the last chapter of *Pseudodoxia Epidemica* seems to retreat in despair before an annihilating tendency which irretrievably damages the project of reassembly apparently represented by the rest of the book. His fascination with the fragmentary is a function of the belatedness of antiquarian assemblage, the fact that it attempts to replicate an irreplicable original. For Browne this is the essential figure of its imperfection.

Donne's *Courtier's Library* (*c.* 1594?–1611) and Browne's *Musæum Clausum* (*c.* 1674) are two extended English examples of the curiosity spoof which propose serious ideas about the nature and purpose of collecting and enquiry.[26] Somewhat surprisingly, however, both have attracted from editors merely casual judgements like 'whimsical', 'amusing', and *'jeu d'esprit'*.[27] These exercises are undoubtedly designed partly for entertainment, but it is

---

[26] Donne's is the earliest English example of the freestanding catalogue-in-jest; besides Rabelais, another of its models may have been Johann Fischart's *Catalogus catalogorum perpetuo durabilis* (Strasbourg, 1590); this includes a number of nonsense titles such as *Commentaria commentariorum, cum additionibus additionum, & annotationibus super annotata . . . cui adiunctae glossæ glossarum.*

[27] John Donne, *The Courtier's Library, or Catalogus Librorum Aulicorum*, ed. Evelyn Simpson (London: Nonesuch, 1930), 1; Patrides glancingly characterises *Musæum Clausum* as a parody of indiscriminate collecting practices (C. A. Patrides, ' "The Best Part of Nothing": Sir Thomas Browne and the

also clear that they carry altogether more serious burdens. Each is precisely situated within the social framework of learning – Donne's *Library* is in fact a Latin work – to which the very form of the library or collection catalogue is familiar and self-explanatory. The imagined audiences of each of these works are ones already well-acquainted with the format and purpose of such lists, and with the habit of assemblage practised by genteel individuals. Each adapts the rhetorical energy of the spoofs in order to propose serious and unsettling ideas about the nature and purpose of collecting and enquiry. They rely on many of the same comic assumptions and stereotypes which are guyed in the spoofs – economic futility, purposeless and trivial curiosity, and the social or domestic disruption which are functions of curious pursuits; however with their altogether darker conclusions, they may fairly be counted as meta-parodies, send-ups of the satirical spoof-genre, using its nuances and conventions to condemn them by implication of frivolity, as if the spoofs, acute as they are, miss the most important and telling meanings of curiosity.

Donne's is a collection, as its preface makes clear, 'not for sale', but available to a certain courtly echelon which he seems to know all too well. This tract is designed as a sort of bluffer's guide to erudition: the average courtier hasn't read much, but has to behave as though he had. Donne advises against recourse to the epitomes that everyone reads for the purpose of disguising scant attainments; instead, the really adept ignoramus should master works so obscure that quotation from them will be bound to impress 'people who previously fancied they knew everything' when they 'hear of authors entirely new to them'.[28] Sniping at the vacuousness of courtly attainments (he notes that with their late hours and their elaborate *toilettes*, most courtiers haven't much time for reading anyway), Donne reminds his coterie audience simultaneously of its exclusivity and its superficiality. Although the preface begins with a standard Ciceronian complaint against an age of illiteracy and the incompleteness of knowledge, the work seems to propose itself as a typical comic squib.

Some of the items are purely amusing: there is the lampooned mysticism and hermetic philosophy of Pico and Dee in a work explaining the significant patterns of the hairs on the tail of Tobit's dog; a treatise credited

Strategy of Indirection' in Patrides *Approaches*, 33); Marjorie Swann interprets it within the networks of social exchange and status-building (*Curiosity and Texts: The Culture of Collecting in Early Modern England* (Philadelphia: University of Pennsylvania Press, 2001), 132–3). Although Donne's satire has at least had a meticulously annotated edition by Evelyn Simpson, Browne's has been almost entirely ignored except by Bent Juel-Jensen in a helpful but brief bibliographic article ('*Musæum Clausum, or Bibliotheca Abscondita*: Some Thoughts on Curiosity Cabinets and Imaginary Books', *Journal of the History of Collections* 4 (1992), 127–40).

28 Donne, *Courtier's Library*, 42.

to the unreliable polymath Cardano called *On the Nullibiety of Breaking Wind*; the more reliable encyclopaedism of Aldrovandi behind the prolix and vaunting title *Quis Non? Or, a Refutation of all the errors, past, present, and future, not only in theology but in the other branches of knowledge, and the technical arts of all men dead, living, and as yet unborn*, a work described by Donne as having been 'put together in a single night after supper by Dr Sutcliffe'.[29] A book explaining the sexing of atoms, and another purportedly by Walter Cope, a well-known antiquary, on testing the age and authenticity of antiquities, accuse experimental and antiquarian curiosity at a surprisingly early moment in England. Naughtily entitled *Believe in Thy Havings and Thou Hast Them*, the Cope book is a clear thrust at the trash being acquired as legitimately antique by wilfully deluded curiosi.

Many of the items in *The Courtier's Library* are, however, far from comic. This learned spoof is tartly acidulated with exact and vengeful scorn against the named authors of various religious and political outrages, especially various Protestant enforcers and informers.[30] One book on anti-Catholic persecutions is said to be written by Richard Topcliffe, the ruthless inquisitor of recusants, a man so notorious that an imaginary Italian verb, *topcliffizzare*, was coined in England with the sense of 'to inform against'. Foxe's massive *Book of Martyrs*, regarded as a series of lies by English Catholics, is here reduced to something the size of a penny-piece by copying out only its truthful elements. *Anything out of Anything, or the art of deciphering and finding some treason in any intercepted letter* is a book said to have been written by Walsingham's dirty-tricks expert, Thomas Philips; Sutcliffe, author of the preposterous *Quis Non?*, was also a well-known anti-Catholic controversialist. Most biting are two works associated with the trial and execution of Donne's hero, Essex, one of them on Francis Bacon's perfidy as Essex's erstwhile friend and subsequent prosecutor. Works, in short, on intrigue, betrayal, persecution, ignorance, pomposity, and flattery are all listed as appropriate and efficient holdings in such a collection, and Donne implicitly derides it: these are stupid and useless books written mainly by or about – and by extension, for – terrible people; he mocks the intelligence and character of his imagined audience even by suggesting such reading material to them. The typical early-modern curiosity

[29] This is reminiscent of Aldrovandi's *Acanthologia, sive historia universalis omnium rerum quae modo aliquo spinis sunt præminitae* (see Lodovico Frati, *Catalogo dei Manoscritti di Ulisse Aldrovandi* (Bologna: N. Zanichelli, 1907), items 86–7).

[30] Evelyn Simpson reads it in a far lighter vein (*Courtier's Library*, 24–5); John Carey, however, describes it as 'a bitter little satire' (*John Donne: Life, Mind and Art* (London: Faber, 1981), 21).

spoof, with its emphasis on social confusion, is harnessed by Donne to political and religious grievances and to persecutions which have generated chaos and tragedy; the relatively harmless and unmalicious virtuosi of the typical spoofs are here converted into the collaborators of wickedness and division, so that this library of bad memories, regrets, stupidities, insults, and horrors ultimately makes melancholy and uncomfortable reading.

If *The Courtier's Library* is ultimately a work of retribution or vengeance, by contrast Browne's *Musæum Clausum* (purportedly the catalogue of a vanished collection of books, pictures, and curiosities) is one of attempted reparation and restoration. Unpublished in his lifetime, *Musæum Clausum, or Bibliotheca Abscondita* (the locked (concealed) museum, or the lost library) probably dates, on internal evidence, from the mid-1670s, the last decade of his life, and more than half a century after Donne's catalogue. At this time his reputation as a polymath and savant had long since secured him a wide-ranging and flourishing correspondence with the leading scientists, scholars, and antiquarians of his day, and *Musæum Clausum* is addressed as a thank-you note to a learned friend – possibly Walter Charleton, the naturalist and founder-member of the Royal Society – for scholarly cooperation and consultation. Like other cabinet-spoofs, *Musæum Clausum* displays learned scepticism about certain items, shows knowledge of real cabinets, and contains jokes about the more ludicrous areas of scholarly debate. It is prefaced by a brief epistolary section which, unlike Donne's, is a cheerful note of friendliness and gratitude rather than a scathing derogation, in which Browne returns with thanks the borrowed catalogue of an unnamed collection of books, rarities, and 'Singularities of Art and Nature', a catalogue which he compares to those of Aldrovandi, Calceolari, Moscardi, and Worm, as well as to famous ducal and imperial collections.[31] In other words, the setting of *Musæum Clausum* is that of the civil exchange of material and information associated with gentility, as we would expect between Browne and his correspondents, a reminder of the self-appointed task of cooperating 'advancers' as expressed in *Pseudodoxia Epidemica*, to reinstate the sum of knowledge. The allusions to half a dozen or more of the most celebrated Continental collections suggests easy familiarity on

---

[31] The eighteenth-century sale catalogue of the combined libraries of Thomas and Edward Browne contains a number of these catalogues (see *A Catalogue of the Libraries of Sir Thomas Browne and Dr Edward Browne, His Son* [facsimile of 1710 auction catalogue], ed. Jeremiah S. Finch (Leiden: E. J. Brill/Leiden University, 1986), 18, 23). *PE* and other works make further references which indicate that Browne was familiar with still other catalogues which he may not have owned. Marjorie Swann thinks that Browne's remark to Charleton 'what in this kind I have by me' refers to his own possession of curiosities, but in fact it refers to other catalogues, not curios themselves (132–3).

both sides with such catalogues, and possibly even with the collections themselves.[32] The catalogue of *Musæum Clausum*, offered as a return for an initial favour, is inspired by the occasion and practices of intellectual civility familiar to cabinet-collectors and naturalists all over Europe, and is introduced as a vignette of the values and impulses of scholarly civility, just as Donne's insults in *The Courtier's Library* are an uncivil response to the abettors of incivility.

Musæum Clausum is, like *The Courtier's Library*, a straightforward catalogue list, but where Donne's consists only of books, Browne has artefacts as well. Like many of the great collections (for instance, Aldrovandi's), Browne's doesn't segregate books and objects in separate collections.[33] Divided into three sections – books, pictures, and antiquities and rarities – the list reflects the variety and peculiarity of the 'collectible', and none of the sections has any obvious thematic consistency. Its textual curiosities include famous conundrums, corrected histories, and lost books. There is 'an exact account' of the death of Averrhoes from an over-enthusiastic colic-cure;[34] 'a punctual relation' of Hannibal's crossing of the Alps, especially of the type and quantity of vinegar he used to break the rocks;[35] lost plays by Diogenes the Cynic; Seneca's epistles to St Paul; two books by Julius Caesar; and a letter to Cicero from his brother in Britain. The pictures in this museum are either technically marvellous, deploying astonishing light-effects to suggest moonlight, snowscapes, and submarine scenes; or they represent marvels – great events such as battles and banquets, or curious artefacts such as leaning towers, caricatures of the famous, and facial likenesses ('Charles the First and one Osborn, an hedger' or 'Henry IV of France and a miller of Languedock'). Among the typical antiquities and random rarities are some slightly unusual medals and inscriptions, Italian souvenirs, and an ancient clock, as well as weirder wonders: an ostrich egg engraved with the battle of Alcazar, a stone febrifuge, sargasso salt (an antiscorbutic), an alarming receipt for a laxative purge called 'Diarrhizon

---

[32] Whether Browne had access to any of the Italian collections during his studies at Padua in 1632 is unknown, but he seems to know a great deal about the contents of the Emperor's collection at Vienna when he writes about alchemy to his son Edward, then travelling in that part of Europe, and later to discuss the collection as he had seen it in *An Account of Several Travels* (1677) (Thomas Browne to Edward Browne, 23 December 1668 (Keynes IV, 39)).

[33] See my discussion of this phenomenon in Chapter Three. See also Bann, 84; and Laurencich-Minelli, 22.

[34] Like many items in *Musæum Clausum*, this one can be found under discussion in Browne's miscellaneous notes and notebooks. The nature of Averrhoes's death has been obscured by an error of identifiable origin (the Italian poet Marini); Browne expects Kircher to discover the truth of the matter (Keynes III, 250).

[35] Browne had already pronounced authoritatively in *Pseudodoxia*: 'an ocean of vinegar too little for that effect!' (*PE* VII.xviii.600).

mirificium', and 'Batrachomyomachia, or the Homerican Battel between Frogs and Mice, neatly described upon the Chizel Bone of a large Pike's Jaw' (*MC*, 119).

Browne's humour, if recondite, is unmistakable to those familiar with collecting and with specific collections. The *Batrachomyomachia* sends up the fad for microscopic manufactures such as hundreds of heads carved on a cherrystone, or the narrative engraving of gems so familiar from existing cabinets. Some of the items are overtly fanciful, such as Seneca's letters to Paul,[36] and the aetherial salts so volatile that they can only be examined by the light of the Bononian Stone, or Galileo's barium sulphide (probably a glance at the fascination with natural fluorescence mentioned by Shadwell and investigated by Hooke and Boyle).[37] The eagle stone (a geode containing loose fragments, thought to avert miscarriage),[38] souvenirs of specific events such as the Doge's ring found in the belly of a fish caught in the Adriatic, and various naturalia like squid ink (against hysteria) – all these are actual or generically typical elements of contemporary collections.

Browne's acquaintance with the catalogues of some of the great Continental cabinets is certain; however, collecting ideally also promoted more local networks of civil exchange, and *Musæum Clausum* shows that Browne and his correspondent were aware, probably through John Evelyn, of the modest cabinet of Canon John Bargrave of Canterbury, who had travelled on the Continent at mid-century.[39] In most respects a typical tourist's collection, Bargrave's had at least one odd curio – the finger of a Frenchman bought in Toulouse in about 1646. The Franciscan church of the Cordeliers at Toulouse had human remains for sale from its vaults, and Bargrave was initially offered the entire body of a baby which he had to decline as too large a souvenir to be acquired on the outward journey. He selected the finger instead.[40] Browne caricatures this somewhat disconcerting item as:

---

[36] There was an attractive but apocryphal tradition in which Seneca and Paul corresponded, a tradition doubtless fostered by the clear Stoic influences upon the Apostle, and possibly by his connexion with Seneca's elder brother, an imperial administrator in Achaia (Acts 18:12).

[37] The Bononian stone is credited by Browne in *PE* II.v.138.

[38] This and other mineral wonders are covered in *PE* II.v.

[39] Although he went into holy orders, Bargrave matriculated at Padua in 1647 and probably had interests in common with Browne, including anatomical studies: and among the items in his cabinet is a model eye purchased there (Bann, 15).

[40] Browne almost certainly had no direct contact with Bargrave, but the genteel intermediation of other savants is the obvious channel of information. John Evelyn knew and visited both Bargrave and Browne, and as a member of the Royal Society also knew Walter Charleton, the presumed recipient of *Musæum Clausum*. See Bann, 69, 76; also Sturdy and Henig, [14]. Browne had, however, visited the vaults of the Cordeliers and knew of their trade in dried body-parts (*OA*, 340).

Mummia Tholosana; or, The complete Head and Body of Father Crispin, buried long ago in the Vault of the Cordeliers at Tholouse, where the Skins of the dead so drie and parch up without corruption that their persons may be known very long after, with this Inscription, *Ecce iterum Crispinus* [behold Crispin anew]. (*MC*, 119)

What sort of joke is this? Why would Browne's imaginary, ideal collection contain a French corpse? One answer might be the fascination with miraculously preserved bodies which occupied many investigators throughout the century, and was speculated on by divines and scientists alike, including Browne.[41] He and Aubrey, for example, were both interested in reports of uncorrupted bodies exhumed. When the choir of St Paul's fell down in 1666, the body of Bishop Braybrook tumbled out of its coffin and was found to be uncorrupted ('except the ears and the pudenda', as Aubrey scrupulously reports).[42] In *Urne-Buriall* Browne notes that Thomas, Marquis of Dorset who died in 1530 was found in 1608 to be 'perfect and nothing corrupted, the flesh not hardened, but in colour, proportion, and softness like an ordinary corpse newly to be interred' (*UB* III, 156);[43] also, he refers in his notebooks to 'a bodye wh. had been buried some hundreds of yeares in St Paul's, as I have observed in the vault of the Cordeliers of Tholouze, as in dried bodies in the sows [i.e., pickled]' (*OA*, 340). And he was probably amused by fake relics, of which the gullible (or greedy) Bargrave possessed thirty-four: that the pious reassembly of, and reverence for, the scattered parts of martyrs made not one but many saints of the same name was an unintentional parody of divine creation and resurrection. The indiscriminate tourist's appetite for vulgar and worthless souvenirs as authentications of past personal experience may also have appealed to him as a subject for satire.

The relation between Bargrave's real finger and Browne's imaginary corpse is, of course, speculative, a joke relying, like much of its learned comedy, on a punchline not actually given in *Musæum Clausum*. Assuming that Charleton and Browne knew of Bargrave's cabinet – not only the French body-part, but *confitti di Tivoli* ('so like sugar-plums that they will deceive any man', says Bargrave) and lewd medals appear in *Musæum Clausum*[44] – the joke depends upon an intertext – or, more precisely, an 'interfact' – exterior to the boundaries of the catalogue itself. That interfact is the Bargrave collection, and more specifically the Frenchman's finger it contains. Although Bargrave attached no name to the owner

<hr />

[41] For example, Hakewill makes an extensive list of such prodigies beginning with classical and mythological antiquity (Hakewill, 191).
[42] Aubrey, *Monumenta Britannica* II, 750.
[43] Browne is citing William Burton, *The Description of Leicestershire* (1622).
[44] Both collections also contained *aetites*, the eagle stone, although this was a generic item common to many cabinets.

of his French finger, Browne christens his relic Crispinus. The phrase
'*Ecce Crispinus*' is Horace's personification of the babbler;[45] '*Ecce iterum
Crispinus*' is Samuel Butler's epigraph against Sidrophel, a thoughtless
and grasping virtuoso in the style of Sir Nicholas Gimcrack, enthusias-
tically resisting 'wholesome sense and Nurture'.[46] The Frenchman's body
in *Musæum Clausum* is a comic fantasy evolved from knowledge of the
bizarre trophy held by Dr Bargrave, from Browne's reading of Butler, and
from his recollection of Horace. Intertext and interfact, the Horace–Butler
Crispin and the body nominated as Crispin's allude to a network of common pursuit, literary community, and social habit, to the joined-together
quality of early-modern civil intellectual and informational exchange. But
it is a unitary quality that is in fact at odds with *Musæum Clausum*
itself.

The Bargrave finger is undoubtedly silly, and Browne's Father Crispin –
a babbling, desiccated carcass – pokes fun, perhaps, at antiquarian frivolity.
But this interfact is also implicated in a network through which Browne's
Frenchman, initially Bargrave's nameless and disembodied finger, is 'translated' into an entire, identified persona. The anonymous owner of Bargrave's digit is resurrected by Browne in his whole body. The key word here
is *iterum* –'anew', or 'again' – and the move from '*Ecce*' to '*Ecce iterum*' is
from epitaph to resurrection, the difference between the interred Crispin
and the risen one. The antiquary as resurrectionist – if that's what this is –
is an idea present in the dedicatory letter of *Urne-Buriall*, whose purpose
is 'to keep men out of their urnes'(*U-B*. Le Gros, 132). This note is also
seconded by others in the period. Thomas Philipot describes the antiquary
in 1646 as one who

> from that rude and blended Masse, can bring
> Their dead remembrance out, and can new wing
> Those thus rais'd up to life,
> . . . can peece up mens scatter'd dust [.][47]

---

[45] Horace, *Satires* I, ll. 120–1. The phrase *Ecce Crispinus* appears in IV, 13–14. Jonson presents a cruel
portrait of Marston under this name in *Poetaster* (1600–1; in *The Complete Works of Ben Jonson*, ed.
Herford *et al.*), IV.

[46] *Ecce iterum Crispinus* is also the opening line of Juvenal, *Satires* IV. The Juvenalian Crispinus is a
gluttonous plutocrat, and Butler may be blending Horace's babbler with Juvenal's gourmand. Browne
doesn't, however, seem to be alluding to Juvenal in his rendition of Crispin. Butler's 'Heroical Epistle'
appeared in 1674, a date which may help us to establish the date of *Musæum Clausum* ('The Heroical
Epistle of Hudibras to Sidrophel' in Samuel Butler, *Hudibras*, ed. John Wilders (Oxford: Clarendon
Press, 1967), l. 36). That Browne was well aware of the spoof tradition is evident not only from
Crispin's Hudibrastic epitaph, but also from a note 'Upon Reading Hudibras' in which he traces the
history of parody and notes that 'an Excellent Parodie there is of both Scaligers upon an Epigram of
Catullus' (*ON*, 245–6).

[47] Thomas Philipot, 'On the Sight of some Rare Pieces and Monuments of Antiquitie, in an Antiquaries
Studie', ll. 24–33, in *Poems* (1646), 23.

The antiquary, in this vision, has power to 'peece up' mankind like a cento; his study 'is the publike Ark / In which the memories of men embark'.[48] A later elegy on John Selden turns this antiquarian into a redeemer: 'that brave recorder of the world when age and mischief had conspired and hurled vast kingdoms into shattered heaps; who could redeem them from their vaults of dust and mould'.[49] Browne himself, in an undergraduate poem on the death of Camden, asked 'how dost thou, cruel England, / Suffer him to die, *through whom thou livest whole?*', [my italics].[50] For Browne the Bargrave finger is a signature of resurrection, cognate with his thinking about the scattered wilderness of forms to be called out at the Last Day by the voice of God. But equally it is a pathetic funereal fragment, the finger as the scattered final testament of a life now 'parched up', of a world of words (in this case, the prolixity of the imagined Crispinus) reduced to a single, perhaps deictic, body part which forms a wordless gesture. This is a theme familiar from *Urne-Buriall*, where the reductive power of death makes Methusaleh's *age* his only chronicle, 'spares the epitaph of Adrian's horse, confounds that of himself' (*UB* iv, 167). The Bargrave finger is a reduction which initially attracts mirth and even satire from Browne; but this mirth retreats before a more thoughtful and equivocal sense of the meaning of the purely reliquary.

The lone, shrivelled bit of flesh in Bargrave's cabinet grown into a body labelled by Browne as the semi-resurrected Crispin is one of a range of more disturbed, melancholic ideas which insistently disrupt the ludic quality of *Musæum Clausum*. This museum, lost from view and knowledge, contains many items which are themselves famously absent from history: works by Ovid, Pytheas, Scaliger, Cicero, Aristotle, Diogenes, Democritus, Solomon, Confucius, and others; things, and pictures of things, which can no longer be seen or have never been seen, nor ever can be – the photosensitive aetherial salt, or the icescapes and submarine pieces; illegible inscriptions, incredible objects, and recollected horrible events – the box containing the *unguentum pestiferum* which caused the great plague of Milan,[51] the skin

---

[48] *Ibid.*, ll. 37–8.

[49] R. Fletcher, 'On the much to be lamented death of that gallant Antiquary . . . John Selden Esquire', in *Ex Otio Negotium* (1656), 232.

[50] 'Camden Insignia' ('Vivat sepultus, dura quid pateris mori, / Quo tota vivis, Anglia?') in Keynes iii, 146–7.

[51] In a series of *quaeres* about plague in his *Observations and Notes*, Browne asks 'An detur pestis Artificialis, uti fertur de pulvere et unguento pestifero in peste Mediolanensi?' [Whether an artificial plague can be produced, such as was delivered as powder and as pestilent ointment in the plague of Milan?] (Keynes iii, 252). In another note he wonders whether this infectious ointment was manufactured from dead bodies (Keynes iii, 296).

of a snake bred out of human spinal marrow, and a description of various tortures; some things no longer extant, some completely fanciful.

Like *Urne-Buriall*, *Musæum Clausum*'s lexical precision is burdened with images and ideas of scattering, fragmentation, loss, dissolution, and forget-fulness. Many of the items reputed to be 'exact' and 'punctual' relations – oddly emphatic phrases for such obscure matters – are also said to have been left accidentally in foreign lands; shipwrecked; stolen or sold during wars; or reported to be, but never precisely located, in old, remote, unspec-ified libraries in difficult-to-reach or now-ruined places. The insistence on accuracy and authority in words like 'exact', 'punctual', and 'particular' is a helpless antagonist of the forces of dispersal, decay, and accident which have occulted the collection. This cabinet of fugitive, mislaid, immaterial, represented, and described things might have been enrolled in a work listed by Donne in *The Courtier's Library*, Pancirolli's *Libro de rebus perditus*, or *The Book of Things Lost*.[52]

Browne's categories of loss are varied. The Cicero letter which has turned up in *Musæum Clausum* 'wherein are described the Country, State, and Manners of the Britains of that Age' (*MC*, 110) – a letter whose loss Browne says in *Urne-Buriall* 'we much deplore' (*U-B* 11, 145) – might have supplied precious information to those antiquarians and historiographers engaged in the authentication of English national identity and English custom by recourse to classical, specifically Roman, influence and legitimacy. It's a let-ter, indeed, which might have spared Browne's own error in *Urne-Buriall* where he incorrectly designates the Walsingham urns as Roman rather than Saxon. Another item is 'a *particular* narration' of the famous eighth-century English expedition to North Africa and the sack of Arzilla, an otherwise wholly fabulous exploit but for the Arabic account of it,[53] itself wrested from the King of Fez and lost in a ship full of books and rarities being transported by the King of Spain to the Escorial. Not only is this startling suggestion of early English daring and naval capability utterly specious, with 'the English' hardly in existence at this point; the allusion to such a profound catastrophe as a shipload of books at the bottom of the sea produces a pang only a little less thrilling than the burning of the library at Alexandria. Indeed, that primal bibliographical disaster is also invoked

---

[52] Donne lists several addenda to Pancirolli's *Libro de rebus perditis* and *Libro de rebus inventis*.

[53] The story was familiar from Leo Africanus, and may concern the (possibly mythological) Berber leader Khwlan ('Gayland') who occupied Asilah in the early eighth century. I am most grateful to Professor David Abulafia and to Dr Raphael Lyne for advice on this item.

when Browne casually mentions 'an old library at Alexandria containing eight thousand volumes' (*MC*, 112). The lost correspondence between Paul and Seneca is one of those remarkable possibilities which is temptingly plausible (Seneca's brother was the Roman administrator who declined to prosecute Paul[54]) but sadly inexistent: contact between Browne's two heroes is the wishful fantasy of a thoughtful seventeenth-century intellectual who knows exactly how much has been lost from the edifice of Western learning, and dreams of it as an impossible benefit which no ransacking of old libraries can ever unearth. An imagined correspondence between two such figures is, moreover, an emblem of that meeting of minds which, at their very best, the practices of curiosity and investigation could foster.

When Browne thinks about the frailty of human understanding – cæsuras and misapprehensions whose origin he locates in the systemic damage occasioned by the Fall of Man – he thinks about reparations which can be activated only by what he calls 'reminiscentiall evocation' (*PE*. Reader, 1), a process of strenuous recollection, or re-membering of scattered, splintered, and incomplete structures of knowledge. To recombine these is the intellectual project he addresses in his major works after *Religio Medici*. In *Urne-Buriall* the anthological impulse of the cento only plaintively suggests the joining together or completion of the subject. If collections like libraries, encyclopaedias, and natural history compendia, and the ancillary phenomenon of the cabinet, are an orderly reconvening of scattered fragments which together again make something approaching a conceptual totality, in *Musæum Clausum* the reconstitution and ordering of the collection, and the superficial humour of many of the descriptions, belies a darker and altogether more serious set of ideas about dismemberment and dissolution. Here, a regrouped anthology of precious, formerly lost things is being proposed as *itself* now lost. *Musæum Clausum*, cataloguing what either no longer exists or never existed, is ultimately a tract on the lovely but false materiality of the world under heaven, a materiality perhaps naively celebrated by the cabinet and the museum. Pitching an exceptionally material item like the French finger against aetherial salts, evanescent histories, and lost libraries, Browne notifies us, as he has already done in *Urne-Buriall*, of how little can in fact be salvaged, displayed, and known. *Musæum Clausum*, as an imaginary cabinet, offers

---

[54] Acts 18:12.

imaginative space to represent what real cabinets cannot or dare not show. If all creation is an analect,[55] 'that little compendium of the sixth day' in which we behold 'the scattered and dilated pieces of those five before' (*RM* 1.50, 54), *Musæum Clausum* simultaneously enacts the compendium and its dilation.

Browne writes in *Pseudodoxia Epidemica* that with our understandings 'eclipsed . . . we must betake our selves to wayes of reparation . . . for thus we may in some measure repair our primarie ruins, and build our selves men againe' (*PE* 1.v.30). But *Pseudodoxia*'s initially hopeful project of reparation, the sense of the collection as reminscence, as the gathering up of fragments as tokens of a lost compendium, is a project which *Urne-Buriall* and *Musæum Clausum* tell us is unlikely to be fulfilled by humankind. Browne muses in his notes on obscure works 'knowne only to some libraries, or else some Arabick writer, the Arabians being very carefull to preserve the workes of the Greekes wch they often translated, and sometimes fathered other works upon the best of them wch are now very rare or quite lost among us' (*OA*, 250). This passage is a route-map through the varieties of human dereliction and error: books are lost, difficult to come by, translated (perhaps well, perhaps poorly), or invented and falsely attributed to Greek writers, even by the Arabs who in other respects were the conservators of ancient culture and writings. To reconvene or re-member available information about what had become a ruined, broken coherence, the 'remains of a greater whole', is ultimately the task of the Creator, not the antiquary or the naturalist. Remembrance itself is fraught with uneasy complexities, and Browne's work is a conspectus of that uneasiness. Consigning certain fearful truths to Pancirolli, *Pseudodoxia Epidemica* gestures in its final chapter toward the forgetfulness of the self-cancelling of *Urne-Buriall*, which dismisses its own recollective project while enacting it; and *Musæum Clausum* extends this with a collection which tells us only of the failure to preserve it. It might be possible to ascribe this state of mind to Browne's advancing years: he was fifty-three when *Urne-Buriall* was published, but had achieved his three score years and ten when he produced *Musæum Clausum*, his last formal word on the subject of curiosity. It is a word perhaps tempered by the wisdom of a long life in learning: probably the world can never be recollected and reminisced, he says in *Urne-Buriall*; the optimism and declarative energy of *Pseudodoxia* have fled. What remains

---

[55] Meaning 'gathering up of gleanings' (*Shorter OED*, sb., pl.); or 'crumbs that fall from the table' (*OED* sb.2, 54).

is a wistful evocation in *Musæum Clausum* of the ambitions of curiosity and a delicately comic demonstration of their futility.

Urne-Buriall's companion work, *The Garden of Cyrus*, conveys an altogether different idea of the state of the world, however, an ebullient and imaginatively liberated vision of creation which seems unrelated to the saturnine humour of its partner. It is to that work that I now turn.

CHAPTER 6

The epitome of the earth: The Garden of Cyrus and verdancy

[Apple-trees] would bee placed in such artificiall rowes that which
way soever a man shall cast his eyes, yet hee shall see the trees every
way stand in rowes, making squares, alleyes, and divisions, according
to a mans imagination [.]
Gervase Markham, *The English Husbandman* (1635), part II, 123.

HORTULAN SAINTS AND
SEVENTEENTH-CENTURY GARDENERS

Browne imagines the end of the world as the time when human remains
will sprout into new life, as 'that great Autumn', when 'the graves shall shoot
up their concealed seeds' and 'men shall spring up, and awake from their
Chaos again' (*PE* VI.i.442). It is an event, moreover, which is miraculously
to occur not in springtime, but in the season of decline and death. Browne's
interest in seeds and generation, both literal and metaphorical, is the subject
of *The Garden of Cyrus* (1658), a work which mines his extensive reading
of the outstanding English biologists of the early and middle parts of the
century – including Harvey and Highmore on generation – as well as his
own accumulated observations in embryology and germination.[1] *Cyrus*,
in other words, shows us Browne in his most rigorously scientific mode.
As he discusses the structure, vegetation, and generation of plants, seeds,
eggs, insects, and higher animals, the enormous range of his biological,
botanical, anatomical, and physiological expertise becomes obvious. It is,
moreover, Browne's most *native* work: in his discussion of plant generation
in *Cyrus's* third chapter he produces, in effect, a flora of the East Anglian
countryside.

And yet this science is sometimes hard to see because the essay is also
Browne's most playful, the one most given to rhetorical sleight-of-hand,
structural complexity, and mystical, metaphorical exercises, almost as if he

[1] Harvey, *De Generatione Animalium* (1651) and Nathaniel Highmore, *The History of Generation* (1651).

were deliberately gainsaying the Baconian command to simplify and purify the expression of natural philosophy and natural history. *Cyrus's* extensive treatment of its ostensible subject – figures of five, or the quincunx – has been read as occult, Platonic, millenarian/prophetic, cabbalistic, and even musical (some of these encouraged by the tract itself, whose title-page announces that the quincunx is to be 'artificially, naturally, mystically considered' (*GC* 1, 173)).[2] Many of these motives may be present in the essay but all of them are modes – rhetorical and conceptual – which support its central purpose and meaning as a work of natural philosophy concerned with the most important development in early-modern biological science. To read *Cyrus* adequately, we must examine the ways in which it addresses and incorporates puzzles and discoveries in generation and yokes them to an overriding teleological theme.

Cyrus, the 'lord of gardens' for whom Browne's essay is named, is the Persian prince who declared that husbandry and warfare are equal accomplishments in a ruler: 'it is useless to have broad acres under tillage unless there are men to defend them; and next to them, those who stock and cultivate the land best ... [E]ven stout-hearted warriors cannot live without the aid of the workers'.[3] Among the several anecdotes of Cyrus the Younger, Xenophon includes the regular, quincunxial planting system of his orchard which inspires Browne, and the prince's proud boast that he himself has been its 'manual planter' (*GC* 1, 181), that, indeed, he never 'sat down to dinner when in sound health, without first working hard at some task of war or agriculture'.[4]

Why, other than as the source of the horticultural quincunx, does Browne commemorate and linger on Cyrus? That prince arises out of a society characterised by Browne as almost aggressive in its 'botanical bravery' (*GC* 1, 180); indeed, Cyrus' more notable military exploit recounted in Xenophon's *Anabasis* is admitted and then summarily dismissed by Browne in favour of his accomplishment as a 'splendid and regular planter' who nevertheless 'dispos[ed] his trees like his armies in regular ordination' (*GC* 1, 181). The military metaphor in planting is one he also notices in Aristotle's *Politics*, and in the tactical ingenuity of various Greek and Roman armies, analysed as quincunxial (*GC* 1, 183; 11, 189–90). As if to make the

---

[2] See Huntley, '*The Garden of Cyrus* as Prophecy', 133–41; Thomas C. Singer, 'Sir Thomas Browne's "Emphaticall Decussation, or Fundamentall Figure": Geometrical Hieroglyphs and *The Garden of Cyrus*', *English Literary Renaissance* 17 (1987), 85–102; Huntley, *Sir Thomas Browne*, 206–7; and Chalmers, 'That Universal and Publick Manuscript', 414–30.

[3] Xenophon, *Oeconomicus* in *Memorabilia, Oeconomicus*, trans. E. C. Marchant (Cambridge, MA: Harvard University Press/Loeb Classical Library, 1923), 396–7 (IV.15–16).

[4] *Ibid.*, 398–401 (IV.24).

military-horticultural simile unmistakable, he notes that the etymology of the Hebrew word for 'garden' also yields the word 'buckler' (shield) (*GC* I, 180). Nothing, it seems, could be more violently yoked together than warfare and garden fruits, and Cyrus is Browne's convenient signature for that conjoining of apparently exclusive categories.

The hortulan art, in these seemingly incompatible categories of war and gardening, has dual and sometimes antithetical meanings. This yoking is delicately linked to two separate but related traditions of seventeenth-century botanical writing. It is a partial example of the first, the extensive genre of treatises on fruit-trees, practical guides in the georgic mode very often enriched with metaphorical, Christian readings of the garden and orchard, a genre which also includes herbals and botanical-medicinal works. Hartlib's *Designe for Plentie* (1652), a practical guide to effective arboriculture, is coupled with *The Reformed Spirituall Husbandman* (1652), in which devotion is likened to 'the sowing of a heavenly Seed', and good spiritual husbandry will reap 'the fruits of life everlasting'.[5] Ralph Austen's Hartlibian answer, *A Treatise of Fruit-Trees* (1653), was printed together with *The Spirituall Use of an Orchard* (1653),[6] and, like almost all the practical treatises, claims social utility: the effective growing of produce will enhance the commonwealth.[7] In *The Art of Simpling* (1656) William Coles declares that good horticulture will elevate London as 'the great Empory of the world'.[8] But most also invoke the more resonant symbolic readings of natural theology, the demonstration of God's power and perfection through the study of his works.[9] In *Adam in Eden* (1657), a signaturist, Paracelsian herbal providing remedies from local English plants, Coles intends to restore 'that happinesse which Mankind lost by the Fall of *Adam*, . . . to render thee an exact Botanick, by the knowledge of so incomparable a Science as the Art of *Simpling*, to re-instate thee into another *Eden*, or, *A Garden of Paradise*'.[10] The catalogue of the Oxford Physic Garden refers to Adam as 'the great Simpler' (because by giving these plants their right names

[5] Samuel Hartlib, *The Reformed Spirituall Husbandman* (1652), A3^{r-v}.
[6] This work was dedicated to Hartlib as a grateful response to Hartlib's *Designe for Plentie* (1652). Austen, too, invokes Cyrus as a kingly precedent for apple-growing (Ralph Austen, *A Treatise of Fruit-Trees . . . Together with the Spirituall Use of an Orchard* (1653), 10).
[7] Austen, ¶1^{v}. See also Evelyn, *Sylva*, c1^{r}, 112–20; Anon., *The Fruiterers Secrets* (1604), A2^{v}; Anthony Lawrence and John Beale, RS, *Nurseries, Orchards, Profitable Gardens, and Vineyards Encouraged* (1677), t.p.; and Markham, A4^{r}.
[8] William Coles, *The Art of Simpling* (1656), 17.
[9] See David M. Knight, 'The Rise and Fall of Natural Theology' in *his Natural Science Books in English 1600–1900* (London: Portman Books, 1972; reprinted 1989), 47.
[10] William Coles, *Adam in Eden: or Natures Paradise* (1657), a1^{r}.

he 'declare[d] their nature' as medicinal ingredients).[11] The neo-Vergilian georgic tradition, in reassigning the vain hope of a restored golden age instead to a happy, laborious husbandry which mimics that tidy paradisial moment, insists, as Evelyn does, that we make our gardens in 'resemblance of that blessed Abode' in preparation for the world to come.[12] The civility of the Edenic state, when neither man nor animal preyed upon one another, is extended to the vegetable kingdom, where plants 'live in a faire Communitie togeather, . . . while everie flower is contented with its owne estate, nor would the Dazie wish to be a Rose, nor yet the Rose contemnes the meanest flower'.[13]   Such paradise metaphors abound, with well-ordered gardens as epitomes of Eden, and gardeners as the types of Adam and of Christ. Thomas Savile names the gardener as 'the happie second Adam, . . . who is the *Creator, Restorer*, and *Repairer* of the whole attainder'.[14] Austen insists that Adam in his innocence was a planter of fruit-trees, and understands Eden itself to have been specifically an orchard.[15] Orchard- and fruit-growing manuals elevate orchard produce, especially cider, to sacred status, and associate the production and consumption of it with national blessings, innocent virtue, and economic power.[16] Paradise on earth, as William McClung has suggested, is the locus in which 'an immaterial vision and a material structure or system of relationships are brought together and depend upon each other'.[17] If the orchard-treatises couple the visionary and the eschatological with the homely (in the form of cider, perry, and cordials) and the downright economic (in the forwarding of the national interest), this binding together of the practical and the emblematic to yield Edenic conceptions of individual and communal welfare is also a process which informs *The Garden of Cyrus*, where the elementary structural unit (the quincunx) refers both to a pragmatic arboricultural

---

[11] Philip Stephens and William Browne, *Catalogus Horti Botanici Oxoniensis* (1658), ¶5[r–v]. See also Coles, *Art of Simpling*: 'there was no Plant whereof *Adam* understood not the name or vertue before his Fall, yet after that, as the world grew elder in time, so grosser in ignorance: this kind of Philosophy was almost, if not altogether, forgotten' (10).

[12] John Evelyn, *Kalendarium Hortense* (1669), 9. See also R. B., *Herefordshire Orchards* (1657), 48.

[13] Hartlib, *Reformed Spirituall Husbandman*, 6.   [14] Thomas Savile, *Adam's Garden* (1611), A3[v].

[15] Austen, ¶4[v], 8, 12. That Adam looked after orchards was, according to Austen, an emblem and reminder of the occasion of the Fall (130). Genesis mentions no plants in Eden except trees (noted by Andrew Cunningham, 'The Culture of Gardens' in *Cultures of Natural History*, ed. N. Jardine, J. A. Secord, and E. C. Spary (Cambridge: Cambridge University Press, 1996), 39).

[16] Goodman makes an interesting if grumpy counter-argument, however: the robbing of orchards is one of the first crimes of children, when they 'ceaz[e] upon forbidden fruits'. The eating of this booty gives them worms, upsets their digestive systems, and makes 'their tender yong bodies . . . quicke Sepulchres'. Orchards and apples give us 'the first token and assurance of their mortalitie, *morte morieris*' (Goodman, 330).

[17] William McClung, *The Architecture of Paradise: Survivors of Eden and Jerusalem* (Berkeley: University of California Press, 1983), 1.

technique and to a reproduction of the orderliness of the divine model.[18]

Purchas reminds his readers that 'civil life should imitate nature which is the best instructer';[19] and the civil order of plants is, by extension, to be mirrored by the civility of gardeners. Gervase Markham enjoins husband-men to practise courtesy[20]; other horticulturalists castigate the 'Effeminate Phantasticks' who ruin themselves and the country by importing foreign drink instead of encouraging the production of healthful native cider, and the universities are enjoined to promote by civil 'invest[ment] in a Golden Grove [i.e., a botanical garden]' the general progress and welfare of the kingdom.[21] But the civility of the horticultural arts is often not so public, and this is the other, less obviously pragmatic tradition to which *Cyrus* gestures. Browne describes the treatise in the dedication as 'this garden discourse' (*GC*. Bacon, 136). To write about gardens in 1656–8 is hardly a neutral act: the proliferation of poems about gardens in the 1640s and 50s, especially by militant and moderate Royalists like Cowley and Marvell, is an Epicurean trope of retirement from the fray, of nostalgia for a lost (pre-regicidal) innocence.[22] Whether or not *The Garden of Cyrus* was written in direct response to the civil disorder of the 1640s and mid-1650s, as has been argued, some of its features associate it with the larger genre of hor-tulan poetics in the manner of John Denham and Andrew Marvell.[23] Yet Browne is in no sense a landscapist: he is not concerned with its political symbolism, nor does he make, as Bacon does, aesthetic prescriptions for the proper elements of a planned pleasure-garden. His idea of the garden and its meanings is not presented topographically as it is in *Coopers Hill*

---

[18] For the history of the idea of paradise, see A. Bartlett Giammatti, *The Earthly Paradise and the Renaissance Epic* (Princeton: Princeton University Press, 1966); McClung, 2; John Prest, *The Garden of Eden: The Botanic Garden, and the Re-Creation of Paradise*, 2nd edn (New Haven: Yale University Press, 1988); Stanley Stewart, *The Enclosed Garden: The Tradition and the Image in Seventeenth-Century Poetry* (Madison: University of Wisconsin Press, 1966); Terry Comito, *The Idea of the Garden in the Renaissance* (New Brunswick: Rutgers University Press, 1978). Anthony Low, in his *The Georgic Revolution* (Princeton: Princeton University Press, 1985), discusses English poetry of work in the sixteenth and seventeenth centuries, although he has little to say about the practical georgic treatises discussed above.

[19] Markham, 17. For a discussion of the alignment between the material and the political worlds, see Rogers, 8–10.

[20] Markham, 6. [21] Lawrence and Beale, 8.

[22] See James Turner, *The Politics of Landscape: Rural Scenery and Society in English Poetry, 1630–1660* (Cambridge, MA: Harvard University Press, 1979), 7 ff. Houghton observes that the characteristic English virtuoso of the seventeenth century lived at his country estate rather than in town or at Court (62).

[23] Huntley believes it to be a comment on current events ('*The Garden of Cyrus as Prophecy*', 135); and Post suggests it is a retirement tract (143). Singer, however, insists that *GC* is not an occasional piece (86). On the retirement trope in English, see Turner, 4–93.

(1642) or *Upon Appleton House* (*c.* 1654), nor is he, like the orchardists, concerned with an actual or proposed garden. Browne's horticulture rests on altogether more fundamental level of botanical understanding – the very bases of verdure. Cultivation is the artificial counterpart of natural generation, and in this sense *Cyrus* is centred on what is wild, not what is tame; it is *anti*horticultural.[24]

Maren-Sofie Røstvig notes the post-Restoration appropriation of the Horatian *beatus ille* theme and of the Vergilian celebration of georgic enterprises as enunciated by Cowley in the late 1660s, by sectarians, and by the prosperous middle class who could finally approve of pious country pursuits formerly associated with Royalist retreat;[25] she also suggests that the retirement ethos of the late-seventeenth and eighteenth centuries was, after its use as a political statement had passed, yoked to the rise of Ray-inspired natural theology.[26] It is certainly possible to extend the chronological range of this latter development back to a somewhat earlier point, with *Cyrus* in the mid-1650s an early instalment of this tendency: Browne, 'retired' at least from London and national politics, writes of the East Anglian countryside and the natural signatures of his rural theology not, perhaps, as garden or cultivated plot, but as Edenic repository of divine messages which as botanist he must decipher. The selection of Cyrus as eponymous soldier-become-gardener subjugates worldly, social ambition to the delights of agricultural retirement. Browne's Cyrus, like Marvell's gardener who 'has the soldier's place', leaves war for planting, the answering opposite of Marvell's Cromwell, who gave up planting bergamot to become God's soldier.[27]

Horticultural concerns were the province of both the Royalists and their antagonists, and both strands of garden-writing are governed economically (or better, *œconomically*, with its root in οἶκός, 'household') – that is, each positions itself within the framework of a kind of domestic order, 'domestic' referring as well to the nation as to the household. The retreat-œconomy substitutes the disorder of the unmanageable public, political sphere with the carefully disposed and managed green-world of Appleton House and other highly controlled and retired landscapes, where the

[24] Merton claims, though without instantiation, that Browne was himself a fruit-grower ('Botany', 167).

[25] Maren-Sofie Røstvig, *The Happy Man: Studies in the Metamorphoses of a Classical Ideal*, 2nd edn, vol. II: *1700–1760* (Oslo: Universitetforlaget/ New York: Humanities Press, 1971), 15.

[26] Røstvig, II, 21.

[27] Andrew Marvell, *Upon Appleton House*, l. 337, in *The Complete Poems*, ed. Elizabeth Story Donno (Harmondsworth: Penguin, 1972), 75–99. See also Carew's 'To My Friend G.N. from Wrest' (1639) in *The Poems of Thomas Carew*, ed. Rhodes Dunlop (Oxford: Clarendon Press, 1949), 86–9; Marvell's 'Upon Hill and Grove at Bill-Borrow' (*c.* 1650s); and *An Horatian Ode Upon Cromwell's Return from Ireland*, ll. 29–36, both in *Complete Poems*, ed. Donno, 71–3 and 55–8.

natural effulgence of the plant kingdom, under strict maintenance and design, yields profitable mental peace and a microcosmic social order, as well as the usual agricultural products. The godly production-œconomy, by contrast, initiates agricultural techniques that will boost output to benefit the realm, and especially the lower orders, the very unmanageable elements on whose behalf certain sectarian groups agitated, but which also restore, under the aegis of piety, the original bounty of the unrestricted Edenic paradise. The production/utility argument was not the exclusive domain of Parliamentarian voices, any more than retirement belonged solely to Royalists. But in the almost total absence of personal data and correspondence from the pre-1660 period of his life (referred to in Chapter One), Browne's political allegiances and reactions are difficult to assess except in the broadest outlines, and it is therefore risky to claim outright that *Cyrus* contributes specifically to the retirement or to the godly horticultural impulses of the period; rather, within it both are at least residually present.[28]

Browne's relation to these various horticultural positions and traditions is complex. *Cyrus*'s emphasis on the geometric order of the quincunx – at least in its opening pages on gardening – could certainly be read as part of the tranquil hortulan retreat-œconomy; on the other hand, although Browne makes no practical suggestions for the fruiterer, the carefully observational data on seeds, sprouts, and plants are potentially helpful in the manner of the orchard- and fruit-writers. The orderliness of the quincunx, the clear vistas and ergonomic advantages which plantations of this diagonal design produce, can naturally be read as oppositional responses to the difficulties and disruptions of its moment, with *Cyrus* as an intellectual retreat, if not into a garden, then into a theory of planting and propagation which is itself as precisely laid out as a botanical plot. But other than a reference to 'this ill-judging age' in the essay's prefatory letter, not a word is spoken or an image offered that can with confidence be construed as a protest against civil disorder. By the same token, for all the evidence of Browne's practical knowledge of plants, their generation and habitat, beyond the reminder that plants given sufficient air, light, and space do well if arranged quincunxially, he makes no precise suggestions to the working gardener or orchard-keeper. *The Garden of Cyrus* is, to use a botanical metaphor, partly a hybrid of these two kinds of writing, the potential of arboricultural efficiency and nutritional plenty in the public sphere and the trope of garden-order and retirement in the private sphere presented as a starting-point

---

[28] Kevin Dunn points out that, even after the Restoration, the Royal Society maintained a sometimes difficult equilibrium consisting of these same competing Puritan ideas about social function and aristocratic ones about retirement (134).

only, a pair of recessive traits only allusively present in the essay. *Cyrus* is thus very distinct from the two garden traditions: it is rhetorically pretending order while being essentially wild, or at least unmanaged, a botanical lesson in unregulated, spontaneous, rampant procreativity that resists any hortulan or horticultural ideology of cultivation. The quincunx, as an elaboration of the divine natural signature, is the framework of a restored, Edenic order which scientifically generated gardens of the time were exemplifying and which symbolised the redemptive possibilities of empirical investigations, a framework grounded in the most fundamental of all studies, the miracle of generation.

STRICTER BOTANOLOGY: BROWNE'S NATURAL PHILOSOPHY

The essay's primary concern is thus natural-historical rather than œconomic or spiritual; however, in order to assess this claim, Browne's own scientific credentials need to be established. How serious and reputable was his natural history, and is it appropriate to describe him, in however minor a role, as a natural philosopher? These questions and distinctions, latent in all his major works, are essential in judging *Cyrus*, the work that seems to provide us with the most direct evidence, outside of his notes and correspondence, of his scientific undertakings.

In the broad spectrum of 'curious' persons in the seventeenth century, some groups were concerned with natural philosophy (investigative, experimental, analytical, theoretically backed science), a discipline governed most characteristically by method of one kind or another. This category is exemplified in the extreme by William Harvey early in Browne's adult life, and by Robert Hooke and Robert Boyle in mid- and late-century. At the other end of the spectrum, various kinds of curiosity prompted collection – some of it discriminating, taxonomical natural history – often but not always linked to something resembling method or paradigm. The more intellectually rigorous versions of this kind of curiosity are represented by Ulisse Aldrovandi in the late-sixteenth century and Nehemiah Grew, Olaus Worm, and Athanasius Kircher in the seventeenth; their less rigorous, but in many respects equally interesting, counterpart is represented by John Aubrey, an indefatigably curious but somewhat undisciplined connoisseur of fact. Although the distinction is not always clear in the period, the difference is between philosophy and history, with experimental philosophers performing tasks quite different from those of the natural historians.[29]

[29] Harold Cook contrasts natural history and natural philosophy, defining them respectively as descriptive and causally analytical ('The Cutting Edge', 48–9).

Marie Boas Hall, who has addressed the question of Browne's science, places him squarely in the ranks of the 'pure' natural historians, a group she characterises as collectors 'of every sort of fact'.[30] While this does indeed describe him in part, it hardly does him justice. Certainly, some of Browne's most meaningful, serious, and original contributions to the science of his day were the assemblage of observations of English plants and animals in aid of the great taxonomical projects of John Ray and Christopher Merrett, and for Ray's editions of Francis Willughby; his assistance to Evelyn's *Sylva* was also partly that of the accomplished naturalist. But Hall wrongly suggests that Browne was, like Burton, mainly a connoisseur of book-learning rather than of experimental practice and observational data, that he demonstrated little or no interest in method, or in the leading theories and discoveries of the day. She appears, for example, to take as equivocal Browne's references to heliocentrism and to the circulation of the blood.[31] A great many of Browne's more scientifically, empirically distinguished contemporaries were not entirely convinced by Copernicus, and Browne at least honours the importance of the Copernican theory by explicitly withholding judgement. As an associate of a number of distinguished Harveians and a dedicated anatomist in the Harveian tradition, he certainly knew and understood the theory of circulation, to which he refers in his own writings several times; moreover, as a master's candidate at Oxford when *De Motu Cordis* appeared in 1628, it is almost inconceivable, knowing what we do about his huge range of reading and acquaintance with scientists of many sorts, that he could have failed to pay close attention to so profound a development as this one. Browne deeply admired Harvey's other great work, *De Generatione Animalium* (1651), and appears to have been reading its first section in 1638, long before its publication, further suggesting close connexions with Harveian circles.[32] If Browne were a proper investigative scientist, Hall assumes, he would be citing Harvey and others constantly. It is far more likely, however, that Harvey's

---

[30] Marie Boas Hall, 179. Robin Robbins also makes this assessment in respect of *PE* (Robbins *PE* I, xxxix). Hall does not explain what she means by 'pure' natural history.

[31] Hall takes Browne's remark to Henry Power – 'Dr Harvey's piece *De Circul. Sang.*; which discovery I prefer to that of Columbus' (Thomas Browne to Henry Power, [1646] in Keynes IV, 255) – to refer to the Paduan anatomist Realdo Columbo rather than to the explorer of the New World, and thus to be a faint commendation (Hall, 182). Keynes and Huntley both conclude that 'Columbus' is the explorer (Keynes IV, index reference; Huntley, *Sir Thomas Browne*, 82). But the Columbus crux is essentially of little import, since Browne's admiring preference for Harvey over his nearest competitor clearly signals sound, learned respect rather than the faint enthusiasm detected by Professor Hall.

[32] Charles Webster, *The Great Instauration: Science, Medicine and Reform, 1626–1660* (New York: Holmes and Meier, 1976), 137; Huntley, *Sir Thomas Browne*, 81; and Frank, *Harvey*, 35. In *PE* III.xxviii.288 and 300, Browne venerates Harvey, specifically citing 'the new and noble doctrine of the circulation of the blood'.

accomplishment – not to 'discover' the circulation, as is often claimed, but to explain and demonstrate it experimentally[33] – was immediately obvious and correct to Browne, who subsequently had nothing to add.[34] Having judged Browne to be a scientific collector rather than a thinker, she is necessarily astonished that he should have owned and read early Galileo, even though astronomy, as she notes, was not one of his central interests.

The emerging portrait, in short, is not of someone content to maintain a generalist's acquaintance with new developments. As Jeremiah Finch observes, most of the medical authorities Browne recommends to the young Henry Power in 1646 are either contemporary or quite recent.[35] The evidence points to a naturalist with scientific and medical interests who has read and absorbed the major works of specialists even in fields not of the first congeniality to him – Copernicus, Bacon, Galileo, Harvey, and Gilbert (not to mention Highmore, Boyle, Hooke, Mayow, and Lower) – and is clearly continuing to do so throughout his publishing career, as witnessed by the revisions and additions to *Pseudodoxia Epidemica*, and the extensive notes in his unpublished papers. This reading, furthermore, generates experiments and observations from him that, to judge by his correspondence, continued to the end of his life in 1682. It is true, as Hall says, that Browne cited Aristotle more frequently than any other natural historian; but in an era whose greatest Aristotelian was Harvey, this can hardly be thought surprising. And Aristotle, especially in *Pseudodoxia Epidemica*, is as likely to be the subject of Browne's correction as he is to be an undisputed authority in natural history. It is clearly, therefore, incorrect to characterise him as the plodding but worthy fact-gatherer of Hall's portrait.

It is more reasonable to describe him as somewhere in the middle of the spectrum which has Hooke and Boyle at one end and Aldrovandi and Ray at the other. Browne's proficiency in gathering information is clear in every major work after *Religio Medici*, and this constant compilation, contained by a meditative framework, is at the heart of his literary production. His collecting spans natural and human history, as did Aldrovandi's, but his extensive correspondence with Merrett about animal nomenclature and comparative anatomy, and his connexion with an English resident of Iceland of whom he made minute enquiries in natural phenomena (probably in aid of Hooke's various undertakings in the Royal Society) show that it was far from indiscriminate, and that it was fundamentally analytical.

---

[33] See Frank, *Harvey*, 2 and 9–11.

[34] This seems to be Huntley's view of the matter (*Sir Thomas Browne*, 81).

[35] Finch, *Sir Thomas Browne*, 169. Webster also regards Browne's reading as very current. Hall, on the other hand, takes Browne's citation of Hippocrates and Galen as 'fathers and fountains of the faculty' as singularly indicative of Browne's somewhat backward scientific disposition (Hall, 183).

Nevertheless, his participation in the enterprise of gathering and sharing basic information is essentially Baconian and compendious.

The Baconian promotion of utile knowledge in aid of developing technologies likely to benefit the kingdom is nowhere to be found in Browne's writing; and, beyond his practical interest in improved medical diagnosis and treatment, nowhere is there the least indication of commitment to this ideal. His treatise 'Of Garlands' is a response to Evelyn's call for help in producing *Sylva*. It is hard to imagine a more pragmatic essay than Evelyn's, a work encouraging more efficient arboriculture to produce, among other products, better timber for the construction of the fleet; yet Browne's remarks could come straight out of *Urne-Buriall* – they are an antiquarian's survey of 'coronary' plants and their uses over the past several thousand years in several continents. Not only is Browne's science un-Baconian in this condition of utility; indeed it is, if anything, more 'pure', more disinterested, more Boylean than Baconian. Browne's own experimental behaviour may not be original, in the sense that Harvey's dissection and analysis in examining circulation, or Boyle and Hooke's investigation and explanation of air pressure, were original. That it tended to confirm rather than to discover merely tells us that Browne lacked the brilliant scientific talent of some of his great contemporaries.[36] But he worked on a number of theoretical (rather than purely technical) problems which also absorbed the attention of the leading English experimentalists: like Hooke he was interested in the physics of bubbles, in the acoustics of echoes and of whispering galleries, in the nature of fossils, and in bodies in motion.[37] His extensive biological work – anatomies of birds and animals, and especially his far-reaching investigations into plant-germination and fruition – fulfills all the requirements of investigative, often experimental, methodical science as it was being practised by its more notable exponents. He discovered, he notes with some pride, a new, apparently pulmonary, feature of frogs 'not yet observed by any' (*GC* 111, 206). Later in *The Garden of Cyrus* he enunciates, but of course does not understand the full meaning of, what we have since learned to

---

[36] Joseph Needham, the preeminent modern historian of the subject, nevertheless regards Browne's work in embryology as pioneering: 'his significance in [chemical embryology] has so far been quite overlooked, and it is time to recognise . . . his originality and genius in his field' (*A History of Embryology*, 2nd revised edn (Cambridge: Cambridge University Press, 1959), 133).

[37] See Browne's 'Notes on Bubbles' (Keynes 111, 438–40), 'Notes on the Motion of Bodies and Ebullition' (Keynes 111, 432–7), and 'Echoes' (Keynes 111, 242–3). See Hooke, who wrote copiously on fossils, beginning with *Micrographia* (1665), and on bubbles (Thomas Birch, *History of the Royal Society of London* (London, 1765–7), 111, 29. On Hooke's interest in acoustics, see Stephen Inwood, *The Man Who Knew Too Much: The Strange and Inventive Life of Robert Hooke, 1635–1703* (London: Macmillan, 2002), 131.

call Darwinian specialisation: 'every plant breeds its peculiar insect . . . the great variety of flies lies in the variety of their originals' (*GC* III, 199).

Pseudodoxia Epidemica shows detailed evidence of Browne's investigations. A rough count of his own 'certain and experimented truths' (*PE* VII.xviii.605) (not including items which Browne says he has merely 'observed') show at least twenty instances of experimental activity, including work on the magnetic properties of various substances, on the nature of ash, on magnification, various anatomical investigations of animal generation (in vipers, frogs, and insects), on animal behaviour (in toads, earwigs, and spiders), on plant generation (in mistletoe and grains), and on various proverbial truths, such as the flotation of corpses and the relative weights of the living and the dead body.[38] The notebooks and tracts are crammed with such material. Although more biologically oriented, this list has the range and variety of Hooke's enterprises.

One of Browne's typical experiments is featured in his essay on the common error that 'Crystall is nothing else, but Ice or Snow concreted' (*PE* II.i.81–2), and it has the extreme simplicity of some of the best enquiries. In cold weather he sets a glass of water covered with an inch of oil on its surface outdoors to demonstrate that water will freeze even if denied contact with air, a problem that arises partly from the debate about the origin of fossils. In another, that a pot of ashes can absorb as much water as the empty pot would hold is disproved by 'the strictest experiment I could ever make', in which he demonstrates that the unabsorbed ash has volume; he extends the experiment by trying it with snow, sugar, and sponge (*PE* II.v.128). He observes, however, that ashes more 'reverberated' by fire are more porous, and thus more absorbent. He dissects a horse, a dolphin, a deer, and a porpoise to establish the truth of various authoritative assertions about the presence of gall (dolphins and porpoises lack it, but the rest do not, he says) (*PE* III.ii.165; III.ix.193–4).

These are simple demonstrations which can hardly, or only just, be called 'experiments'; they are perhaps more reasonably to be termed 'directed observations'. Nevertheless, he sometimes combines observation, reading, and trial in more ambitious projects. An ancient belief holds that mistletoe grows where thrushes and ringdoves drop its seeds. Browne immediately points out that the theory does not explain why mistletoe only grows in certain species of tree rather than in all trees where these birds alight. He also

[38] On magnetism, *PE* II.ii.86; on ashes, *PE* II.v.128; on magnification, *PE* II.vii.153; on vipers, frogs, and insects, *PE* III.xvi.221, III.xiii.212–13, and III.vii.182; on toads, earwigs, and spiders, *PE* III.xxvii.280–1; on mistletoe and grains, *PE* II.vi.147-8 and III.xxvii.285; on the flotation of dead bodies, *PE* IV.vi.312; on the weight of dead and living bodies, *PE* IV.ii.296.

notes that the growth habit of mistletoe (downward, from the underside of branches) make the bird/seed theory most unlikely, and anyway, the berries of mistletoe, he knows by trial, will not grow if sown. This combination of information allows him to suggest logically that the birds associated with mistletoe eat its berries, which is why they are always seen near it, but that mistletoe, because it does not grow from its seeds, must be a parasite or 'super-plant' which feeds on the sap of certain trees (*PE* 11.vi.147–8). He is thus able, from looking at trees, observing the behaviour of birds, and experimentally sowing seeds, to conclude that mistletoe is associated with certain *trees* rather than with certain *birds*, and to suggest reasons for this association. In another trial he wants to verify that because frogs have lungs and breathe they can drown. He keeps a frog underwater for six days until it dies – whether from suffocation or inanition he does not say – and he thus reckons the experiment to be 'not answerable' (a complex word meaning either 'adequate', or 'accordant', or 'commensurate', making it difficult for us to know whether he thinks the experiment proves the opposite of the contention, or fails to give a clear result); he goes on to note that frogs are generally difficult to kill (*PE* 111.xiii.213). Not all his experiments, in other words, successfully yield conclusive results, and he finishes his remarks on frogs by declaring himself prepared to try some further tests. A similarly unsuccessful experiment was one performed on vipers to see if the young really do eat their way through the belly of the mother. But this trial could not be sustained because he could not manage to keep the female vipers alive through to parturition, even though 'we have thrice attempted it' (*PE* 111.xvi.221).

This sample of his experimental activity shows a range of projects and of reasoning, from the empirically simple (looking inside animals to find if they have gall, or watching vipers) to the somewhat more complex (applying his knowledge of air and water to make an experiment on ice) to the rationally sophisticated, if experimentally simple (the logic of mistletoe). He is alive to the ambiguity of some experimental results (for example, the frog experiment), and seems to have a consistent and modern approach to method. The experiments cited above are from *Pseudodoxia*, and all arise from a debatable or downright erroneous proposition which Browne usually considers first by recourse to received opinion, and later tests or investigates experimentally or ocularly; he finally concludes what he can from his results. This is an interesting deductive-inductive approach, where a theory (already, in *Pseudodoxia*, presented as erroneous) is proposed and then tested 'experientially'. It is a deductive pattern which is inflected by his essentially inductive sensibility: in the notebooks we see this much more vividly than in *Pseudodoxia*, in his observation of 'every sort of fact'. How much he was affected by Cartesian method (which he certainly understood from an early moment) is difficult to estimate. His subtle but pragmatic blend of Baconian induction and Cartesian deduction is well illustrated by the work on mistletoe. He is certainly willing to test a hypothesis either experimentally or logically.[39] A short discussion of cetaceous animals derives most of its information from the dissection of a dolphin (indeed, of *two* dolphins, as he says with a certain satisfaction) (*NE*, 348). His observations of frogs record experiments with frogspawn and copulation (*NE*, 352).

Perhaps his most extended surviving investigative notes are those concerning the ostrich, which mix direct observation of the bird he kept for a time in his garden with a survey of ancient and modern descriptions and ostrich-lore. In 1681 the ambassador of the King of Fez and Morocco presented Charles II with a gift of many ostriches – so many, indeed, that there was clearly some difficulty knowing what to do with them: Browne speculates that they might be released into St James's Park, or given away to great landowners with extensive acreage, and reckons that a pretty brisk trade in pulverised ostrich-eggshells could be established among the apothecaries if only they would add the substance to their pharmacopoeia. Browne's son Edward, by now well established in London and at Court as one of the King's physicians, acquired one of the birds, which came to live in Thomas's Norwich garden for a time, an episode Browne referred to as the 'oestridge buisinesse'.[40] Father and son corresponded about the bird (with Edward clearly observing the London ostrich contingent), letters which are a frequently hilarious mixture of learned allusions to the classical authorities and clever tips on practical ostrich-keeping. 'This oestridge though a female was above seven foot high and some of the masles were higher, ether exceeding or answerable unto the stature of the great porter unto King Charles the first', Browne writes with notable precision in his miscellaneous papers.[41]

When it first came into my garden it soone eat up all the gilliflowers, Tulip leaves, & fed greedily upon what was green, as Lettuce, Endive, Sorrell: it would feed upon oates, barley, pease, beanes, swallowe onyons, eat sheepes lights and livers ... When it tooke downe a large onyon it stuck awhile in the *Gula* & did not descend directly, butt wound backward behind the neck whereby I might perceave that the Gullett

---

[39] Chalmers also describes Browne's methodology as dual in this way ('Thomas Browne', 53–8).

[40] Thomas Browne to Edward Browne, 10 February 1681/2 (Keynes IV, 208). It would be most interesting to know how an ostrich was transported from London to Norwich in the late-seventeenth century.

[41] *NE*, 354. The porter was Sir John Millicent, who played Goliath and other giant roles in masques for James I.

turned much, butt this is not peculiar unto the oestridge, butt the same hath been observed in the stork when it swallowes downe froggs & prettie bigg bitts. It made sometimes a strange noyse, had a very odde note especially in the morning & perhaps when hungry.[42]

This noise he describes in a letter to Edward as like 'the cryeing or schriking of a hoarse child butt ... more mournfull & dismall'.[43] He suggests trying it on beer, bits of iron wrapped in pastry,[44] worms, small eels, milk, bay leaf, and an olive. He notes the Latin and Greek names for the ostrich, the shape of its head and feet, its fabled antipathy to horses, the colour of its feathers, the use of those feathers in millinery, the likelihood of the fashion of feathers in hats coming back, the African tradition of eating ostrich, how to cook them (with dates and apricots, according to Leo Africanus and Apicius), the possibility of hunting them with falcons, the craft of turning their eggs into drinking cups, the watchfulness of the ostrich, its acute hearing, and the accuracy of the drawings of ostriches in the ornithologies of Aldrovandi, Bellonius, and Jonston. This is a thorough anatomy of the bird, using every kind of information he can lay hands on. Either the English cold or the peculiar English diet killed the unlucky bird, and it was afterwards literally anatomised by Edward, and its skeleton preserved, '[t]his being, I thinck, the first oestridge dissected in England'.[45] The latitude of this series of thoughts, *quaeres*, and descriptions of the ostrich is apparently indiscriminate, with folklore and social speculation jostling with anatomical fact and natural history. But to have undertaken the keeping of such an exotic bird for the purpose of gathering as much information as possible about its behaviour and morphology is itself an adventurous and relatively rigorous project;[46] and the somewhat chaotic categories of ostrich fact merely alert us to exactly what had not already been established, to how needy these early investigators were of some organising principle for such assemblages. The seemingly random ostrich facts are similar to the abundant and unexpected ramifications of the quincunx itself.

Even if Browne is not a brilliant experimentalist and theorist, and even if his *Pseudodoxia* is largely derivative, he is far from being merely a 'curious' person. With his extensive training and practice in medical observation,

---

[42] *NE*, 355. [43] Thomas Browne to Edward Browne, 10 February 1681/2) (Keynes IV, 209).
[44] Goodman explains the wearing of ostrich-feathers by warriors by reference to the bird's willingness to eat iron: 'she lends her feathers to the campe for their beutie and ornament, as being the excrement of their weapons' (Goodman, 93).
[45] Thomas Browne to Edward Browne, 10 February [1681/2] (Keynes IV, 208).
[46] This was not the first such bird Browne had seen: he notes that he first saw a cassowary or emu belonging to King James at Greenwich when he was still a schoolboy (Thomas Browne to Edward Browne, 22 August [1680] (Keynes IV, 156)).

diagnosis, and therapy, he could not but be well-versed in the rigours of method and intellectually inclined toward serious and orderly empirical undertakings. He is neither simply a 'busy gather[er] of information', nor can he be called a 'substantial' contributor to experimental science,[47] and this important medial position – typical of the more ambitious virtuosi – is a crucial determinant of his work.

Jonathan Post has observed that Browne was most comfortable in the study of small things.[48] Browne confirms this in a well-known passage of *Religio Medici* when he says 'I could never content my contemplation with those general pieces of wonders, the flux and reflux of the sea, the increase of the Nile, the conversion of the needle to the north; and have studied to match and parallel those in the more obvious and neglected pieces of nature' (*RM* 1.15). Although he was interested in meteorological phenomena, and had enough mathematics to make and understand astronomical measurements, he is rapturous about the structures of seeds and the anatomy of plants and insects, and about insect eggs – indeed, virtually all aspects of the organic world.[49] 'He that would behold the shoppe of a bees mouth needs observing eyes and good magnifying glasses, whereby he may behold one of the rarest artifices in nature' (*ON*, 247),[50] he remarks in his notebook, anticipating the microscopist Swammerdam's sense that the profoundest indications of divine power are to be seen in the smallest things.[51] And because it is likely that microscopic, rather than expensive telescopic, lenses were more readily available to him, such observations were easily performed. He appears to have been familiar with microscopes, and perhaps possessed one,[52] and he certainly had strong magnifying glasses

---

[47] Robbins, *PE* I, xxxviii.   [48] Post, 38.

[49] Robbins notes that precise measurement 'does not seem to have appealed to Browne' (Robbins *PE* II, 725), even though it is clear that he understood a certain amount of mathematics. He claims rather too summarily that Browne had 'no grasp' of astronomy (Robbins *PE* I, xxxviii), and suggests that biology, which did not then entail the sort of careful measurement required in astronomy and physics, therefore appealed to him more. It seems more likely to have appealed because of its intimate connexion with his profession.

[50] A variant of this passage occurs in *GC* III, 202, which indicates that Browne may have been using some form of magnifying lens in the first half of the 1650s.

[51] See Marion Fournier, *The Fabric of Life: Microscopy in the Seventeenth Century* (Baltimore: Johns Hopkins University Press, 1996), 63; and Harold Cook, 'The Cutting Edge', 56.

[52] See Browne's comments on microscopic enlargement in Thomas Browne to Edward Browne, 6 July, [1678] (Keynes IV, 85). Browne's own remarks throughout his works do not support Robbins, who without explanation says that Browne 'neglected' magnifying glasses and compound microscopes (Robbins *PE* I, xxxviii). Marion Fournier is not sure whether Browne possessed a microscope, even if he clearly knew quite a lot about their capacities; she points out that most microscopes in use before 1680 were very likely to be homemade, a fact which may support the assumption that Browne had one of his own (see Fournier, 26, 47).

which he used to watch the transformation of maggots into flies.[53] He refers in *Pseudodoxia Epidemica* to the pioneering work of Cesi (in the 1620s) on plants and insects (*PE* II.vii.155).[54] He had read (and owned) Hooke's *Micrographia* (1665), and was certainly well aware of Leeuwenhoek's claims for microscopic observations of animalcules in liquids in 1679,[55] and of some of Swammerdam's work.[56] Above all, his long friendship and shared scientific interests with his former pupil Henry Power FRS, the first published English microscopist, makes it highly probable that by the 1660s, at the latest, he had seen and used various magnifying implements.[57] As he says of spectacles, 'things of common use may bee passed over in silence' (*ON*, 245), and none of this evidence can absolutely establish Browne's practical microscopy, especially before 1665; however, it strongly suggests an ongoing interest in the technology of looking at tiny things.

With his longstanding attention to generation and germination, and his lifelong activity in simpling, the generation of seeds was perhaps the perfect subject for someone of Browne's keen observational faculties who, without an extensive laboratory, may have found experimentation on and dissection of plants more convenient than work on animals. With relatively little equipment he could work carefully on plants and their seeds, and his seminal tract might with justice have been called *The Laboratory of Cyrus*.

The microscopic problem he returns to again and again, and to which he made minor contributions, is that of generation. Although the great biological advancers like Harvey and Highmore were concerned with reproduction, partly as a consequence of questions about the foetal and embryonic heartbeat which arose in the wake of the theory of the circulation of blood, a more fundamental debate about the nature and sequence of generation was current: do organisms exist from the creation of the universe (a theory known as 'pre-existence'); are they preformed in their entirety before conception in one or the other parent, with sexual conjunction merely initiating growth ('preformation'); do they come into being immediately upon conception in a sudden transformation ('metamorphosis'); or do they develop slowly, after conception ('epigenesis')? Pre-existence, preformation, metamorphosis, and epigenesis all had seventeenth-century adherents, and certain organisms seemed to be proof of one or the other.

[53] See *NCB*, 329.   [54] This is an addition to the 1672 edition.
[55] Thomas Browne to Edward Browne, 22 September [1680] (Keynes IV, 165).
[56] In Swammerdam's *Miraculum Naturae* (1672); Thomas Browne to Edward Browne, 9 December [1679] (Keynes IV, 142).
[57] Power was, however, based in Yorkshire after 1654, and may well not have had the opportunity to share his microscopes with his mentor. See Charles Webster, 'Henry Power's Experimental Philosophy', *Ambix* 14–15 (1967–8), 157–8.

Insects, for example, seemed obviously to be formed metamorphically, especially those who undergo aurelian (i.e., pupal) transformation from larva to insect. It is metamorphic generation that is at the root of the theory of spontaneous generation, and Browne was especially interested in aurelian metamorphosis, which he 'account[s] in the first ranck of the wonders of nature' (*NE*, 356). Viviparous and oviparous animals clearly did not develop metamorphically; but it was not, on the other hand, clear how they might develop epigenetically since this would apparently attribute to mere matter a purpose and aim normally reserved for God. Harvey and Highmore, following Aristotle, favoured epigenesis, a form of mechanism; Gassendi, Swammerdam, and Malebranche promoted pre-existence, Descartes and Leeuwenhoek preformation, as did Browne, at least in plants, although he is elsewhere equally interested by epigenesis, as is clear in *Pseudodoxia* when he records his observations of the development of the tadpole, 'the strange indistinction of parts . . . how succesively the inward parts doe seem to discover themselves, untill their last perfection'. He concludes, 'what a long line is runne to make a Frogge' (*PE* III.xiii.213).[58]

Although Browne interested himself in many aspects of generation, considering the opinions of ancients and moderns alike – Aristotle, Hippocrates, Fabricius, Highmore – and performing his own experiments on chicken eggs (*PE* II.i.76), if he has a serious, truly scientific, specialisation, it is in plant generation, and secondarily in the generation of insects, whose eggs seem so like seeds. We have already noted his interest in the apparently miraculous revivification of plants in *Religio Medici* and in discussion with Henry Power in the late 1640s. In his experimental notes, which are full of the results of trial germinations, he proposes to himself a set of investigations about the longevity of seeds:

To manifest how lasting the seminall principles of bodyes are, how long they will lye uncorrupted in the earth, or how the earth that hath been once impregnated therewith may retaine the powers thereof unto opportunity of actuation or visible production. A remarkable garden where many plants had been, being digged up

---

[58] It is not always easy to characterise the views of some of these scientists with complete confidence: at times Descartes seems to promote epigenesis, and Gassendi preformation. Browne himself speaks of the 'seminall principall' contained in the seed as the '*idæa*' of the adult organism, a Platonic term which was used in discussions of epigenesis. But he also speaks of the 'epitome' of the organism within the seed, a term associated with preformation. In his letter to Henry Power on the subject of plant generation he makes clear his belief in preformation when he says, 'it is not improbable that the plant is delineated from the beginning,. . .& that these unto the eye of nature are butt soe many yonge ones hanging upon the mother plant' (Thomas Browne to Henry Power, [8 June 1659] (Keynes IV, 268), BL MS Sloane, 3515, f. 60). These terms and ideas are very suggestive of modern genetic models, but Browne and his colleagues had, of course, no real sense of the seed as a fertilised ovule, nor of the causal connexion between the flower and the seed (see Merton, 'Botany', 163–4).

& turned a fruitlesse ground, after ten yeeres being digged up, many of the plants returned wh. had layne obscure; the plants were *blattaria, stramonium hyoscyamus, flore Albo*, &c., & litle lesse have wee observed that some plants will maintaine their seminallity out of the earth, as wee have tried in one of the least of seeds, that is of marjorame. (*NE*, 363)

The mysterious agencies and structures of seeds occupied major investigators like John Ray, who asks a series of fundamental questions about seed germination and generation which he, like Browne, cannot fully answer. A number of his *quaeres* are ones Browne had already been asking in the 1650s.[59] The problem of generation from seeds embraced a huge range of items and examples. The germinative agency in seemingly inert matter is a primary mystery, as this passage indicates. Ralph Austen's peroration on seeds is typical:

Will it not cause *Admiration* to consider that a huge and mighty body (the biggest of all bodies whatsoever that have life) does arise of a small *kernell or seed, that that seed* should containe in it (*virtually or potentially*) a great *Tree*, with all the properties of it, and retaine its nature exactly in every particular?[60]

An equivalent mystery is 'plurall germination' (one grain of corn producing many shoots (*PE* vii.ii.541)); so too is the phenomenon of corruptive reproduction, of insects possibly created by and formed from rotting matter. Even the inorganic was subject to generative theorising, fossils and other 'formed' stones being thought by the Vitalists to be generated from seeds planted by God in the earth to mimic known organisms.[61] Browne's own investigations of seeds, as we shall see, yield some mixed ideas of plant generation; likewise, his natural inclination to the theory of corruptive reproduction is sometimes, but not always, displaced by his experiments with and observations of insects. On the question of fossils and formed stones, his remarks in *Pseudodoxia* suggest that he is an unreconstructed Vitalist.[62] He is aware that 'the elements are full of the seeds of putrefaction' (*PE* ii.vii.154), that creatures 'having their seeds and principles in the wombe of nature, are every-where the power of the Sun is' (*RM* i.15), and that 'dewes, froaths, or water, Even rayne water, whc seemeth simple, contains the seminalls of animals' (*NE*, 364).[63] Browne so specifically likens

---

[59] Ray, *The Wisdom of God*, 74–86. Ray approvingly cites *The Garden of Cyrus*.   [60] Austen, 28.

[61] For views on the seminal nature of fossils and other stones, see Rossi, 7–10.

[62] For Browne's Vitalist expressions concerning stones, see *PE* ii.i.81–3.

[63] Pyle, 234. The advent of powerful microscopes after 1660 showing animalcules where none had been suspected tended to quash the theory of spontaneous generation, but even Hooke persisted with it although he had made microscopic observations to disprove it (Alice Stroup, *A Company of Scientists: Botany, Patronage and Community at the Seventeenth-Century Parisian Royal Academy of Sciences* (Berkeley: University of California Press, 1990), 149).

the organic to the inorganic seed that it is worth quoting *Pseudodoxia* to understand precisely his catholic sense of seeds:

> yet is there unquestionably, a very large Classis of creatures in the earth farre above the condition of elementarity: And although not in a distinct and indisputable way of vivency, or answering in all points the properties or affections of plants, yet in inferiour and descending constitutions, they do like these containe specificall distinctions, and are determined by seminalities; that is created, and defined seeds committed unto the earth from the beginning. (*PE* 11.i.83)

Later in *Pseudodoxia* he refers to this sense of divine implantation of botanical seeds: 'God ... hath with variety disposed the principles of all things, wisely contriving them in their proper seminaries, and where they best maintaine the intention of their species' (*PE* vi.vii.487). Seeds, and seed-like phenomena, lurk everywhere, and the natural world seems to be organised on the basis of germination, with plants, fossils, and human remains all ready to arise. The biological miracle of germination and generation functions also as a divine signature of everlasting life.

CREATURES OF THE THIRD DAY: EDENISM AND NATURAL SIGNATURES

The signature under which he is able to conjoin the biological and the divine is the quincunx. Although diagonal or decussive plantings were, and remain, a very widespread practice, 'quincunx' seems hardly to have been used before *Cyrus* except as an astronomical term. Other than R. B., who describes it as a feature of 'our best Orchards', the quincunx is not mentioned by any other English writer of prose or poetry before Browne, who quite simply appropriates an ancient and obscure concept, and from the simplicity of orchards ramifies it throughout the natural and artificial worlds.[64] The arcane significance he attaches to it is often as obscure as the most specialised hermetic, alchemical, or numerological theories. The quincunx is, to quote the *OED*, 'an arrangement or disposition of five objects so placed that four occupy the corners, and the fifth the centre, of a square or other rectangle'.[65] Using parataxis as the rhetorical analogy of

---

[64] *OED* 'quincunx', 1., cites William Lilly's *Christian Astrology* (1647) as describing a particular planetary aspect as a quincunx. R. B.'s *Herefordshire Orchards*, published two years before *Cyrus*, might have been the source of Browne's interest in the quincunx, although the uncertain chronology of *GC*'s composition makes it possible that it predated R. B. By 1677 the term is current among the practical orchardists – see, for example, Lawrence and Beale, 12.

[65] *OED*, 'quincunx', 2.

Baconian compilation, Browne finds this figure in the constellation Hyades, the disposure of artichoke leaves, the skin of the pineapple, the beaver's tail, Christ crucified, the reticulated bedsprings of the Greeks, forceps and nutcrackers, and Macedonian battle formations, to rehearse only a tiny sample. Browne's use of the quincunx is in certain respects straightforwardly numerological: it is the sovereign number, the middle digit in the sequence of primary Arabic numerals one to nine;[66] it is the 'conjugal number',[67] and its Roman form, the v, is half a quincunx which, joined with another, becomes x or the Greek χ, the first or fundamental letter of Christ's name (*GC* 1, 181), and is therefore associated with generation and regeneration. More broadly, the decussis, or central point of the quincunx, governs the 'ambient' figure produced by the remaining four points, a feature to which Lawrence Breiner attributes spatial and conceptual, as well as numerological, power.[68] It is, moreover, an 'irreducible hieroglyph' which mimics paradise itself, where the tree of knowledge was situated in the middle, decussive, place. As Janet Halley observes, the severe and infinite regularity of the quincunxial network is a comely order which can easily be disrupted by the imperfection of the human condition, so that by choosing it – as a poet might choose to make a metrical inversion – Browne creatively deforms his narrow quincunxial themes with many irregularities by which he figures his innate inability to achieve or maintain paradisial perfection and order.[69]

On a very much larger scale, the early-modern botanical garden, embodiment of the text of nature, was organised to display, among other things, such natural hieroglyphics. Characterised as Edenic, an epitome of the 'happy garden state',[70] the garden in Bacon's estimate was 'the greater perfection' of civilisation, and he advances a planting scheme to achieve *ver perpetuum*, a paradisial, constant spring.[71] Spatially organised by various different paradigms – by parts of the world, by seasons, by remedial and therapeutic qualities – it became the herbaceous equivalent

---

[66] See Alastair Fowler, *Triumphal Forms: Structural Patterns in Elizabethan Poetry* (Cambridge: Cambridge University Press, 1970), 17.
[67] So called because it combines, in Pythagorean theory, the female number, two, and the male number, three (Singer, 95).
[68] Lawrence Breiner, 'The Generation of Metaphor in Thomas Browne', *Modern Language Quarterly* 38 (1977), 264–8.
[69] Janet E. Halley, 'Sir Thomas Browne's *The Garden of Cyrus* and the Real Character', *English Literary Renaissance* 15 (1985), 103–5.
[70] Harold Cook, 'The Cutting Edge', 54. See also Paulus Hermann, *Paradisus Batavius* (Leiden, 1698).
[71] Francis Bacon, 'Of Gardens' in *Essays*, ed. John Pitcher (Harmondsworth: Penguin, 1985), 197–8.

of the formal curiosity cabinet, with the crucial difference that its arrays and categories, while proposing order from the chaotic verdure of plant-life, also had a specific technical, practical purpose in the training of doctors and apothecaries.[72] John Ray believes that God approves of the 'comely order' of 'regular Gardens and Orchards'[73] as the imitation or adornment of an innate, divine order. Except for Oxford, whose Physic Garden (1621) had been endowed but not created when he matriculated there as an undergraduate,[74] each of Browne's universities possessed such a fully functioning and long-established encyclopaedic garden. Padua's, with Pisa's the oldest in Europe (1544–5), was close to a hundred years old when Browne arrived, and Montpellier's (1597) was only slightly less venerable. One of the first modern (i.e., clinically essential) botanical gardens associated with a European medical faculty was established at Leiden in 1587, the university which granted Browne his M.D. in 1633. We must presume that he knew these gardens very well indeed; and, although he claimed to be no gardener, his relatively unusual interest in active simpling – the gathering of herbs for uncompounded remedies which was normally overseen but not actually performed by trained physicians, who delegated it to apothecaries and simpling countrywomen[75]– suggests a more than ordinary attention to growing things, both cultivated and wild. He recalled his own simpling expeditions in and around Cheapside in his London boyhood;[76] he had clearly instructed the young Henry Power to do the same.[77] The botanical garden, as the formal embodiment of prelapsarian nature, of the garden in which there was 'no Plant whereof Adam understood not the name or vertue before his Fall',[78] would have represented to a trained physician the book of remedial nature, making the

---

[72] It is important to remember, as Prest reminds us, that the original impulse of the encyclopaedic garden had nothing to do with the developing scientific culture of the period and its concentration on the collection of data, but rather concerned the desire to re-establish the Garden of Eden, or its nearest equivalent, in the post-lapsarian world (Prest, 6).

[73] Ray, *The Wisdom of God*, 114–15.   [74] Frank, *Harvey*, 25, 49–50.

[75] 'Simples' were so called because they were not elaborately compounded with exotic (often metallic) substances, the preserve of learned, Galenic medicine. On the relation of simpling to learned medicine, see Andrew Wear, *Knowledge and Practice in English Medicine, 1550–1680* (Cambridge: Cambridge University Press, 2000), 46–67.

[76] 'I know most of the plants of my country and of those about me; yet methinks I do not know so many as when I did but know an hundred, and had scarcely ever simpled further than Cheapside' (*RM* 11.8). Robbins glosses the remark as a reference to the stalls selling herbs for cooking and healing (*Sir Thomas Browne*, 75), but in the early-seventeenth century there were gardens, churchyards, and fields in the vicinity to which Browne may be referring.

[77] Henry Power to Thomas Browne, [15 September 1648] (Keynes IV, 259). In this letter Power assures Browne, 'I have traced yr commands, & simpled in the woods, meadows & Fields instead of Gardens'.

[78] Coles, *Art of Simpling*, 100.

botanical garden a kind of pun, offering both spiritual and physiological salves.[79] The natural theology of these highly organised gardens is also evident in a less organised, more mystical form in certain kinds of natural history. The providential messages – signatures – inscribed in the living manuscript of nature are ones to which Browne as well as the next generation of scientists, including Ray and Boyle, was highly attentive, as he famously declares in *Religio Medici* (1.16), and his quincunxially arranged natural world – from orchard-layout to the head of the common thistle – seems to adhere to some such 'comely order'.[80] 'The greatest mystery of religion', he says in *Cyrus*, 'is expressed by adumbration' (*GC* IV, 218); such adumbration is partly fulfilled by natural signatures, a Pythagorean-Cabbalistic 'reading' of literal signs – hieroglyphical, alphabetical, or broadly metaphorical – embedded in the creation. Browne's signaturism yields metaphysical meditations, or what has been described as a 'set of Anglican gestures' made in order to impose unity and to reconvene the fragmented authority of the established church. However, the reconvening of fragments is, as I have been arguing, a primary impulse in the practices of curiosity and especially of the wider 'Baconian' programme of the advancement of learning and the resurrection of knowledge, and not especially Anglican or restrictive.[81] Such signaturist reading would instead have come to Browne from several other sources: the Florentine neo-Platonists of Ficino's school, whose interest in hermetic philosophy extended to occult sympathies and antipathies, magic effluvia, and signatures;[82] the sixteenth- and seventeenth-century Italian mystical tradition which extends from Piero Valeriano to Emanuele Tesauro, with its almost palaeo-Romantic celebration of the world as a heraldic blazon of God's glory;[83] the 'curious' tradition of Gaffarel;[84] the Paracelsian medics

---

[79] In the same year as *Cyrus*, a eulogising poem celebrating Philip Stephens's and William Browne's catalogue of the Oxford Botanical Garden offered this summary of its encyclopaedism:

> We have our Stephens and what's more renown,
> They have their vulgar errors, we have Brown.
> (Capell Wiseman, in Stephens and Browne, ¶6ᵛ)

[80] Ray, however, although he is interested by signatures and finds them attractive as a way of thinking about providential wisdom, declares himself doubtful of their authenticity as divine design (*The Wisdom of God*, 221).

[81] The phrase is Nigel Smith's. Signaturism was, it is true, particularly attractive to certain kinds of Anglican intellectuals in this period (one thinks not only of Browne, but also of Hall and Ray); however, it is especially characteristic of the Continental Paracelsians and of the Calvinist hortulan specialists, none of whom was Anglican (*Literature and Revolution in England, 1640–1660* (New Haven: Yale University Press, 1994), 128).

[82] Hunter, *John Aubrey*, 20.   [83] See Tesauro; and Piero Valeriano, *Hieroglyphica* (Basle, 1556).

[84] For signatures in plants and stones, see James Gaffarel, *Unheard-Of Curiosities*, trans. Edmund Chilmead (1650), 35–7.

such as Porta, Croll, Gerard, and Coles who, like more conservative naturalists, carefully collected a herbarium of remedies and the pathologies they
would address based upon various systems of analogy between plants, other
substances of the pharmacopoeia, and symptoms and causes of disease;[85]
and the practical gardeners, for whom the planting of orchards and the
making of healthful fruit-based drinks was a kind of godly, innocent labour
attended and confirmed by vegetable hieroglyphics, who naturally inclined
toward hermetic and Paracelsian cures.[86] Browne was not a Paracelsian
medic, yet he was interested by some aspects of that method, which related
the look of a herb to the part of the human body for which it was a specific,
and which in its astrological-medical signaturism attached starry influences
on the body to plant signatures alluding to them.[87] As 'a Protestant with
Platonic tendencies',[88] he was interested in, if not entirely convinced by,
hermetic uses of herbs and the *materia medica* according to their outward
forms or habits: saxifrage, for instance, as a 'stone-breaker' was deemed
efficient in the treatment of gall- and kidney-stones; the bloodstone, red-
dish or flecked with red, would stanch bleeding.[89] He takes care to correct
erroneous signaturist analogies: the fungus of the elder tree known as Jew's
ear, he explains, 'concerneth not the Nation of Jews' but is a corruption
of Judas, who was said to have hung himself from an elder, making Jew's
ear a specific in 'Quinsies, sore throats, and strangulations' (*PE* 11.vii.156).
Paul's bettony, likewise, refers not to the Apostle, but to an obscure ancient
physician. Discovering false etymologies to demolish signaturist therapies,
he is, if not completely sceptical of Paracelsian medical therapies, at least
anxious that true signatures, rather than mistaken ones, be established.[90]

[85] See Chalmers, 'That Universal and Publick Manuscript', 415. Gerard (publishing in 1597) was
England's first herbal signaturist (Prest, 63).
[86] For example, Austen, †3ʳ – ††1ʳ; see also Coles, *Art of Simpling*, 88; and S. A. E. Mendyk, *'Speculum
Britanniae': Regional Study, Antiquarianism, and Science in Britain to 1700* (Toronto: University of
Toronto Press, 1989), 129–30.
[87] See Wear, 98; and Allen Debus, *The English Paracelsians* (New York: Franklin Watts, 1966), 19–20,
and 20, n.11.
[88] John R. Knott, 'Sir Thomas Browne and the Labyrinth of Truth' in Patrides *Approaches*, 26.
[89] This was either the heliotrope (green jasper spotted with red jasper) or the sanguine hematite
(sesquioxide of iron).
[90] We have observed this already in Browne's treatment of the Peterfish (see Chapter One). Although
he points out the interesting fact that the numerological centre of *Cyrus*, the thirty-first of sixty-
one paragraphs in the third chapter, reads 'though not in this order, yet how nature delighteth
in this number', Singer in his discussion of Browne's signaturism in *Cyrus* insists too strongly on
Browne's exclusive interest in mathematical relations and figures, and thus upon Pythagorean and not
Paracelsian signatures (92–8). The distinction, however, is not one Browne makes; nor is he especially
interested in mathematics. He is only peripherally concerned with real 'geometry', a word he tends
to use merely to mean 'shapes' or 'figures'. Chalmers, unaccountably, thinks Browne was essentially
dismissive of Pythagoreans, signaturists, and Cabbalists altogether (Chalmers, 'That Universal and
Publick Manuscript', 430).

He wishes, like Paracelsus, 'that every plant might receive a name according unto the disease it cureth', and regrets the fanciful and arbitrary naming of plants after saints and apostles (*PE* ii.vii.156). Browne's professional attitude toward Paracelsian signatures appears to have been equivocal. Although in one place he notes disapprovingly the signatures of Croll and Porta, whose 'semblance is but postulatory' to careful inspectors (*PE* ii.vi.141), he based almost all of the first chapter of *The Garden of Cyrus* on one of Porta's agricultural treatises, and in his famous 1646 letter to the young Henry Power advised him to read Croll and other Paracelsian 'Chymistators'.[91] Despite his ongoing interest in natural signatures, the typically Galenic tenor of his surviving medical opinions and prescriptions does not point to any particular enthusiasm for signaturist pharmacopoeia, but does not rule out more general moral signatures from his range of concerns.[92]

Although he says that there is often 'obscuritie in discovering the true intentions of figure', this phrase makes clear Browne's assumption of some intention or other in biological signatures. As the notebooks show, he is always on the lookout for signatures. He makes a list of 'hidden' plant signatures from his own botanising in his notebooks, signs in the roots and pores of plants: various incisions he has made reveal stellate, triangular, circular, and flower-shaped figures in oak sprouts, fig stalks, root vegetables, and verbascum, as well as the sign of Pisces, of a tree, and of 'notable white characters' in water-ferns and 'yong green walnutts' (*ON*, 248). He delivers learned opinions about these signs and compares them with those of other writers, and most of them subsequently appear in *The Garden of Cyrus*. He has seen the figures of snakes and cockles in stones, and bulls' heads in animal entrails. He is interested by an egg sent to him by one of his correspondents with the 'notable signature of the figure of a duck soe fully detail'd as to the body, head, eye & bill ... not made out by phancy butt apprehended by every eye'; he has not, however, been so impressed by a goose egg of Aldrovandi 'with man's head & hayre spred furie-like & terminating in some shape of gees heads ... I suspected much made out by fancy in that description' (*NE*, 353).[93] Browne was especially watchful for geometrical or shaped figures, rather than emblematic figures or words in ancient languages – the words *aiaiai*, *viuviu*, *lilil* found inside sedges,

---

[91] Finch, *Sir Thomas Browne*, 188. The treatise was *Villa* (1592). Browne to Power, [1646] (Keynes iv, 255).

[92] Huntley, *Sir Thomas Browne*, 77.

[93] It is not clear whether this Aldrovandi specimen is one Browne inspected, or simply read about (or saw an engraving of). He says 'I have very intentively looked upon [it]', and it is possible that he had visited Aldrovandi's massive collection in Bologna, which survived in the seventeeth century, during his student sojourn in Italy in the early 1630s. See my note on this possibility in Chapter Five.

or the five brethren of the dog-rose[94] – which were more typical of other signaturists, as if the mere presence of design were sufficient indication of heavenly purpose.[95]

What was Browne looking at when he looked at these marks in nature? The signatures of the natural world, said William Mewe, are 'Relicks of His goodness',[96] fragments of that paradisial moment when Adam could scout the inherent names and properties of things, when the natural world proclaimed its own order,

> Where evry plant did in its lustre shine,
> But did not grow promiscuously there,
> They all dispos'd in such rich order were
> As did augment their single native grace [.][97]

That the world is 'God's library',[98] 'a booke in *Folio*, printed for all / With God's great Workes in Capitall',[99] that 'nature geometrizeth' (*GC* III, 203), meant that mystics, naturalists, and medics could actively search its text for signals, not only of therapeutic properties in plants and minerals, but for more solemn moral – even eschatological – messages. Kenelm Digby read the swelling and splitting of the bean-cod during germination as a political signature expressing the rebellion of 'inferiour members that should study nothing but obedience', and germination itself as a signature of 'our bleeding nation'.[100] The natural world was to some observers producing signatures of its own decay: Godfrey Goodman decides that complex Galenic physic (compared to the simple natural medicine of wild animals) is a signature of our fallen natures, and the rise of the urban 'Paris-Garden' or public pleasure-ground an 'undoubted mark[e] of corruption'; he thinks the

---

[94] The plant containing the strange words is thought by Robbins to be a sedge, but αιαι is traditionally the flower said to have sprung from the earth where Hyacinth's blood fell, and the phrase ('alas') that of Apollo in his grief. The flower might therefore be either an iris or a hyacinth. See also William T. Stearn, 'The Five Brethren of the Rose: An Old Botanical Riddle', *Huntia* 2 (1965), 180–4.

[95] This geometric tendency is discussed by Chalmers, 'That Universal and Publick Manuscript', 426, and Singer, 98.

[96] William Mewe, quoted by Samuel Hartlib in *The Reformed Commonwealth of Bees*, 47.

[97] [Allen Apsley,] *Order and Disorder: or, the World Made and Undone* (London, 1679), 28. This work has recently been attributed to Apsley's sister, Lucy Hutchinson. See Lucy Hutchinson, *Order and Disorder: or, the World Made and Undone*, ed. David Norbrook (Oxford: Blackwell, 2001); and David Norbrook, 'Lucy Hutchinson and *Order and Disorder*: The Manuscript Evidence', *English Manuscript Studies: 1100–1700* 9 (2000), 257–91. I am grateful to William West for bringing this development to my attention.

[98] Purchas, A2r.

[99] Guillaume Du Bartas, *The Divine Weeks and Works of Guillaume de Saluste Sieur du Bartas*, trans. Josuah Sylvester, ed. Susan Snyder, 2 vols. (Oxford: Clarendon Press, 1979), I, 'The First Week; The First Day', ll. 173–4.

[100] Kenelm Digby, *Discourse on the Vegetation of Plants* (1661), II.

cooking of meat, and thunder and lightning, are 'tokens and forerunners of the last general combustion'.[101] That the end of the world was likely to be imminent prompted the millenarian to discover confirmation of the world's fallenness, as well as to perform signaturist investigations which would confirm the developing 'instauration' or renewal which was supposed to herald the last day, an unfolding of knowledge which would release mankind from the full consequences of the Fall.[102] Less gloomy prognosticators like Browne read the world and find signatures of resurrection. In his preface to Moufett's work on insects, Theodore Mayerne reads the silkworm's transformation from larva to winged butterfly via the 'tomb' of the chrysalis as the flight of the heaven-bound soul after death and burial.[103] Thomas Heywood finds such messages in the diurnal seasonal cycle which portends death and rebirth;[104] and Browne, although naturally sceptical of the signatures he chooses to 'correct' in *Pseudodoxia*, concedes that the legend of the phoenix, even if only an 'alogy', is an allowable signature of resurrection (*PE* III.xii.204). Later, less mystical naturalists used the essential idea of ensignment that belongs to signatures for practical ends (surely what Hartlib, who combines the intensely practical view of the technologist with the spiritual awareness of last things and man's final days, has in mind when he quotes Mewe's sense of signatures as relics): John Aubrey, Hartlib's admirer, claims that certain herbaceous profiles of localities indicate the presence of subterranean minerals (hazel and betony signal freestone beneath; oak signals iron; holly and oak together signal coal),[105] even if he is not immune to less pragmatic signals, such as Nathaniel Highmore's analysis of the reproduction of trees by frost as a signature of resurrection.[106] Hartlib's own eschatological and chiliastic interests promoted this grafting of the technological and pragmatic onto the mystical and emblematic, so that Austen, that severely practical fruiterer, nevertheless regards much of his agricultural practice as emblematic: he believes that the technique of grafting arose from the separation of stocks and grafts at the Fall of man, separated entities which will be reunited at the end of the world in the general resurrection of whole bodies,[107] and that

[101] Goodman, 96, 21, 397, 291. Whether the world *was* in decline was the subject of considerable debate. See my discussion in the Introduction.

[102] Jacob, 34.   [103] Moufett, Ffff 4r.

[104] Thomas Heywood, *The Hierarchie of the Blessed Angells* (1635), 383.

[105] Hunter, *John Aubrey*, 117. As Hunter points out, Aubrey's evidence seems to contradict itself on a number of occasions, but the fundamental signaturist idea is nevertheless present.

[106] Hunter, *John Aubrey*, 124. Aubrey was quoting from Highmore's *Corporis Humanii* (1651); this signature was also promoted by Digby, *Discourse on Vegetation*, 76.

[107] Prest, 85.

trees themselves stand as saints in the orchard and convey 'notions' to the understanding.[108]

Signaturism is in some hands a millenarian tool, and whatever his reservations as a doctor and naturalist may be about its medical and practical uses, Browne offers through it his distinctively and explicitly millenarian ideas in *The Garden of Cyrus*.[109] If fruitfulness, as the millenarians claimed, had been abbreviated by the Fall and by the saltwater inundation of the Flood, Browne's natural theology found a reassuring plenitude, to an almost preposterous degree, of signatures in the plant world, signatures both artificial and natural, the greatest of these being the signature of the seed. His elegant signature of the plant revived from its ashes (in *RM* 1.48), or 'palingenesis', seems to combine the Platonic magic of 'representing the very forme of plants by their ashes philosophically prepared'[110] with the well-known phenomenon of pyrogenous germination; and a quite different laboratory demonstration in which the distilled essence of certain roots mixed with *sal nitri* or *sal amoniac* will produce figures of 'filicular shaped plants'.[111] *The Garden of Cyrus*, which begins gravely enough as a history of a certain quincunxial method of orchard plantation (and at one or two points early on might have developed into a horticultural textbook in the manner of Austen or R. B.), spreads and ramifies like a plurally germinating handful of corn until figures of five seem to colonise the entire world.[112]

Part of Browne's signaturist enthusiasm emerges from his primitive delight in looking at things and recording their physical characteristics, a delight wholly on display in his commonplace books, notes and observations, and experiments; and one way of understanding *Cyrus* is to recognise it as a formal excuse for gathering together a variety of observational data which he has been collecting, a vegetable chorography of the English countryside which is a prelude to that great English work of plant classification, Ray's *Catalogus Plantarum Angliae* (1670). In the prefatory letter he claims to have 'industriously declined illustrations from rare and unknown plants' (*GC.* Bacon, 176), and no plant mentioned in *Cyrus* is other than a common English specimen, often a weed rather than a

---

[108] Austen, †3ʳ. This is originally an Augustinian conceit (Augustine, *City of God against the Pagans*, ed. and trans. R. W. Dyson (Cambridge: Cambridge University Press, 1998), Book XIII, ch. 21, 'Of Paradise').

[109] Huntley says categorically that '*The Garden of Cyrus* is a more religious and millenarian document than has been hitherto recognized' (Huntley, '*The Garden of Cyrus*', 133).

[110] Henry Power, BL MS Sloane 1334, ff. 33, 'Experiments and Subtilties'. Digby also discusses palingenesis in *Discourse on Vegetation*, 74–6, 80.

[111] See Chapter Three, n. 49.

[112] Webster describes Austen's book as 'the puritan counterpart of *The Garden of Cyrus*' (Webster, *Great Instauration*, 508).

cultivar. It is Browne's contribution to the natural history of Britain (a work not intended as a 'survey' but reminiscent of one) and, more importantly, to the reconvening of knowledge and the reordering of the world implied by that contribution. Another way to regard it, however, is as an act of devout and learned imitation: Browne the natural theologian hopes to find messages about the resurrection of the world in the fallen one he inhabits; these, when he finds them, form a repeated structure (the quincunx) which seems to suggest a hopeful pattern after all still latent in the world, an architectonic fragment of a larger lost structure announcing the world to come. To study signs in plants is 'to *Restore* To us, what Adam knew before',[113] and that discovery would, in turn, suggest a structure of the celebratory work which describes it. If spiders make virtuously right-angled nets, and plants arrange their leaves and flowers quincunxially, *The Garden of Cyrus* itself is a figure, a signature of resurrection. Like fractals or crystals, the essay recapitulates its quincunxial micro-structure in its macro-architecture.

A BYE AND BARREN THEME: MODESTY AND PLAYFULNESS IN *THE GARDEN OF CYRUS*

Browne's prefatory remarks, as we have already noted, are often among his most revealing. The dedicatory preface to *The Garden of Cyrus* is addressed to Nicholas Bacon, a collateral descendant of the great Francis. This is highly appropriate: of all his formal, published works, *The Garden of Cyrus* is Browne's most purely Baconian undertaking.

Like Browne's other prefaces, this one is careful to establish apparently modest disclaimers which identify the writer as intellectually 'civil'.[114] It is full of paralipses, the figure of concise omission, which overtly serve the rhetorical function of abasement and effacement;[115] indeed, this preface is most notable for insisting upon everything that it does not do, upon all that it cannot claim to be. It is *not* a herbal, nor a taxonomy of plants, Browne is *not* a gardener, it is *not* new material, and the theme itself is *not* fruitful, but 'bye and barren' (*GC*. Bacon, 175). All this is, of course, almost comically disingenuous. *The Garden of Cyrus* offers richly instantiated taxonomic

---

[113] Coles, *Adam in Eden*, b2r.
[114] The courteous reference at the end of the preface to Nicholas Bacon's being 'not new set, but long rooted in such perfection' may be mischievous: Bacon's grandfather was the first baronet, one of the notoriously large number of Jamesian creations, and Nicholas himself was created baronet by Charles II in 1660 (Finch, *Sir Thomas Browne*, 186). The nobility of the Bacon family is nothing if not 'new set'.
[115] Discussed by Breiner, 269.

evidence from the Norfolk hedgerows. We know that Browne had at least one large arable plot in Norwich under cultivation, not to mention the gardens at his various Norwich houses. The theme of the quincunx, if not precisely new, is so elaborated as to make Dr Johnson exclaim that if not on guard one would think 'decussation was the great business of the world'.[116] And the great central digression of the work (for which Browne sheepishly asks indulgence) is anything but barren, being entirely about generation and fruition.

Indeed, in the midst of all his paraliptic effacements, he announces his intention to digress, to 'admit of collateral truths, though at some distance from their principals'. Thus the largest paraliptic claim of all is the one which establishes the quincunx as an uncontainable signature: 'subjects so often discoursed confine the imagination, and fix our conceptions unto the notions of fore-writers' (*GC.* Bacon, 175), and so this treatise, he announces, will occupy an empty plot, one so barren that it recommends itself only in being uncolonised by others. This radical vacancy, moreover, will prove fecund: it will be the soil in which the unconfined imagination will take root and flourish in the promised 'excursions' and 'collateral truths' with the extravagant life of verdure.

The paraliptical signposts do not, therefore, efface the subject by deferral; rather, like the clearing of quincunxial orchards to allow light and air, they make plain the tract's central subject, and they intensify our recognition of all that is, after all, to be included in the form of full-blown digressions and digressive asides. In one sense, by limiting himself to the apparently narrow range of the quincunxial form in nature, *Cyrus* is Browne's most focused composition, the one which most thoroughly colonises and ransacks its subject, even more exactly than *Urne-Buriall*. In another, by selecting procreation, the great business of the world, he allows himself an extreme latitude of enquiry which at least equals, if it does not exceed, the rambling range of *Religio Medici* and the encyclopaedic one of *Pseudodoxia Epidemica*. The preface sounds, in this respect, almost as if he wished to delude his reader, to spring his intricate understanding of the book of nature on an unsuspecting audience prepared for, at best, a 'low delight' (*GC.* Bacon, 177). The force of this unexpected richness of range and instance is itself one of *Cyrus*'s primary effects. Particularly in its digressive tendencies, tendencies which Browne likens to the practice of enhancing gardens with artificial objects and contrivances (*GC.* Bacon, 176), the essay germinates and ramifies far beyond its stated subject.

[116] Johnson, 494.

Despite the modesty (or the cunning) of his hedging in the preface, he hints at the size of his true purpose. The noblest gardens, he says, are 'the epitome of the earth' (*GC.* Bacon, 176); moreover, though the Muslims believe that the life to come will be a garden, in fact paradise is everywhere in this life, and even if theologically 'the delightful world comes after death', nevertheless 'the verdant state of things is the symbol of the Resurrection, and to flourish in the state of glory we must first be sown in corruption' (*GC.* Bacon, 177). The early perfection of the world, he implies, when paradise existed on earth and nothing was yet sown in corruption, is still with us in this verdure, in the subject of generation which from the first sentence of the preface seems to govern the essay. If early-modern natural historians were partly animated by the wish to re-perfect natural knowledge in taxonomies and phytologies, and curious collectors thought to represent prelapsarian order in their arrays and assemblages, Browne assesses this task as the marshalling of natural signs of rebirth into the delightful world. The primary signature of that world and that rebirth is, as he says, 'the verdant state of things'; his green thoughts lead him to examine, as a naturalist, its germs and motives. With this treatise, he marries his longstanding interest in the developing science of generation with his devotional love of natural signatures, and with his antiquarian, polymathic facility in assembling textual evidence from his large learning. Generation itself, not the quincunx, is the great central signature of *The Garden of Cyrus.*

The formal purpose of the work is proposed as the discovery of natural signatures indicating the remnants of Eden in the fallen world of the naturalist, and the essay uses the figure of five, the quincunx, to frame this discovery. But because verdure and effulgence, which do not always present themselves quincunxially, are Browne's true theme, it is the central third chapter with its learned digression on generation which is its heart. So, although the quincunx is the titular and through-running leitmotif of *Cyrus*, it functions in fact as a harbinger – being the conjugal number, as the *logos* which brings rebirth and resurrection – of the natural fecundity that signifies God's grace. Thus Browne allows himself latitude within this programme for a great deal that is not quincunxial, or only forcedly so. Not that quincunxial signatures and generation are divergent: as in so much of Browne's thought, the mystical tends to second and support the findings and observations of the naturalist. It is clear from this central digression that he presents his material – the fruits of his own local observations and experiments – as a scientist presenting results to an informed audience of fellow naturalists. His exculpatory disclaimer in the dedicatory letter to

Bacon – that 'such discourses allow excursions, and venially admit of collateral truths, though at some distance from their principals[;] [w]herein, if
we sometimes take wide liberty, we are not single, but err by great example'
(*GC*. Bacon, 175–6) – is in fact not an excuse but a preparation for what
is to be the major element of the essay. Digressions, therefore, of which
there are many in *The Garden of Cyrus*, are not 'excessive irrelevancies'[117]
but structural signals, enactments, signatures, even, of the theme of generation: just as seeds germinate and multiply, and as the figure of the quincunx
comes to comprehend the entire creation, so the management of the argument of *Cyrus* ramifies and burgeons with offshoots and tendrils reaching
in many directions. Janet Halley has helpfully formulated Browne's digressive structure in *Cyrus*: '[He] defines a major stumbling block to human
mental activity: its inability to discern "rules without exceptions", to create
mental forms that contain natural diversity . . . Formally, Browne promises
anomalies and digressions because he will prefer an encyclopaedic render-
ing of nature in its irreducible plenitude to any specious accomplishment
of his formal aims.'[118]

That *The Garden of Cyrus* was published together with *Urne-Buriall*, and
that both works have five chapters, has needlessly governed much critical
attention to *Cyrus*. The two essays are usually described as 'companion
pieces', mainly on the strength of this first appearance in print, because
they make a convenient death-life pairing, and because Browne tells Bacon
that 'the delightful world comes after death' and could perhaps be referring to the sequential ordering of the two subjects. But this is not strong
evidence that Browne designed them to be read contiguously. On the contrary, the corollary of the post-mortem 'delightful world' is that 'gardens
were before gardeners', that the delightful world of Eden preceded human
life. And if it is true, as has been claimed, that *Cyrus* was the earlier work
and was interrupted unexpectedly by the discovery of the Walsingham urns
which are the ostensible subject of *Urne-Buriall*, it is even harder to argue
that Browne had any serious overarching design for the pair.[119] It is important to establish the slenderness of the pairing argument, since it has tended
to obscure the individual design (and merit) of the less accessible *Cyrus*,
which has lived in its companion's shadow for almost its entire history.

Unlike *Urne-Buriall*, whose five chapters move inexorably from the
coldly factual to the rhapsodically mystical, *Cyrus*'s five chapters allow

---

[117] Huntley, '*The Garden of Cyrus*', 141.   [118] Halley, 101.
[119] This assertion by Huntley, who believes *The Garden of Cyrus* was being planned and written at least
two years before it was registered in 1657/8, is made without supporting evidence, and its validity
is impossible to assess (Huntley, '*The Garden of Cyrus*', 134).

Browne to make – in keeping with the quincunxial theme – a more balanced, regular, and geometrically determined shape, with the longest, central chapter acting as the thematic centre of the essay. If *Urne-Buriall* is not centred like *Cyrus*, it is because it is perpetually reaching toward conclusion – to rhetorical conclusion but also to the conclusions to which all earthly things tend. *Cyrus*, on the other hand, is not about finality and endings, but about beginnings, balance, shapeliness, and recurrence. To borrow Alastair Fowler's term, *Cyrus* is written in the 'triumphal' form, with the 'middest' chapter on seeds and generation accruing 'the sovereign and triumphal associations of the central place'.[120] This particular shapeliness is peculiarly apt for the regular, endlessly recapitulated and interlocking quincunx, a shape geometrically controlled and liberated by its central point.

If Chapter III of *Cyrus* is its quincunxial centre – and this centrality will be discussed shortly – the other chapters are evenly disposed thematically around it. The first chapter suggests the history of the quincunx and its range of incidence; the second discusses artificial quincunxes; the third begins with natural quincunxes, but quickly extends this to discuss generation; the fourth rummages among more abstruse natural phenomena for metaphorical figures of five; and the fifth, as if inverting the scholarly and declarative first chapter, insists on a huge catalogue of *quaeres*, of questions rather than statements or answers (see diagram).

I: quincunxial history and facts		II: artificial quincunxes
	III: natural quincunxes/ generation	
IV: metaphorical quincunxes		V: quincunxial questions

It is a design which shows a self-consciously chiasmic patterning, a mirroring effect in which artificial and natural, question and answer, certainty and mystery, and fact and fancy, interact and reflect each other, all filtered through the central quincunxial axis of the third and focal chapter.

To understand the whole of *Cyrus*, therefore, we must understand its middle chapter, the astonishing, digressive, decussive, virtuosic display which effulgently enacts the theme of germination. Browne announces in the first paragraph of the essay that it is to be concerned with the creatures of the third day of creation (i.e., the vegetable kingdom) (*GC* I, 179).[121] In order

---

[120] Fowler, 65.
[121] It may be significant that the creatures of the third day are most profoundly considered in the third chapter.

to support the creations of subsequent days – animals and man – not only did the plant kingdom appear in the Garden of Eden as 'the primitive food of animals', but, as he tells us in *Religio Medici*, all animals are themselves 'but the hearbs of the field, digested into flesh' (*RM* 1.37). Vegetation, represented at first in gardens, seems to comprehend the whole creation.

The Garden of Eden stands as a divine signature of cultivation (artificial effulgence) *and* generation (natural effulgence), of paradise, and ultimately of natural renewal. The third chapter's opening remarks recapitulate the order of creation up to the third day: quincunxes in the heavens, in the earth (in the form of minerals), and in land- and sea-vegetation, provide an introduction to the general principles of quincunxial plant morphology, which in turn leads to the digression for which he apologises, on generation, a digression which, like the fecund Garden of Adonis endlessly germinating at the centre of Book III of *The Faerie Queene*, seems to colonise and command the central chapter of *The Garden of Cyrus*.[122] And it is a huge digression, a massive instantiation of the physiology and morphology of pods, cods, acorns, cones, beans, stones, pips, nebs, nuts, and kernels. If readers have been readied for only a 'low delight', the barren plot of the quincunxial subject will be fecundated in a rhetorical task posed as a horticultural one: in such unpromising soil Browne's unconfined notice of natural signs will take root and flourish in extravagant, almost unmanageable, verdancy. The series of digressions on various aspects of natural and horticultural history is licensed by the figure of five, a canny means of allowing him to import an enormous and often only distantly related range of remarks, and his expressions of regret for his own freedom are accordingly hard to take seriously. So too are the continued litotes or paralipses of this and the preceding chapters – at a rough count there are thirty-five such figures in *Cyrus*, usually forebearing discussion of other, perhaps digressive, topics in phrases like 'we shall decline', 'to omit', and 'we shall not insist'. In other words, an essay which seems litotically to highlight all the digressions it is not making creates by this means a rhythm, almost from the outset, of deferred or resisted by-ways which immediately become central and notable; and its central digression (from which the paralipsis virtually disappears),[123] apologetically offered as if diversionary, becomes its primary theme.

---

[122] The digression on generation begins about a third of the way into Chapter III, with the sentence (appropriately digressive-sounding), 'Where, by the way, he that observeth the rudimental spring of seeds shall find strict rule, although not after this order' (*GC* III, 196), and ends with a series of 'queries which might enlarge but must conclude this digression' (*GC* III, 200).

[123] I count only one besides the concluding remark.

The miracle of seeds which most interests Browne is their *ex nihilo* life, emblematically reminiscent of God's initial creative act. 'The exiguity and smallness of some seeds, extending to large productions', he remarks, 'is one of the magnalities of nature, somewhat illustrating the work of the Creation, and vast production from nothing' (*GC* iii, 199). Seeds in their various stages of dormancy and germination have received his close ocular and experimental attention. He has seen, probably using magnifying lenses, how 'the rudimental leaf and root are discoverable' in some pulses, a piece of evidence which seems to confirm the generative theory of preformation. He is also able to detect the way in which the developing root and stalk are differentiated within the seed, and the distinctive way these two parts of the plant sprout, whatever the aspect of the seed within the ground. Again and again his observations have amazed him with signs of the miraculous regeneration of life in apparent death or extreme barrenness, as when a newly germinated seed, having had its stalk and roots stripped, will nonetheless regerminate, or when seeds long dormant – in fallow land, or even in the gizzards of birds – 'produc[e] themselves again' (*GC* iii, 198).

The *ex nihilo* aspect of seed-generation brings him, once again, to the animal production nearest to plant seeds – that of insects – and the digression on generation extends to the 'equivocal' production of insects from plants and other animals, whose seminalities are often, like seeds, 'undiscernible'. As the 'rudimental stroke' of duckweed is a seed 'the bigness of a pin's point', so from a glass of water 'a watchful eye may also discover the puncticular originals of periwinkles and gnats' (*GC* iii, 199). This is a subject he touches on in each major work: in *Religio Medici*, for example, the metaphor of bee-generation out of dead matter is turned into a figure of intellectual civility; *Pseudodoxia*, however, reminds us that 'even ... in the body of man from putrid humours, and peculiar wayes of corruption, there have succeeded strange and unseconded shapes of wormes' (*PE* iii.vii.184). In *The Garden of Cyrus* the potentially monstrous capabilities of spontaneous generation are salved by his recognition that 'undiscernible seminalities' (*GC* iii, 199) – the stupendous number of animalcules and seeds being discovered in water, for example – account for all kinds of life, so that the death of some animals, in sponsoring life to new ones, becomes yet another resurrection signature, a further cyclical reading of the processes of life, death, and decay in the natural world which supports his theological understanding of the divine pattern. Whether the miracle of animal-seeds ultimately exceeds that of plants is still open to question, however: the 'seeds of some plants are less than any animal's', yet for the most part 'the biggest of vegetables exceedeth the biggest of animals' (*GC* iii, 199). The digression concludes with a further series of *quaeres* concerning eggs and seeds.

Many of the signatures Browne 'discovers' in *The Garden of Cyrus* can seem playful and even strained. When, in the final chapter, the relentless and almost absurdly inventive list of quincunxes (the five acts of Greek drama, the five pebbles of David against Goliath, the five spots of the ladybird, and so on) leaves the strictly geometrical quincunx for more metaphoric or purely numerical ones, we recognise a scientist who has effectively integrated his natural history with his theology. The Paracelsians, pragmatically looking for remedies, used such similitudes purely pragmatically; the natural philosophers, not seeking such precise theological messages in their investigations, do not usually organise the world along these patterns. Only Browne, genuinely looking at seeds and reproduction, finds a lesson and converts what he knows as a scientist to be true of organisms into a reminder of his faith and a prefiguration of glory. What Browne humorously calls 'inexcusable Pythagorism' (*GC* v, 221) is precisely the method of *The Garden of Cyrus*, a tract which nevertheless encourages the proper and sober Baconian attitudes of 'sense and ocular observation' as 'the surest path to trace the labyrinth of truth' (*GC* v, 226); and his determination to break the bounds of his own quincunxial propriety, to o'erflow the measure of subject and of structure, is an enactment of the very fecundity, the effulgence, the brimming revivification that the natural world offers at every turn.

I have suggested that *Cyrus*, though neither a horticultural nor a hortulan tract, has an oblique relation to both traditions. It is – strikingly among Browne's works – the least governed by the well-established conventions of learned civility. Indeed, in his single-minded attention to the vegetable kingdom in the third chapter, Browne presents himself as the solitary fieldworker gathering specimens in hedgerows, and as the attentive, retired naturalist peering through his magnifying glass at germinations and tiny dissections. His botanical miniaturism is appropriate: in modesty he does not dream of offering large methods or cosmologies; these assessments of the green world are figures of an essentially personal, partly private engagement with salvationary learning. This Browne, though backed by his wide networks of learned associates and printed authorities, seems for the moment to have exhausted civil exchange, to have retreated from large considerations of civility, error, and mutability into the field of the apparently negligible miracle. Perhaps it is a recognition that ultimately only the relentlessly observational naturalist, seeking the innocent knowledge of first-hand, direct inspection, can hope to effect a real reclamation of the true natural epitome.

CHAPTER 7

The fruits of natural knowledge: the fugitive writings and a conclusion

It is a vulgar error to suppose that you have tasted huckleberries who never plucked them.

[Thoreau, *Walden*, 1854]

Browne's working papers are wonderfully inconclusive. Full of the particular humility of the sincere enquirer, they are necessarily open-ended and indefinite. In form and in investigative content they exude the immediacy of ongoing projects, the never-ending variety of interrogations into the nature of the world. Most of them cannot be securely dated, but it is clear that they derive from all the periods of his career, from undergraduate poems (evidence, alas, of one literary facility he did not possess) to scraps from the later 1670s, within a few years of his death. They are an appropriate conclusion to this discussion of Browne. Although he ceased, after the late 1650s, to produce original new work,[1] he was revising and adding to *Pseudodoxia*, carrying out experiments and observations, and maintaining his extensive correspondence until his death in 1682 at the age of seventy-seven.

Fortunately, unlike his completed manuscripts which he seems to have destroyed when works went into print, a very large number of the miscellaneous working papers connected to these activities survive and are held mainly in the British Library and in the Bodleian, in the Sloane and the Rawlinson collections respectively. It is a piece of good fortune that we possess such evidence of Browne at work, a glimpse of a writer so rare in this period; the survival of these fragile monuments to his life in learning and enquiry rebukes his own sense of dissolution and loss in *Urne-Buriall* and *Musæum Clausum*. It is an irony he himself might cheerfully have likened to the surviving epitaph of Hadrian's horse.

[1] The date of *Letter to a Friend* is debated. Formerly attributed to the mid-1670s and Browne's old age, it has more recently (and convincingly) been reassigned to the 1650s (see Huntley, *Sir Thomas Browne*, 184–203).

The papers represent a veritable seed-bed of items, contemplations, stray facts, *quaeres*, and propositions or considerations in rough draft, where germs and kernels were sown and germinated, lifted, and transplanted into the greater and more coherent works. This fugitive material, however, is not itself compositionally coherent. As its editor Sir Geoffrey Keynes indicates, the large selection published in the *Works* (1964) is a helpful but entirely arbitrary editorial disposition of disparate material into manageable generic categories – as commonplace collections, as natural historical notes, as experimental data, and so on – which are not Browne's own. Nor could they be: they have been much tampered with and rearranged over the past 250 years. Some of the most interesting material in them is little more than scribbling and note-taking, although this is also punctuated by more composed fragments, proto-essays, and letters. That the collection is in no particular order in respect of Browne's own practices is bibliographically insignificant but thematically felicitous: intellectually, the contents of the papers are effulgently disordered and consequently they are wonderfully energetic.

This randomness of enquiry in the papers is nevertheless somewhat at odds with the orderliness of Browne's polished output. A writer and natural philosopher whose inclination is for quincunxial design and Baconian categories of thought is one whom we might expect, even in rhetorical 'undress', to arrange his primitive thoughts and formulations in some discernible if latent pattern. What is instead clear is the way in which the papers represent, in Browne's progressive development of thoughts, a chaos gradually regulated and systematised. The relation of the papers to the final works, and to Browne's overarching conception of his intellectual project, is that same marshalling, that same vigorous coordination of stray and scattered creation implicit in contemporary encyclopaedic textual and material arrays and demonstrated throughout his great published compositions.

A section designated by Keynes as additional material for the *Miscellany Tracts* will illustrate this movement from disarrangement to order. This section of six folios in BL MS 1827 is a set of replies to a varied set of queries from an unidentified correspondent.[2] Browne solves the riddle of an Irish soldier who in delirium cried out in an unknown language which Browne finds to be Russian; he explains the iconic depiction of St Corbinian riding a bear; he considers without conclusion the origin of the idiom 'to count noses'; he runs through a number of epitaphs, asking 'whether Jocular & ænigmaticall epitaphs bee allowable' and noting ones on Prince

---

[2] Thomas Browne, 'A Brief Reply to Severall Queries' [an addition to *Miscellany Tracts*] in Keynes III, 224–9.

Doria's dog and on Hadrian's horse; he thinks about where the phrase *hic jacet* originates, and why most of the inscriptions in Gruter commemorate the young. He suggests writing a dialogue spoken by an epitaph and a funeral oration, perhaps as a kind of *paragone* between the two forms, and concludes with a series of notes on medals. It seems, in other words, that the order in which he answers the initial queries leads him to a further consideration of epitaphs and epigraphy of various kinds, so that what begins as responses to an eccentrically random set of queries settles with the last ones on a topic dear to his heart which generates a much greater field of information. To this extent there is at least thematic coherence: the variety of examples of epitaphs and inscriptions, from both textual and material sources, native and foreign, curious and famous, are mingled with more general interrogations – should comic epitaphs be permitted; is *siste viator* ['pause, traveller'] a proper locution for church sepulchres – and all this beckons toward a greater whole in an evolutionary process of assembly; these are notes toward an authoritative disquisition such as *Urne-Buriall*.

Indeed, there is no formal, published work of Browne's which lacks some primitive or initial version of one or more of its sections in the notes. The worry about the epitaph of Hadrian's horse Boristhenes surfaces as a figure of tragicomic transience in *Urne-Buriall*. Throughout his observations and notes he mentions plant signatures and the quincunx itself, so prominently featured in *The Garden of Cyrus*; and several passages of *Cyrus* are found in embryo form in the notebooks. The commonplace book has familiar items: he proposes 'a dialogue between two Twinns in the womb concerning the world they were to come into', a fantasy also proposed in *Urne-Buriall*;[3] a note about those who die or achieve some notable thing on their birthdays is found more fully developed in *Letter to a Friend*;[4] and a number of curiosities in *Musæum Clausum* originate here as jottings.[5] The regeneration of plants, the miracle of aurelian metamorphosis in insects, the signature spots of the Peterfish, even a remark about the supposed atheism of doctors – 'though in poynt of devotion & pietie physitians do meet with common obloquie, yet in the Roman Calendar wee find no lesse then 29 saints & martyrs of that profession', which may have informed the title and purpose of *Religio Medici*[6] – appear in the papers.

---

[3] On a nineteenth-century pastiche based on this idea, see my Introduction.
[4] *LF*, 104–5.   [5] *ON*, 250–2.
[6] *NCB*, 320. Although it seems likely from internal evidence that the papers represent work from nearly the entire span of Browne's adult career, it may be too much to insist that the paper bearing this comment about the religion of doctors dates from the time of *Religio Medici's* composition or even its publication, but that work from his undergraduate days persists among them makes this assignment not impossible.

It is interesting to observe the compositional process itself. The following passage shows Browne thinking almost as he writes:

> it had been a . . . fancy for me to think of Platoe's yeare and the revolution after the heavens unto ther first place; after motion in the hevens themselves had not continued so long to weare out like a garment; the earth had been destroyed before it had been so widely discovered. America might have been a perpetuall *terra incognita* and never arose unto us.

> . . . it is not to your . . . that his goodnesse his patience hath thus so long continued it. How that carried the earth in the early dayes of the first man drowned the same before 16 hundred yeares, should still deferre the last flames and should still contend with itt and yet deferre the last flames. And surely if the patience of heaven were not proportionable unto the provocations from earth, theer needed a mediator for its duration as well as transgression hath the duration of it, and the world had come short of our present computation. It had been a chymericall phancy to have dreampt of Platoes yeare; the north starre had not stood within 2 degrees and half of the pole and the iter palans of the same had never attayned unto cancer; the earth would have been destroyed before it had been descovered. America had been a perpetuall *terra incognita* and never arose unto us.[7]

These two paragraphs, incomplete and here and there indecipherable, are worth untangling. In them we see Browne's subtle shifts of emphasis in revamped phrases which correct or extend their initial versions. Plato's year – the belief, asserted in *Timæus*, that time repeats itself and the stars return to their original equinoctial places every 25,000 years – is dismissed at the outset: the wearing-out process of such a long revolution would, Browne argues, have destroyed the earth long since, long before we made the recent discovery of the New World.

The damaged opening of the second paragraph assigns the survival of the earth to God's wisdom and mercy, although Browne seems to qualify this when he wonders how a Maker who sent the Flood in anger and punishment 1,600 years after Adam could support its continuation rather than destroy it in fire. This thought is revised mid-sentence when the '*still*' of 'still deferre the last flames' is reassigned to 'and should still contend with itt', and the first phrase is revamped as 'and *yet* deferre the last flames.' He wants the ongoing mercy of God to be foremost, with the two prepositions 'still' and 'yet', temporal extensions, doubly emphasising His forbearance. The commensurability of heaven's patience with earthly provocations is an easy enough formula, although a missing comma in 'theer needed a mediator for its duration as well[,] as transgression hath the duration of it' makes the whole phrase otherwise somewhat difficult to understand. He

---

[7] *ON*, 267–8. I am indebted to Andrew Zurcher for his help in deciphering the MS of this passage.

seems to say that except for that commensurability, there would have to be an intercessor to seek an extension for earth's existence, since otherwise it is controlled by transgression and would not have been allowed to last as long as it has. He then returns with a revised and re-situated remark about Plato's year, where the phrase 'it had been a [chymicall?] fancy for me to think' becomes 'it had been a chymicall phancy to have dreampt', an alteration perhaps depersonalising the cosmic Platonic idea, or perhaps simply relocating it with greater rhetorical force at the end rather than the beginning of the passage. The scientific Browne then intervenes when he notes that the Platonic calculation is not supported by astronomical observations, which show that the stars are in the wrong places and that the earth should have ceased to exist long ago. Finally he converts the failure to discover America into the destruction of the earth itself 'before it had been descovered'. The first allusion to America is merely one which indicates the actual chronology of the earth, which has lasted long enough for the New World to be discovered; the second allusion deepens the force of the figure by suggesting that the world itself, and not just America, would, but for God's mercy, have been *terra incognita*. The revisions in this passage seem to show us a little of how Browne developed a thought, and remind us how careful a stylist he is, rearranging in the course of the two paragraphs both the order of argument and more minor but telling semantic emphases.

The richness of their contents makes it impossible to list the full range of information and enquiry to be found in the papers. Included in them are a few complete essays, such as 'On Dreams',[8] or the account of Charles VIII's itinerary in Italy, or brief but fully instantiated discourses on plagues and on the Pharsalian Fields, or anatomical essays on the ear, the navel, the skin, and so on.[9] Much more of the papers consist of jottings and notes on plants, birds, animals, history ancient and modern, medicines, medals, bubbles, experimental method, probability, and meteorology. Some information is anecdotal, as, for instance, the account of a centenarian woman in Yarmouth afflicted by a voracious appetite which had to be supplied by the parish, an account prepared for the Royal Society but not lacking in the practising physician's essentially humane and pragmatic approach: 'Though I am ready to extend my charity unto her', he remarks, 'yet I should be loath to spend a peece of Ambregris I have upon her, and to afford her 6 graines for every dosis, till I found some effect thereof, though that bee esteemed a specifick in her condition'.[10] The vaunted charity of the second part of *Religio Medici* is not, it seems, without practical limits. Other anecdotes concern the measurement of a Norwich steeple

[8] Discussed in Chapter Two above.   [9] *OA*, 333–44.   [10] *ON*, 243.

('14 yards higher then Grantham steeple' he remarks with civic pride) and a thrilling account of a terrific thunderstorm which generated fireballs and substantially damaged his house in two places: 'The noyse & lightening were so terrible that they putt the whole citty into an Amazement, & most unto their prayers.' He goes on to say that in a similar storm a few days later a woman and her horse were killed by lightning near Bungay, an event attested to by the groat-sized pieces of her 'shivered' hat which were sent to him as a curiosity.[11] He records the consequences of binge-drinking in the case of one Robert Hutchinson, a regular at the Wheatsheaf in his own parish in Norwich. For reasons perhaps not wholly experimental, Hutchinson drank a gallon of brandy in fourteen hours, fell into a fever, and complained of a burning in his stomach, but recovered within a week ('with a great louthing of brandie after'). Another man did the same, but his additional consumption of beer seems to have saved him from any ill effects.[12] Strolling in the countryside outside Norwich, and seeing a cottage wreathed in honeysuckle belonging to 'a right good man', Browne was prompted to make a Latin poem in which the honeysuckle celebrates humble, healthy country life above the contagion of cities:

> I adorn the kindly door of my master and mistress,
> A house where enters neither force nor guile.
> Such, if the gods came down to earth from heaven,
> Is the cottage which Jupiter and Mercury would enter.[13]

This charming conceit is especially interesting because Browne remarks that he has in his house a copy 'from a draught of Reubens' of this visitation of the two gods to the elderly couple Baucis and Philemon. Countryside observations, featuring so largely in the miscellaneous notes, could yield more than natural history.

A tantalising sense of learned community and vigorous intellectual exchange also resides in these extremely various papers. Like the *Miscellany Tracts*, mostly addressed to correspondents, the papers show Browne responding to queries and gathering up information to give to others. The notes everywhere address a reader, often informally: 'Butt before I dismisse you I shall not omitt to entertaine you with a few other Queries whereof perhaps you have not taken much/strict notice', he tells the addressee of

---

[11] 'Account of a Thunderstorm' in Keynes III, 239–40.   [12] *NCB*, 276.
[13] *NCB*, 281–2, trans. Keynes.

> *At domini dominæque meæ pia limina adorno*
> *Et quam non intrant visque dolusque domum.*
> *Talem, si peterent de cælo numina terras,*
> *Jupiter intraret Mercuriusque casam.*

his notes on plagues.[14] 'How like you that argument of Mahomet Bassa [who prevented, by reasoning with Selimus, a massacre of Christians]', he enquires in his notes on naval fights.[15] 'I have been so often earnest with you to learne, read & remember all you can', he admonishes the young Edward Browne on his early travels.[16] A great many lists of things to look into appear in the papers – whether it is true that 'to make urine upon the earth newly cast up by a mole, bringeth downe the menses', 'what kind of motion sliding is', 'to cleanse & cleere pearles by washing or steeping them in may dewe taken from lettuces';[17] these may be the record of queries presented to him by others as well as his own investigations.

The correspondence between Browne and his son Edward concerning the ostrich has already been discussed. The other principal example of such exchange is the correspondence with and notes for Christopher Merrett, with whom Browne had extended conference about British birds in aid of the revised version (never published) of Merrett's *Pinax Rerum Naturalium Britannicarum* (1667–8). He had offered to supply Merrett with information about Norfolk birds, and at first he gives an overview of the birdlife he has been observing in his district for years, with the habits of eagles, kites, cranes, gannets, skuas, swans, ospreys, and others detailed in a letter-like composition. These notes become more list-like in succeeding folios, however, as Browne considers species of whose identity he is unsure, and the ongoing exchange with Merrett, of which we possess evidence in both epistolary form and as working notes, becomes a remarkable consultation between the two men as they try to establish correct Latin names for a number of species which have quite distinct local names in various parts of the country. Some of Browne's notes seem purposed merely to establish a pre-existing nomenclature:

Larus cinerus . . . commonly called sternes.

Platea, or shovelard . . .

Bernacles, Brants, *Branta* . . .

Sheldrakes, *sheldracus Jonstoni*.

Barganders, a noble coloured fowle, *vulpanser* . . .

Wild geese, *Anser ferus*.

Scoch goose, *Anser scoticus*.

Goshander, merganser.[18]

[14] *ON*, 252. [15] *ON*, 254. [16] *ON*, 266. [17] *NCB*, 296, 297, 302. [18] *NHN*, 403–4.

The difficulty of establishing a reliable scientific nomenclature is one by which Browne, with his longstanding connexions with the fowlers, countrymen, and fishermen who brought him specimens, is particularly troubled. 'Many sorts of wild ducks', he tells Merrett, 'passe under names well knowne unto fowlers though of no great signification, as smee, widgeon, Arts, ankers, noblets.'[19] In one of the letters which emerged from these consultations, Browne says, 'I confesse . . . I am much unsatisfied on the names given . . . by countrymen, and uncertaine what to give them myself . . . as yet of uncertaine classe or knowledg.'[20] He has to describe birds for whom there are no known Latin names: 'A may chitt, a small dark gray bird litle bigger then a stint [a sandpiper], of fatnesse beyond any. It comes in may into marshland & other parts, & abides not above a moneth or 6 weekes. Another small bird somewhat bigger than a stint, called a churre, & is commonly taken among us';[21] 'Ringlestones, a small white & black bird like a wagtayle & seemes to be some kind of *motacilla marina*'.[22] The bewildering and strangely named wealth of hoop-birds, shooing-horns, yarwhelps, chocks, hobbies, whinbirds, chippers, trussers, pokers, seapyes, puets, barkers, and scramblers native to or migrant through the bird-rich marshy and sandy Norfolk coast clearly require expert assignment to their proper categories, since, as Browne notes elsewhere, 'countrymen are not the best nomenclators' (*PE* III.xxvi.272).

Perhaps even more exciting to the naturalist was the discovery of a true non-descript:

On XIIII of May, 1664, a very rare bird was sent mee, kild about Crostwick, wch seemed to bee some kind of Jay. The bill was black, strong, and bigger then a Jayes, somewhat yellowe clawes tippd black. 3 before and one clawe behind, the whole bird not so bigge as a Jaye. The head, neck, & throat of a violet colour; the back upper parts of the wing of a russet yellowe, the fore & part of the wing azure, succeeded downward by a greenish blewe, then on the flying fethers bright blewe; the lower parts of the wing outwardly of a browne, inwardly of a merry blewe; the belly a light faynt blewe; the back toward the tayle of a purple blewe; the taile eleven fethers, of a greenish coulour, the extremities of the outward fethers thereof white with an eye of greene.[23]

The bird, later sent on to Merrett, was a garrulous roller (*garrulus argentoratensis*). The description, however, is good enough to locate it in a modern bird encyclopaedia. 'Have you *mustela mas et fœmina*', he asks,

[19] *NHN*, 404.

[20] Thomas Browne to Christopher Merrett, 6 February 1668/9 (Keynes IV, 356). This was a common complaint: William Coles calls these country names 'improper, bastard, and insignificant' (Coles, *Adam in Eden*, a3ʳ).

[21] *NHN*, 406.   [22] *NHN*, 407.   [23] *NHN*, 410.

'a kind of wild fowle, lesse then a duck, from the head calld wesels ...
? Have you sea phaisant, another kind of duck, so called from the long
pheasants in the tayle ... Have you receaved any further notice of cricke
teale, or crackling teale.'[24] Merrett's names are equally confusing: 'I do not
find any fish you call a Pope', Browne writes, 'butt one called a Pout ... I
send you the figure'.[25] Without a systematic zoology, teasing out the correct
identity of birds, not only their proper Latin designations but also the more
elementary agreement that they were referring to the same creature in the
first place, was a long and careful process.[26]

Demotic names were only part of the trouble. There was scholarly error,
as well: Browne warns Merrett that a printed description of *anas arctica clusii*
('the same we call a puffin') incorrectly makes it exclusive to the Faroe Islands
though it is in fact found in Wales, too.[27] Browne himself has to apologise
for labelling as a barker the picture of a yarwhelp, the confusion arising
from the similarity of their calls.[28] The texture of question and answer,
give and take, and the informal mixture of different sorts of information, is
very suggestive of the Baconian compiling and establishing of terms which
must have been common among the learned and the curious throughout
the realm. These notes and observations show us the intellectual underpinning of Browne's formal and artful public productions; and the vignette
of two naturalists putting their heads together in the cause of organising
information can stand for a kind of learned sociability and mutuality which
must have been the very texture of Browne's investigative existence.

Cross-fertilisation (to use a generative metaphor Browne could *not* have
understood) by cooperative exchange of ideas and information is everywhere in his work, from the largest and most finished compositions to
these random surviving papers, the mere detritus of an investigative career. His works, like the papers, function as the earth itself functions, as a
seminarium, a place of intellectual germination and fruition. Beyond the
pattern of this intellectual verdancy, it is dangerous to insist on a deliberate
and clear shape for the progression of Browne's works: *Religio Medici* was
probably only partially 'wrought', its author surprised by publicity; *Pseudodoxia* evolved over many editions and was a work-in-progress for two
decades; *Urne-Buriall* and *The Garden of Cyrus* may or may not have been
designed in tandem, and even the order of their composition is in doubt;
the tracts, notebooks, commonplace books, and other assorted compendia

---

[24] *NHN*, 414, 416.   [25] *NHN*, 416.
[26] The history of this process is partly given in Keith Thomas, *Man and the Natural World: Changing
Attitudes in England, 1500–1800* (Harmondsworth: Penguin, 1983), Chapter 11.i.
[27] *NHN*, 405.   [28] *NHN*, 413.

of observations, experiments, and theories observe no rule of organisation, and function instead like elements to be inserted in the completed compositions. Throughout this book I have tried to suggest that the intellectual structures of Browne's keenest scientific and antiquarian interests govern the literary and thematic structures of his work, to maintain that analogies between the civil and material cultures of empiricism and the rhetoric of Browne's thought are reliable routes into his dense, idiosyncratic writings. Although Browne's particular blend of the strictly empirical and the more freely analogical puts him on the cusp of two intellectual epochs and allows him the latitude to use the practical and spiritual paradigms of investigation and assemblage more energetically than most, the same freedom and the same influence are latent in some of his predecessors, and fully, if differently, evolved in his inheritors. Further consideration of these features in Browne's writings would attend also to those of Aldrovandi, Camden, Burton, Casaubon, Aubrey, Evelyn, Grew, Boyle, and Hooke, for each of whom, since 'mankind fell by tasting of the forbidden Tree of Knowledge, so we, their Posterity, may be in part restor'd by the same way, not only by beholding and contemplating, but by tasting too those fruits of Natural knowledge, that were never yet forbidden'.[29]

Perhaps justly, the historians of science have overlooked Browne; with less reason, the admirers of the great conceitful or polemical writers like Donne and Milton regard him as (apparently) complacent, apolitical, and insufficiently agonised. Moreover, the overwhelming primacy of *Religio Medici* among his works, together with the current interest in Renaissance concepts of self, has tended to promote discussion of this single contribution to 'life-writing' at the expense of the themes and purposes of his later, more typical, mature work. Browne's influences, especially the practical and visual components of seventeenth-century investigation, have been passed over by literary students, and deemed too slight for the students of scientific history. Inconveniently situated between art and science, and resisting any obvious generic or polemical category, the architectonic and rhetorical analogies between his literary craft and his investigative activities (for example, collecting, or practical medicine) have been largely ignored. But the shape and construction of Browne's works through these investigations, this training, and this reading helps us to understand the emerging structures of knowledge in his lifetime.

No one can claim for Browne some undetected scientific originality which would elevate him to the first rank of English scientists; instead, by

---

[29] Hooke, *Micrographia*, b2r.

situating his great powers of synthesis within an intellectual and literary ferment, we remind ourselves that the greatest movements and shifts in human history are often best illustrated at least as clearly by the responses of minor and marginal figures as by the great minds. In this respect, to understand what occurred in the development of science in the seventeenth century is to notice the engagement of Browne and others like him, crucial members of a sometimes undifferentiated society of sincere and ingenious enquirers whose fame, like the civil bee celebrated in *Religio Medici,* survives in communal rather than individual accomplishment, and Browne is representative rather than unique. To this extent, the history of early-modern investigation is usefully inflected by these minor reputations.

As a writer of the first rank, however, Browne needs no apology. It is not easy to name another author of the period who at once combined interests so wide with a habit of expression rich, vigorous, and supple enough to meet stringent intellectual demands. One aim of this book has been to analyse what might be called Browne's 'investigative poetics', the formal and the syntactical rhythms of enquiry in his major works, a way of approaching new problems and new knowledge in which empirical thought-patterns, practical enquiry, and the freedom of his instinctive prose are a single, powerful instrument. It is a poetics which grants him Adamic access to those fruits of natural knowledge that were never yet forbidden.

Bibliography

MANUSCRIPTS

BL MS Sloane 1334 (Thomas Browne Notes and Correspondence)
BL MS Sloane 1847 (Thomas Browne Notes and Correspondence)
BL MS Sloane 1911–13 (Thomas Browne Notes and Correspondence)
Bodleian MS Top. Gen.c.24 (John Aubrey, *Monumenta Britannica*)

MARGINALIA

Browne, Thomas. *Religio Medici* (1642) with Browne's marginal corrections (Robert Taylor Collection, Firestone Library, Princeton University)

PRIMARY SOURCES

Unless otherwise noted, the city of publication is London.

Aldrovandi, Ulisse. *De quadrupedibus digitatis* (Bologna, 1645)
Anon. *The Fruiterers Secrets* (1604)
Anon. *True News from Norwich* (1641)
[Apsley, Allen.] *Order and Disorder: or, the World Made and Undone* (1679) [see also Hutchinson, Lucy]
Aristotle. *De Generatione Animalium*, trans. A. Platt (Oxford: Clarendon Press, 1910)
  Historia Animalium, trans. A. L. Peck, 3 vols. (London: Heinemann, and Cambridge, MA: Harvard University Press, 1970)
Astell, Mary. 'The Character of a Vertuoso' in *An Essay in Defence of the Female Sex* (1696), 96–110
Aubrey, John. *Brief Lives*, ed. Oliver Lawson-Dick, 2nd edn (London: Mandarin, 1992)
  Monumenta Britannica, ed. John Fowles and Rodney Legg, 2 vols. (Sherborne: Dorset Publishing Co., 1982)
  The Natural History of Wiltshire, ed. John Britton (London: Wiltshire Topographical Society / J. B. Nichols, 1848)
  Remaines of Gentilisme and Judaisme in *Three Works*, ed. John Buchanan-Brown (Fontwell: Centaur, 1972), 127–304
  Three Works, ed. John Buchanan-Brown (Fontwell: Centaur, 1972)

223

Augustine. *The City of God against the Pagans*, ed. and trans. R. W. Dyson (Cambridge: Cambridge University Press, 1998)

Austen, Ralph. *A Treatise of Fruit-Trees . . . Together with The Spirituall Use of an Orchard* (1653)

Bacon, Francis. *The Advancement of Learning*, ed. Brian Vickers (Oxford: Oxford University Press, 1996)

The Essays, ed. John Pitcher (Harmondsworth: Penguin, 1985)

New Atlantis, ed. Arthur Johnston (Oxford: Clarendon Press, 1974)

Parasceve in *The Philosophical Works of Francis Bacon*, ed. and trans. James Spedding and John M. Robertson (London: George Routledge and Sons, 1905), 388–412

Basset, Robert. *Curiosities; Or, the Cabinet of Nature* (1637)

Birch, Thomas. *History of the Royal Society of London for Improving of Natural Knowledge*, 4 vols. (1756–7)

Bodin, Jean. *Methodus ad facilem historiarum cognitionem* (1566)

Republique (1576)

Bosio, Antonio. *Roma sotterranea* (Rome, 1632)

Boyle, Robert. *A Proemial Essay . . . Touching Experimental Essays* (1661)

'Some Observations about Shining Flesh, Both of Veal and of Pullet' (1672) in *Early Science in Oxford*, ed. R. T. Gunther, 2nd edn, vol. vi: *The Philosophical Society* (London: Dawsons, 1968), 99–101

'Two Essays concerning the Unsuccessfulness of Experimentes' in *The Works of the Honourable Robert Boyle*, 5 vols. (1744), i, 204–27

Brome, Alexander. *Songs and Other Poems* (1664)

Browne, Edward. *An Account of Several Travels through a Great Part of Germany: In Four Journeys* (1677)

Browne, Thomas. *Christian Morals* (1716) in *The Works of Sir Thomas Browne*, ed. Geoffrey Keynes, 2nd edn, 4 vols. (Chicago: University of Chicago Press, 1964), i, 243–95

The Garden of Cyrus (1658) in *The Works of Sir Thomas Browne*, ed. Geoffrey Keynes, 2nd edn, 4 vols. (Chicago: University of Chicago Press, 1964), i, 175–227

Hydriotaphia, or Urne-Buriall (1658) in *The Works of Sir Thomas Browne*, ed. Geoffrey Keynes, 2nd edn, 4 vols. (Chicago: University of Chicago Press, 1964), i, 131–72

Letter to a Friend (1690) in *The Works of Sir Thomas Browne*, ed. Geoffrey Keynes, 2nd edn, 4 vols. (Chicago: University of Chicago Press, 1964), i, 101–21

Miscellaneous Notes from Commonplace Books in *The Works of Sir Thomas Browne*, ed. Geoffrey Keynes, 2nd edn, 4 vols. (Chicago: University of Chicago Press, 1964), iii, 272–330

Miscellany Tracts (1683) in *The Works of Sir Thomas Browne*, ed. Geoffrey Keynes, 2nd edn, 4 vols. (Chicago: University of Chicago Press, 1964), iii, 3–120

Musæum Clausum (*c.* 1674) in *Miscellany Tracts* in *The Works of Sir Thomas Browne*, ed. Geoffrey Keynes, 2nd edn, 4 vols. (Chicago: University of Chicago Press, 1964), iii, 109–19

Notes and Experiments in Natural History in *The Works of Sir Thomas Browne*, ed. Geoffrey Keynes, 2nd edn, 4 vols. (Chicago: University of Chicago Press, 1964), III 347–60

Notes on the Natural History of Norfolk in *The Works of Sir Thomas Browne*, ed. Geoffrey Keynes, 2nd edn, 4 vols. (Chicago: University of Chicago Press, 1964), III, 401–31

Observations and Notes in *The Works of Sir Thomas Browne*, ed. Geoffrey Keynes, 2nd edn, 4 vols. (Chicago: University of Chicago Press, 1964), III, 239–71

Observations in Anatomy in *The Works of Sir Thomas Browne*, ed. Geoffrey Keynes, 2nd edn, 4 vols. (Chicago: University of Chicago Press, 1964), III, 333–44

Pseudodoxia Epidemica (1646), ed. Robin Robbins, 2 vols. (Oxford: Clarendon Press, 1981)

Religio Medici ([1642] 1643) in *The Works of Sir Thomas Browne*, ed. Geoffrey Keynes, 2nd edn, 4 vols. (Chicago: University of Chicago Press, 1964), I, 3–93

Religio Medici and Other Works, ed. L. C. Martin (Oxford: Clarendon Press, 1964)

Repertorium: Tombs of Norwich in *The Works of Sir Thomas Browne*, ed. Geoffrey Keynes, 2nd edn, 4 vols. (Chicago: University of Chicago Press, 1964), III, 123–43

Sir Thomas Browne: 'Religio Medici', ed. Jean-Jacques Denonain (Cambridge: Cambridge University Press, 1953)

Sir Thomas Browne: 'Religio Medici', 'Hydriotaphia', and 'The Garden of Cyrus', ed. Robin Robbins (Oxford: Clarendon Press, 1972)

Sir Thomas Browne: Selected Writings, ed. Geoffrey Keynes (London: Faber and Faber, 1968)

Sir Thomas Browne: The Major Works, ed. C. A. Patrides (Harmondsworth: Penguin, 1977)

Sir Thomas Browne's Works, ed. Simon Wilkin, 4 vols. (London: William Pickering, 1835–6)

Thomas Browne, 'Religio Medici', ed. Vittoria Sanna (Cagliari: Università di Cagliari, 1958)

'To the Deceased Author, upon the Promiscuous Printing of His Poems, the Looser Sort, with the Religious' in *Donne: Poetical Works*, ed. Herbert J. C. Grierson, 2nd edn (Oxford: Oxford University Press, 1971), 340–1

The Works of Sir Thomas Browne, ed. Geoffrey Keynes, 2nd edn, 4 vols. (Chicago: University of Chicago Press, 1964)

Bryskett, Lodovick. *A Discourse of Civil Life* (1606)

Buonanni, F. *Ricreatione dell'occhio e della mente nell'osservation' delle Chicciole* (Rome, 1681)

Burnet, Gilbert. 'Character of a Christian Philosopher' in *Lives, Characters, and an Address to Posterity*, ed. John Jebb (London: Duncan, 1883), 366–7.

Burnet, Thomas. *The Sacred Theory of the Earth* (1689)

Burton, Robert. *The Anatomy of Melancholy*, ed. T. C. Faulkner, N. K. Kiessling, and R. L. Blair, 5 vols. (Oxford: Clarendon Press, 1989)

Butler, Charles. *The Feminine Monarchie* (1609)

Butler, Samuel. *Hudibras*, ed. John Wilders (Oxford: Clarendon Press, 1967)
  Satires and Miscellaneous Poetry and Prose, ed. René Lamar (Cambridge: Cambridge University Press, 1928)

Camden, William. *Britannia* (1586), trans. Philemon Holland (1610)
  Remains concerning Britain (1605), ed. R. D. Dunn (Toronto: University of Toronto Press, 1984)

Cantimpré, Thomas of. *Bonum universale de apibus* in *Thomae Cantipratani . . . miraculorum et exemplorum memorabilium* (Douay, 1605)

Carew, Thomas. *The Poems of Thomas Carew*, ed. Rhodes Dunlap (Oxford: Clarendon Press, 1949)

Chiocco, A., and B. Ceruti. *Musæum Francisci Calceolari Veronensis* (Verona, 1622)

Coleridge, Samuel Taylor. *Marginalia* in *The Collected Works of Samuel Taylor Coleridge* (London: Routledge and Kegan Paul, and Princeton: Princeton University Press, 1985), XII

Coles, William. *Adam in Eden: or, Natures Paradise* (1657)
  The Art of Simpling (1656)

Combe, Thomas. *The Theater of Fine Devices* (1614) [a translation of Guillaume de la Perriere's *Théâter de bons engins* (1539)]

Courtin, Antoine de. *The Rules of Civility* (1678)

Cowley, Abraham. *Essays, Plays and Sundry Verses*, ed. A. R. Waller (Cambridge: Cambridge University Press, 1906)
  Poems (1656)
  Poeticall Blossoms (1633)
  A Proposition for the Advancement of Experimental Philosophy (1661) in Abraham Cowley, *Complete Works in Verse and Prose*, ed. Alexander Grosart, 2 vols. (London: Chertsey Worthies' Library, 1881), II, 281–91

Croll, Oswald. *Tractatus de signaturis internis rerum* in *Basilica Chymica* ([Frankfurt?], 1647), 1–152

Dante. *The Divine* Comedy, trans. Laurence Binyon (London: Agenda, 1947)

Daye, John. *The Parliament of Bees* (1641)

Denonain, Jean-Jacques, ed. *Sir Thomas Browne: 'Religio Medici'* (Cambridge: Cambridge University Press, 1953)

Descartes, René. *Discourse on Method* in *René Descartes: Philosophical Writings*, trans. and ed. Elizabeth Anscombe and Peter D. Geach (Edinburgh: Nelson, 1963), 5–57

Digby, Kenelm. *Discourse on the Vegetation of Plants* (1661)
  Observations on 'Religio Medici' (1643)

Dockray, Benjamin. *Conjectural Restoration of the Lost Dialogue between Two Twins* (London: Cash, 1855)

Donne, John. *The Courtier's Library, or Catalogus Librorum Aulicorum*, ed. Evelyn Simpson (London: Nonesuch, 1930)
  Donne: Poetical Works, ed. Herbert J. C. Grierson, 2nd edn (Oxford: Oxford University Press, 1971)
  Essays in Divinity, ed. Evelyn Simpson (Oxford: Clarendon Press, 1952)

John Donne: Selected Prose, ed. Neil Rhodes (Harmondsworth: Penguin, 1987)

John Donne: The Epithalamiums, Anniversaries, and Epicedes, ed. W. Milgate (Oxford: Clarendon Press, 1978)

Du Bartas, Guillaume. *The Divine Weeks and Works of Guillaume de Saluste Sieur Du Bartas*, trans. Josuah Sylvester, ed. Susan Snyder, 2 vols. (Oxford: Clarendon Press, 1979)

Dugdale, William. *The History of Imbanking and Drayning* (1662)

History of St Paul's Cathedral (1658)

Earle, John. *Microcosmography*, ed. Alfred S. West, 2nd edn (Cambridge: Cambridge University Press, 1951)

Eliot, John. *Poems* (1658)

Evelyn, John. *Diary*, ed. W. Bray, 2 vols. (London: Everyman, 1907)

The Diary of John Evelyn, ed. E. S. de Beer (London: Oxford University Press, 1959)

Kalendarium Hortense (1669)

Publick Employment and an Active Life Prefer'd (1667)

Sylva (1664)

Fairfax, Nathaniel. *A Treatise of the Bulk and Selvedge of the World* (1674)

Finch, Jeremiah S., ed. *A Catalogue of the Libraries of Sir Thomas Browne and Dr Edward Browne, His Son* [facsimile of 1710 catalogue of 1711 auction by Thomas Ballard, bookseller] (Leiden: E. J. Brill/Leiden University Press, 1986)

Fischart, Johann. *Catalogus catalogorum perpetuo durabilis* (Strasburg, 1590)

Fletcher, R. *Ex Otio Negotium* (1656)

Frati, Lodovico. *Catalogo dei manoscritti di Ulisse Aldrovandi* (Bologna: N. Zanichelli, 1907)

Gaffarel, James. *Unheard-Of Curiosities*, trans. Edmund Chilmead (1650)

Gassendi, Pierre. *Vir illustri Nicolai Claudii Fabricii de Peiresc senatoris aquisextiensis vita* (Paris, 1641)

Gerard, John. *Herball or Generall Historie of Plantes* (1597)

Glanvill, Joseph. *Plus Ultra* (1668)

The Vanity of Dogmatizing (1661)

Goodman, Godfrey. *The Fall of Man, or the Corruption of Nature* (1616)

Grew, Nehemiah. *Anatomy of Plants* (1682)

Guazzo, Stephano. *The Art of Complaisance, or the Means to Oblige in Conversation* (1677)

The Art of Conversation (1738) [originally published in English as *Civile Conversation* (1575)]

Hakewill, George. *Apologie of the Power and Providence of God* (Oxford, 1627)

Hall, Joseph. *The Works of the Right Reverend Joseph Hall*, ed. P. Wynter, 10 vols. (1863)

Harrington, James. *The Commonwealth of Oceana*, ed. J. G. A. Pocock (Cambridge: Cambridge University Press, 1992)

Hartlib, Samuel. *Considerations Tending to the Happy Accomplishment of England's Reformation* (1647) in *Samuel Hartlib and the Advancement of Learning*, ed. C. Webster (Cambridge: Cambridge University Press, 1970), 126–39

Designe for Plentie (1652)

The Kingdome of Macaria (1641) in *Samuel Hartlib and the Advancement of Learning*, ed. C. Webster (Cambridge: Cambridge University Press, 1970), 79–90

The Reformed Commonwealth of Bees (1655)

The Reformed Spirituall Husbandman (1652)

Hawkins, H. *Parthenia Sacra* (1633)

Hermann, Paulus. *Paradisus Batavius* (Leiden, 1698)

Hesiod. *Homeric Hymns and Homerica*, trans. Hugh G. Evelyn-White (London: Heinemann, and Cambridge, MA: Harvard University Press, 1967)

Theogony, and Works and Days, trans. Dorothea Wender (Harmondsworth: Penguin, 1973)

Heywood, Thomas. *The Hierarchie of the Blessed Angells* (1635)

The Iron Age (1632)

Hobbes, Thomas. *Leviathan*, ed. Richard Tuck (Cambridge: Cambridge University Press, 1991)

On the Citizen (*De Cive*), ed. and trans. Richard Tuck and Michael Silverstone (Cambridge: Cambridge University Press, 1998)

Hooke, Robert. *A Discourse of Earthquakes* in *The Posthumous Works of Robert Hooke*, ed. Richard Waller (1705), 277–450

The Life and Work of Robert Hooke in *Early Science in Oxford*, ed. R. T. Gunther, 2nd edn, 15 vols. (London: Dawsons, 1968), VI and VII

Micrographia: Or Some Physiological Descriptions of Minute Bodies Made by Magnifying Glasses (1665)

The Posthumous Works of Robert Hooke, ed. Richard Waller (1705)

Horace. *Satires, Epistles, and Ars Poetica*, trans H. Rushton Fairclough (London: Heinemann (Loeb), 1926)

Hutchinson, Lucy. *Order and Disorder: or, the World Made and Undone* (1679), ed. David Norbrook (Oxford: Blackwell, 2001)

Isocrates. *Isocrates*, trans. George Norlin, 3 vols. (London: Heinemann, and Cambridge, MA: Harvard University Press, 1966–8)

Johnson, Samuel. *Life of Sir Thomas Browne* in *Sir Thomas Browne: The Major Works*, ed. C. A. Patrides (Harmondsworth: Penguin, 1977), 481–511

Jonson, Ben. *The New Inn* in *The Complete Works of Ben Jonson*, ed. C. H. Herford, Percy Simpson, and Evelyn Simpson (Oxford: Clarendon Press, 1938), VI

Poetaster in *The Complete Works of Ben Jonson*, ed. C. H. Herford, Percy Simpson, and Evelyn Simpson, 11 vols. (Oxford: Clarendon Press, 1938), IV

Jonston, John. *An History of the Constancy of Nature* (1657)

An History of the Wonderful Things of Nature (1657)

Keynes, Geoffrey, ed. *The Works of Sir Thomas Browne*, 2nd edn, 4 vols. (Chicago: University of Chicago Press, 1964)

Kircher, Athanasius. *Arca Noë* (1675)

Lawrence, Anthony, and John Beale, RS. *Nurseries, Orchards, Profitable Gardens, and Vineyards Encouraged* (1677)

Levett, John. *The Ordering of Bees: or, the True History of Managing Them* (1634)

MacKenzie, George. *A Moral Essay Preferring Solitude* (1665)

Mandeville, Bernard. *The Fable of the Bees* (1714)

Markham, Gervase. *The English Husbandman* (1635)

Marmion, Shakerley. *The Antiquary* (1636) in *Dodsley's Old English Plays*, ed. Carew Hazlitt, 15 vols. (1875), XIII, 417–523

Marvell, Andrew. *The Complete Poems*, ed. Elizabeth Story Donno (Harmondsworth: Penguin, 1972)

Milton, John. *The Complete Prose Works of John Milton*, ed. Ernest Sirluck, 8 vols. (New Haven: Yale University Press, 1953–82)

   Paradise Lost, ed. Alastair Fowler (London: Longmans, 1968)

Montaigne, Michel de. *The Essayes of Michel Lord of Montaigne*, trans. John Florio, ed. A. R. Waller, 3 vols. (London: J. M. Dent and Sons/Everyman,1910)

Mornay, Philippe de. *Traité de la vérité de la religion chrétienne* (1581)

Moufett, Thomas. *Insectorum sive minimorum animalium theatrum* in *The History of Fourfooted Beasts and Serpents . . . whereunto is now added The Theater of Insects*, by Edward Topsell (1658)

Nashe, Thomas. *Pierce Penilesse His Supplication to the Devil* (1592) (Harmondsworth: Penguin, 1972)

Norris, John. *Reflections upon the Conduct of Human Life* (1690)

Patrides, C. A., ed. *Sir Thomas Browne: The Major Works* (Harmondsworth: Penguin, 1977)

Peacham, Henry. *Compleat Gentleman* (1612), ed. Virgil B. Heltzel (Ithaca, NY: Cornell University Press for the Folger Shakespeare Library, 1962)

Philipot, Thomas. *Poems* (1646)

Plot, Robert. *The Natural History of Staffordshire* (1686)

Plutarch. *The Lives of the Noble Grecians and Romans*, trans. John Dryden (New York: The Modern Library, [n.d.])

Poe, Edgar Allen. *Marginalia* (Charlottesville: University of Virginia Press, 1981)

Porta, Giovanni Battista della. *De Humana Physiognomia* (Naples, 1598)

   Phytognomica (Naples, 1588)

Power, Henry. *Experimental Philosophy* ([1663] 1664)

Procopius, *History of the Wars*, ed. H. B. Dewing, 3 vols. (Cambridge, MA: Harvard University Press, and London: Heinemann, 1961)

Purchas, Samuel. *A Theatre of Politicall Flying-Insects* (1657)

Ramsey, William. *The Gentleman's Companion* (1672)

Ray, John. *Miscellaneous Discourses concerning the Dissolution and Changes of the World* (1692)

   The Wisdom of God Manifested in the Works of Creation (1691)

R. B. *Herefordshire Orchards* (1657)

Remnant, Richard. *A Discourse or History of Bees* (1637)

Robbins, Robin, ed. *Pseudodoxia Epidemica*, by Thomas Browne, 2 vols. (Oxford: Clarendon Press, 1981)

   Sir Thomas Browne: 'Religio Medici', 'Hydriotaphia', and 'The Garden of Cyrus' (Oxford: Clarendon Press, 1972)

Ross, Alexander. *Medicus Medicatus* (1645)

Rusden, Moses. *A Further Discovery of Bees* (1679)

Savile, Thomas. *Adam's Garden* (1611)

Seneca. *Ad Lucilium epistulae morales*, trans. Richard M. Gunmere, 3 vols. (Cambridge, MA: Harvard University Press, 1917)

De Beneficiis in *Moral Essays*, trans. John W. Basore, 3 vols. (Cambridge, MA: Harvard University Press/Loeb, 1989), III

Seneca's Troades: A Literary Introduction with Text, Translation, and Commentary, trans. Elaine Fantham (Princeton: Princeton University Press, 1982)

Thyestes in *Four Tragedies and Octavia*, trans. E. F. Watling (Harmondsworth: Penguin, 1966)

Shadwell, Thomas. *The Virtuoso* (1675), ed. Marjorie Hope Nicolson and David Stuart Rodes (London: Edwin Arnold, 1966)

Shakelton, Francis. *A Blazyng Starre* (1580)

Shakespeare, William. *The Complete Works*, ed. Alfred Harbage (London: Penguin, 1969)

Sidney, Philip. *The Countesse of Pembroke's Arcadia*, ed. Albert Feuillerat (Cambridge: Cambridge University Press, 1912)

A Defence of Poetry in *The Miscellaneous Prose of Sir Philip Sidney*, ed. Katherine Duncan-Jones and Jan van Dorsten (Oxford: Clarendon Press, 1973), 73–121

Spenser, Edmund. *A View of the State of Ireland*, ed. Andrew Hadfield and Willy Maley (Oxford: Blackwell, 1997)

Sprat, Thomas. *The History of the Royal Society*, ed. Jackson Cope and Harold Whitmore Jones (St Louis, MO: Washington University Studies, 1958)

Stephens, Philip, and William Browne. *Catalogus horti botanici Oxoniensis* (1658)

Stowe, John. *Survey of London* (1635)

Stubbe, Henry. *The Plus Ultra Reduced to a New Plus* (1670)

Stubbes, Philip. *Anatomy of Abuses* (1583)

Swammerdam, Jan. *Historia insectorum generalis* (Leiden, 1669)

Miraculum Naturae (1672)

Tesauro, Emanuele. *Il Cannochiale Aristotelico* (Rome, 1664)

Thoreau, Henry. *Walden*, ed. J. Lyndon Shanley (Princeton: Princeton University Press, 1971)

Tirinus, Jacobus. *Biblia magna* (Paris, 1644)

Topsell, Edward. *The History of Fourfooted Beasts and Serpents . . . whereunto is now added The Theater of Insects* (1658)

Tradescant, John. *Musaeum Tradescantium: or, a Collection of Rarities Preserved at South-London* (1656)

Twain, Mark. *The Innocents Abroad* (New York: New American Library, 1966)

Valeriano, Piero. *Hieroglyphica* (Basle, 1556)

Vergil. *Georgics*, trans. John Dryden (New York: Cheshire House, 1931)

Webster, Charles, ed. *Samuel Hartlib and the Advancement of Learning* (Cambridge: Cambridge University Press, 1970)

Webster, Noah. *The Letters of Noah Webster*, ed. Harry H. Warfel (New York: Library Publishers, 1953)

Weever, John. *Ancient Funerall Monuments* (1631)

Wilkin, Simon, ed. *Sir Thomas Browne's Works*, 4 vols. (London: William Pickering, 1835–6)

Wilson, John. *The Projectors* (1665)

Wither, George. *The Schollers Purgatory Discovered in the Stationers Commonwealth* [1624]

Wood, Anthony à. *Athenae Oxonienses, to which are added the Fasti*, ed. Philip Bliss, 5 vols. (1815)

Xenophon. *Oeconomicus* in *Memorabilia, Oeconomicus*, trans. E. C. Marchant (Cambridge, MA: Harvard University Press, 1923), 362–525

SECONDARY SOURCES

Adolph, Robert. *The Rise of Modern Prose Style* (Cambridge, MA: Harvard University Press, 1968)

Ashworth, William. 'Marcus Gheeraerts and the Aesopic Connection in Seventeenth-Century Scientific Illustration', *Art Journal* 44 (1984), 132–8

Bann, Stephen. *Under the Sign: John Bargrave as Collector, Traveler, and Witness* (Ann Arbor: University of Michigan Press, 1994)

Barbour, Reid. *English Epicures and Stoics: Ancient Legacies in Early Stuart Culture* (Amherst: University of Massachusetts Press, 1998)

Barkan, Leonard. *Unearthing the Past: Archaeology and Aesthetics in the Making of Renaissance Culture* (New Haven: Yale University Press, 1999)

Barnaby, Andrew, and Lisa J. Schnell. *Literate Experience: The Work of Knowing in Seventeenth-Century English Writing* (New York and Basingstoke: Palgrave Macmillan, 2002)

Bennett, Kate. 'John Aubrey's Collections and the Early Modern Museum', *Bodleian Library Record* 17 (2001), 213–45

Bennett, Jim, and Scott Mandelbrote. *The Garden, the Ark, the Tower, the Temple: Biblical Metaphors of Knowledge in Early Modern Europe* (Oxford: Museum of the History of Science and the Bodleian Library, 1998)

Birken, William. 'The Social Problem of the English Physician in the Early 17th Century', *Medical History* 31 (1987), 201–16

Blom, Philipp. *To Have and to Hold: An Intimate History of Collectors and Collecting* (London: Allen Lane, 2002)

Blum, Abbe. 'The Author's Authority: *Areopagitica* and the Labour of Licensing' in *Re-Membering Milton: Essays on the Texts and Traditions*, ed. Mary Nyquist and Margaret W. Ferguson (New York and London: Methuen, 1987), 74–96

Bodemer, Charles W. *Embryological Thought in Seventeenth Century England* in *Medical Investigation in Seventeenth Century England* (Los Angeles: University of California/William Andrews Clark Memorial Library, 1968), 3–25

Brauer, George C. *The Education of a Gentleman: Theories of Gentlemanly Education in England 1660–1775* (New York: Bookman Associates, 1959)

Breiner, Lawrence. 'The Generation of Metaphor in Thomas Browne', *Modern Language Quarterly* 38 (1977), 261–75

Brooks, Douglas, ed. *Printing and Parenting in Early Modern England* (Aldershot: Ashgate Press, 2004)

Bryson, Anna. *From Courtesy to Civility: Changing Codes of Conduct in Early Modern England* (Oxford: Clarendon Press, 1998)

Byron, Glennis. *Dramatic Monologue* (London: Routledge, 2003)

Carey, John. *John Donne: Life, Mind and Art* (London: Faber, 1981)

Catling, Brian. *Tending the Vortex: The Works of Brian Catling*, ed. Simon Perril (Cambridge: CCCP Books, 2001)

Chalmers, Gordon Keith. 'That Universal and Publick Manuscript', *Virginia Quarterly Review* 26 (1950), 414–30

'Thomas Browne, True Scientist', *Osiris* 2 (1936), 28–79

Comito, Terry. *The Idea of the Garden in the Renaissance* (New Brunswick, NJ: Rutgers University Press, 1978)

Cook, Elizabeth. 'The First Edition of *Religio Medici*', *Harvard Library Bulletin* 2 (1948), 22–31

Cook, Harold. 'The Cutting Edge of a Revolution? Medicine and Natural History near the Shores of the North Sea' in *Renaissance and Revolution: Humanists, Scholars, Craftsmen and Natural Philosophers in Early Modern Europe*, ed. J. V. Field and Frank A. J. L. James (Cambridge: Cambridge University Press, 1993), 45–61

Cope, Jackson I. 'Sir Kenelm Digby's Rewritings of His Life' in *Writing and Political Engagement in Seventeenth-Century England*, ed. Derek Hirst and Richard Strier (Cambridge: Cambridge University Press, 1999), 52–68

Croll, Morris. '"Attic Prose" in the Seventeenth Century' in *Style, Rhetoric, and Rhythm*, ed. J. Max Patrick *et al.* (Princeton: Princeton University Press, 1966), 51–101

'The Baroque Style in Prose' in *Style, Rhetoric, and Rhythm*, ed. J. Max Patrick *et al.* (Princeton: Princeton University Press, 1966), 207–33

Cuddon, J. A. *A Dictionary of Literary Terms and Literary Theory*, 4th edn (Oxford: Blackwell, 1998)

The Owl's Watch-Song: A Study of Istanbul (London: Barrie and Rockliff, 1960)

Cunningham, Andrew. 'The Culture of Gardens' in *Cultures of Natural History*, ed. N. Jardine, J. A. Secord, and E. C. Spary (Cambridge: Cambridge University Press, 1996), 38–56

'Sir Thomas Browne and His *Religio Medici*: Reason, Nature, and Religion' in *Religio Medici: Medicine and Religion in Seventeenth-Century England*, ed. Ole Peter Grell and Andrew Cunningham (Aldershot: Scolar Press, 1996), 12–61

Daston, Lorraine. *Classical Probability in the Enlightenment* (Princeton: Princeton University Press, 1988)

Datta, Kitty Scoular. 'Sir Thomas Browne and *Vox Norwici*', *Notes and Queries* 231 (1986), 461

Dear, Peter. 'A Mechanical Microcosm: Bodily Passions, Good Manners, and Cartesian Mechanism' in *Science Incarnate: Historical Embodiments of Natural Knowledge*, ed. Christopher Lawrence and Steven Shapin (Chicago: University of Chicago Press, 1998), 51–82

'Narratives, Anecdotes, and Experiments: Turning Experience into Science in the Seventeenth Century' in *The Literary Structure of Scientific Argument*, ed. Peter Dear (Philadelphia: University of Pennsylvania Press, 1991), 135–63

Debus, Allen. *The English Paracelsians* (New York: Franklin Watts, 1966)

Denonain, Jean-Jacques, ed. *Sir Thomas Browne: 'Religio Medici'* (Cambridge: Cambridge University Press, 1953)

Dion, Mark. *Natural History and Other Fictions* (Birmingham: Ikon Gallery, Hamburg: Kunstverein, and Amsterdam: De Appel, 1997)

Dobbs, Betty Jo. 'Studies in the Natural Philosophy of Sir Kenelm Digby', *Ambix* 18 (1971), 1–25

Drake, Ellen Tan. *Restless Genius: Robert Hooke and His Earthly Thoughts* (New York: Oxford University Press, 1996)

Dunn, Kevin. *Pretexts of Authority: The Rhetoric of Authorship in the Renaissance Preface* (Stanford: Stanford University Press, 1994)

Evans, Robert C. *Jonson, Lipsius and the Politics of Renaissance Stoicism* (Wakefield, NH: Longwood Academic, 1992)

Evans, R. J. W. *Rudolf II and His World: A Study in Intellectual History 1576–1612* (Oxford: Clarendon Press, 1973)

Finch, Jeremiah. 'The Norfolk Persuaders of Sir Thomas Browne: A Variant Copy of the 1712 Posthumous Works', *Princeton University Library Chronicle* 11 (1950), 199–201

    Sir Thomas Browne: A Doctor's Life of Science and Faith (New York: Henry Schuman, 1950)

Findlen, Paula. 'Jokes of Nature and Jokes of Knowledge: The Playfulness of Scientific Discourse in Early Modern Europe', *Renaissance Quarterly* 43 (1990), 292–331

    Possessing Nature: Museums, Collecting, and Scientific Culture in Early Modern Italy (Berkeley: University of California Press, 1994)

Fisch, Harold. 'The Scientist as Priest: A Note on Robert Boyle's Natural Theology', *Isis* 44 (1953), 252–65

Fish, Stanley E. *Self-Consuming Artifacts: The Experience of Seventeenth-Century Literature* (Berkeley: University of California Press, 1972)

    Seventeenth-Century Prose: Modern Essays in Criticism (New York: Oxford University Press, 1971)

Forster, E. M. 'The Celestial Omnibus' in *Collected Short Stories of E.M. Forster* (London: Sidgwick and Jackson, 1948), 38–58

Foucault, Michel. *The Order of Things: An Archaeology of the Human Sciences* (London: Tavistock, 1982)

Fournier, Marion. *The Fabric of Life: Microscopy in the Seventeenth Century* (Baltimore: Johns Hopkins University Press, 1996)

Fowler, Alastair. *Triumphal Forms: Structural Patterns in Elizabethan Poetry* (Cambridge: Cambridge University Press, 1970)

Frank, Robert G., Jr. *Harvey and the Oxford Physiologists: A Study of Scientific Ideas* (Berkeley: University of California Press, 1980)

    'The Physician as Virtuoso in Seventeenth-Century England' in *Papers Read at a Clark Library Seminar* (5 February 1977) (Los Angeles: William Andrews Clark Memorial Library, 1979), 57–114

Freedberg, David. *The Eye of the Lynx: Galileo, His Friends, and the Beginnings of Modern Natural History* (Chicago: University of Chicago Press, 2002)

Gardiner, Samuel R. *History of the Great Civil War 1642–1649*, 4 vols. (London: Longmans, Green, 1904)

Gasking, Elizabeth. *Investigations into Generation, 1651–1828* (London: Hutchinson, 1967)

Giammatti, A. Bartlett. *The Earthly Paradise and the Renaissance Epic* (Princeton: Princeton University Press, 1966)

Godwin, Joscelyn. *Athanasius Kircher: A Renaissance Man and the Quest for Lost Knowledge* (London: Thames and Hudson, 1979)

Gottlieb, Sidney. '*Elegies Upon the Author*: Defining, Defending, and Surviving Donne', *John Donne Journal* 2 (1983), 23–38

Grafton, Anthony. *Joseph Scaliger: A Study in the History of Classical Scholarship*, 2 vols. (Oxford: Clarendon Press, 1983)

Grell, Ole Peter, ed. *Paracelsus: The Man and His Reputation, His Ideas and Their Transformation* (Leiden: E. J. Brill, 1998)

Grey, Robin. *The Complicity of Imagination: The American Renaissance, Contests of Authority, and 17th-Century English Culture* (Cambridge: Cambridge University Press, 1997)

Guibbory, Achsah. *Ceremony and Community from Herbert to Milton: Literature, Religion, and Cultural Conflict in Seventeenth-Century England* (Cambridge: Cambridge University Press, 1998)

Gunther, R. T. ed. *Early Science in Oxford*, 2nd edn, vol. IV: *The Philosophical Society* (London: Dawsons, 1968)

Hall, Marie Boas. 'Thomas Browne, Naturalist' in *Approaches to Sir Thomas Browne: The Ann Arbor Tercentenary Lectures and Essays*, ed. C. A. Patrides (Columbia, MO: University of Missouri Press, 1982), 178–87

Hall, Michael L. 'The Emergence of the Essay and the Idea of Discovery' in *Essays on the Essay: Redefining the Genre*, ed. Alexander Butrym (Athens, GA: University of Georgia Press, 1989), 73–91

Halley, Janet E. 'Sir Thomas Browne's *The Garden of Cyrus* and the Real Character', *English Literary Renaissance* 15 (1985), 100–21

Harris, Victor Irwin. *All Coherence Gone: A Study of the Seventeenth Century Controversy over Disorder and Decay in the Universe*, 2nd edn (London: Frank Cass, 1966)

Havenstein, Daniela. *Democratizing Sir Thomas Browne: 'Religio Medici' and its Imitations* (Oxford: Clarendon Press, 1999)

Helgerson, Richard. *Self-Crowned Laureates: Spenser, Jonson, Milton and the Literary System* (Berkeley: University of California Press, 1983)

Henkel, A., and A. Schöne. *Emblemata* (Stuttgart: Metzler, 1996)

Hirst, Derek. *England in Conflict, 1603–1660* (London: Arnold, 1999)

Holmes, Frederick L. 'Argument and Narrative in Scientific Writing' in *The Literary Structure of Scientific Argument*, ed. Peter Dear (Philadelphia: University of Pennsylvania Press, 1991), 164–81

Houghton, Walter E. 'The English Virtuoso in the Seventeenth Century', *Journal of the History of Ideas* 3 (1942), 51–73

Howart, David. 'Sir Robert Cotton and the Commemoration of Famous Men', *British Library Journal* 18 (1992); reprinted in *Sir Robert Cotton: Essays on an Early Stuart Courtier and His Legacy*, ed. C. J. Wright (London: British Library, 1997), 40–67

Huebert, Ronald. 'Privacy: The Early Social History of a Word', *Sewanee Review* 105 (1997), 21–38

Hughes, Trevor. 'The Childhood of Sir Thomas Browne: His Relationship to His Mother and Stepfather', *London Journal* 23 (1998), 21–9

Hunter, Michael. 'The Conscience of Robert Boyle: Functionalism, "Dysfunctionalism" and the Task of Historical Understanding' in *Renaissance and Revolution: Humanists, Scholars, Craftsmen, and Natural Philosophers in Early Modern Europe*, ed. J. V. Field and Frank A. J. L. James (Cambridge: Cambridge University Press, 1993), 147–59

John Aubrey and the Realm of Learning (London: Duckworth, 1975)

'Latitudinarianism and the "Ideology" of the Early Royal Society: Thomas Sprat's *History of the Royal Society* (1667) Reconsidered' in *Philosophy, Science and Religion in England 1640–1700*, ed. R. Kroll, R. Ashcraft, and P. Zagorin (Cambridge: Cambridge University Press, 1992), 199–229

Science and Society in Restoration England (Cambridge: Cambridge University Press, 1981)

Huntley, Frank Livingstone. '*The Garden of Cyrus* as Prophecy' in *Approaches to Sir Thomas Browne: The Ann Arbor Tercentenary Lectures and Essays*, ed. C. A. Patrides (Columbia, MO: University of Missouri Press, 1982), 132–42

Sir Thomas Browne: A Biographical and Critical Study, 2nd edn (Ann Arbor: University of Michigan Press, 1968)

Impey, Oliver, and A. MacGregor, eds. *The Origins of Museums: The Cabinet of Curiosities in Sixteenth- and Seventeenth-Century Europe* (Oxford: Oxford University Press, 1985)

Inwood, Stephen. *The Man Who Knew Too Much: The Strange and Inventive Life of Robert Hooke, 1635–1703* (London: Macmillan, 2002)

Jacob, Margaret C. *The Cultural Meaning of the Scientific Revolution* (Philadelphia: Temple University Press, 1988)

Jagodzinski, Cecile. *Privacy and Print: Reading and Writing in Seventeenth Century England* (Charlottesville: University of Virginia Press, 1999)

Jones, R. F. 'Science and English Prose Style, 1650–1675' in *Seventeenth-Century Prose: Modern Essays in Criticism*, ed. Stanley E. Fish (New York: Oxford University Press, 1971), 53–89

Juel-Jensen, Bent. '*Musæum Clausum, or Bibliotheca Abscondita*: Some Thoughts on Curiosity Cabinets and Imaginary Books', *Journal of the History of Collections* 4 (1992), 127–40

Knight, David M. *Natural Science Books in English 1600–1900*, 2nd edn (London: Portman Books, 1989)

Knott, John R. 'Sir Thomas Browne and the Labyrinth of Truth' in *Approaches to Sir Thomas Browne: The Ann Arbor Tercentenary Lectures and Essays*, ed. C. A. Patrides (Columbia, MO: University of Missouri Press, 1982), 19–30

Kroll, R., R. Ashcraft, and P. Zagorin, eds. *Philosophy, Science and Religion in England 1640–1700* (Cambridge: Cambridge University Press, 1992)

Kushner, Tony. *Hydriotaphia* in *Death and Taxes: Hydriotaphia and Other Plays* (New York: Theatre Communications, 2000)

Langbaum, Robert. *The Poetry of Experience: The Dramatic Monologue in Modern Literary Tradition* (London: Chatto and Windus, 1972)

Laurencich-Minelli, Laura. 'Museography and Ethnographical Collections in Bologna during the Sixteenth and Seventeenth Centuries' in *The Origins of Museums: The Cabinet of Curiosities in Sixteenth- and Seventeenth-Century Europe*, ed. Oliver Impey and A. MacGregor (Oxford: Oxford University Press, 1985), 17–23

Levine, Joseph H. 'Latitudinarians, Neoplatonists, and the Ancient Wisdom' in *Philosophy, Science and Religion in England 1640–1700*, ed. R. Kroll, R. Ashcraft, and P. Zagorin (Cambridge: Cambridge University Press, 1992), 85–101

Levi-Strauss, Claude. *The Savage Mind* (London: Weidenfeld and Nicolson, 1966)

Love, Harold. *The Culture and Commerce of Texts: Scribal Publication in Seventeenth-Century England*, 2nd edn (Amherst, MA: University of Massachusetts Press, 1998)

Low, Anthony. *The Georgic Revolution* (Princeton: Princeton University Press, 1985)

Lugli, Adalgisa. *Wunderkammer* (Torino: Umberto Allemandi, 1997)

McClung, William A. *The Architecture of Paradise: Survivals of Eden and Jerusalem* (Berkeley: University of California Press, 1983)

McCrea, Adriana. *Constant Minds: Political Virtue and the Lipsian Paradigm in England, 1584–1650* (Toronto: University of Toronto Press, 1997)

MacGregor, Arthur. 'The Cabinet of Curiosities in Seventeenth-Century Britain' in *The Origins of Museums: The Cabinet of Curiosities in Sixteenth- and Seventeenth-Century Europe*, ed. Oliver Impey and A. MacGregor (Oxford: Oxford University Press, 1985), 147–58

Marotti, Arthur F. *Manuscript, Print, and the English Renaissance Lyric* (Ithaca, NY: Cornell University Press, 1995)

    'Shakespeare's Sonnets as Literary Property' in *Soliciting Interpretation: Literary Theory and Seventeenth-Century English Poetry*, ed. Elizabeth D. Harvey and Katherine Eisaman Maus (Chicago: University of Chicago Press, 1990), 143-73

Mendyk, Stanley A. E. '*Speculum Britanniae*: Regional Study, Antiquarianism, and Science in Britain to 1700* (Toronto: University of Toronto Press, 1989)

Merton, Egon Stephen. 'The Botany of Sir Thomas Browne', *Isis* 47 (1956), 161–71

    'Old and New Physiology in Sir Thomas Browne: Digestion and Some Other Functions', *Isis* 57 (1966), 249–59

    Science and Imagination in Sir Thomas Browne (New York: King's Crown Press, 1949)

    'Sir Thomas Browne as Zoologist', *Osiris* 9 (1950), 413–34

Milgate, W. *John Donne: The Epithalamiums, Anniversaries, and Epicedes* (Oxford: Clarendon Press, 1978)

Miller, Elizabeth. '[Stoker's Research]' in *Three Vampire Tales*, ed. Anne Williams (Boston: Houghton Mifflin, 2003), 47–51

Miller, Peter N. *Peiresc's Europe: Learning and Virtue in the Seventeenth Century* (New Haven: Yale University Press, 2000)

Mirlees, Hope. *A Fly in Amber: Being an Extravagant Biography of the Romantic Antiquary Sir Robert Bruce Cotton* (London: Faber, 1962)

Mulryne, J. R. 'The Play of Mind: Self and Audience in *Religio Medici*' in *Approaches to Sir Thomas Browne: The Ann Arbor Tercentenary Lectures and Essays*, ed. C. A. Patrides (Columbia, MO: University of Missouri Press, 1982), 60–8

Nathanson, Leonard. 'Sir Thomas Browne and the Ethics of Knowledge' in *Approaches to Sir Thomas Browne: The Ann Arbor Tercentenary Lectures and Essays*, ed. C. A. Patrides (Columbia, MO: University of Missouri Press, 1982), 12–18

The Strategy of Truth: A Study of Sir Thomas Browne (Chicago: University of Chicago Press, 1967)

Needham, Joseph. *A History of Embryology*, 2nd revised edn (Cambridge: Cambridge University Press, 1959)

Nicholl, Allardyce. 'Kenelm Digby, Poet, Philosopher, and Pirate of the Restoration', *Johns Hopkins Alumni Magazine* 21 (1933), 330–50

Niebyl, Peter H. 'Science and Metaphor in the Medicine of Restoration England', *Bulletin of the History of Medicine* 47 (1973), 356–74

Norbrook, David. 'Lucy Hutchinson and *Order and Disorder*: The Manuscript Evidence', *English Manuscript Studies: 1100–1700* 9 (2000), 257–91

Oakeshott, Michael. *Hobbes on Civil Association*, 5th edn (Oxford: Blackwell, 1975)

Olmi, G. 'Science-Honour Metaphor: Italian Cabinets of the Sixteenth and Seventeenth Centuries' in *The Origins of Museums: The Cabinet of Curiosities in Sixteenth- and Seventeenth-Century Europe*, ed. Oliver Impey and A. MacGregor (Oxford: Oxford University Press, 1985), 5–16

Oppenheimer, Jane. 'John Hunter, Sir Thomas Browne and the Experimental Method', *Bulletin of the History of Medicine* 21 (1947), 17–32

Parry, Graham. *The Trophies of Time: English Antiquaries of the Seventeenth Century* (Oxford: Oxford University Press, 1995)

Patey, Douglas Lane. *Probability and Literary Form: Philosophic Theory and Literary Practice in the Augustan Age* (Cambridge: Cambridge University Press, 1984)

Patrides, C. A. '"The Best Part of Nothing": Sir Thomas Browne and the Strategy of Indirection' in *Approaches to Sir Thomas Browne: The Ann Arbor Tercentenary Lectures and Essays*, ed. C. A. Patrides (Columbia, MO: University of Missouri Press, 1982), 31–48

'Renaissance and Modern Thought on the Last Things: A Study in Changing Conceptions', *Harvard Theological Review* 51 (1958), 169–85

Patrides, C. A., ed. *Approaches to Sir Thomas Browne: The Ann Arbor Tercentenary Lectures and Essays* (Columbia, MO: University of Missouri Press, 1982)

Pearce, Susan M., ed. *Interpreting Objects and Collections* (London: Routledge, 1994)

On Collecting: An Investigation into Collecting in the European Tradition (London: Routledge, 1995)

Pebworth, Ted-Larry. 'Wandering in the America of Truth: *Pseudodoxia Epidemica* and the Essay Tradition' in *Approaches to Sir Thomas Browne: The Ann Arbor*

Tercentenary Lectures and Essays, ed. C. A. Patrides (Columbia, MO: University of Missouri Press, 1982), 166–77

Pelling, Margaret. *The Common Lot: Sickness, Medical Occupations, and the Urban Poor in Early Modern England* (London: Longman, 1998)

Perril, Simon, ed. *Tending the Vortex: The Works of Brian Catling* (Cambridge: CCCP Books, 2001)

Petersson, R. J. *Sir Kenelm Digby* (Cambridge, MA: Harvard University Press, 1956)

Piggott, Stuart. *Ancient Britons and the Antiquarian Imagination: Ideas from the Renaissance to the Regency* (London: Thames and Hudson, 1989)

Post, Jonathan F. S. *Sir Thomas Browne* (Boston: Twayne Publishers, 1987)

Prest, John. *The Garden of Eden: The Botanic Garden and the Re-Creation of Paradise*, 2nd edn (New Haven: Yale University Press, 1988)

Preston, Claire. *Bee* (London: Reaktion Press, 2005)

'In the Wilderness of Forms: Ideas and Things in Thomas Browne's Cabinets of Curiosity' in *The Renaissance Computer: Knowledge Technology in the First Age of Print*, ed. Neil Rhodes and Jonathan Sawday (London: Routledge, 2000), 170–83

'The Jocund Cabinet and the Melancholy Museum in Seventeenth Century English Literature' in *Curiosity and Wonder from the Renaissance to the Enlightenment*, ed. Alexander Marr and R. J. W. Evans (Aldershot: Ashgate, 2005)

' "Unriddling the World": Sir Thomas Browne and the Doctrine of Signatures', *Critical Survey* 5 (1993), 263–70

Pyle, A. J. 'Animal Generation and the Mechanical Philosophy: Some Light on the Role of Biology in the Scientific Revolution', *History and Philosophy of Life Sciences* 9 (1987), 225–54

Ransome, Hilda M. *The Sacred Bee in Ancient Times and Folklore* (Burrowbridge: Bee Books Old and New, 1937)

Righter, Anne [Barton]. 'Francis Bacon' in *Essential Articles for the Study of Francis Bacon*, ed. Brian Vickers (Hamden, CT: Archon Books, 1968), 300–21

Robbins, Robin. 'Browne's Cosmos Imagined: Nature, Man, and God in *Pseudodoxia Epidemica*' in *Approaches to Sir Thomas Browne: The Ann Arbor Tercentenary Lectures and Essays*, ed. C. A. Patrides (Columbia, MO: University of Missouri Press, 1982), 155–65

Rogers, John. *The Matter of Revolution: Science, Poetry, and Politics in the Age of Milton* (Ithaca, NY: Cornell University Press, 1996)

Rose, Mark. 'The Author as Proprietor: *Donaldson v. Becket* and the Genealogy of Modern Authorship', *Representations* 23 (1988), 51–85

Rosenheim, James M. *The Townshends of Raynham* (Middletown, CT: Wesleyan University Press, 1989)

Rossi, Paolo. *The Dark Abyss of Time: The History of the Earth and the History of Nations from Hooke to Vico*, trans. L. G. Cochrane (Chicago: University of Chicago Press, 1984)

Roston, Murray. 'The "Doubting" Thomas' in *Approaches to Sir Thomas Browne: The Ann Arbor Tercentenary Lectures and Essays*, ed. C. A. Patrides (Columbia, MO: University of Missouri Press, 1982), 69–80

Røstvig, Maren-Sofie. *The Happy Man: Studies in the Metamorphoses of a Classical Ideal*, 2nd edn, 2 vols. (Oslo: Universitetforlaget, and New York: Humanities Press, 1971)

Rudwick, Martin J. S. *The Meaning of Fossils: Episodes in the History of Palaeontology*, 2nd edn (New York: Neale Watson Academic Publications, 1976)

Ruestow, Edward G. *The Microscope in the Dutch Republic: The Shaping of Discovery* (Cambridge: Cambridge University Press, 1996)

Sandler, Florence. '*The Faerie Queene*: An Elizabethan Apocalypse' in *The Apocalypse in English Renaissance Thought and Literature: Patterns, Antecedants, and Repercussions*, ed. C. A. Patrides and Joseph Wittreich (Manchester: Manchester University Press, 1984), 148–74

Sargent, Rose-Mary. 'Bacon as an Advocate for Cooperative Scientific Research' in *The Cambridge Companion to Bacon*, ed. Markku Peltonen (Cambridge: Cambridge University Press, 1996), 146–77

Saunders, Jason Lewis. *Justus Lipsius: The Philosophy of Renaissance Stoicism* (New York: The Liberal Arts Press, 1955)

Schultz, E. 'Notes on the History of Collecting and of Museums' in *Interpreting Objects and Collections*, ed. Susan M. Pearce (London: Routledge, 1994), 175–87

Sebald, W. E. *The Rings of Saturn* (1995), trans. Michael Hulse (London: Harvill, 1998)

Seelig, L. 'The Munich Künstkammer, 1565–1807' in *The Origins of Museums: The Cabinet of Curiosities in Sixteenth- and Seventeenth-Century Europe*, ed. Oliver Impey and A. MacGregor (Oxford: Oxford University Press, 1985), 76–89

Sessions, Ina. *A Study of the Dramatic Monologue in American and Continental Literature* (San Antonio: Alamo Printing Co., 1933)

Shapin, Steven. '"The Mind is its Own Place": Science and Solitude in Seventeenth Century England', *Science in Context* 4 (1990), 191–218

'Pump and Circumstance: Robert Boyle's Literary Technology', *Social Studies of Science* 14 (1984), 481–520

'"A Scholar and a Gentleman": The Problematic Identity of the Scientific Practitioner in Early Modern England', *History of Science* 29 (1991), 279–327

A Social History of Truth: Civility and Science in Seventeenth-Century England (Chicago: University of Chicago Press, 1994)

Shapiro, Barbara J. *Probability and Certainty in Seventeenth-Century England: A Study of the Relationships between Natural Science, Religion, History, Law, and Literature* (Princeton: Princeton University Press, 1983)

Sharpe, Kevin. *Sir Robert Cotton, 1586–1631: History and Politics in Early Modern England* (Oxford: Oxford University Press, 1979)

Sinfield, Alan. *Dramatic Monologue* (London: Methuen, 1977)

Singer, Thomas C. 'Sir Thomas Browne's "Emphaticall Decussation, or Fundamentall Figure": Geometrical Hieroglyphs and *The Garden of Cyrus*', *English Literary Renaissance* 17 (1987), 85–102

Sirluck, Ernest. 'Milton's Pamphlets' in *The Complete Prose Works of John Milton*, ed. Sirluck, 8 vols. (New Haven: Yale University Press, 1953–82), II, 137–216

Smith, Nigel. *Literature and Revolution in England, 1640–1660* (New Haven: Yale University Press, 1994)

Stearn, William T. 'The Five Brethren of the Rose: An Old Botanical Riddle', *Huntia* 2 (1965), 180–4

Stewart, Stanley. *The Enclosed Garden: The Tradition and the Image in Seventeenth-Century Poetry* (Madison: University of Wisconsin Press, 1966)

Stroup, Alice. *A Company of Scientists: Botany, Patronage and Community at the Seventeenth-Century Parisian Royal Academy of Sciences* (Berkeley: University of California Press, 1990)

Sturdy, David, and Martin Henig, *The Gentle Traveller: John Bargrave and His Collection* [Abingdon: Abbey Press, 1983]

Swaim, Kathleen M. *Before and After the Fall: Contrasting Modes in 'Paradise Lost'* (Amherst: University of Massachusetts Press, 1986)

Swann, Marjorie. *Curiosity and Texts: The Culture of Collecting in Early Modern England* (Philadelphia: University of Pennsylvania Press, 2001)

Thomas, Keith. *Man and the Natural World: Changing Attitudes in England, 1500–1800* (Harmondsworth: Penguin, 1983)

Tribby, Jay. 'Cooking (with) Clio and Cleo: Eloquence and Experiment in 17th-Century Florence', *Journal of the History of Ideas* 52 (1991), 417–39

Turnbull, G. H. *Samuel Hartlib: A Sketch of His Life and His Relations to J. A. 'Comenius'* (Oxford: Oxford University Press, 1920)

Turner, James. *The Politics of Landscape: Rural Scenery and Society in English Poetry, 1630–1660* (Cambridge, MA: Harvard University Press, 1979)

Tylden-Wright, David. *John Aubrey: A Life* (London: HarperCollins, 1991)

Waddington, Raymond B. 'The Two Tables in *Religio Medici*' in *Approaches to Sir Thomas Browne: The Ann Arbor Tercentenary Lectures and Essays*, ed. C. A. Patrides (Columbia, MO: University of Missouri Press, 1982), 81–99

Warnke, Frank. 'A Hook for Amphibium: Some Reflections on Fish' in *Approaches to Sir Thomas Browne: The Ann Arbor Tercentenary Lectures and Essays*, ed. C. A. Patrides (Columbia, MO: University of Missouri Press, 1982), 49–59

Warren, Austin. 'The Style of Sir Thomas Browne', *Kenyon Review* 13 (1951), 674–87

Wear, Andrew. *Knowledge and Practice in English Medicine, 1550–1680* (Cambridge: Cambridge University Press, 2000)

Webber, Joan. *The Eloquent 'I': Style and Self in Seventeenth-Century Prose* (Madison: University of Wisconsin Press, 1968)

Webster, Charles. 'English Medical Reformers of the Puritan Revolution: A Background to the "Society of Chymical Physitians"', *Ambix* 14–15 (1967–8), 16–41

The Great Instauration: Science, Medicine and Reform, 1626–1660 (New York: Holmes and Meier Publishers, 1976)

'Henry Power's Experimental Philosophy', *Ambix* 14–15 (1967–8), 150–78

Webster, Charles, ed. *Samuel Hartlib and the Advancement of Learning* (Cambridge: Cambridge University Press, 1970)

Wechsler, Lawrence. *Mr Wilson's Cabinet of Wonder* (New York: Vintage Books, 1995)

Wilding, Michael. '*Religio Medici* in the English Revolution' in *Approaches to Sir Thomas Browne: The Ann Arbor Tercentenary Lectures and Essays*, ed. C. A. Patrides (Columbia, MO: University of Missouri Press, 1982), 100–14

Wiley, Margaret. *The Subtle Knot: Creative Scepticism in Seventeenth-Century England* (London: George Allen and Unwin, 1952)

Willey, Basil. *The Seventeenth-Century Background* (New York: Columbia University Press, 1934)

Williamson, George. *The Senecan Amble: A Study in Prose Form from Bacon to Collier* (Chicago: University of Chicago Press, 1951)

Wise, James N. *Sir Thomas Browne's 'Religio Medici' and Two Seventeenth-Century Critics* (Columbia, MO: University of Missouri Press, 1973)

Woolf, D. R. *The Idea of History in Early Stuart England: Erudition, Ideology, and 'The Light of Truth' from the Accession of James I to the Civil War* (Toronto: University of Toronto Press, 1990)

Yates, Frances. *The Art of Memory*, 2nd edn (London: Ark, 1984)

Zakin, Sergei. 'Inside the Book of the World: Issues of Textual Interpretation in Mid-Seventeenth-Century Discourse on Knowledge', unpublished PhD thesis, University of Cambridge (1998)

WEBSITES

http://penelope.uchicago.edu [complete works of Sir Thomas Browne and other related materials]

Index

Page numbers in italics refer to illustrations.